Contracts Stories

Introduction

In this book, eleven contracts scholars return to the cases that lie at the heart of the canon, revisit their underlying facts, and place them in their legal, social, and political context.

The first two chapters examine cases from the middle of the Industrial Revolution. Richard Danzig's essay on *Hadley v. Baxendale* and its broken mill shaft shows how the famous delay arose in a world in which the transportation system in England was in transition from canals to railroads. Commerce was expanding at an unprecedented rate, yet only fifteen judges sat in courts of general jurisdiction. They had to handle commercial litigation for the entire country. The law had to keep pace. *Hadley*, in short, is a story of judicial innovation accompanying technological innovation.

Raffles v. Wichelhaus with its two ships *Peerless* also involves a market undergoing dramatic change. The case centers on the question why it made a difference that cotton came on one ship rather than another. Brian Simpson explores the world that gave rise to the litigation, one in which the Civil War in the United States made the price of cotton especially volatile. A futures market in cotton was coming into being, and the identification of the ship by name in the contract was the way in which parties set a time for performance.

The next two chapters explore the emergence of doctrine in more recent times. In his essay, Robert Scott provides a detailed examination of the story behind *Hoffman v. Red Owl Stores*. On closer inspection, it appears that this case, like *Raffles*, grew out of a misunderstanding. Professor Scott suggests that the misunderstanding in *Red Owl* is emblematic of the larger problems associated with applying promissory estoppel to precontractual negotiations, problems that courts have been quicker to understand than academics. Richard Epstein uses *ProCD v. Zeidenberg* to explore the doctrine of offer and acceptance and larger questions of the relationship between contract and property in a world of mass markets. He shows how two able judges can approach the same set of facts from radically different perspectives, one doctrinal and one functional, and reach opposing legal conclusions.

Carol Sanger examines *Baby M,* a case that asks whether contracts with surrogate mothers are legally enforceable. As with *Hadley* and *Raffles,* this case is one that arises in a nascent market. The litigation would not have taken place either ten years earlier or later. By locating *Baby M* in its own distinct time and place and showing how this peculiar baby-making contract arose, Professor Sanger is able to explore the subtle interactions between market and family, commerce and altruism.

The next chapter revisits *Hamer v. Sidway,* the case in which an uncle promises $5,000 to his fifteen-year-old nephew if he does not smoke, drink, or gamble until he is twenty-one. This essay tries to uncover the larger family drama that lies beneath the surface and explore the limits on what the law can do to sort out relationships inside the family and outside the marketplace.

Robert Gordon uses *Britton v. Turner* to showcase the wealth of recent work in legal and social history. At the same time, Professor Gordon shows how the doctrine in this case is a piece of a broad tapestry, one in which definitions and ideologies of "freedom" in contracting, particularly as applied to the contract of employment, is still being made.

Lea VanderVelde reviews the reception of the doctrine of *Lumley v. Wagner* in this country. The case involves a singer who breaks her promise to perform at one opera house in order to appear at another. Professor VanderVelde shows in a still different way how doctrine cannot be separated from time and place. Our legal culture in the nineteenth century embedded within it problematic conceptions of women and the role they were supposed to play. These decisively shaped the legal doctrine that emerged here, as well as elsewhere.

The last three chapters explore the political, legal, and cultural circumstances that shaped the litigation in three canonical cases. Judith Maute examines the way in which the lawyers and the judges mishandled *Peevyhouse v. Garland Coal & Mining Co.* and left only a token recovery for plaintiffs who had a simple and meritorious breach-of-contract action. Barak Richman looks at *Rockingham County v. Luten Bridge Co.* It is a story of political infighting, one that led a county to build a bridge to nowhere. His story is of a judge who seeks to provide legal stability for local governments who enter into commercial dealings in such environments. In the last essay, Debora Threedy examines the cultural and social forces behind *Alaska Packers' Association v. Domenico,* the paradigmatic case of economic duress. It shows how the case far from being about opportunistic fishermen and sailors is a story in which once again cultures clash and nothing is quite as it seems.

The cases examined in this book span nearly a century and a half. While they remain the vehicles used to introduce first-year students to the law of contracts, this book sounds a useful note of caution. To be sure, cases matter and so too the legal principles they embody, but neither can stand alone. Context always matters, and much is lost when controversies are reduced to simple hypotheticals and black-letter maxims.

The narrative in a judicial opinion occupies a privileged place, but we should not forget that there are other possible narratives, sometimes many others. These essays provide a window into the wonderfully diverse world of modern legal thought and show that great stories are worth retelling.

Douglas G. Baird
Chicago, Illinois
October 2006

1

Richard Danzig*

Hadley v. Baxendale: A Study in the Industrialization of the Law

Hadley v. Baxendale is still, and presumably always will be, a fixed star in the jurisprudential firmament.
—GRANT GILMORE, THE DEATH OF CONTRACT 83 (1974)

Of the many thousands of students who graduate from American law schools every year, probably all save a few hundred are required to read the 1854 English Exchequer case of *Hadley v. Baxendale*.[1] It is, indeed, one of a startlingly small number of opinions to which graduates from law school will almost assuredly have been exposed even if they attended different institutions, used a variety of textbooks, and opted for disparate electives. The exceptional pedagogical centrality of the case is further underscored by the similarly widespread attention the case receives in the curricula of all Commonwealth law schools.

But if the case is unusually widely read, it is typically narrowly studied. In the first-year law curriculum, where the opinion usually appears, cases are normally treated like doctrinal fruits on a conceptual tree: some bulk large, some are almost insignificant; some display a wondrous perfection of development, others are shown to be rotten at the core; some are further out along conceptual branches than others;

* Nunn Prize Fellow at the Center for International Strategic Studies (Washington, D.C.). An earlier version of this essay appeared in Richard Danzig, *Hadley v. Baxendale*: A Story in the Industrialization of Law, 4 J. Legal Stud. 249 (1975), published by the University of Chicago. Copyright 1975 by The University of Chicago. All rights reserved.

[1] 9 Ex. 341, 156 Eng. Rep. 145 (1854).

but all are quite erroneously treated as though they blossomed at the same time, and for the same harvest.

This ahistorical view may have some didactic advantages, but it overlooks much that is important. Cases are of different vintages; they arise in different settings. It matters that *Hadley v. Baxendale* was decided in 1854 in England, and not in 1974 in California. Without reflecting on the ramifications of these facts of timing and setting, perhaps teachers and students can understand black-letter law as it now is, but neither can comprehend the processes of doctrinal innovation, growth, and decay.

By focusing on one central case in its historical setting I hope in this article to provide an experiential supplement to the legal reader's steady diet of logic. My theme is that *Hadley v. Baxendale* can usefully be analyzed as a judicial invention in an age of industrial invention. After describing the facts and the holding of *Hadley v. Baxendale* in the first section that follows, my concern in succeeding sections is to discuss why the "rule of the case" was invented in its particular form and in this particular case; to assess the relationship between this judicial invention and the existing legal and economic technology; to underscore the impact of the rule in effecting a specialization of judicial labor and a standardization, centralization, and mass production of judicial products; and to demonstrate that the rule of the case became widely known and generally accepted because, as with other successful inventions, it was well advertised and marketed. I shall conclude by suggesting that although this invention was useful for the age in which it was created, it is very possible that it is now of limited significance and in need of modernization.

I

In Gloucester, England, on Thursday, May 12, 1853, the engine shaft at City Flour Mills broke, preventing the further milling of corn. On May 13, the mill proprietors, Joseph and Jonah Hadley, dispatched an employee to Pickford and Co., "common carriers," to inquire as to the fastest means of conveying the shaft to W. Joyce and Co., Greenwich, where it would serve as a model for the crafting of a new shaft. A Pickford employee, Mr. Perrett, represented that it would be delivered "on the second day after the day of . . . delivery" to Pickford.

The shaft was delivered to Pickford on Saturday, May 14, but it did not, in fact, reach W. Joyce and Co. until May 21, because at the last stage of voyage the shaft was shipped with a consignment of iron bound for Joyce and Co. by canal rather than by rail. In consequence, the Hadleys calculated that the steam mill stoppage was prolonged an unnecessary five days, at a cost in lost profits of £300.[2] When Pickford refused to make good these losses, the Hadleys brought suit before the Queen's judges, sitting in the Assize Court for Gloucester, naming Joseph Baxendale, the London-based managing director of Pickford, as the defendant. (Baxendale was personally liable for the failings of his unincorporated business.) Baxendale paid £25 into court as a settlement offer, but this was spurned, and the case went to trial before a "special jury" (about which more later) in August, three months after the alleged damages were inflicted. The Hadleys, now claiming "near £200" damages,[3] presented witnesses to show the nature of their understanding with Pickford and the magnitude of the damages they incurred as a result of the delay. (It developed that the witnesses testified to only £120 in damages.) The well-known barrister, Sir Henry Singer Keating, then summarized the plaintiff's case:

> The issue they [the jury] had to try was extremely simple, and peculiarly fitted for them to decide, namely, whether what he could not help designating the paltry sum of £25 was sufficient to compensate them [the Hadleys] . . . . The defendants Messrs. Pickford and Co., were common carriers, and as such possessed certain rights, and took upon themselves certain obligations.

Against this the defendants argued that the damages incurred were "too remote."

Sir Roger Crompton, the new but by all accounts careful and competent Assize judge,[4] instructed the jury

> to consider what, under the circumstances was a reasonable time for delivering the shaft; and next, what was the damages caused to the Plaintiffs by the delay in the delivery. . . . They should give their damages for the natural consequences of the defendant's breach of contract, and with that view they would

---

[2] 9 Exch. at 343, 156 Eng. Rep. at 146.

[3] Gloucester Journal, Supplement August 13, 1853, at 1, col. 4.

[4] "On the bench he proved himself to be a very sound lawyer and a good judge." 13 WILLIAM S. HOLDSWORTH, A HISTORY OF ENGLISH LAW 437 (7th ed., rev. 1956). A contemporary recorded his impression: "Crompton, J., was remarkable for learning, depth and acuteness and was painfully conscientious about speaking accurately when he spoke judicially. I believe also that he never recognized the notion that the common law adopts itself by a perpetual process of growth to the perpetual roll of the tide of circumstances as society advances." SIR W. ERLE, MEMORANDUM ON THE LAW RELATING TO THE UNITED STATES 38–39 (1869). I am indebted to Professor William Cornish for this reference.

have to consider whether the stoppages of the Plaintiff's works
was one of the probable and natural consequences of that
breach of contract, and then, looking to all the circumstances of
the case and the position of the parties, to say what was the
amount of the damages occasioned by the stoppage of the
works.[5]

So instructed, the jury retired for about half an hour and returned with
a compromise verdict: Damages were assessed at £50.

Baxendale promptly appealed. The case was heard in the Exchequer
on February 1 and 2, by Barons Alderson, Parke, and Martin, and
then, after "great pains were bestowed upon" the question,[6] Baron Alderson delivered an opinion on February 23, 1854. This opinion, the
only one rendered in *Hadley v. Baxendale* (for no further appeal was
taken), refashioned the substantive law of contract damages by effecting a subtle but significant change in the contemporary understanding
of the rule that damages be awarded only for the "natural consequences" of a breach. Other judges, and indeed, this same Exchequer
bench at other times, read the limitation as a simple rule tending by
the criterion of "naturalness" to exclude that portion of damages which
the plaintiff had himself exacerbated (and thus unnaturally sustained),
and by the criterion of "consequence" to exclude those injuries which
could not, in fact, be causally related to the breach. In contrast, Baron
Alderson here read the phrase "natural consequences" as though it
meant normal consequences and thus predictable consequences—
obviously a more rigorous standard. In the most critical sentence of the
opinion, he said:

> Where two parties have made a contract which one of them has
> broken, the damages which the other party ought to receive in
> respect of such breach of contract should be such as may fairly
> and reasonably be considered either arising naturally, i.e., ac-
> cording to the usual course of things, from such breach of con-
> tract itself, or such as may reasonably be supposed to have
> been in the contemplation of both parties, at the time they
> made the contract, as the probable result of the breach of it.[7]

Not content with simply ordering a new trial after the articulation
of the standard, Baron Alderson went on to "apply the principles above

---

[5] Gloucester Journal, *supra* note 3.

[6] Chief Baron Pollock later remarked: "The argument took place several
weeks before the judgment was given, and I know that great pains were bestowed upon it." Wilson v. Newport Dock Co., 35 L.J. Ex. 97, 103 (1866).

[7] 9 Ex. at 354, 156 Eng. Rep. at 151.

laid down" to the case at hand, and advanced three rather remarkable propositions. First, he asserted that "the only circumstances here communicated by the plaintiffs to the defendants" at the time the contract was made were that they were millers whose mill shaft was broken. According to Baron Alderson, there was no notice of the "special circumstances" that the mill was stopped and profits would be lost as a result of delay in the delivery of the shaft. Thus the Baron concluded that damages for lost profits could not be awarded under the contemplation branch of the rule.

Second, Baron Alderson held that "it is obvious that in the great multitude of cases of millers sending off broken shafts to third persons by a carrier under ordinary circumstances"[8] the mill would not be idle and profits lost during the period of shipment. Millers, he held, ordinarily would have spare shafts or, at any rate, if their mills were stopped it would usually be a consequence of other difficulties as well. Thus there could be no recovery for lost profits under the "usual course of things" branch of the rule.

Third, Baron Alderson held "that the Judge ought, therefore, to have told the jury, upon the facts before them, they ought not to take the loss of profits into consideration at all in estimating damages."[9]

The first of these propositions is remarkable because it flies in the face of what the reporter of Baron Alderson's decision apparently thought was established by the record. The reporter's headnote says unequivocally that the defendant's clerk "was told that the mill was stopped, that the shaft much be delivered immediately, and that a special entry, if necessary, must be made to hasten its delivery...."[10]

The second and third propositions are remarkable because they hold that the trial judge, and in case of his error, the appellate judge, ought to preempt a local jury in determining commercial error, even though the issue appears to be one of fact and not one of law. These latter propositions serve to underscore an important, although generally less noticed, procedural innovation corresponding to the substantive change effected by *Hadley v. Baxendale*: the case not only modifies instructions to juries, it also directs judges to keep some issues from the jury.

II

The novelty of the changes effected in procedural and substantive law by *Hadley v. Baxendale* suggests that the opinion may be exam-

---

[8] 9 Ex. at 356, 156 Eng. Rep. at 151.

[9] 9 Ex. at 356, 156 Eng. Rep. at 151.

[10] 9 Ex. at 344, 156 Eng. Rep. at 145.

ined as an invention. The innovation effected in the law is here unusually stark. Baron Alderson, in support of the central proposition he advanced, cited no precedent and invoked no British legislative or academic authority in favor of the rule he articulated. Nor was this due to oversight. The opinion broke new ground by establishing a rule for decision by judges in an area of law—the calculation of damages in contracts suits—which had previously been left to almost entirely unstructured decision by English juries.

Chitty's preeminent 1826 treatise on contracts, for example, even in its 771-page 1850 edition, had allocated only 13 of its pages to the subject of damages, and virtually all of those pages concerned issues associated with penalty clauses. As to damages in the normal run of cases, Chitty had only one comment to offer:

> When the parties have not furnished the criterion of damages by stipulating for a liquidated sum to be paid as such, it is, in general, entirely the province of the jury to assess the amount, with reference to all the circumstances of the case.[11]

Similarly, Smith's *Law of Contracts,* prominent in the same period, mentioned damages not at all,[12] and Smith's general collection of leading law cases touched on damages only in the context of tort.[13] Thus the Hadleys' counsel seems to have fairly summarized the state of prior thinking on the subject when he argued that "the difficulty which . . . exists in the estimation of the true amount of damages, supports the view . . . that the question is properly for the decision of a jury" without elaborate instruction or review.[14]

The strikingly novel nature of the innovation of English law effected by *Hadley v. Baxendale* must have been particularly apparent to the participants in the case because among the cases outmoded by this opinion, one decided seven years earlier involved this same Baxendale and these same judges. In *Black v. Baxendale,*[15] Pickford was two days late in the delivery of "five bundles of haycloths," thus causing Black's employee to incur both wasted time (valued at a little more than one pound per day) and an otherwise unnecessary "removal cost" of ten

---

[11] JOSEPH CHITTY, A PRACTICAL TREATISE ON THE LAW OF CONTRACTS 768 (4th ed. 1850).

[12] JOHN W. SMITH, THE LAW OF CONTRACTS (1847). See also the second edition (1855), which similarly omits the subject.

[13] JOHN W. SMITH, A SELECTION OF LEADING CASES ON VARIOUS BRANCHES OF THE LAW 430ff. (Henry S. Keating & James S. Willes eds., 3d ed. 1849).

[14] 9 Ex. at 347, 156 Eng. Rep. at 148.

[15] 1 Ex. 410, 154 Eng. Rep. 174 (1847).

shillings. At trial, Chief Baron Pollock "directed the jury that they were at liberty to give these expenses as damages if they should think fit."[16] Inexplicably the jury awarded damages of ten pounds— apparently more than the amount the most generous calculation of damages would have justified. Baron Martin, who was to sit on the panel that decided *Hadley v. Baxendale*, argued the case on appeal for Baxendale, claiming, *inter alia*, that the jury verdict should be overturned because Pickford "had no notice for what purpose the goods were sent"[17] or what expenses would ensue on failure to deliver. Neither Baron Parke nor Baron Alderson, both later to sit with Baron Martin in *Hadley v. Baxendale*, would accept this argument. Baron Parke said, "The defendants are responsible only for reasonable consequences of their breach of contract. It was a question for the jury whether [the expenses were] . . . reasonable."[18] And Baron Alderson added, "[w]hether these expenses were reasonable was entirely a question for the jury."[19] Had the sum been larger both judges would have reversed on grounds of miscalculation of the expenses, but both (joined by the rest of the court) agreed that the type and limit of the liability incurred was exclusively a matter for the jury. This view, of course, was what *Hadley v. Baxendale* rejected.

In a lecture given at the Seldon Society while this article was in draft,[20] Professor A. W. B. Simpson pointed out that both Pothier's treatise on the French Civil Code (translated into English in 1806)[21] and Sedgwick's American treatise in its first and second editions of 1847 and 1852 argued for rules of contract liability essentially like that adopted by the Court in *Hadley v. Baxendale*.[22] Further, Professor Simpson noted that Baron Parke remarked in the course of the argument in *Hadley v. Baxendale* that he thought that "the sensible rule appears to be that which has been laid down in France . . . and which is . . . translated by Sedgwick. . . ."[23] From this Professor Simpson con-

---

[16] 1 Ex. at 410–11, 154 Eng. Rep. at 174–75.

[17] 1 Ex. at 410–11, 154 Eng. Rep. at 174–75.

[18] 1 Ex. at 410–11, 154 Eng. Rep. at 174–75.

[19] 1 Ex. at 410–11, 154 Eng. Rep. at 174–75.

[20] A. W. B. Simpson, Innovation in Contract Law (unpublished manuscript available from Professor Simpson).

[21] ROBERT JOSEPH POTHIER, A TREATISE ON THE LAW OF OBLIGATIONS, OR CONTRACTS, pt. I, ch. II, art. III, §§16ff. (William David Evans trans., 1806).

[22] THEODORE SEDGWICK, A TREATISE ON THE MEASURE OF DAMAGES 67 (2d ed. 1852).

[23] 9 Ex. at 346, 156 Eng. Rep. at 147.

cludes that "the moving spirit behind *Hadley v. Baxendale* was surely Baron Parke"[24] and argues, more generally, that this illustrates a proposition advanced in his lecture: that innovation in the law in the nineteenth century was largely prompted by the quiet absorption of the observations of treatise writers, particularly treatise writers influenced by the civil law, into the decisions of English common law judges.

There is much to be said for this position. But Professor Simpson's otherwise admirable discussion seems insufficient in two ways. First, in looking to Baron Parke as the animating force behind the decision, Simpson neglects to consider the role of Baxendale's counsel, Sir James Shaw Willes. As we shall see, the fact that Willes was a principal actor in the case was of no small significance in effecting the spread of the rule.

Contemporary descriptions convey a portrait of Willes as extraordinary on three counts, all of which must have operated to his advantage in this litigation. He was reputed to be the ablest commercial lawyer of his time; he was co-editor of the most prominent annotated volume of British legal cases;[25] and he was remarkably cosmopolitan. It was said of Willes that he spoke seven languages, many of them so fluently that when, for example, he was accused in Spain of having murdered a coachman who fell under the horses of a carriage in which Sir James was riding, Sir James successfully defended himself before the Spanish Court without assistance. It seems clear that his commercial interests combined with his academic orientation and his cosmopolitan outlook caused Willes to be thoroughly familiar with the French Civil Code's provision on damages and with the similar views of Sedgwick, then the outstanding American commentator on the subject. Indeed, the official report of the arguments before the appellate bench makes it clear that the counsel on both sides came to court well primed on Pothier and Sedgwick and that they cited them to the judges more often than vice versa.

I shall return to Willes's influence later. Obviously, the fact that Willes had read Pothier and especially Sedgwick only reinforces Mr. Simpson's point as to the influence of treatise writers. Two years after the case was decided, when Willes had occasion to comment on it in his next edition of Smith's *Leading Cases*, he underscored Sedgwick's influence:

> [T]he subject is discussed at length in the very learned work of Mr. Theodore Sedgwick "On the Measure of Damages" Ch. 3

---

[24] Simpson, *supra* note 20, at 48.

[25] SMITH, *supra* note 13.

.... The suggestion of Mr. Sedgwick . . . seems to agree in substance with the decision of the Court of Exchequer in the case of *Hadley v. Baxendale* and others. . . .[26]

However—and this is the second, more significant regard in which Professor Simpson's discussion can be faulted—if an understanding of the rule in *Hadley v. Baxendale* must begin with some recognition of the influence of foreign models on British thinkers, it need not end there. As Friedman and Ladinsky note in another context, an interest in foreign ideas may be prompted by "dissatisfaction" with the existing law. "A foreign model here sharpens discussion and provides a ready made plan. Yet the felt need for such [a law change] has domestic origins."[27] Why was there a felt need for an innovation in the law of damages at the time of *Hadley v. Baxendale*? The search for a more satisfactory answer than that provided by reference to foreign treatise writers requires us to look further.

III

To understand the origins and the limitations of the rule in *Hadley v. Baxendale* we must appreciate the industrial and legal world out of which it came and for which it was designed. In 1854 Great Britain was in a state of extraordinary flux. Between 1801 and 1851 its population rose from 10.6 to 20.9 million. By 1861 its population was 23.2 million and its GNP £668 million. Contemporaries saw the magnitude of this change and were aware of its impact on the law. As one writer, surveying the scene in 1863, put it:

What our law was then [in 1828], it is not now; and what it is now, can best be understood by seeing what it was, then. It is like the comparison between England under former, and present, systems of transit, for persons, property, and intelligence: between the days of lumbering wagons, stage coaches, and a creeping post—and of swift, luxurious railroads and lightening telegraphs. All is altered: material, inducing corresponding moral and social changes.[28]

Arising squarely in the middle of the "industrial revolution" and directly in the midst of the "Great Boom" of 1842–1874, *Hadley v. Bax-*

---

[26] JOHN W. SMITH, A SELECTION OF LEADING CASES ON VARIOUS BRANCHES OF THE LAW 430–31 (Henry S. Keating & James S. Willes eds., 4th ed. 1856).

[27] Lawrence M. Friedman & Jack Ladinsky, *Social Change and the Law of Industrial Accidents*, 67 Colum. L. Rev. 50, 78 (1967).

[28] SAMUEL WARREN, A POPULAR AND PRACTICAL INTRODUCTION TO LAW STUDIES 12 (3d ed. 1863).

endale was a product of those times. The case was shaped by the increasing sophistication of the economy and the law—and equally significantly by the gaps, the naïveté, and the crudeness of the contemporary system.

The raw facts of the case should alert the reader to the half-matured
and unevenly developing nature of the economy in which the decision
was rendered. For example, the Hadley mill was steam-powered. While
it was not hand-run, animal-driven, wind-powered, or water-powered,
as in an earlier age, it was also not powered by electricity as it would
be in the next century. So with the now famous broken shaft. It was a
complicated piece of machinery, manufactured by a specialized company on the other side of England. But it was neither a standardized
nor a mass-produced machine. It was hand-crafted. Thus the transaction in *Hadley v. Baxendale*: The old shaft had to be brought to eastern
England as the "model" for the new one.

The circumstances of the breach similarly reflect a half-way mod-
ernized society. The breach occurred because the shaft was sent by canal, the early industrial transport form, rather than by rail, the mature industrial transport form. That both co-existed as significant
means of shipment suggests the transitional nature of the period. The
ready acceptance of the notion that delay gave rise to damages, that
time meant money, suggests the affinity of the modes of thought of this
age to our own. But the units of account for measuring time in *Hadley
v. Baxendale* suggest the distance between our period and this one:
Speed for a trip across England was measured in days, not hours.

If the facts offer us a glimpse of an economic world in transition,
what of the legal system which had to deal with that transition? This
system was also modernizing, but, at the time of *Hadley v. Baxendale*,
it was still strikingly underdeveloped. The case itself indicates the rudimentary and uneven development of the commercial law of the period. *Hadley v. Baxendale* is frequently described as a case involving a
claim for damages consequent on a breach of a negotiated contract for
especially quick delivery of a consigned package; but in fact, although
this was the first of two counts on which the Hadleys initially pressed
their suit, both the official and the contemporary press reports make it
clear that before going to trial against Baxendale they abandoned all
claim to damages based on a specific contract. Instead their pleadings
claimed damages arising as a consequence of Pickford's failure to effect
delivery "within a reasonable time" as it was obliged to do because of
its status as a common carrier. If, as Maine posited ten years after
Hadley v. Baxendale, the process of modernization involves a move-

ment from status to contract,[29] this most famed of modern contract cases is peculiarly antiquarian!

The pleadings' emphasis on status rather than contract appears to have been related to the underdeveloped nature of the law of agency in England at the time. The *Gloucester Journal* report of the Assize trial comments:

> The declaration had originally contained two counts; the first charging the defendants with having contracted to deliver the crank within the space of two days, which they did in truth do, but there was a doubt how far Mr. Perrett, the agent of the defendants, had authority to bind them by any special contract which would vary their ordinary liability. It was therefore thought not prudent to proceed upon that count, but upon the count of not delivering within a reasonable time.[30]

The Hadleys' counsel apparently reasoned that a jury verdict against Baxendale predicated on what was said to or by Pickford's clerk might be upset by an appellate court on a theory that personal liability could not be imputed to Baxendale through comment to or by an agent. The situation was summarized by Baxendale's counsel in the argument on appeal:

> Here the declaration is founded upon the defendants' duty as common carrier, and indeed there is no pretense for saying that they entered into a special contract to bear all the consequences of the non-delivery of the article in question. They were merely bound to carry it safely, and to deliver it within a reasonable time. The duty of the clerk, who was in attendance at the defendants' office, was to enter the article, and to take the amount of the carriage; but a mere notice to him, such as was here given, could not make the defendants, as carriers, liable as upon a special contract. Such matters, therefore, must be rejected from the consideration of the question.[31]

Baxendale's counsel here overstates the case, but at the least it appears that there was an uncertainty in the rudimentary law of agency as it existed at the time.

This uncertainty may explain Baron Alderson's surprising assertion that the Hadleys failed to serve notice that the mill operations were dependent on the quick return of the shaft. It may be that as a factual

---

[29] HENRY MAINE, ANCIENT LAW 165 (1864).

[30] Gloucester Journal, *supra* note 3, at 1, col. 3.

[31] 9 Ex. at 352, 156 Eng. Rep. at 150.

matter the Hadleys never served notice on Pickford's clerk of their extreme dependence on the shaft, and that the Court reporter simply
erred in asserting that notice had been served to this effect. But it is
also possible that Baron Alderson saw the case as Pickford's counsel
urged: "[A] mere notice . . . was here given . . . [but it] could not make
the defendants liable . . . [and therefore it was to] be rejected from the
consideration of the question."[32]

This agency problem underscores the fact that the case is *Hadley v.
Baxendale*, not *Hadley v. Pickford's Moving Co.*; in other words, that
the opinion was handed down at a time and in a situation in which
principals were personally liable for the misfeasance of their companies. Although the principle of limited liability was already recognized
in England for exceptional "chartered" companies, it was not until 1855
that Parliament extended the right to ordinary entrepreneurs, and it
was not until 1901 that Pickford (and many other companies) incorporated. In 1854 the desirability of limiting personal liability for corporate debts was a major item of parliamentary debate and the legal
world's most hotly disputed subject. This contemporary ferment was
fed by, and in turn reinforced, related areas of concern about the run of
liability: A Royal Commission was meeting in 1854 to consider expanding the right to petition for bankruptcy; the right to limit liability for
torts by means of a prior contract was being pondered in the courts;
and the alleged right of common carriers to limit liability for property
loss by mere prior notification was being keenly debated.

Under these conditions the concept of a severe restriction on the
scope of damages in contract actions must have seemed both less alien
than it would have appeared to a judge a decade earlier, and more important than it would have seemed to a judge a decade later. For in
1854 judges were, at one and the same time, confronted with a growing
acceptance of the idea of limited liability and yet with a situation of
unlimited personal liability for commercial misfeasance. This was a
time, moreover, when commercial interactions involved increasing ag-
glomerations of capital and a pyramiding and interlocking of transactions, so that any error might lead to damages that could significantly
diminish annual profits or even destroy the personal fortunes of those
sharing in thinly financed ventures.

Two particular aspects of the incomplete evolution of ideas about
limited liability appear to be especially intertwined with the litigation
in *Hadley v. Baxendale*. A quarter of a century before the litigation,
Parliament had addressed the question of substantial claims against

---

[32] 9 Ex. at 352, 156 Eng. Rep. at 150.

coach and canal carriers for loss of sealed boxes that contained jewels, currency, and the like but whose exceptional value was not superficially apparent and that were consequently carried for regular fees and with no more than regular care. Parliament's solution in the Common Carriers Act of 1830 was to declare that shippers of "articles of great value in small compass" were required to give notice of that value or otherwise have their right of recovery limited to ten pounds.[33]

That the act did not control *Hadley v. Baxendale*—a case involving a bulky object—must have been evident. But it is doubtful that the Act was irrelevant to *Hadley v. Baxendale*. If the Hadleys' agent went out of his way to assert that the mill's operations depended on the speedy return of the shaft, it may have been because of the pattern established by the Act's notice requirement. It is yet more probably that by the time of litigation the lawyers involved had turned to the Act as the first legislative referent in cases involving loss by a common carrier such as Pickford. Further, it is worth noting that Baron Parke, a member of the *Hadley v. Baxendale* panel, was the author of the authoritative opinion on the 1830 Act.[34] Given this familiarity, it seems reasonable to suggest that in their emphasis on the interplay between notice and liability and in their ready acceptance of the notion of the desirability of limiting damages for cases that are not signaled as (if the pun will be forgiven) more than run-of-the-mill affairs, the *Hadley v. Baxendale* judges followed patterns already established by Parliament.

Viewed from this perspective, the common law innovation promulgated in *Hadley v. Baxendale* may be seen as a technical adaptation of an older idea to new circumstances. The Act of 1830 may have been sensibly phrased given the state of carriers' and shippers' businesses when it was enacted, but by mid-century commerce was more complicated. Bulk shipments had increased with the advent of the railroad, and it may reasonably be supposed that this increase was not so much the product of increases in shipments of horses, cows, produce, and other things easily recognized and valued as it was a consequence of more shipments of machinery which—like the Hadleys' mill shaft—performed complex functions and was of uncertain worth and importance. By 1854 it must have been strikingly apparent that an item did not have to be of "small compass" to be "of uncertain value."

If from one vantage point *Hadley v. Baxendale* simply effected a judicial extension of the Act of 1830, from another vantage point *Hadley v. Baxendale* stands as an example of a tension between Parliament

---

[33] 1 Will. 4, c. 68 (1830).

[34] Walker v. Jackson, 10 M. & W. 161, 152 Eng. Rep. 424 (1842).

and the judiciary. This tension grew from an ambiguity in section 6 of
the Act of 1830. That section was open to the interpretation that by
posting notice carriers could limit their liability for loss or injury to ten
pounds. The consequent railroad practice of limiting liability by published handbills or printed notice on tickets or bills of lading aroused
much public anger. A modern British legal historian has summarized
the situation:

> [W]hile it could be said that many carriers had the check of
> competition to oblige them to take an accommodating line with
> dissatisfied customers, the railways could afford to face claims
> for loss and injury with the disdainful wave of an exemption
> clause. By the early 1850s there had been a number of well
> publicized refusals to pay which made the railways extremely
> unpopular with the press and in Parliament.[35]

In 1852, the Exchequer, in an opinion by Baron Parke in *Carr's Case*,[36]
held effective the practice of limiting liability by notice as within the
meaning of the 1830 Act. By the time of *Hadley v. Baxendale*, a year
and a half later, it was clear that this would not be allowed to continue.
"The effect of nineteenth century parliamentary reform was to compel
the parties to have competitive legislative programmes on every subject,"[37] and this issue was no exception. In December 1852 a Parliamentary Select Committee was charged with considering revision of
the 1830 Act, and by July 1853 it had held hearings and submitted five
reports, urging revision of the 1830 Common Carriers Act. Although
the Committee had not focused on Carr's case, and the bill effecting
reversal of the case was not passed until April 1854, as *Hadley v. Baxendale* was being argued and decided in January and February 1854 it
must have seemed very probably that this legislation was coming. Seen
in this light *Hadley v. Baxendale* effected a judge-made limitation on
damages as a matter of public law just as Parliament was about to in-
hibit severely carriers' capacities to limit their liability as a matter of
private law.

Other more comprehensive studies of Victorian judges and legisla-
tors will have to explore this tension between Parliamentary and judicial disposition toward the entrepreneur, and particularly the common
carrier, but insofar as a case study can shed any light on the matter, it
is worth noting that the predisposition of this panel seems clear. Two

---

[35] William Cornish (unpublished, untitled manuscript available from Professor Cornish, Magdalene College, University of Cambridge).

[36] Carr v. L & Y Ry., 7 Ex. 707, 155 Eng Rep. 1133 (1852).

[37] ALAN HARDING, A SOCIAL HISTORY OF ENGLISH LAW 337 (1966).

of the three Exchequer judges were tied to Pickford in contexts likely to make them sympathetic to the company. Baron Martin had represented Pickford before ascending to the bench, and Baron Parke's brother had been the managing director of the company before Baxendale.

The opinion in *Hadley v. Baxendale* is written in general terms and has had a broad impact on the law of contracts down to the present day. But at the time of its conception it was probably seen and shaped by its authors in the context of uncertainties about the law of agency and conflicts about the shape of the law of liability—particular common carriers' liability—that are now generally forgotten.

IV

An understanding of the relationship of the rule in *Hadley v. Baxendale* to the contemporary law affecting common carriers may be a predicate to comprehending the impulse behind the rule and its form, but standing alone it tells only a part of the story. I think the rule in *Hadley v. Baxendale* may have had its most significant contemporary effects not for the entrepreneurs powering a modernizing economy, but rather for the judges caught up in their own problems of modernization.

By the middle of the nineteenth century Parliament had acted to modernize the judicial system in a number of important ways. Successive law revision commissions and ensuing enactments had effected changes in the substantive laws of tort, debt, criminal law, and, as we have seen, contractual liability. Antiquated aspects of pleading and procedure were similarly remodeled. But the size and case disposition capacity of the common law courts remained remarkably stagnant.

In 1854 the entire national judiciary of Britain and Wales sitting in courts of general jurisdiction numbered fifteen. These judges, distributed equally between three benches—the Court of Common Pleas, the Queen's Bench, and the Exchequer—sat individually to hear all cases in London and at Assize (court held in major provincial towns) for two terms of about four weeks each year. They convened as panels of three or four to hear appeals in London at other times. They sat in panels usually numbering seven (confusingly denominated as the Exchequer Chamber) to hear appeals from the panels of three or four. Only appeals from the panels of seven would be heard by another body of men: The House of Lords.

A quarter of a century earlier, in a famous speech in the House of Commons, Lord Brougham had asked: "How can it be expected that twelve judges can go through the increased and increasing business now, when the affairs of men are so extended and multiplied in every direction, the same twelve, and at one time fifteen, having not been much more than sufficient for the comparatively trifling number of causes tried two or three centuries ago?"[38] Brougham's call for more judges was answered in 1830 by the addition of one judge to each court. But even with this improvement, it was apparent that there was a severe limitation on the number and intricacy of the trials and appeals that these judges could process. Indeed over the fifty years surrounding the decision in *Hadley v. Baxendale* the number of cases brought to trial in the common law courts each year remained remarkably stable and low (around 2,400 cases) despite the extraordinary increase in commercial transactions over the period. Although the modern observer is likely to approach this situation with his view colored by images of the endless, enervating litigation described in Dickens's *Bleak House* (published in 1853), this stability in case processing apparently was not achieved by allowing a case backlog to accumulate. Extant docket sheets show that at any given Assize no more than half a dozen cases would typically be held for later sittings. The *Hadley v. Baxendale* litigation is suggestive of this speed in disposition. The Hadleys suffered their injury in May; they brought their suit and received prompt jury trial and judgment in August. Baxendale appealed on the fifth of November, had the appeal argued on the first of February, and received a favorable decision by the end of that month.[39]

Probably the most critical factor in enabling the Courts at Common Law to operate on so intimate a basis was the reconstruction, by act of Parliament in 1846,[40] of the haphazardly functioning local "Courts of Requests" into an extensive and competent court system capable of handling a large volume of cases. This system of "county courts" was rendered inferior to the Common Law Courts (which began being called the "Superior Courts") by permitting appeal from County Court judgments to a Common Law Court and by limiting County Court claims to sums less than twenty pounds. Further, the intent of the legislature to effect a transfer of minor cases away from the Superior Courts was manifested by the enactment of a statute assessing costs against even a victorious plaintiff in Superior Court if his recovery in a contract case amounted to no more than twenty pounds, or in a tort case to five pounds.

---

[38] 18 Parl. Deb. (2d ser.) (1828) 127, 140.

[39] The precise dates may be found in 22 L.T.O.S. 91, 262, 276 (1843–54), and 23 L.T.O.S. 69 (1854).

[40] 9 & 10 Vict., c. 95 (1846).

After their creation in 1846, the County Courts immediately became the journeyman carriers of the judicial workload. Within their first year of operation they reported receiving 429,215 cases.[41] In 1857 they dealt with 744,652 "plaints."[42] We are properly cautioned to discriminate between substantial judicial business and routine administrative debt-collection cases in assessing the significance of caseloads over this period. This advice is particularly apt because the County Courts were initially conceived as debtor-creditor courts and always drew the bulk of their business from this context. But it seems clear that the County Courts also quickly began handling a substantial number of more substantial lawsuits, and this development was strongly reinforced by an Act of Parliament in 1850 that expanded County Court jurisdiction to encompass claims of up to fifty pounds. By the time of *Hadley v. Baxendale* the County Courts were very probably handling many times the number of tort, contract, and other nondebt cases then being processed by the Superior Court judges at Assizes.

Against this backdrop the rule in *Hadley v. Baxendale* can be seen to have had significant contemporary implications that are normally invisible to the modern observer. The bifurcation of the County and Superior Court systems effected a specialization of labor insofar as it tended to discriminate between unimportant and important cases at least on the basis of the amount of recovery they involved. This division of labor was perfectly sensible so long as County Court work was almost exclusively concerned with debts, because in that form of litigation the amount likely to be awarded can be ascertained with great certainty. But by 1854 the events I have sketched probably prompted an increase in contract litigation in the County Courts. If brought in Superior Courts these cases were pressed at the peril of securing only minor recovery and then having that success washed out by the burden of costs. Under such conditions it is not surprising that previously ignored questions of the calculation of damages in contracts cases began to receive attention, not so much because these rules were considered important as matters of substantive law as because they were important as rules of jurisdiction. By identifying the criteria by which damages were to be assessed, the *Hadley v. Baxendale* court enhanced the predictability of damages and therefore the correct allocation of cases between the systems. Moreover, since the rule of the case coupled this enhanced predictability with an assertion of limitations on recovery, it

---

[41] Harry Smith, *The Resurgent County Court in Victorian Britain*, 12 Am. J. Legal Hist. 126, 128 (1969).

[42] WARREN, *supra* note 28, at 46.

tended to shunt cases from the Superior Courts toward the County Courts and thus protect the smaller system from at least a portion of the workload that if untrammeled would overwhelm it.

Some standardization of court decisions was implicit in these developments. But this standardization afforded more advantages than simply those associated with caseload allocation and (because of enhanced predictability of outcome) caseload reduction through settlement. Standardization was a means by which the Superior Courts could enhance their authority over County Courts at the very moment they were yielding primary jurisdiction to them.

In 1854 it must have been apparent to the fifteen judges who composed the national judicial system that they had no hope of reviewing half a million cases or even that fraction of them which dealt with genuinely contested issues. Moreover, the relatively small stakes involved in County Court cases left all but a miniscule proportion of litigants disinclined to incur the costs of appeal. Under these conditions it is not surprising that *ad hoc* review gave way to attempts at a crystallized delineation of instructions for dispute resolution that more closely resembled legislation than they did prior common law adjudication.

In its centralization of control, the judicial invention here examined paralleled the industrial developments of the age. The importance of the centralization of control is particularly evident when the rule is put back into the context in which it was promulgated: in terms of judges' control over juries. Told at its simplest level, *Hadley v. Baxendale* is the tale of a litigation contest between two local merchants and a London-based entrepreneur in which the local jury decided for the local merchants and the London judges asserted the priority of their judgment for the national entrepreneur. The tension inherent in the conflict of perspectives between the two decision-making centers—local juries and appellate judges—is underscored when one focuses on the particular decision makers in this case. It was a *special* jury that rendered a verdict for the Hadleys. Special juries were drawn, at the request of a party (probably on assertion of unusual complication in the litigation),[43] from a limited list of property owners. At the Baxendale trial nine of the twelve jurors were designated "merchants." Three were labeled simply "Esquire."[44] If life in the mid-nineteenth century was anything like life in our times, the jury members, themselves local

---

[43] THOMAS E. TOMLINS, THE LAW-DICTIONARY, s.v. Jury (4th ed. 1835) (no pagination): "Special juries were originally introduced in trials at bar, when the causes were of two [*sic*] great nicety for the discussion of ordinary freeholders. . . ."

[44] Gloucester Journal, *supra* note 3.

merchants who must have suffered frustration or injury from the then frequent occurrence of carrier error, probably sympathized much more readily with the Hadleys than with Baxendale. In contrast, the panel that heard the case on appeal was "special" in a way quite different from the jury. Two of the panel's members had experienced the difficulties and adopted the perspective of Pickford at one time or another. Under these conditions the invention of the case must have seemed particularly appealing to its promulgators. It led not simply to a resolution of this case for Baxendale, but also, more generally, to a rule of procedure and review that shifted power from more parochial to more cosmopolitan decision makers. As Baron Alderson put the matter, "we deem it to be expedient and necessary to state explicitly the rule which . . . the jury [ought] to be governed by . . . for if the jury are left without any definite rule to guide them, it will, in such cases as these, manifestly lead to the greatest injustice."[45]

From a less personal perspective the invention also effected a modernization by enhancing efficiency as a result of taking matters out of the hands of the jurors. Whatever its other characteristics, jury justice is hand-crafted justice. Each case is mulled on an *ad hoc* basis with reference to little more than, as Chitty put it, "the circumstances of the case."[46] In an age of rapidly increasing numbers of transactions and amounts of litigation, a hand-crafted system of justice had as little durability as the hand-crafted system of tool production on which the Hadleys relied for their mill parts. By moving matters from a special jury—which cost twenty-four pounds, untold time to assemble, and a half hour to decide—to a judge, the rule in *Hadley v. Baxendale* facilitated judicial production. And by standardizing the rule that a judge employed, the decision compounded the gain—a point of particular importance in relation to the County Courts where juries were rarely called.

Thus the judicial advantages of *Hadley v. Baxendale* can be summarized: After the opinion the outcome of a claim for damages for breach of contract could be more readily predicted (and would therefore be less often litigated) than before; when litigated the more appropriate court could more often be chosen; the costs and biases of a jury could more often be avoided; and County Court judges and juries alike could be more readily confined in the exercise of their discretion. Clearly the rule invented in the case offered substantial rewards to the judges who promulgated it and in later years reaffirmed it.

---

[45] 9 Ex. at 353–54, 156 Eng. Rep. at 150.

[46] CHITTY, *supra* note 11.

V

How does an opinion whose primary functions seem to correlate with a quarrel over an 1830 transport act and with the needs of a judicial system in the 1850s come to be viewed as "a fixed star in the jurisprudential firmament" so many years later?[47]

The fame and widespread acceptance of the innovation effected by this case seems particularly remarkable when we remember that this was a decision by one of three equal intermediate courts. Other Exchequer opinions were vulnerable to rejection or recasting by Queen's Bench and Common Pleas judges sitting either in their appellate capacity as the Exchequer Chamber, or within their own systems as Assize and nisi prius judges. Why did this case escape overruling and anonymity? The theme of invention suggests an answer. For an invention to be widely employed it must not only fill a need and be well fabricated; it must also be marketed. In mid-nineteenth century England it was perhaps easier than ever before for a judge-created rule to take hold and influence other judges and lay conduct. Prompt press reporting of opinions and an expanding bar served to transmit at least the gist of commercial opinions to those likely to be affected by them. More important, an increasing professionalization of the system of court reporting made the then common tactic of "doubting" the accuracy of an adverse reported opinion more difficult, and thus enhanced the power of precedent.

There was another factor at play that has been lost sight of by modern observers. Sir James Shaw Willes, overlooked by Professor Simpson but to whom I have ascribed much of the responsibility for the invention in the case, appears to have been remarkably situated to effect the marketing of the invention by virtue of his position as co-editor of the foremost legal textbook of the time: Smith's *Leading Cases*. Yet more remarkably—and this underscores the already mentioned intimacy of the mid-century British legal world—Willes's opposing counsel on appeal (and the counsel for the Hadleys at trial), Sir Henry Singer Keating,[48] was the other editor of Smith's *Leading Cases*.

The two "editors" wasted no time in converting their litigation arguments into an academic analysis, so that a primary difference between the 1852 edition of Smith's *Leading Cases* and the 1856 edition was a lengthy description of and commentary on *Hadley v. Baxendale*. The impact of such notoriety cannot, of course, be precisely ascer-

---

[47] GRANT GILMORE, THE DEATH OF CONTRACT 49 (1974).

[48] *See generally* 30 DICTIONARY OF NATIONAL BIOGRAPHY 275, s.v. Sir Henry Singer Keating (Sidney Lee ed., 1892).

tained, but it seems fair to surmise that it was substantial. The breadth of the book's readership and the respect with which it was regarded can be inferred in part from the frequency with which it is noted as referred to by judges in the official reports. Our rudimentary sources, moreover, show Smith's note on *Hadley* quoted by litigants in cases where the *Hadley* rule might apply and in public discussion of the rule.[49]

Nor did Sir Henry and Sir James end their association with *Hadley v. Baxendale* upon enshrining the opinion in Smith's *Leading Cases*. Both culminated illustrious careers by elevation to the Superior Courts; and Sir James, in particular, in his capacity as an appellate judge had frequent occasion to endorse and expound on the opinion in *Hadley v. Baxendale*. Within a year of arguing for Baxendale he was one of three judges offering an opinion in the case in which the Court of Common Pleas accepted the Exchequer rule. Over the next decade Willes established himself as the outstanding commercial law judge of the latter half of the century. He then crafted the most significant nineteenth-century opinion interpreting and endorsing *Hadley v. Baxendale*,[50] and followed it, four years later, with the next most often cited elaboration of the rule[51]—in this instance in an opinion reviewed and sustained by the Exchequer Chamber.

In sum, Sir James was a central actor in the importation, spread, and interpretation of the rule in *Hadley v. Baxendale*; and he contributed toward these ends as an academic, as a litigator, and as an esteemed appellate judge. If the common law is thought to be some "brooding omnipresence" working itself pure, it obviously acquired some substantial human assistance in this instance.

VI

But if we have some idea of the first causes of the spread of the invention, what explains its staying power? Here, I think, the histories of industrial and legal inventions part company. As a rule industrial inventions are prized in proportion to their use. If, like the model T Ford, some inventions remain valued long after they have lost their general utility, it is only because some aficionados treasure them as acknowledged antiques. The present curricular predominance and asserted intellectual centrality of *Hadley v. Baxendale* suggests that this is not so

---

[49] See, for example, the argument of counsel for the defendants in British Columbia Saw-Mill v. Nettleship, 3 C.P. 499, 505 (1868).

[50] Fletcher v. Tayleur, 17 C.B. 20, 28 (1855).

[51] Horn v. Midland Rail Co., 7 C.P. 583 (1872).

in the law. For as presently taught and ensconced in the Uniform Commercial Code, the rule is almost as irrelevant to the modern age as are those artifacts—the Hadley hand-crafted shaft and the Baxendale canal barge—that provided the occasion for its articulation.

I have suggested that the rule's utility for nineteenth-century judges and entrepreneurs was as a control mechanism. It tended to make damages both predictable and limited by constraining them to the bounds of the normal, in the absence of special notice leading to advance contemplation of an abnormal state of affairs. In another context Richard Posner suggested that the rule is of societal advantage because it increases the chances of optimization of precaution-taking. He describes the "general principle" of the case as "that where a risk of loss is known to only one party to the contract, the other party is not liable for the loss if it occurs," and then suggests that this principle "induces the party with knowledge of the risk either to take any appropriate precautions himself or, if he believes that the other party might be the more efficient loss avoider, to disclose the risk to that party."[52]

He illustrates this advantage by the following hypothetical:

> A commercial photographer purchases a roll of film to take pictures of the Himalayas for a magazine. The cost of development of the film by the manufacturer is included in the purchase price. The photographer incurs heavy expenses (including the hire of an airplane) to complete the assignment. He mails the film to the manufacturer but it is mislaid in the developing room and never found.
>
> Compare the incentive effects of allowing a photographer to recover his full losses and of limiting him to recovery of the price of the film. The first alternative creates little incentive to avoid similar losses in the future. The photographer will take no precautions. He is indifferent as between successful completion of his assignment and the receipt of adequate compensation for its failure. The manufacturer of the film will probably not take additional precautions either; the aggregate costs of such freak losses are probably too small to justify substantial efforts to prevent them. The second alternative, in contrast, should induce the photographer to take precautions that turn

---

[52] RICHARD A. POSNER, ECONOMIC ANALYSIS OF LAW 61 (1972). See also John H. Barton, *The Economic Basis of Damages for Breach of Contract*, 1 J. Legal Stud. 277, 296 (1972); LAWRENCE FRIEDMAN, CONTRACT LAW IN AMERICA 126 (1965) ("avoidable consequences must be abided by those with power to avoid them; it would distort the market system to allow an offender against this principle to cast his losses upon another party. . . .").

out to be at once inexpensive and effective: using two rolls of film or requesting special handling when he sends the roll in for development.[53]

It should be obvious that the rule's achievement of the advantages Posner described, or the benefits I have noted earlier, has been and continues to be premised on the viability of its underlying concepts of normalcy and notification. Yet the manner in which these concepts were pressed into service by the Exchequer panel is characteristic of the halfway-industrialized period in which the case arose.

On the one hand, the panel helped to bring the law in phase with the industrializing economy. By its presumption of normalcy the rule invented in the case eroded the prior legal deference to idiosyncrasy and opened the prospect of a standardization of damages as a concomitant of the standardization of transactions effected by mass production. Moreover, in its emphasis on contemplation as the only alternative to natural damages, the rule signaled an evolution away from the pre-industrial emphasis on status and toward the more modern volitional concepts of contract. On the other hand, as developed in *Hadley v. Baxendale*, these concepts were tainted by anachronism, and as they were applied over the following years their antique aspects became more salient.

Consider, first, the notification or "contemplation" branch of the rule. Willes and some other—in America, most notably Holmes—interpreted this as requiring at least a tacit agreement or assumption of risk as a prerequisite to recovery of abnormal consequential damages. This interpretation of the rule has, however, been rejected in both England and America. It is now almost universally recognized that, in the words of the Uniform Commercial Code, if at the time of the making of the contract the seller has "reason to know" of possible consequential damages, that is enough to make him liable for recovery of those damages.

Whether viewed as a simple "notice" or a more exacting "contemplation" requirement, however, this portion of the rule in *Hadley v. Baxendale* runs counter to the tide of an industrializing economy. It was already somewhat out of date when expressed in the Exchequer opinion. For in *Hadley v. Baxendale* the court spoke as though entrepreneurs were universally flexible enough and enterprises small enough for individuals to be able to serve "notice" over the counter of specialized needs calling for unusual arrangements. But in mass-transaction situations a seller cannot plausibly engage in an individualized "con-

---

[53] POSNER, *supra* note 52, at 60–61.

templation" of the consequences of breach and a subsequent tailoring of a transaction. In the course of his conversion of a family business into a modern industrial enterprise, Baxendale made Pickford itself into an operation where the contemplation branch of the rule in *Hadley v. Baxendale* was no longer viable. Even in the 1820s the Pickford operations were "highly complex."

The bulk of Pickford's traffic was of an intermediate kind, which came on to the main north-south route from east and west. This was directed to certain staging points, sorted, and thence dispatched to its destination. Cross-traffic of this kind was tricky to organize and required very clear methods of procedure. According to Joseph Baxendale, then a senior partner in Pickford, a cargo of fifteen tons might involve up to 150 consignees and thus the same number of invoices.[54]

By 1865 the business had grown to the point where it left that contemporary chronicler of industry, Henry Mayhew, without words to "convey . . . to the reader's mind a fair impression of the gigantic scale upon which the operations of the firm are conducted." This was "an enormous mercantile establishment with a huge staff of busy clerks, messengers and porters. . . . It is divided into innumerable departments, the employees in each of which find it as much as they can comfortably do to master its details without troubling themselves about any other."[55]

A century later most enterprises fragment and standardize operations in just this way. This development—and the law's recognition of it—makes it self-evidently impossible to serve legally cognizable notice on, for example, an airline that a scheduled flight is of special importance or on the telephone company that uninterrupted service is particularly vital at a particular point in a firm's business cycle.

In its comments about "normal" damages the Exchequer panel speaks in terms that again seem singularly antique. Businesses are assumed to be so straightforward as to admit of a rule of damages that characterizes a single mode of operation as "normal" and one set of consequences as "predictable." This leads the panel to announce, apparently on the basis of nothing more than its a priori impressions, that it "is obvious that . . . millers sending off broken shafts to third persons" would not normally be dependent on the prompt return of these shafts for the operation of their mills.[56] Further, the panel implies that if mill-

---

[54]G. Turnbull, *Pickfords and the Canal Carrying Trade, 1780–1850*, 6 Transport History 14 (1973).

[55] H. MAYHEW, THE SHOPS AND COMPANIES OF LONDON 50–55 (1865).

[56] 9 Ex. at 356, 156 Eng. Rep. at 151.

ers were normally dependent on the return of shafts, then one could readily assess the run of damages which would normally follow from delay.

Contemporary British cases indicate that this approach was freighted with enormous difficulties at the time it was conceived. A survey of the most recent American cases brings home the fact that as the economy has become more diverse and complex, the rule has become less viable. Elements of standardization in the modern economy produce some regularities in dealing, but by and large the normalcy rule does not now function so as to afford anything like the certainty that would optimize risk planning or render litigation unnecessary because outcomes were predictable.

The inadequacies of the rule are masked by still more fundamental phenomena that render the case of very limited relevance to the present economy. At least in mass-transaction situations, the modern enterprise manager is not concerned with his corporation's liability as it arises from a particular transaction, but rather with liability when averaged over the full run of transactions of a given type. In the mass-production situation the run of these transactions will average his consequential-damages payout in a way far more predictable than a jury's guesses about the payout. In other words, for this type of entrepreneur—a type already emerging at the time of *Hadley v. Baxendale*, and far more prevalent today—there is no need for the law to provide protection from the aberrational customer; his own market and self-insurance capacities are great enough to do the job.

Another modern development has yet further displaced *Hadley v. Baxendale*. Though the right to limit liability by agreement was disputed at the time of the case, the entrepreneur now has the undoubted capacity to set a ceiling on his liability by a contract clause.[57] Almost without exception large-scale entrepreneurs now avail themselves of that privilege. In consequence, they limit as well as normalize damages on their own initiative.

Even Posner's hypothetical is belied by the ubiquitous limitation-of-liability clause. For when a case approximating this hypothetical arose in the real world, the developer (Kodak) apparently readily conceded the magnitude of the consequential damages due (the cost of retaking

---

[57] *See* UCC §2-719(3): "Consequential damages may be limited or excluded unless the limitation or exclusion is unconscionable. Limitation of consequential damages for injury to the third person in the case of consumer goods is *prima facie* unconscionable but limitation of damages where the loss is commercial is not."

photographs in Alaska) and rested its case instead on the scope of its limitation-of-liability clause.[58]

It is only for small-volume sellers, those who deal in custom-made transactions or with a small number of customers—i.e., for those transactions most like early nineteenth-century commerce—that the rule invented in *Hadley v. Baxendale* is arguably of commercial significance. These sellers also, of course, may limit their liability by contract or cushion their liability by insurance, but since their sales transactions are less routinized (and also often less professionalized) they are more likely to miscarry and their miscarriage is less likely to have been provided for through economic precautions such as insurance or legal precautions effected as a result of consulting farsighted counsel. As unexpected difficulties arise these small-volume sellers may therefore be most likely to feel the impact of the residual common law of contracts and thus of the *Hadley v. Baxendale* rule.

Even within this realm, however, it can be doubted that the rule much affects economic life. It is doubtful that it affects information flow at the time of the making of the contract, because by hypothesis the parties are not very accurate or self-conscious planners. A more sophisticated rationale for the rule in this context might focus on its effect on a seller not at the time of his entering a contract but rather at the time of his deciding whether to voluntarily breach or to risk breaching. Only at that time and only where an option exists as to whether to breach or to increase the risk of breach does it seem likely that a seller who has not opted for a limitation-of-liability clause will consult a lawyer and consequently be affected by the legal rules. It can be argued that the societal gain from the rule in *Hadley v. Baxendale* stems from its improvement of the seller's calculus about whether to breach in this situation.

To put this observation in context, consider the position of a truck owner, *A*, who has a contract to sell his truck to *B*, and assume that *B* would suffer a "normal" net loss of $200 if the truck were not made available as scheduled. If *C* arrives on the scene and bids to preempt the truck for an urgent need, *A* can estimate the damages he will "normally" owe *B*. He will presumably sell to *C* only if the new sale price will exceed the old sale price plus $200 in damages. If *C* is willing to buy for such a high price, it is to everybody's advantage to let him do so. *C* benefits because he values the truck more highly than he values the money he is paying for it; *B* benefits because he receives his ex-

---

[58] Willard Van Dyke Productions, Inc. v. Eastman Kodak Co., 189 N.E.2d 693 (N.Y. 1963).

pected profits by way of damages; *A* benefits because he makes more money, even after paying damages, than he would have made had the truck not been sold to *C*. Society benefits because one party, *C*, has gained while no other party has lost. If *B* were in an abnormal situation and so expected to suffer greater damages than $200, the rule of *Hadley v. Baxendale* would coerce him into signaling these higher damages, so that the proper damage calculation and subsequent truck allocation would be made. Thus, in theory, by facilitating an accurate calculus of the breach, the rule optimizes resource allocation.

But if this is its modern rationale, it is apparent that considerable thought ought to be given to restructuring the rule. Resting the seller's liability on whether the type of damages incurred was "normal" (or, in the UCC's words, whether it was a type of damage of which the seller had "reason to know") seems undesirable because it lets an all-or-nothing decision ride on an indicator about which many sellers cannot, at the time of breach, speculate with confidence. Further, if the recoverability of a type of damages is established, a seller may often have no reasonable basis for determining the magnitude of the damages involved. On this dimension—obviously critical to any calculus of the care warranted to avoid breach—the rule has nothing to say. Lastly, if the rule were truly finely geared to optimizing the allocation of resources, it would place its emphasis on the damage known to the seller at the time of breach rather than at the time of contract, at least where the breach was voluntary. When the rule was framed stress had to be placed on communication at the time of the making of a contract because that was the only occasion on which information exchange could be coerced without fear of imposing enormous transaction costs. Now the telephone and vastly improved telegraphic facilities make it possible to mandate discussion at the time of breach. Would it be desirable to move the focus of rule to this point? On this question some empirical evidence would be desirable. Do the average transaction costs associated with information exchange at the time of the contract multiplied by the number of instances in which such information is exchanged exceed the average transaction costs of information exchange at the time of voluntary breach multiplied by the number of occasions when breach is seriously considered? If so, there is much to be said for a revision in the rule.

Of course, the rule may be defended on purely equitable grounds. Even if its economic repercussions are trivial or counterproductive, when the parties do not prospectively or retrospectively agree on damages, this may be the fairest means of assessing them. But is it? Why should the courts look exclusively to whether a defendant could foresee a type of damages (e.g., lost profits from the stoppage of a manufacturing enterprise), but not attend to whether he could foresee their magnitude? Does the recovery of tens of thousands of dollars, where most parties would have anticipated hundreds of dollars, comport with our sense of fairness? Conversely, is the analysis of fairness so well developed in contract law that we can say with confidence why, in the above hypothetical, *A* rather than *B* ought, on equitable grounds, to obtain the special profits from dealing with *C*?

This brief discussion of the functioning of *Hadley v. Baxendale* in the modern world is not intended to resolve arguments about how UCC §2-715(2) or the common law consequential-damages rule ought to be phrased or interpreted. Rather, it is intended to provoke such arguments. I do not think anyone can explain why we should now accord this mid-nineteenth-century rule such curricular predominance, much less explain how it functions, and still less how it ought to function, in the modern world. Yet it retains its place because it seems as though it has always held this place. It seems, as one English judge at the time of *Hadley v. Baxendale* wryly commented in another context, that when "a rule is well established by decisions, it is not necessary to give any reasons in its support, or to say anything to show it to be a good and useful one."[59]

VII

My aim in this article has been to supplement the years of doctrinal explication lavished on the text of *Hadley v. Baxendale* with a sufficient understanding of context to afford some insights—albeit speculative ones—into the process of law-change. I would hope that this discussion would serve as a counterpoise to the tendency to regard some rules of law as "fixed stars" in our legal system. Judicial rules are more like inventions, designed to serve particular functions in particular settings. I have tried to demonstrate that an analysis of the original setting and functions of one particular rule will enhance an understanding of that rule even when it has long outlived that setting and those functions. Further, I have sought to suggest that if a rule is to be regarded as an invention, then it ought to be subject to review, lest we make too big an investment in it even as it is becoming outmoded.

---

[59] Judge Maule in Emmens v. Elderton, 4 H.L. Cas. 624, 658, 10 Eng. Rep. 606, 619 (1852).

2

A. W. Brian Simpson[*]

Contracts for Cotton to Arrive: The Case of the Two Ships *Peerless*

Some leading cases only achieve their special status posthumously, and *Raffles v. Wichelhaus*[1] is a striking example. It was decided by the Court of Exchequer on January 20, 1864, and the judges who heard the case, Chief Baron Pollock and Barons Martin and Pigott, thought the solution to the problem presented to them to be so obvious that they gave judgment for the defendants without troubling to give any reasons for their decision. Indeed, they cut short the argument of defendants' counsel, George Mellish Q.C. and Arthur Cohen, thinking it unnecessary to hear them complete it.[2] The case was reported by Edwin T. Hurlstone and Francis J. Coltman, and by the *Law Journal*, perhaps because of the curiosity of the facts; otherwise it seems to have caused no immediate ripples in the contemporary legal world.

Since 1868 the case has been under continuous discussion, and it has come to be one of the best-known old chestnuts of the common law. Perhaps the best-known modern discussion is that of Grant Gilmore in the *The Death of Contract*.[3] No student of the law of contract could regard his education as complete without either reading the case in the

---

[*] Charles F. and Edith Clyne Professor of Law, University of Michigan Law School. Reprinted with permission of the publisher from *Cardozo Law Review*, vol. 11, pages 287–333.

[1] The case of *Raffles v. Wichelhaus* is reported in 2 H. & C. 906, 159 Eng. Rep. 375 (Ex. 1864); and in 33 L.J.N.S. 160 (Ex. 1864).

[2] *See* GRANT GILMORE, THE DEATH OF CONTRACT 39 (1974).

[3] *Id.* at 35–44 (1974). For a more recent discussion, see Robert L. Birmingham, *Holmes on 'Peerless': Raffles v. Wichelhaus and the Objective Theory of Contract*, 47 U. Pitt. L. Rev. 183 (1985).

reports themselves or, more commonly, acquiring some acquaintance with the case from one of the abbreviated, and sometimes garbled, accounts that appear in the legal casebooks or hornbooks. Yet in spite of the incredible number of hours which, since 1864, must have been devoted to discussing the case, virtually nothing is known about it.

Raffles v. Wichelhaus in the Law Reports

As reported, the action brought by Raffles was for failure by the defendants to accept and pay for 125 bales of Surat cotton, "guaranteed middling fair merchant's Dhollorah," which had, at some unspecified date, been sold to them at a price of 17¼ pence a pound, the cotton "to arrive ex 'Peerless' from Bombay." *Peerless* was, of course, the name of a ship. The name of the type of cotton is spelled Dhollerah or Dhollera, this being a type of cotton grown in the Achmedabad district of Bombay. Surat is the name of a port from which cotton was at one time shipped, and came to be the name applied to all cotton shipped from Bombay. The cotton was to "be taken from the quay . . . at the rate of 17¼d. per pound, [to be paid] within a certain time then agreed upon after the arrival of the said goods in England." A bale of cotton from India ideally contained some 400 pounds of cotton, or a little under.[4] So something of the order of 50,000 pounds of cotton, at a substantial price of £3,593 15s 0d.,[5] was involved in the contract.

Raffles alleged that the cotton had indeed arrived at Liverpool on the ship *Peerless*. He had been willing to perform his side of the bargain, and tendered performance, but the defendants had not been willing to accept and pay for the cotton. The defendants replied with two pleas.

The first plea was not quoted in the reports, and its form is now undiscoverable. It may perhaps have merely averred, in effect, that the seller did not tender delivery, without the explanatory matter about the two ships included in the second plea. If so, it would have left the dispute to surface at trial in evidence to the jury, and would not have been demurrable. For it was the inclusion of this matter in the plea that served as an invitation to raise the question of law by way of demurrer at that stage in the proceedings. Conceivably this question had been mooted in negotiations before the matter went to litigation, and

---

[4] *See* THOMAS ELLISON, THE COTTON TRADE OF GREAT BRITAIN 91 (1886); MAURICE WILLIAMS, THE COTTON TRADE OF 1861 AND 1862, at 21 (1863).

[5] There is no sensible way of converting the sum into modern terms, but if one thinks of $100,000, this will give an impression.

the plea may have been deliberately framed to allow the matter to be adjudicated.

The second plea stated that in the contract (which, the plea implied, had been made in writing) the defendants intended to refer to a ship called *Peerless* which had left Bombay in October. The plaintiff had not offered to deliver cotton from this ship, but only cotton which had arrived from another ship, also called *Peerless*, which had sailed from Bombay in December. The plea did not assert that Raffles had intended to refer to the October ship; it makes no averment as to his intention or understanding. The pleadings and reports do not indicate in which year these sailings occurred, nor when or in what order the ships arrived, but imply that the October ship had in fact arrived at Liverpool.

The plaintiff objected that, even if true, there was no answer in law to the claim. In technical language Raffles demurred, not disputing the truth of the facts alleged by his opponents, but raising a purely legal question. This would be decided by the judges sitting *en banc,* that is, as a multi-judge court, in London. According to the principles of pleading accepted at this period, Raffles, by demurring, admitted the truth of Wichelhaus and Busch's factual claim; he conceded that they had indeed meant to refer to the October ship. It does not necessarily follow that this was in reality true (though it probably was) but only that for the purpose of deciding the case the matter was placed beyond argument.[6] The case was decided on the demurrer. Essentially the question that the court had to decide was whether the defendants' story, as set out in the plea, and thereby conceded to be true for the purpose of the argument, was *capable* of furnishing a defense. If so, the plaintiff's demurrer must fail. His only hope of success would have been to join issue on the plea, raising a question of fact to be submitted to a jury. But it was now too late to do that.

In substance the plaintiff argued that he had offered to perform exactly and precisely the contract he had made: to deliver Surat cotton, of appropriate type and quality, from a ship called *Peerless*, sailing from Bombay. He had done just that. The fact that the defendants might have intended to refer to some other ship of the same name was neither here nor there:

> The contract was for the sale of a number of bales of cotton of a
> particular description, which the plaintiff was ready to deliver.

---

[6] "With respect to the *effect* of a demurrer—it is first, a rule, *that a demurrer admits all such matters of fact as are sufficiently pleaded.*" HENRY J. STEPHEN, A TREATISE ON THE PRINCIPLES OF PLEADING IN CIVIL ACTIONS 142 (1867).

> It is immaterial by what ship the cotton was to arrive, so that
> [today we would say "so long as"] it was a ship called the "Peer-
> less."[7]

The force of this argument was enhanced, at a doctrinal level, by the
general rule that if a contract is written, as this one was, the law would
usually resist attempts to modify or amplify its terms through the admission of oral evidence as to what either party claims to have "really"
meant. "The defendant has no right to contradict by parol evidence a
written contract good upon the face of it."[8] Indeed the advantage of
putting contracts into writing would, it was then thought, be lost if the
law, at least in general, did not exclude such assertions. Since the Victorian period this doctrine has, for better or for worse, been much re-
laxed.

Clement Milward, who presented this argument for William Winter
Raffles, put his case vigorously, but the judges were against him; he
has found a sympathetic defender in more recent times in Grant Gilmore, who portrays the judges involved as stupid.[9] For the moment,
however, I shall defer considering Gilmore's views and concentrate on
the text. The report shows that Milward was in difficulty. He had to
concede that the identity of the carrying ship was relevant in one respect, for if the ship had foundered, it was the understanding that the
contract was off, the loss being no doubt normally covered by insurance.[10] From this alone it seemed to follow that the contract was for
cotton on a unique ship, not any ship which happened to have the right
name, much less any ship at all. According to the *Law Journal* he also
made another curious concession: "If the defendants had said their
speculation had fallen through in consequence, it might have been different."[11] He went on to assert, correctly enough, that "[t]he time of the

---

[7] Raffles v. Wichelhaus, 2 H. & C. 906, 907, 159 Eng. Rep. 375, 375 (Ex.
1864).

[8] The quotation is from the report by Hurlstone and Coltman, *Raffles,* 2 H.
& C. at 907.

[9] GILMORE, *supra* note 2, at 37–38.

[10] This concession reflected a customary understanding in the trade, which
was to be codified in 1863.

[11] Raffles v. Wichelhaus, 33 L.J.N.S. 160, 160 (Ex. 1864). It is not immediately obvious what he meant by this remark; traders are in the business to
make profits, and unless the defendants were going to lose by accepting delivery, why should they contest the action at all? One might assume that it was
obvious from the fact of litigation that "their speculation had fallen through in
consequence." *Id.* The explanation for Milward's remark will appear later.

sailing of the ship was no part of the contract,"[12] meaning that it was not specified in the text, but then added, somewhat desperately, "and, for the purposes of the plea, we must take it that both ships sailed on the same day."[13] This strange remark indirectly concedes an important point, which is that the specific identity of the ship might be relevant because it obliquely indicated the sailing date, and this was how the judges saw the matter. The commercial sense in the judges' attitude lay in the fact that the identity of a particular ship, which would sail at a particular moment, affected the time at which the cotton would arrive at Liverpool and thus become available for resale in the spot market. Cotton prices, of course, did not remain constant. Knowledge of the date of sailing or, if the contract was made during the voyage, knowledge of the ship's progress might make it possible to form a useful estimate of its probable date of arrival; as we shall see, such knowledge could be had.

This was the point made by Chief Baron Pollock when, according to the report by Hurlstone and Coltman, he intervened to say, "[o]ne vessel sailed in October and the other in December."[14] Viewing the matter from a legal standpoint, the judges seem to have thought that once it appeared that there were two ships that answered the contractual description, and no way of telling, from the written terms, which of the two was intended, the contract was latently ambiguous; a jury should therefore be allowed to hear the evidence and decide whether the parties meant the same ship (and, if so, which ship) or different ships. Thus in the *Law Journal* report Chief Baron Pollock is recorded as saying, "Whether the same Peerless was meant by the plaintiff and the defendants is a matter of evidence for the jury."[15] In the account by Hurlstone and Coltman, Mellish argued, "[T]here is a latent ambiguity, and parol evidence may be given for the purpose of shewing that the defendant meant one 'Peerless' and the plaintiff another."[16] As has been explained, the plea put in by the defendants does not say anything as to the plaintiff's intentions. In an earlier case, *Smith v. Jeffryes,*[17] decided in 1846, Baron Alderson explained the concept of "latent ambiguity": "A latent ambiguity is, where you show that words apply equally to two different things or subject-matters, and then evi-

---

[12] *Id.*

[13] *Id.*

[14] 2 H. & C. at 907, 159 Eng. Rep. at 376.

[15] 33 L.J.N.S. at 160.

[16] 2 H. & C. at 908, 159 Eng. Rep. at 376.

[17] 15 M. & W. 561, 153 Eng. Rep. 972 (Ex. 1846).

dence is admissible to shew which of them was the thing or subject-matter intended."[18]

Obviously, if an identical case went to a jury, and the jury found that the agreement referred to the October ship, the plaintiff would lose, and if the reference was to the December ship the plaintiff would win. If, however, a jury found that the parties meant different ships and that it was impossible to say to which ship the contract referred, the claim again might fail, and a judge in such a case would have to direct the jury as to an appropriate decision. But there was no need for the court in *Raffles v. Wichelhaus* to investigate these possibilities and say what a suitable direction would be to dispose of the action. It was enough that the plea, if true, could in law furnish an answer to the action; if so, the plaintiff's legal objection to it failed. So, as the report laconically puts it, "[t]here must be judgment for the defendants."[19]

What remains open to question is whether the decision in the case, laconically expressed though it is, indicates what view the judges would have taken in a trial if it emerged that one party meant one ship and the other meant the other, and there was, as it were, no way of identifying the ship to which "the contract" referred. Mellish and Cohen certainly argued that if one party meant one ship and the other the other, as might be assumed as a matter of common sense to be the story behind the case, there would be no contract at all; they used the expression *consensus ad idem*, agreement as to the same thing, arguing by implication that this *consensus* was essential in a contract. Although their argument was stopped at this point, it does not necessarily follow that the three judges agreed with it; the judges might not have seen any need to go into the matter, or they might have accepted the idea with some qualifications. In the absence of any judicial explanation of the decision it is to some degree speculative why the case was decided in the way it was. Given the doctrinal context, the limited explanation I have given is as reasonable and economical a deduction from the evidence as can be made, but some doubt must always remain. This fact was to be important in the subsequent history of the uses to which the case was put.

The Maritime Background

There were reports of at least eleven ships called *Peerless* sailing the seven seas at the time, for the name was a popular one. The *Mercantile Navy List* for 1863 lists nine British registered sailing vessels of that

---

[18] 15 M. & W. at 562, 153 Eng. Rep. at 972–73.

[19] 2 H. & C. at 908, 158 Eng. Rep. at 376.

name, their ports of registration being London, Aberystwyth, Dartmouth, Greenock, Halifax, Windsor (Nova Scotia), Hull, and Liverpool, which boasted two such ships. There were also two American ships named *Peerless* from Boston and Baltimore. The existence of so many vessels of the same or a similar name could obviously cause confusion in shipping movement reports. There was nothing unusual, however, in this state of affairs. Ships commonly shared the same name, particularly popular names such as *Annie*. But the two vessels with which we are concerned can readily be identified as the two that were registered at Liverpool. At the time it was the practice in the shipping press to differentiate vessels bearing the same name by the names of their captains, not, as one might expect, by using their unique registered number. Contrary to assumptions often made, for example, by those impressed by the economic analysis of law, commercial practices in this period at least seem to have been governed as much by tradition and conservatism as by cold rationality.

Our ships are *Peerless* (Major) and *Peerless* (Flavin). *Peerless* (Major), registered as number 20279, was a three-masted sailing vessel, ship rigged (that is, square rigged on all three masts, unlike a barque), of 841 tons register. She was of wooden construction and carried a female figurehead. She had been built in 1857 at Bridport in Dorset, England, by E. Cox and Company for a number of members of the Prowse family. Half the sixty-four shares in her were originally owned by William Prowse of Bridport. At the time of her voyage to Bombay she was described as being owned by J. Prowse and Co. of Ansdell Street, Liverpool, at which port she had been registered on October 28, 1857. Her captain, Robert Major, was a Yorkshireman, born in 1817, who had commanded her since she was built. His previous and first command had been the *Duke of Lancashire* (1852–1857), and he had obtained his master's certificate of competence in 1852. Of the official ship's papers connected with the voyage in question, only one survives, and this is in the Memorial University of St. John's, Newfoundland. Known as "List C," it provides on a standard form information about the engagement and discharge of the crew of the ship, their conduct, and various other details. At the end of the voyage, Robert Major had to deliver this document to the shipping master at Liverpool within forty-eight hours. It was so delivered on February 21, 1863.

From this and other documents it appears that after signing off the crew from his previous voyage on September 8, 1861, Robert Major had engaged a new crew comprising two mates, a carpenter, boatswain, steward, and cook, thirteen seamen, and six apprentices. This was on November 15 of that year, and he put to sea on November 19. The average age of his seamen was about twenty-six, and they included two Norwegians, a Swede, and a German. Only four of the seamen had been on the previous voyage. List C does not specify rates of pay, but from documents preserved from her previous voyage we can guess that they would run from about seven pounds a month for the first mate, John Judson, down to two pounds ten shillings for seamen. In Calcutta, to which the vessel initially sailed, five of the crew were discharged, two on account of sickness. They included the second mate, Walter Wilson of Scarborough. Since his conduct and ability were recorded only as "good," not the more usual "very good," the captain may have felt himself well rid of him, but his replacement, James T. Prescott of Deal, was apparently worse, for the captain declined to give him any testimonial whatsoever.

From the official log of her previous voyage to India, which lasted from about November 17, 1860, to September 12, 1861, we may guess that Robert Major was a disciplinarian who did not run a happy ship. As the ship lay in the river Mersey at the start of the voyage, one sailor was discharged while another sailor and an apprentice contrived to abscond. The official log describes an unpleasant slanging match between the captain and one of his disgruntled sailors, which took place when the ship lay at Calcutta on St. Patrick's Day in 1861. From the log description, I imagine the sailor used threatening and abusive language, which the captain acted upon, propelling the sailor on his way, though the captain would not, of course, record this.

On the voyage with which we are concerned five replacement seamen were engaged at Calcutta, some on May 30, and some on June 5, 1862. One of the apprentices also left the ship there on April 11 but was not replaced. From List C, we can tell that the *Peerless* was lying at Calcutta between April 11 and June 5, but this document does not show that she went to Bombay at all.

The *Lloyd's Lists* do not show her reaching Bombay. *Lloyd's Lists* were the regularly published reports from the local agents established at this time by Lloyd's of London to report shipping movements. Agents noted the arrival and departure of ships and collected information from ship's masters on sightings of vessels. Their reports were consigned to London through the mails. From *Lloyd's List* it was possible to reconstruct the voyage of *Peerless* (Major) in more detail. Having sailed from Liverpool on November 19, 1861, she was "spoken" on January 1, 1862, in 9 north, 21 west, a position off what is now Liberia. She was next reported from Calcutta on April 3 as having entered the port the previous day, after encountering heavy weather off Madagascar on February 22 and again in the Bay of Bengal on March 25, apparently as she lay outside the port. In these storms she was damaged, losing bulwarks, and some hundred bales of her cargo were damaged by leakage from cases of chloride of lime, which had been misdescribed when shipped as "general merchandise." Presumably in consequence it had been incorrectly stowed. On June 21 she was reported from Calcutta as having left the port of Bombay, which she reached on August 13, 1862. On October 20 she set sail for Liverpool at about the time when the northeast monsoon began.

Her departure was noted in England in *Lloyd's List* in a report from Lloyd's agent in Bombay, dated October 27, the day mails left Bombay. They arrived, via Marseilles, on November 20, 1862. It thus became generally known in the commercial world, including Liverpool on that day. The information could have been available a little earlier, for Maurice Williams, who was a cotton broker, in his *Cotton Circular* of November 19, notes that the most recent information available to him from Bombay was of October 20. Of course it was also possible for individuals to receive information much earlier by the use of cables, or through private sources of information such as ship's captains. Since 1857 there had existed a telegraphic service covering most of the way to India, albeit unreliably. *Peerless* (Major) safely arrived in the river Mersey on February 14, 1863, and docked on the eighteenth, as appears from List C; there could have been some delay in finding a vacant berth in the port. This *Peerless* was not reported in *Lloyd's List* while on passage, that is between October 20, 1862, and February 14, 1863. Except in emergencies or to receive orders, sailing vessels on such a voyage remained well away from land, both for reasons of safety and to conform to wind systems. It is, of course, possible that private information about her voyage did reach Liverpool in the course of this voyage, but we have no way of knowing.

Peerless (Flavin), whose official number was 41935, was a somewhat larger Liverpool-registered wooden sailing vessel of 1,005 tons. She too was three-masted, ship-rigged, and carried a female figurehead. Her history was rather more complex. She was built in Quebec by P. Brunelle in 1858, and was first registered at Quebec on September 23, 1858. As European timber resources dwindled, a prosperous shipbuilding industry was established in the new world, and Quebec was a center of this trade. She was then in the sole ownership of one James Gillespie of that city. In 1859 she was wrecked, apparently on her maiden voyage, but she was sold, recovered, repaired, and registered *de novo* at Halifax, Nova Scotia, where presumably the repair work was done. On May 5, 1862, her registration had been transferred to Liverpool, and, at the time of the voyage in question, her first as a Liverpool ship, she was owned by Messrs. Dixon and Wynne of 39 Oldhall Street. Her captain was Thomas Flavin, an Irishman born in 1823 in County Waterford. His first command had been *Zetland* (1854–1856) on a voyage to the South Pacific; then he had commanded *Sardinia* and *Panola* in the North American trade. Between 1858 and 1859 he had commanded the schooner *Lizzie Flavin* in the coastal trade; she was so named, presumably, after his wife or daughter. Thomas Flavin had obtained his master's certificate, number 16023, at Liverpool in 1857, where he lived at 53 Bridgewater Street, and had become *Peerless*'s captain in 1861 after his previous ship, *Erin-go-brogh*, was lost on December 9, 1860.

For the voyage with which we are concerned the only surviving document is the ship's articles, on form AC, *Agreement and Account of Crew (Foreign Going Ship)*. Of the crew of twenty-five, which included, in addition to three mates, a carpenter, boatswain, sailmaker, and cook, six crew members came from Waterford, the captain's home—an indication of his good repute with seamen—and five more were Irishmen. The crew signed or made their marks (seven of the crew were wholly illiterate) on June 7, 1862, to be on board on June 10 by nine o'clock a.m. Perhaps they were in a somewhat frail state of health after spending their month's advance of pay in the traditional bibulous and amorous manner. For this or some navigational reason, *Peerless* did not put to sea until June 12. The crew's pay ranged from six guineas a month for the first mate, Evan Evans, down to one pound a month for first voyagers James Gleven and Patrick Flaherty; only two seamen had been on her previous voyage. They were, typically, in their late teens or early twenties; seamen did not last long in Victorian days. *Peerless* sailed direct to Bombay, where she was reported on October 11 as having arrived at the port on the eighth. From her articles it can be established that she entered the port on October 10; the master had to hand them over to the temporary care of the shipping master, a Mr. Hayman. Two days later Charles Francis, the oldest seaman on board, aged thirty-five, died there of tuberculosis, a relatively common cause of death among seamen. Her arrival at Bombay became known in Liverpool on November 5, where it had been known since September 22 that the other *Peerless* was also lying in the port.

Her articles were returned to Captain Flavin on December 22. He put to sea two days later, on Christmas Eve 1862. The news that he had sailed was available in Liverpool on January 21, 1863, in an issue of *Lloyd's List* that carried a report from Bombay dated December 27, the day the mails regularly left. On March 27 the same publication reported that she had been sighted off Ascension Island in the South Atlantic, and on February 26 she had spoken by the Edmund Kaye at 1 south, 20 west, a position that is well off the African coast and northwest of Ascension. On April 16 she put into Queenstown (now Cobh) in Cork harbor in Ireland; this stop at a "port of call" would be to enable her to receive orders as to her port of discharge through the telegraph system. This suggests that the vessel's instructions were to sail from Bombay "to Cork for orders," not necessarily for Liverpool, though the purpose of the call may have merely been to receive instructions on some other matter. We may be sure that she would at this point be in telegraphic communication with Liverpool. She sailed the same day, arriving at the port on April 19, 1863. Her papers were signed on April 23 as delivered on that day to the shipping master.

It was cotton from this vessel, *Peerless* (Flavin), that Raffles offered to deliver to Wichelhaus and Busch and that they refused to accept. This offer would probably have been made somewhere between April 23 and May 10, when the vessel was unloading in Queen's Dock, a process that could take some considerable time. There would be a customary period of notice, perhaps ten days, before payment would be due. Raffles had earlier failed to tender delivery of cotton from *Peerless* (Major), which, as we have seen, had docked in Liverpool almost exactly two months earlier, on February 18, presumably discharging her cargo in the course of the following three weeks or so. And, so the defendants claimed, it was *Peerless* (Major), the October ship, which they had intended to specify in the forward delivery contract into which they had entered. Whether Raffles owned any cotton on this vessel cannot now be determined; during argument in the case Clement Milward indicated, probably correctly, that he had not. Of course, if he had none it might still have been possible for him, though to his loss, to have acquired cotton of equivalent type and grade in the spot market, though it would not have been in any sense *ex Peerless*, and would also have been probably of a different crop.

The Commercial Background: Speculation in Cotton

The immediate commercial background to the transaction litigated in *Raffles v. Wichelhaus* was the Lancashire cotton famine, created by the blockade of the Southern American states during the Civil War.[20]

---

[20] Before the war, the Southern states had been the principal source of high-quality raw cotton; the blockade drastically reduced the supply. E. Donnell, who was very active in the cotton trade and who was much involved with the establishment of the New York Cotton Exchange, gives figures. In 1861, 1,842,000 bales of cotton entered Britain from the Southern states. EZEKIEL DONNELL, CHRONOLOGICAL AND STATISTICAL HISTORY OF COTTON 507 (1872). In 1862, the quantity fell to a mere 72,000 bales. *Id.* at 517.

There are many accounts of the cotton famine. For this article, I have relied on R. ARNOLD, THE HISTORY OF THE COTTON FAMINE (1865); ELLISON, *supra* note 4; D. A. FARNIE, THE ENGLISH COTTON INDUSTRY AND THE WORLD MARKET, 1815–1896 (1979); W. O. HENDERSON, THE LANCASHIRE COTTON FAMINE, 1861–1865 (1934); JOHN WATTS, THE FACTS OF THE COTTON FAMINE (1866); MAURICE WILLIAMS, SEVEN YEARS HISTORY OF THE COTTON TRADE (1868). This last work comprises trade circulars issued by Maurice Williams, a cotton broker during the famine, to his clients; they were reissued in book form to make a history.

Spinners were forced to turn to other sources of supply, particularly to India, and the price of cotton from all sources rose sharply and became extremely volatile. The year 1862 saw the sharpest rise. In consequence there was much speculative dealing in the cotton market. Because of cotton's highly variable character, the purchasing and sampling of the raw material was left to expert brokers working on commission to fulfill specific orders from spinners. But speculative purchases, whether by brokers or other entrepreneurs, were not made to fulfill known orders. Instead they were made in the uncertain "bullish" hope that the cotton could later be sold more profitably in a rising market, or the rights assigned. The individuals engaged in the litigation were obviously active in this lucrative but hazardous trade. It was widely believed that there existed in the Southern states a huge stock of cotton that would be released onto the market if the war ended. In reality, when the war did end, much cotton had been destroyed, and prices did not collapse as expected.

As well as providing a chance to make (or lose) a fortune, the famine caused much hardship. The rise in the production costs of yarn caused many spinners to close their mills or reduce production; there was heavy unemployment in the Lancashire mill towns, and in consequence widespread distress.[21] There were also many bankruptcies; the Liverpool figures rose from 175 in 1861 to 370 in 1862, fell in 1863 to 261 and rose in 1864 to 387. Naturally any rumor of peace brought fear of a collapse in the price and created panic among speculators in the cotton market, who were holding stocks of cotton.

Dealings in cotton might be dictated by actual demand for material by cotton spinners, or for re-export, or they might be speculative, entered into with a view to sell if the market moved favorably. Market reports from as early as 1816 recorded sales weekly in these three categories. For example, sales for the week ending January 6 in that year were 6,778 bales for consumption, 5,020 on speculation, and none for export. Later market reports reproduced in Ezekiel Donnell's book or published, for example, in the *Economist* follow this practice and at times show very large speculative purchases. For example, in 1825 Liverpool purchases for consumption totaled 622,106 bales, those on speculation 302,000. There was massive speculation in 1825, 1849, 1852, and 1855, and explanations provided by Donnell make it clear that this was "bull" speculation, based on the belief that the price of

---

[21] To cap it all the reservoir made famous by the case of *Rylands v. Fletcher* burst, closing a coal mine and thereby both putting more people out of work and adding to the worries of Rylands, the largest employer of labor in the industry. *See Rylands,* 3 H. & C. 774 (Ex. Ch. 1865), 3 L.R. 330 (H.L. 1868).

cotton would rise. On January 1, 1825, the cotton stock was half what it had been thought to be; naturally prices rose. The statistics do not record the contractual form of these dealings, but the majority would probably have been in "spot" cotton, that is, in specific identifiable bales of cotton present in Liverpool and available for inspection, weighing, and delivery, and purchased to be held in store against future demand. In the early nineteenth century factors that militated against any considerable trade in cotton that was not on the spot were the great variations in quality and type of the material as well as the weights of bales. Such variations made inspection before purchase essential. The problems that discouraged trade in cotton that was not on the spot were eventually solved by the evolution of sophisticated grading, and by the use of samples, and by cheap arbitration together with arbitrated price adjustments both to solve disputes and to cope with variations from the contract description. In the early half of the century these devices had not been much developed.

Nevertheless, in spite of the difficulties, there existed a trade in cotton *in transitu*, purchased for forward delivery.[22] The contracts involved were called "contracts to arrive" or "arrival" contracts. They do not appear to have been common until the 1850s. There are references in the *Economist* as early as 1851, and later in the decade they are more common. By the 1860s reference to them became standard form in market reports. Such contracts were attractive to speculators since they avoided warehousing costs if the cotton was promptly sold on arrival or if the rights of the purchaser were assigned. In the absence of prepayment they also avoided locking up capital.

The explanation for their development, claimed J. Todd in 1934, was technological rather than legal.[23] The invention of the steamship and its use in the Atlantic trade by the Cunard line, formed in 1840, made it possible for news of the American crop size and for samples of cotton to be conveyed across the Atlantic ahead of the slower sailing vessels that carried bulk cotton from the principal source of supply, the Southern states: "Merchants were advised of cotton coming by certain ships, and transactions took place in cotton 'to arrive,' which accounts for the fact that in certain offices in Liverpool today the futures department is

---

[22] For a discussion of the law of arrival contracts, see J. P. BENJAMIN, A TREATISE ON THE LAW OF SALE OF PERSONAL PROPERTY; WITH REFERENCES TO THE AMERICAN DECISIONS AND TO THE FRENCH CODE AND CIVIL LAW 497 (J. C. Perkins ed., 1st American ed. 1875).

[23] JOHN A. TODD, THE MARKETING OF COTTON (1934).

still called the Arrivals Department."[24] Quite apart from the steam-ship, telegraphs and railways also enabled news of a vessel's progress, cargo, and bills of lading to travel faster than the vessel. Thus, as we have seen, there were "ports of call" such as Falmouth in England or Cork in Ireland where sailing vessels, including our *Peerless* (Flavin), called or reported for orders and were placed in touch with the markets by telegraph; since 1852 Cork had been in direct touch with Liverpool.

The extension of international telegraph services enhanced the pos-sibilities. The telegraph between England and India, which passed down the Persian Gulf, was not effectively connected until February 1865, but parts of the distance were serviced before this. Lines at the European end reached Corfu and Malta by 1857 and Aden by 1859. The Red Sea cable from Suez to Karachi was connected in 1860 but frequently failed.

In addition, the practice of mutual speaking and reporting of ships on passage often enabled news of the progress of a particular vessel to be available in Britain before the vessel arrived. Thus in a variety of ways information traveled more rapidly than bulk cargoes. Although writers such as Todd emphasize the importance of steamships in the Atlantic trade, a noticeable feature of early references to "contracts to arrive" is that they seem to relate more commonly to East Indian rather than American cotton. This was so in 1857 before there existed an Indian telegraph covering the whole distance. It is easy to see why. By as early as 1849, mail traveling by steamship could reach Britain from Bombay in about a month, while cargo on sailing vessels, neces-sarily passing round the Cape of Good Hope, took about four months. Mail, carried on luxury passenger vessels, traveled on the so-called overland route, using the railway to cross the isthmus to Alexandria. The considerable time savings as compared with American trade en-couraged such dealings in East Indian cotton. The Suez Canal opened in 1869, reducing the distance to Bombay from about 11,000 miles to around 6,300, but steamships serving the overland route, together with railways and telegraph services, sped communication by the mails long before this. Indeed the canal made no significant difference. Bulk cargo could not, of course, be economically transported on the overland route. Even after the canal opened, sailing vessels did not use it, and they long continued to be more economical for the carriage of nonperishable cargoes than steamships. The *Times* on December 3, 1869, published a note by Thomas Ellison on the possibility that cotton might be shipped

---

[24] *Id.* at 66.

by the canal on steamships,[25] but it was not until May 31, 1870, that it published reports of several cotton-carrying vessels, including the *Bywell Castle,* using this route.

The Form of Arrival Contracts

A contract for cotton "to arrive" was a contract for forward delivery, or, as it is sometimes called, a "time contract." One might expect that such a contract would normally specify a time for delivery. For it is the moment when the goods become available in the market that is of paramount importance to the purchaser, particularly if the purchaser wants the goods for use. But the world in which such contracts originated was one in which this was not really possible. Although one could discover, after an interval, when a sailing ship had left or, more approximately, proposed to leave its port of departure, it was very uncertain when, if ever, it would arrive at its destination. Even when it did arrive, there were uncertain delays in finding a berth to unload its cargo. Hence such contracts did not originally specify the time of arrival, much less delivery, even within some fixed period. All they did was to identify which shipment of cotton was being sold; presumably the rationale of this was that the buyer, so long as he knew which shipment was being sold, would be able to form his own estimate of the probable time of arrival. This would not, of course, be a point in time but a period. It is said that originally such contracts were made only when arrival was imminent, the ship typically having been reported off Point Lynas, which is on the north coast of Anglesey, some fifty miles from Liverpool. Presumably there was a signal station there. No doubt also cotton was sometimes sold as the ship lay in the river, waiting to berth. In such cases the date of delivery could be guessed with some precision, though a square-rigged vessel, if it did not employ a steam tug, could take a long and unpredictable time to cover even fifty miles.

There were no doubt various contractual forms used in the early days and various possible ways of identifying the shipment that would directly or indirectly indicate the date of departure and make possible an estimate of the approximate date of arrival. One technique was to name the ship. These were "ship named" contracts. From this, and knowledge of the port of departure, and through the system of reporting ships' movements, the probable date of arrival could be estimated. In addition, the port of origin could be named in the contract—*ex Peerless* Bombay. A contract could also specify the time of departure, not a precise day but a period—*ex Peerless* Bombay guaranteed October

---

[25] The Times (London), Dec. 3, 1869, at 8.

shipment—and what a tragedy that would have been! Even more precise identification of the parcel of cotton within the cargo involved declaring the marks on the bales, only possible if the documents arrived
before the ship, or the ship had docked; this was done before delivery,
but the marks were apparently never incorporated in the original contract. Thus the declaration of the marks did not relate to the time element in the contract.

In the absence of surviving texts of contracts, market reports are the
best evidence of the practices followed. Those published in the *Economist*, which I have used, are fuller for the London market than for the
Liverpool, but there is no reason to suppose that practices in the markets differed significantly. Those for 1862 indicate that in the early
part of that year, up to mid-June, there was little trade in cotton "to
arrive," except in late February, when there was "an extensive inquiry
for Tinnevelly afloat."[26] Thus in the week ending March 15 only a hundred bales were sold in this way. The reports quote type and sometimes
quality, but they mention neither month of shipment, projected date of
arrival, nor whether the ship is named. I suspect that these sales are
for cotton in vessels that were nearly at their destination and thus
about to arrive. This might explain why the reports do not mention the
time of sailing from the port of origin; since the ships' arrival was imminent, the departure date from the foreign port would be of no commercial interest to readers.

In July 1862, in response to the imminent cotton famine, the cotton
market became very excited. By August 30 it was reported that it "bor-
dered on wildness."[27] On September 6 it was reported of the London
market that "[t]he speculation has been enormous, and very wild."[28] In
these conditions dealings in cotton "to arrive" became more common;
no doubt some were purely speculative, but others represented attempts by or on behalf of spinners to safeguard future supplies. Market
reports for the first time quote dates in addition to type, quality, and
price. The dates of shipment show sailing by month, and they indicate
some dealings in cotton that were not due to arrive for some considerable time. In July there is even a report of a sale of cotton, August
shipment: This would not arrive until December 1862 or January 1863.
By late August the market reports settle into a more or less standard

---

[26] *See* The Economist, Feb. 22, 1862, at 216. The reference is to a type of
East Indian cotton.

[27] The Economist, August 30, 1862, at 971. The reference is to the Liverpool
market.

[28] The Economist, Sept. 6, 1862, at 981.

form, quoting shipment dates from April up to August in single months, and in one instance in coupled months (July and August). All these contracts involved East Indian cotton, and one suspects that some were based on information received as to the ship's arrival in the East Indian ports of Bombay or Calcutta. Once it was known that a ship had reached an Indian port, its likely date of departure could be guessed within broad limits. These contracts were probably ship-named contracts, but it is impossible to be sure about this. Whether the contracts employed merely specified the ship or additionally the date of shipment cannot certainly be told. We do not possess texts of such contracts. It may seem more probable that they did, the market reports reflecting this. But these reports may conflate information from the contracts themselves with information on ship movements known to the brokers from *Lloyd's List*. P. E. J. Hemelryk, who had personal knowledge of the practice of the slightly later period, 1864–1870, describes the reports as giving the name of the ship, the cotton sold, and the guaranteed quality of the cotton. He also indicates that the text of the contracts named the ship but did not specify sailing dates. There continue to be reports quoting no date.

It is impossible now to tell precisely the form of contract used by Raffles, Wichelhaus, and Busch. The law reports do not provide the full text, and the pleadings are not preserved in the public records. Plainly it was a ship-named and port-named contract. Plainly too it did not specify the date of shipment. If, as I think, this was the usual practice, it may have originated, understandably enough, when such contracts were made only when the vessel was at sea and near arrival, and have, by 1862, fossilized in conservative trade practice. From the sellers' point of view it had the advantage that he was not undertaking that the vessel had or would depart at a particular time, a matter always surrounded with some uncertainty.

The *Peerless* Contract and the Litigation

William Winter Raffles appears in Liverpool street directories of the period as a cotton broker in partnership with a Samuel Marshall Bulley, who was his brother-in-law. William Winter Raffles was probably the son of a noted independent minister, Thomas Raffles, and the brother of a barrister, Thomas Stamford Raffles, who acted as Stipendiary Magistrate in Liverpool. Daniel Wichelhaus and Gustav Busch, who were probably of Austrian extraction, were not cotton brokers or merchants. Rather they were in partnership as general commission merchants, and they had for a time produced their own trade journal. Their participation in the speculative dealings in cotton was itself a reflection of the unusual conditions produced by the Civil War.

Although we do not have a text of the contract made between Raffles and Wichelhaus and Busch we know that the quantity and type of cotton were specified, and the ship and port were named, but the date of sailing was not mentioned. The contract also specified that the cotton was to be taken from the quay, and payment was to be made within a specified period after the arrival of the vessel. In other respects, we may be fairly confident that it would be a brief document, probably on a printed form supplied by Raffles, who, as a broker, would make many such contracts. It would most likely not incorporate in the text the trade customs, one of which was mentioned by Clement Milward in the course of the argument: "The words 'to arrive ex "Peerless," ' only mean that if the vessel is lost on the voyage, the contract is to be at an end."[29] If the text had included this provision he would surely have quoted it, or expressed himself differently in making the point.

Although we are not given the date of the contract, it can be deduced with some confidence. It is unlikely that the contract would have been made before it was known in Liverpool that a ship called *Peerless* had left Bombay. The departure of *Peerless* (Major) from Bombay on October 20, 1862, was recorded in a Lloyd's agent's report dated October 27, 1862, and published in England in *Lloyd's List* on November 21, 1862. October 27, 1862, was the date at which the mails left Bombay; they arrived on November 20. We then have two conflicting possibilities.

The first is this. If the buyers were telling either the truth or a plausible lie, it seems likely that the contract would have been made before the news of the departure of the December *Peerless*, that is *Peerless* (Flavin), had been published in England, that is to say when only one *Peerless* was known in England to be on passage to Liverpool. The report of the second ship's departure was dated December 27, 1862, and was published in England on January 21, 1863. So the contract should have been made between November 20, 1862, and January 21, 1863. This hypothesis would explain and make plausible the claim by the buyers that the October ship, *Peerless* (Major), was the one intended. Indeed, given that both vessels were registered at Liverpool, that vessels bearing the same name were a commonplace and could easily be differentiated by captain's name or registered number, and that the mercantile community had access to information on shipping movements, the failure of the contract to indicate which *Peerless* was intended is not easy to explain in any other way. However, it must be said that I have not come across a single example of a cotton contract

---

[29] 2 H. & C. at 906, 159 Eng. Rep. at 375.

which identifies a ship except by its name alone; of course, in the vast majority of situations this would suffice.

The claim that the earlier ship was really intended by the buyers may also seem more plausible for an independent reason. That ship's earlier voyage, between November 17, 1860, and September 12, 1861, had also been to India, though to Calcutta, not to Bombay. *Peerless* (Flavin), however, had not been a Liverpool-registered ship until May 1862, and her previous voyages under Captain Flavin had been to Australia and North America, not India. If Raffles and Wichelhaus had previously dealt in cotton shipped on a *Peerless* of Liverpool it would have been Captain Major's vessel, not Captain Flavin's.

The second and conflicting possibility is this. If we assume that the seller, Raffles, was either telling the truth or a plausible lie when he acted on the premise that he meant the December ship, he probably would not have entered into the contract before January 21, 1863, when news of the departure of *Peerless* (Flavin) became available in England in *Lloyd's List*. This would suggest that Wichelhaus and Busch blundered in not becoming aware of the second ship's departure; they failed to check the reported shipping movements, perhaps under the mistaken impression that only one *Peerless* was a Liverpool cotton carrier. I say "blundered," but it must be said that there is no evidence, so far as I know, as to whether it would be normal for purchasers of cotton to make such a check, or whether it would have seemed reasonable to rely on Raffles, who was after all a professional cotton broker, to call their attention to any special problem over the identification of the shipment—here the fact that there were two vessels of the same name on passage from Bombay to Liverpool. Raffles might well have been expected to know on which ship his cotton was carried. Of course, Raffles *might* have entered into the contract before January 21, 1863, in reliance merely on the knowledge that *Peerless* (Flavin) had reached Bombay on October 8, 1862, and would, in due course, leave again. He would have known this by November 5, 1862, and could have been informed by mail of the acquisition of the Dhollerah cotton which was to be carried on the vessel at any time thereafter, before the vessel completed loading cargo in the port.

An examination of the state of the cotton market during this period should throw further light on the matter and enable us to choose between the two possibilities. In the latter part of 1862, great gloom and uncertainty hung over the Lancashire cotton industry. On October 15, 1862, a leader in the *Cotton Supply Reporter* headed "What's to Be Done?" posed the question: "Has the cotton trade yet reached its darkest hour?"[30] To this it provided the less than helpful reply that it was a question "no man may answer." So far as prices are concerned, Maurice Williams's cotton circulars provide, in graph form, a complete account of their weekly movement, but he quotes prices for only one grade of Surats, "Dhollerah Fair." There were many grades used by brokers, and the relationship between the prices quoted and the prices relevant to the transaction that gave rise to the litigation is complicated. The system of grading cotton was peculiar to the type of cotton concerned and did not remain constant over time. It also differed as between different cotton markets. It is therefore not easy to establish precisely what the system was for Surats in 1862. Whereas Williams's circulars quote prices for only one grade, "Dhollerah Fair," the *Cotton Supply Reporter* for this time quotes prices for three: "Fair," "Middling," and "Ordinary." In 1863 "Middling" was normally around one penny per pound cheaper than "Fair," and "Ordinary" was a penny less than "Middling." John Watts, in *The Facts of the Cotton Famine*, published in 1866, quotes prices for "Good Fair" as well as "Fair," these running at about half a penny higher. Quotations published in the *Economist* during 1862–1863 employ a scale running downward in quality thus: "Fine" (rarely quoted), "Good," "Good Fair," "Fair," "Middling," and "Ordinary." It is all very confusing, but it appears that "Middling Fair," the quality that Raffles undertook to supply, was a half-grade intermediate between "Fair" and "Middling." There was no constant relationship between prices for grades, but "Middling Fair" fluctuated around a level of somewhere under one penny per pound below "Fair."

"Dhollerah Fair" had reached a record level of 18½d. in the week ending September 5, 1862, and the price then began to fall. For the weeks ending November 21 and 28, 1862, it was stable at 14½d. It then began to rise: 15½d. on December 5, 16d. on December 12, 16¾d. on December 19, 17½d. on December 26, and 17¾d. on December 31. The decline between September and early December was caused by

> the repeated disasters experienced by the Federal armies, creating for a time, considerable doubt in the minds of many as to the practicability of the North continuing the war—whilst it daily became evident that the very serious advantage that had taken place in so short a time, without anything like a corresponding advance in the prices of Yarn and Cloths, was forcing many Spinners to close their mills, and others to diminish their production to the smallest possible extent.[31]

---

[30] The Cotton Supply Reporter, Oct. 15, 1862.

[31] WILLIAMS, *supra* note 4 (foldout graph), at 32.

But, so Williams explained, the decline was halted in November by the realization that there was no prospect of an early end of the war or of any intervention by the European powers, England having declined to join France in an attempt to mediate. On November 19, 1862, in response to pressure, Maurice Williams issued a special circular entitled "The Present State of the Cotton Trade,"[32] in which he firmly indicated his belief that there was no immediate chance of the war ending and that the price of cotton goods would rise. He thought that spinners would be wise to reopen mills and that the supply of cotton would remain inadequate to satisfy likely demand. The price of Surats, he thought, would rise. It is impossible to tell how influential this circular was.

In December 1862, increased demand did in fact lead to the reopening of many mills. Williams later wrote in his year-end circular, dated December 31, 1862, but plainly written a little later:

> Speculators as well as Exporters also became active operators on receipt of the American President's Message, indicating as it did the unfaltering determination of the Government and people to prosecute the war for the restoration of the Union, and the ultimate abolition of Slavery, and which has been confirmed by a vote of the House of Representatives endorsing President Lincoln's Proclamation as to the *freeing* of all Slaves owned by masters in rebellion against the Federal Government on the 1st of January, 1863.[33]

The *Economist* for January 7, 1863, noted the excitement created in the market by the American news of January 7, 1863, which included the report of the Proclamation; out of a total of 54,500 bales sold that week, 26,500 had been "on speculation." The market was bullish.

So prices began to rise. Maurice Williams's cotton circular for 1863, quoting spot prices, shows "Fair Dhollerah" at 17¾d. during the week ending January 9, rising to 18d. by January 16. It then slowly fell—to 17½d. by January 23, 17d. between January 30 and February 13, 16¾d. by February 20, 16½d. by February 27, and 16d. by March 6. The decline was then arrested. The price was 16½d. by March 13, 17d. for the weeks ending March 20 and 27, 17¼d. for April 2 and 10, and 17½d. for April 17 and 24. There was then a slight fall to 17¼d. in the week ending May 1, then a rise to 18d. maintained between May 15 and July 17, followed by a sharp rise to a peak of 24½d. by October 30.

---

[32] MAURICE WILLIAMS, THE PRESENT STATE OF THE COTTON TRADE (1862) (special circular).

[33] WILLIAMS, *supra* note 20, at 33.

The rise in March was in part caused by news of the negotiation of the Confederate loan of three million dollars, which dissipated any lingering hopes, or fears, of an early peace.

It seems plausible to suppose that the contract would have been made at a time when the spot price for "Middling Fair" Dhollerah was about 17¼d., or a little below, the purchasers believing that the price would rise beyond this figure by the time the cotton arrived. This suggests a contract during the week ending January 10, 1863, when spot sales of this type and quality were between 17d. and 17⅜d., a time when we know there was massive speculative dealing and when sales of East Indian cotton, October shipment, were being made. As it happens there is also evidence of sales of such cotton for December shipment at this time, contracts made therefore before it was known that the vessel had sailed. Raffles must have been one of those who made such contracts, for which the traditional contractual form, which did not uniquely identify the ship, happened to be particularly inappropriate. That *Peerless* (Flavin), the December vessel, had reached Bombay on October 8, 1862, was known in Liverpool by November 5, 1862, as we have seen. The somewhat tardy departure is probably explained by the fact that the new crop of cotton was the intended cargo, and this imposed a delay.

The fluctuations of the market therefore suggest that the contract was made before the departure of the second *Peerless* was known in Liverpool—the first of the two possibilities discussed above. They also indicate the probable time of contracting.

Peerless (Major) duly arrived on February 18, 1863, and on February 26, 1863, *Gore's General Advertiser* reported her docked and unloading in the Albert dock. She did not lack for cotton. Her cargo included, in addition to 414 bales for designated Liverpool merchants, 3,439½ bales of the material; indeed it principally consisted of cotton. The cotton market at this period was reported to be quiet. The *Times* of February 19, 1863, reported that "[t]he cotton market continues peculiarly dull and inanimate, and this day's sales do not exceed 1500 bales—500 on speculation."[34] The *Economist* quotes the London spot prices for Dhollerah "Middling" on February 21, 1863, as 15¼d. and on February 28 as 15d. So the Liverpool market price would be well below the contract price at the time the vessel was discharging, for prices continued to fall. Given the state of the market and level of prices, it is very difficult to understand why Raffles, if he had cotton of appropriate type and quality on the vessel, would fail to tender delivery, since it would

---

[34] The Times (London), Feb. 19, 1863, at 7, col. 5.

clearly have been in his economic interest to do so. We must conclude that he genuinely believed the contract did not relate to a shipment on this vessel. In all probability he would not have had cotton on this ship, as was indicated in argument by his counsel, Clement Milward, "[h]ere it does not appear that the plaintiff had any goods on board the other 'Peerless.' "[35]

Plainly Wichelhaus and Busch could at this point have complained over Raffles's failure to tender delivery, or indeed they might even have sued. But it is easy to see why they had no economic motive for doing so. As matters stood they had made a bad bargain.

The second vessel, *Peerless* (Flavin), arrived off Liverpool on Sunday, April 19, 1863, and *Gore's General Advertiser* reports her unloading in Queen's dock on April 23, 1863. Her cargo was more exotic, including eleven tons of buffalo horns, but again it principally consisted of cotton—1,079 bales for specified merchants (one of whom must have been Raffles) and 3,723 bales and two half bales not bespoke. By now the Liverpool price of Dhollerah cotton was slightly better than it had been; "Dhollerah Fair" stood at 17½d. on April 24 and then fell to 17¼d. in the following week, according to some sources. The *Economist* has Dhollerah in the London market at 16d. for "Middling" and 17¾d. for "Fair," noting a sale of 200 bales of "Middling Fair" "to arrive" at 16⅝d.; "Middline Oomrawattee" at Liverpool stood at 15d., and "Fair" at 17¾d. This level of prices would still not have enabled the purchasers to break even, for "Middling Fair" would fetch around 16¾d.; they would have suffered a substantial loss, though not so great a loss as in late February and early April. Prices over the next four weeks rose slightly, but not enough to give the buyers a profit. There was in consequence no economic advantage to them in accepting delivery from Raffles off the second ship, *Peerless* (Flavin); obviously if there had been they would have done so. Nor was there by now any chance of Raffles being able to sue them for failing to accept delivery from the first ship, *Peerless* (Major). Delivery had never been tendered, and it was now too late to remedy this. In any event, Raffles had in all probability no cotton from the ship to deliver.

To litigate a dispute in the cotton trade in Liverpool was by no means unknown, but it was very unusual; the customary practice was to arbitrate disputes, and this custom was specifically incorporated in the text of the standard form agreement of 1863.[36] Disputes over cotton

---

[35] 2 H. & C. at 906, 159 Eng. Rep. at 375.

[36] This form, by a fortunate chance, became the subject of a correspondence in *The Times* in November 1863. *See* The Times (London), Nov. 12, 1863, at 6.

itself seem to have always been arbitrated, there being no conceivable reason why anyone would go to court over such a dispute. Quite apart from the delay and cost involved, it would have been ridiculous to accept a jury decision, necessarily based on evidence from expert brokers, rather than to accept the direct decisions of a panel of experts.

The text of the standard-form contract can be read as requiring submission to arbitration only in the normal type of dispute, a dispute over quality. Other types of disputes were arbitrated, but the system in the early records, which, so far as I can tell, was still in force in 1863 when the ships *Peerless* were on passage, was different. The arbitrators were the president, the vice president, and an umpire selected by the parties, not the "two respectable brokers" mentioned in the standard-form contract. At the period with which we are concerned, though the customary practice was to keep cotton disputes entirely out of the courts, submission to arbitration appears to have been in effect voluntary. Why, however, did this particular dispute reach the courts?

Any answer to this question must be somewhat speculative. Part of the background to the case is undiscoverable—for example, when did the confusion come to light? In all probability, Raffles, as a broker, would have noted the daily published reports of the arrival of ships, and when *Peerless* (Major) docked he would have realized that there were in fact two ships of the same name carrying cotton that year from Bombay. At some point—we cannot tell when—there must have been communication between the parties, which was probably weakened by two factors. First, Wichelhaus and Busch were not cotton brokers and were thus interlopers in the close-knit world of the members of the Cotton Brokers' Association. Second, Raffles appears to have been a somewhat quarrelsome person.

Now suppose the matter had been arbitrated by professionals. What solution would have been reached? There are, of course, a number of possibilities, but one would have been particularly attractive and is, I think, hinted at in the reports of the case. Assuming there to have been a genuine misunderstanding, neither side initially realizing that there were two vessels of the same name loading cotton in Bombay, what harm had this done to Wichelhaus and Busch? If cotton had been delivered to them from *Peerless* (Major), the vessel they claimed to have intended, they would have suffered a *larger* loss than they would incur by now taking delivery from *Peerless* (Flavin). The misunderstanding had in a sense worked in their favor (*en passant* I cannot but wonder whether some contracts teacher has ever thought of this "hypo" when teaching the case). They had nothing to complain about. This is the point behind counsel's remark, reported only in the *Law Journal*: "If

the defendants had said their speculation had fallen through in consequence, it might have been different."[37] The defendants' speculation
had indeed failed, in the sense of failing to be profitable, because the
price had not risen as they had expected, and Milward would know
that and so would the judges. Milward could not have been trying to
suggest the contrary. But the consequence of the misunderstanding
that led to tender of cotton from the second ship had reduced their loss,
not increased it, and so their speculation had not failed because of the
misunderstanding at all. This surely is the point Milward is making.

Had the matter been settled in the normal way arbitrators might
well have decided that the sensible and decent way to handle the problem, the equitable solution, would be to require Wichelhaus and Busch
to take delivery from Raffles,[38] or even, though this would be less favorable to them, to do something that courts are always reluctant to
do—split the difference. Furthermore, if Wichelhaus and Busch deliberately kept quiet when no cotton was tendered by Raffles from *Peerless* (Major), hoping that when the second ship arrived, the price would
have moved in their favor, it would hardly seem fair to allow them both
to have their cake and eat it by now refusing to accept the cotton when
they discovered that their hopes had been in vain. Raffles may well
have decided to litigate because he was irritated by the failure of
Wichelhaus and Busch to do the decent thing—either accept the cotton
or go to arbitration.

What of Grant Gilmore's discussion of the case in *The Death of Contract?*[39] His speculations as to the background are inevitably miscon-
ceived, being unrelated to evidence. But his principal point was that
the judges in the case foolishly failed to grasp, in spite of Clement Milward's attempts to put the point to them, that in terms of commercial
understanding the identity of the carrying ship was immaterial. Its
only relevance was to the risk of loss. He backs this claim up with a
classic statement of the ahistorical attitude to legal sources: "In commercial understanding, that is exactly what the terms mean today and
there is no reason to believe that they meant anything else a hundred
years ago."[40] And to be sure, Gilmore is correct in saying that there is
no reason if we pay no attention whatever to the historical context in
which the dispute arose. But from what I have said, it is perfectly plain

---

[37] 33 L.J.N.S. at 160.

[38] In terms of a money award, compensate Raffles by paying the difference
between the contract price and market price.

[39] *See* GILMORE, *supra* note 2, at 35–42.

[40] *Id.* at 37.

that in arrival contracts where ship and port were named, the identity of the carrying vessel was of central importance. It was the identity of the carrying vessel that fixed the time of arrival and delivery. In the volatile cotton market, that time was critical to the success or failure of the speculation. The reason why time was not specified directly was technological, and as the technology changed, "shipments" were to be superseded by a new form of contract, "deliveries," which did directly specify time. Out of transactions involving this newer form of arrival contract was to develop the practice of futures trading, but that is another story.

The Rise of *Raffles v. Wichelhaus*

As for those involved in *Raffles v. Wichelhaus,* William Winter Raffles retired in 1868 and died in 1880 or 1881, Daniel Wichelhaus in about 1883, and Gustav Busch in the 1890s. As for the maritime side of the story, Lloyd's *Captains' Registers* record that for both Thomas Flavin and Robert Major, *Peerless* was their last command. Thomas Flavin remained master of his vessel until 1870; she then passed into the ownership of John Hall of Newcastle, who changed her registration to that port, from which she presumably operated as a collier. In 1881 she was sold into French ownership; the ship's articles survive for her last voyage as a British ship. Her eventual fate and final name I do not know, though she continues to be listed by Lloyd's up to the 1885 register as French owned.

Robert Major kept command of his *Peerless* until 1867. She later met, what is for a sailing ship, a more appropriate and dramatic end. On December 9, 1870 she was abandoned in a sinking condition seventy miles north-northwest of Cape Horn.

Both vessels were to enjoy a posthumous fame greater than they had enjoyed in life. For this, the explanation lies partly in the general history of the law of contract, and partly in the history of legal education, particularly a form of it developed at the Harvard Law School in the late nineteenth century.

From around 1800 there took place a very considerable elaboration of the Anglo-American law of contract. Lawyers came to believe that contractual disputes should be analyzed and resolved by reference to general and highly abstract principles of law. It was this process that formed the starting point for Gilmore's *The Death of Contract.* These principles in their turn were thought to elaborate the fundamental notion that contractual obligations all derived from the voluntary agreement of the parties to the contract, from what some called the "meeting of the minds" of the contractors. To a considerable extent the principles of the common law of contract were borrowed from the stock of ideas employed by continental legal writers. They, in turn, had taken them from conceptions developed by the Roman jurists of antiquity, who had conceived the notion that certain forms of contract were consensual. In a consensual contract the obligations of the contractors derived not from the use of some special formality, nor from some action, but simply from the metaphysical fact of agreement, from the *consensus ad idem*. Such old texts of the Roman lawyers as had survived in Justinian's sixth-century restatement of the law, the *Digest*, became an object of study in the European universities from the twelfth century onward. In the nineteenth century the theories based upon them began to permeate the common law. Contractual obligations all derived from the joint wills of the contractors, which became one will through the phenomenon of agreement. Given this scheme of thought, which, of course, was variously developed and received by lawyers, situations in which the parties had misunderstood each other or reached an apparent agreement under some mistake or misapprehension presented a problem. Centuries earlier the Roman jurist Ulpian, writing of the contract of sale which the jurists classified as a consensual contract, had put the point bluntly:

> It is obvious that agreement is of the essence in sale and purchase; the purchase is not valid if there be disagreement over the contract itself, the price, or any other element of the sale. Hence, if I thought that I was buying the Cornelian farm and you that you were selling the Sempronian, the sale is void because we were not agreed upon the thing sold. . . . Of course, if we are merely in disagreement over the name but at one on the actual thing there is no doubt that the sale is good. . . .[41]

Ideas of this character, sometimes categorized as dealing with the effect of mistake *(error)* in contract, came to be received into English and American law and posed a peculiarly acute problem when the parties had appeared to agree. Was apparent agreement sufficient, or must there be a true agreement, a real meeting of the minds?

Nineteenth-century legal thinkers not only elaborated the law of contract; they also believed that it possessed a preeminent social significance. It was through the formation of contracts that free and independent individuals could arrange their mutual affairs to suit their own preferences and choices. Contract could become the legal instrument of progress and social improvement. So when Christopher Columbus Langdell, who had become dean of the Harvard Law School in

---

[41] DIGEST XVIII 1.9.

1870, decided to embark upon a new experiment in legal education, he selected contract law as his subject.

In common with many intellectually minded lawyers of the time, Langdell believed that the case law that had been built up over the centuries in response to contractual disputes was in reality based upon a finite set of legal principles that lurked beneath the apparently disordered farrago of case reports, and invited discovery. Law was a science in the sense that it possessed a deep rational structure, and the legal scientist's function was to identify, formulate, and expound this structure.[42] Langdell married this theory to an educational technique. His law students were to be given the opportunity, under his guidance, to become legal scientists. They would study a limited selection of leading cases and, through analysis and class discussion, discover the principles for themselves.[43] To assist them he decided to publish a selection of such cases. This last idea was not original. An English legal educator, John William Smith, whose two-volume selections of leading cases had appeared in England in 1837–1840, and in America in 1838–1840, was the first person to produce a book around the idea of leading case; the idea had in fact been suggested to him by his friend Samuel Warren, a barrister, legal writer, and novelist. His collection, in its seventh American edition by 1872, had been well received in England and America. There are earlier accounts of American teachers working from cases and, of course, common lawyers had always read cases. But Langdell was perhaps the first person to develop around such a book a special teaching technique, the case class, and to abandon the use of the formal lecture. It was in this that his originality as a teacher consisted. In fact what happened was that the function of the formal dogmatic lecture, which simply told the students what the law was and informed them of the categories within which the matter was to be discussed, came to be discharged by books. Langdell in the second edition of his casebook in 1879 added a summary that performed this function, and in 1880 he published his *A Summary of the Law of Contracts* as a separate book. Armed with this the student could make sense of the classes, and its publication by Langdell reflects his awareness that the pure ideal form of the case system was unattainable. Langdell's *Summary*, significantly titled, is the ancestor of the Gilbert's and other

---

[42] On the history of this belief see my articles *The Rise and Fall of the Legal Treatise: Legal Principles and the Forms of Legal Literature*, 48 U. Chi. L. Rev. 632 (1981), and *Legal Iconoclasm and Legal Ideals*, 58 U. Cin. L. Rev. 819 (1990), and the references there cited to the literature on the subject.

[43] Langdell's theory is set out in the preface to his book C. C. LANGDELL, A SELECTION OF CASES ON THE LAW OF CONTRACTS (1871).

works that still underpin the system to the present day. His technique came to be called the Socratic method, though there is no reason to suppose that Langdell supposed himself to be modelling his behavior on the Platonic dialogues. It has also been given less complimentary names, such as the student-abuse system. Whatever its merits and demerits, it came to be the typical method of American legal education, though, of course, it has developed over time and is not identical as between different law teachers.

Langdell's collection was first published in 1870, but *Raffles v. Wichelhaus* was not one of the cases that he selected for inclusion. Its rise to fame was less straightforward, and effectively began in 1875 when it was discussed by another barrister who practiced on the Northern Circuit, the American exile to the English bar, Judah P. Benjamin.[44] Judah Benjamin was a lawyer of great distinction, and his book was much the fullest treatment of the law of sale that had yet appeared in the common law world. He first mentions the case in Book I of his treatise, which deals with the formation of contract. It appears in Chapter III, which deals with the requirement of "mutual assent." There he states the following derivative principle: "From the general principle that contracts can only be effected by mutual assent, it follows that where, through some mistake of fact, each was assenting to a different contract, there is no real valid agreement, notwithstanding the apparent mutual assent."[45] On the following page appears *Raffles v. Wichelhaus,* and after summarizing the report he adds: "[o]n demurrer, held that on this state of facts there was no *consensus ad idem*, no contract at all between the parties."[46] Later he hedges his view by saying that when the mistake is of one party only,

> [i]t must be borne in mind that the general rule of law is, that whatever a man's *real* intention may be, if he *manifests* an intention to another party, so as to induce the latter to act upon it in making a contract, he will be estopped from denying that the intention as manifested was his real intention.[47]

How this affected his reading of the *Peerless* case he unfortunately does not say. The two principles stated seem, if not to contradict each other, to pull in different directions.[48] Perhaps this was why, in the sec-

---

[44] *See* BENJAMIN, *supra* note 22, at 51–52.

[45] *Id.* at 51.

[46] *Id.* at 52.

[47] *Id.* at 54.

[48] It was part of the tradition of legal science in which Judah Benjamin was writing that the law should be presented as based on a set of compatible prin-

ond English edition of his treatise, published in 1873, he amplified his discussion, explaining that if the parties both intend to refer to two different ships *Peerless,* and there are in fact two such ships, there is no contract. But if there is only one *Peerless*, and one party intended to refer to a ship called *Peeress,* then there would be a good contract: "men can only bargain by mutual communication, and if A.'s proposal were unmistakable, and if it were made in writing, and B.'s answer was an unequivocal and unconditional acceptance, B. would be bound, however clearly he might afterwards make it appear that he was *thinking* of a different vessel."[49] Later in the first edition of his treatise the case turns up again as an illustration of an exception to the parol evidence rule; what the case decided, we are now told, was that

> where a bargain was made for the sale of cotton, "to arrive ex *Peerless* from Bombay," parol evidence was held admissible to show that there were two ships *Peerless* from Bombay, and that the ship *Peerless* intended by the vendor was a different ship *Peerless* from that intended by the buyer, so as to establish a mistake defeating the contract for want of a *consensus ad idem.*[50]

This somewhat more complex account of the case, which, it must be remembered, contains no justificatory or explanatory judicial opinion, must surely have done much to launch the case on its career. In reality, no parol evidence was admitted in the case; it never went for jury trial.

When the English writer Sir Frederick Pollock published his *Principles of Contract at Law and in Equity* in 1876,[51] he must have been familiar with Benjamin's discussion of the case. Now Pollock firmly believed that in the absence of true consent, there could be no contract.

---

ciples. Ronald Dworkin's theory of the "right answer" is a modern expression of this notion. RONALD DWORKIN, LAW'S EMPIRE viii–ix (1986). An alternative view, which I personally prefer and use as a basis for teaching law, is that legal principles, because of the nature of the world in which we live, inevitably point to conflicting solutions in particular instances, just as do moral principles. Life is not packaged in terms of the principles.

[49] J. P. BENJAMIN, A TREATISE ON THE LAW OF SALE OF PERSONAL PROPERTY; WITH REFERENCES TO THE AMERICAN DECISIONS AND TO THE FRENCH CODE AND CIVIL LAW 347–48 (2d ed. 1873).

[50] J. P. BENJAMIN, A TREATISE ON THE LAW OF SALE OF PERSONAL PROPERTY; WITH REFERENCES TO THE AMERICAN DECISIONS AND TO THE FRENCH CODE AND CIVIL LAW 168 (1868).

[51] FREDERICK POLLOCK, PRINCIPLES OF CONTRACT AT LAW AND IN EQUITY (1876).

In setting out the basic elements of contract, conceived of in terms of agreement, he wrote, "The next thing is that these persons [the contracting parties] have a distinct intention, and the intention of both or all of them is the same. Without this one obviously cannot say there is an agreement."[52] Awareness of each other's intention, he explained, was a quite distinct contractual requirement. In the eighth chapter of another book of his, he discussed "[m]istake as excluding true consent,"[53] and, following the Roman jurists, one form of mistake he discussed was error as to the specific thing—what commentators on Roman Law had called *error in corpore*.[54] For Pollock, *Raffles v. Wichelhaus* was something of a godsend, for it was very difficult to find cases which illustrated his theory. "A striking modern case of this kind is *Raffles v. Wichelhaus*," he declared, explaining that

> [t]he plea was held good, for "[t]he defendant only bought that cotton which was to arrive by a particular ship"; and to hold that he bought cotton to arrive in any ship of that name would have been "imposing on the defendant a contract different from that which he entered into."[55]

It will be noted that Pollock's analysis appears to involve the view that the defendants in the case, Wichelhaus and Busch, had in fact bought some cotton, so there must have been a contract, but not for the cotton tendered by Raffles. This analysis was attributed in a footnote to Chief Baron Pollock and Baron Martin. Neither of them had in reality said anything about mistake, or about the need for true consent, though the remark last quoted was uttered by Baron Martin in the course of argument.[56]

Pollock's theory of contract was derived from the German jurist Friedrich Karl von Savigny's *System des heutigen römischen Rechts*.[57]

---

[52] *Id.* at 2.

[53] FREDERICK POLLOCK, PRINCIPLES OF CONTRACT (4th ed. 1888).

[54] *Id.*

[55] *Id.* at 472 (footnote omitted).

[56] Chief Baron Pollock had in fact said, "[i]t is like a contract for the purchase of wine coming from a particular estate in France or Spain, where there are two estates of that name." Raffles v. Wichelhaus, 159 Eng. Rep. 375, 375 (Ex. 1864). Presumably he was trying to make the point that the identity of the ship was commercially relevant, though, of course, the wine example goes to quality, not time.

[57] FRIEDRICH KARL VON SAVIGNY, SYSTEM DES HEUTIGEN RÖMISCHEN RECHTS [SYSTEM OF MODERN ROMAN LAW] (1840–1849).

Pollock adopts Savigny's definition of contract.[58] Sir William Anson, another true consent man, included the case in his very successful treatise on contract, published in 1879,[59] no doubt picking it up from Pollock. So it came about that Langdell, in 1879, also included it in the second edition of his casebook, no doubt influenced by Benjamin and Pollock.[60] In his summary of the law, a dogmatic statement of the principles of contract, he explained that normally the intentions of the parties had to be discovered from what they did, from their acts, so that if they appeared to agree it would normally be presumed that their minds were as one. But in conformity with the true consent doctrine he added that "the performance of the acts will avail nothing, if mutual consent is found to be lacking."[61] *Raffles v. Wichelhaus* was made to serve as an illustration of this dogma. In 1880 it was used in Sir Thomas Erskine Holland's *Elements of Jurisprudence,* then a popular legal work, to illustrate the same thesis.

The case was on its way to join the immortals. Its fame was further enhanced in 1881 when Oliver Wendell Holmes Junior, in *The Common Law,* attacked the interpretation placed upon the case by Pollock, Anson, Langdell, and Holland, developing his own theory that "[t]he law has nothing to do with the actual state of the parties' minds."[62] Nothing so establishes a young thinker as a radical attack on the establishment. And Holmes soon acquired converts to the new faith. In 1886 Holland recanted in the third edition of his *Elements of Jurisprudence,* attributing his change of heart to Rudolph Leonhard's *Der Irrtum bei nichtigen Vertragen,* though the credit, it has been argued, should really belong to Holmes. A letter by Holland to Holmes dated March 21, 1888, refers to the dispute, noting that A. V. Dicey had been persuaded, but that "Anson and Pollock are still obdurate."[63] The case was now cast as the focus of a high theoretical dispute on the basis of

---

[58] *Id.* §140.

[59] WILLIAM R. ANSON, PRINCIPLES OF THE ENGLISH LAW OF CONTRACT 130 (1879).

[60] C. C. LANGDELL, A SELECTION OF CASES ON THE LAW OF CONTRACTS 180, s.v. Mutual Consent (2d ed. 1879).

[61] *Id.* §148, at 1070.

[62] OLIVER WENDELL HOLMES JR., THE COMMON LAW 242 (Mark deWolfe Howe ed., Belknap Press of Harvard Univ. Press 1963) (1881). For a discussion, see GILMORE, *supra* note 2, at 40–42.

[63] Oliver Wendell Holmes Jr., Papers, Harvard Law School Library, MS Box 44, Folder 6.

contractual obligation, and one that, in spite of its very considerable intellectual interest, was of virtually no practical significance.

In time the news of the exciting new system of legal education filtered back across the Atlantic, and in 1886 Gerard B. Finch, who taught law at Queen's College, Cambridge, from 1885, published *A Selection of Cases on the English Law of Contract,* prepared as "a Text-Book for Law Students in the Universities."[64] His introduction extolled the virtues of Langdell's system, which he attempted to introduce to England. He had absolutely no success; the sturdy individualism of English law students, or if you like their idleness, made it impossible to introduce so disciplined and authoritarian a system. Finch inevitably included *Raffles v. Wichelhaus* in his Chapter 5, entitled "Reality of Consent." In the American casebooks, which proliferated as the law schools were Harvardized, the case became a set piece, and in the English treatises too it continues to be included to this day.

The obscurity that has surrounded the facts of the dispute, and the background to it, has proved positively advantageous from an educational point of view, encouraging entertaining and instructive speculation as to what exactly the litigation was all about. The evidence I have set out does not answer all questions. Indeed it raises as many questions as it solves; that is the nature of historical research. But perhaps it makes some aspects of the matter easier to understand. At a doctrinal level the absence of any reasoned judicial opinion inevitably makes the case an empty vessel, into which theories can be poured as desired. It would be sad indeed if my inquiries have dealt the case of the contract for cotton "to arrive" its death blow. But I am confident that it will not have this lamentable effect, and that the tradition of legal doctrinalism will remain proof against the meddlings of historians.

---

[64] GERARD B. FINCH, A SELECTION OF CASES ON THE ENGLISH LAW OF CONTRACT (1886).

3

Robert E. Scott[*]

Hoffman v. Red Owl Stores and the Myth of Precontractual Reliance

The conventional wisdom among contemporary scholars is that courts will impose promissory estoppel liability for reliance investments undertaken prior to any agreement between commercial parties.[1] Evidence of promises made and relied upon during the negotiation process together with a "general obligation arising out of the negotiations themselves" are the supposed grounds for imposing liability even for preliminary negotiations that ultimately break down.[2] But even a casual survey of contemporary case law casts significant doubt

---

[*] Alfred McCormack Professor of Law, Columbia University. This essay benefited greatly from comments by Ken Abraham, George Cohen, Marvin Chirelstein, Victor Goldberg, Jody Kraus, Alan Schwartz, and George Triantis. It is forthcoming in a symposium titled "Commercial Calamities." 68 Ohio St. L.J. 1 (2007).

[1] *See, e.g.*, E. Allan Farnsworth, *Precontractual Liability and Preliminary Agreements: Fair Dealing and Failed Negotiations*, 87 Colum. L. Rev. 217 (1987) ("In recent decades, courts have shown increasing willingness to impose precontractual liability."); Michael B. Metzger & Michael J. Phillips, *The Emergence of Promissory Estoppel as an Independent Theory of Recovery*, 35 Rutgers L. Rev. 472, 496–97 (1983) ("[I]t is clear that promissory estoppel has been used to enforce promises too indefinite or incomplete to constitute valid offers."); RALPH B. LAKE & UGO DRAETTA, LETTERS OF INTENT AND OTHER PRECONTRACTUAL DOCUMENTS 177 ("Liability for action during the precontractual stage of a transaction may be based on the obligation to bargain and to negotiate in good faith."); RESTATEMENT (SECOND) OF CONTRACTS §205, cmt. c (1981) ("Bad faith in negotiations . . . may be subject to sanctions.").

[2] See sources cited *supra* note 1.

on the accuracy of the conventional view. Courts actually make some form of agreement a necessary precondition to a promisee's recovery. The real issues are these: When will a preliminary agreement be found? And how does the nature of such agreement determine when and how a promisee can recover?

These questions have generated a flood of litigation that has been virtually ignored in contemporary contract law courses. One reason that this question is ignored is the misplaced attention given to the decision of the Wisconsin Supreme Court in *Hoffman v. Red Owl Stores, Inc.*[3] As a consequence of a fundamental misunderstanding of the law in action, lawyers bring suits claiming reliance on preliminary negotiations and, to their surprise and that of their clients, they lose. Meanwhile an entire new body of law enforcing certain preliminary agreements has emerged unbeknownst to most lawyers (and legal academics).

The story of this misunderstanding of the law of precontractual liability begins with *Hoffman v. Red Owl*. In *Hoffman*, the court held that even if two parties had never reached agreement on essential factors necessary to establish a contract, a party who relied on representations made during the negotiations could recover sunk costs based on the doctrine of promissory estoppel as expressed in section 90 of the *Restatement of Contracts*. Under this doctrine, the court held that a "promise"—here Red Owl's representation that $18,000 was sufficient capital to secure a franchise—need not be as definite in its terms as a promise that is the basis of a traditional bargain contract.[4]

Putting aside for the moment the dubious accuracy of that holding as a matter of contract doctrine, one fact has become clear in the intervening years during which time *Hoffman* has been ensconced as a favorite in contracts casebooks[5] and analyzed in numerous law review

---

[3] 133 N.W.2d 267 (Wis. 1965).

[4] *Id.* at 275.

[5] *See, e.g.,* RANDY E. BARNETT, CONTRACTS: CASES AND DOCTRINE 732 (3d ed. 2003); JOHN P. DAWSON, WILLIAM BURNETT HARVEY & STANLEY D. HENDERSON, CONTRACTS: CASES AND COMMENT 409 (8th ed. 2003); E. ALLAN FARNSWORTH, WILLIAM F. YOUNG & CAROL SANGER, CONTRACTS: CASES AND MATERIALS 235 (6th ed. 2001); LON L. FULLER & MELVIN ARON EISENBERG, BASIC CONTRACT LAW 573 (7th ed. 2001); EDWARD J. MURPHY, RICHARD E. SPEIDEL & IAN AYRES, STUDIES IN CONTRACT LAW 435 (6th ed. 2003); I STEWART MACAULAY, JOHN KIDWELL & WILLIAM WHITFORD, CONTRACTS: LAW IN ACTION 390 (2d ed. 2003); ROBERT E. SCOTT & JODY S. KRAUS, CONTRACT LAW AND THEORY 204 (rev. 3d ed. 2002).

articles:[6] *Hoffman* is an outlier; the case has not been followed in its own or other jurisdictions.[7] Indeed, a recent case applying the Wisconsin law that governed *Hoffman* refused to award reliance damages on a promissory estoppel claim under similar facts.[8] Courts in other jurisdictions have established strict limitations for imposing promissory liability based on representations made during the negotiation process.[9]

All of this begs for answers to several key questions: How could the court in *Hoffman* find liability where so many other courts could not? And what exactly is the law of contracts in the muddy area of precontractual liability? In this essay, I begin with a close look at the *Hoffman* case. The transcript of the trial reveals a story far different from the conventional understanding of the dispute between Joseph Hoff-

---

[6] *See, e.g.*, Gregory Duhl, Red Owl's *Legacy,* 87 Marquette L. Rev. 297 (2004); Peter Linzer, *Rough Justice: A Theory of Restitution and Reliance, Contracts and Torts,* 2001 Wis. L. Rev. 695, 717–20; Juliet P. Kostritsky, *When Should Contract Law Supply a Liability Rule or Term?,* 32 Ariz. St. L.J. 1283, 1322–23 (2000); Jason Scott Johnston, *Communication and Courtship: Cheap Talk Economics and the Law of Contract Formation,* 85 Va. L. Rev. 387, 494–99 (1999); Avery Katz, *When Should an Offer Stick? The Economics of Promissory Estoppel in Preliminary Negotiations,* 105 Yale L.J. 1249, 1255–57 (1996); Richard Craswell, *Offer, Acceptance and Efficient Reliance,* 48 Stan L. Rev. 481 (1996); *Edward Yorio & Steve Thel, The Promissory Basis of Section 90,* 101 Yale L.J. 111 (1991); Mark P. Gergen, *Liability for Mistake in Contract Formation* 64 S. Cal. L. Rev. 1, 27–42 (1990); Farnsworth, *supra* note 1; Daniel Farber & John H. Matheson, *Beyond Promissory Estoppel: Contract Law and the "Invisible Handshake,"* 52 U. Chi. L. Rev. 903 (1985); Jay M. Feinman, *Promissory Estoppel and Judicial Method,* 97 Harv. L. Rev. 678 (1984); Metzger & Phillips, *supra* note 1; Charles Knapp, *Enforcing the Contract to Bargain,* 44 N.Y.U. L. Rev. 673, 686–90 (1969); Robert Summers, *Good Faith in General Contract Law and the Sales Provisions of the Uniform Commercial Code,* 54 Va. L. Rev. 195, 225 (1968).

[7] Farnsworth, *supra* note 1.

[8] Beer Capitol Distributing, Inc. v. Guinness Bass Import Co., 290 F.3d 877 (7th Cir. 2002). The court denied both promissory estoppel and unjust enrichment claims based on the plaintiff's reliance on defendant's representation during the negotiations that he would recommend plaintiff as the exclusive distributor of defendant's beer for southeastern Wisconsin.

[9] *See, e.g.*, Banco Espirito Santo de Investimento v. Citibank, 2003 U.S. Dist. Lexis 23062 (S.D.N.Y. 2003); R.G. Group v. Horn & Hardart, 751 F.2d 69, 71 (2d Cir. 1984).

man and the representatives of Red Owl Stores.[10] The truth suggests an important lesson for law teachers (and law students): It is dangerous to draw inferences about emerging doctrine from isolated cases and it helps to read cases systematically if one wishes to recover the law in action. By setting the record straight on what really happened in *Hoffman* and pointing where the legal rules governing preliminary agreements have evolved in the years since the case was decided, I hope to encourage a more systematic approach to the "discovery" of new legal doctrines.

The True Facts of *Hoffman v. Red Owl Stores*

The Supreme Court of Wisconsin relied on an edited transcript of the trial as the basis for its decision.[11] But the complete trial transcript of the case[12] paints a very different picture of the relationship between Joseph Hoffman[13] and Edward Lukowitz and the other Red Owl agents headquartered in Minneapolis.[14] This is true even if one endeavors to interpret all facts in the light most favorable to Hoffman as the appellee holding a jury verdict.

The key to unraveling the true story behind *Hoffman* is to ignore the red herring. Specifically, let's put to one side a consideration of the

---

[10] Commentators have been virtually unanimous in accepting the story, as told by the Wisconsin Supreme Court, that Red Owl's escalating financial demands were the proximate cause of the breakdown in negotiations between the parties. Marvin Chirelstein is a notable exception to this uncritical view of the case in suggesting that there is a plausible alternative story to tell about *Hoffman*. MARVIN A. CHIRELSTEIN, CONCEPTS AND CASE ANALYSIS IN THE LAW OF CONTRACTS 57–58 (5th ed. 2006). *See also* Johnston, *supra* note 6, at 497–99.

[11] *See* Brief of the Appellants, Hoffman v. Red Owl Stores, Inc., and Edward Lukowitz, Supreme Court, State of Wisconsin, August Term, 1964, No. 147, Appendix at 101-241.

[12] *Joseph and Shirley Hoffmann v. Red Owl Stores, Inc., and Edward Lukowitz*, Circuit Court, Outagamie County, Wisconsin, File No. 14954, Transcript (Oct. 21, 1963, A. W. Parnell, J.), Trial Record at 77 et seq. [hereinafter Record].

[13] Joseph Hoffmann in fact spelled his name with two *n*'s, thus "Hoffmann," and it was so spelled in the trial transcript and in respondent's brief to the Supreme Court of Wisconsin. *See* Record at 77–78 et seq. The majority opinion of Justice Currie in the Supreme Court misspelled his name and the misspelling has remained ever since.

[14] As I suggest in this essay, the misunderstanding between the parties that led to the dispute cannot be appreciated if one merely reads the edited transcript. Moreover, Red Owl's attorneys did a poor job of highlighting the key facts and their legal relevance either at trial or on appeal.

various actions taken by Hoffman in reliance on statements made by Lukowitz and the other Red Owl representatives during the negotiation process. Rather, let's focus on a single fact. Hoffman claimed to have "about $18,000" available to be set up in a Red Owl franchise.[15] This much is conceded by all. These, then, are the pertinent questions: What was the understanding as to the composition of the $18,000? Was it supposed to be all equity, or was it to be cash composed of some equity and some debt? If the latter, from what sources was Hoffman to obtain his encumbered cash? Finally, how reasonable was Red Owl's reaction to the changing sources of Hoffman's prospective $18,000 contribution as he moved his assets around between September 1961 and January 1962? While these financing questions are complex, they contain the answer to the puzzle that has perplexed students and commentators for years: What explains the behavior of Red Owl officials who, according to the court, repeatedly increased Hoffman's minimum capital requirements, first from $18,000 to $24,000, then to $26,000, and ultimately to $34,000?

1. *The purchase and sale of the Wautoma grocery store and the $18,000 "assurance"*

In the fall of 1959, Joseph Hoffman was restless. He had operated a bakery in Wautoma, Wisconsin, since 1956 but he wanted to do more.[16] So, in November 1959, Hoffman contacted Sid Jansen, the division manager of Red Owl Stores,[17] and inquired about the possibility of acquiring a Red Owl franchise store. Informal discussions continued but without much progress and, by the fall of 1960, Edward Lukowitz had taken over from Jansen as division manager. Around Christmas that year Hoffman had an idea. He thought "it might be a good idea to get a little experience in the grocery business before I go into a bigger store."[18] A friend in Wautoma who was running such a store had suf-

---

[15] Record at 86.

[16] Hoffman had done well in this business and, in February 1959, he had bought the building in which the bakery was located for $10,000 under an installment land contract ($100 down and $100 per month). By September 1961, when he paid off this mortgage, he had paid down the principal liability to about $7,500. *See* Record at 79–81 and note 33 *infra*.

[17] Jansen's responsibilities included "future development" (finding new franchisees and facilitating the process by which they could begin operations as Red Owl franchisees).

[18] Record at 84.

fered a heart attack, and the store was available. Hoffman called Lukowitz, who looked into it and advised him to go ahead.[19]

Hoffman bought the Wautoma grocery store business from his friend for $16,000 in February 1961 and assumed the lease on the building.[20] Things went well even though Hoffman was stretched thin in managing both the bakery and the grocery business at the same time. In May, Lukowitz and another Red Owl employee came to the store to conduct an inventory, and they concluded that the store was running a 3 to 4 percent profit, which they judged as pretty good under the circumstances. Lukowitz thereupon urged Hoffman to sell the business to his assistant, Edward Wrysinski, in order to free up his equity for the larger Red Owl store.[21] Hoffman was reluctant to sell in June because the summer business in the lake country was historically very brisk (an estimated 5,000 tourists would increase the summer population significantly).

At this meeting in May 1961, Hoffman said to Lukowitz and his colleague, "Fellows, you know how much money I got—about $18,000. Will this put me in a bigger operation or won't it?" Lukowitz replied that there would be no problem with that level of investment.[22] There was, however, no discussion then (or at any time thereafter) as to the nature of the $18,000 investment. Was it to be all equity, or was it to be part equity and part borrowed cash?[23] Hoffman clearly assumed the latter. At the time, Hoffman had only $10,500 in cash of his own. He expected the balance to come from a loan to the business by his father-

---

[19] *Id.*

[20] Hoffman paid $7,000 for the business and $9,000 for the inventory and leased the store building for $175 per month. Record at 89. Hoffman's cost in acquiring and operating the grocery business in Wautoma was $18,000. *Id.* at 90. He financed this transaction in part by borrowing $9,500 from the Union State Bank of Wautoma and giving the bank a chattel mortgage on his bakery equipment. Exhibit 41.

[21] There also was evidence that Hoffman and Wrysinski were not working well together and that this might have been a contributing factor in the decision to sell. Record at 119. Though conflicting, the evidence is sufficient to find that Lukowitz urged this move so as to "set Hoffman up" in a bigger Red Owl store.

[22] Record at 86.

[23] On cross-examination, Hoffman was asked, "Was there any discussion at any time as to how this $18,000 was to be made up? That is, was it all unencumbered cash or partly to be borrowed cash?" Hoffman answered, "I don't believe there was any discussion on that." Record at 167.

in-law, Simon Vanden Heuvel, a prosperous local farmer.[24] By saying
he had $18,000, Hoffman treated what he had to contribute to the
business the same as what someone else would lend to it. But a franchisor is hardly indifferent between the two. Red Owl regarded a substantial equity contribution from its franchisees as the key to a successful franchise.[25]

Indeed, Red Owl officials had reason to believe that Hoffman
could and would supply at least $18,000 of his own cash in setting up
the business and would not rely on money lent by others to make that
contribution. On September 11, 1961, Hoffman had provided a financial statement to Lukowitz that was passed on to the home office in
Minneapolis. This statement represented that Hoffman had business
equity of at least $28,000, consisting of $10,000 in cash, $1,500 in in-
ventory in the bakery, $4,500 equity in the bakery building, and
$12,000 equity in his bakery equipment.[26] Thus, from Red Owl's per-
spective, Hoffman would have ample equity provided he liquidated his
bakery business. At that time, however, they did not know that Hoffman had no intention of selling his bakery business in order to free up
his own cash for the new franchise. Rather, he hoped to continue that
business and operate the new Red Owl store at the same time.[27]

The Wautoma grocery store was sold to Ed Wrysinski on June 6,
1961, for $18,000.[28] At the time he sold in June, many details about
establishing Hoffman in a bigger store were unresolved, including
which town would be the best location for the new store, the size and
site of the store building, fixtures needed for a store, etc.[29] Shortly af-

---

[24] *See* Hoffman's financial statement of September 11, 1961 (Exhibit 40).

[25] Equity participation helps to align the interests of a franchisee with those
of the franchisor. *See infra* text accompanying note 81.

[26] *See* Exhibit 40. Financial statement dated September 11, 1961. Although
the statement also reflects a $6,000 equity in his residence in Wautoma, there
was never any indication that personal as opposed to business assets were to
be contributed to the franchise.

[27] Record at 133–34.

[28] Hoffman testified that it was his decision to sell the store business but
that he acted on Lukowitz's advice that he should sell before the summer tour-
ist season in order to prepare for the new store. Hoffman testified, "I told Ed
[Lukowitz that the fellow that was working for me was interested in the business. Ed says: Let's sell it to him now and go into a bigger operation." Record at
94.

[29] On cross-examination Hoffman was asked, "Didn't you know at this time
that in [selling the Wautoma store and] establishing a bigger store there would

terward, Lukowitz suggested alternative locations for the new store—
Lake Mills, Clintonville, Kewaunee, and Chilton. The two of them traveled around looking at these places and finally settled on a lot in Chilton. On August 3, Hoffman acquired a thirty-day option to purchase
the Chilton lot at a price of $6,000 with $1,000 down on exercise of the
option.[30] The plan was that Hoffman would purchase the lot and then
resell it at a profit to the contractor who was building the new store,
taking back a lease at a rental that reflected the enhanced price the
builder agreed to pay.[31] In essence, the sale/leaseback was designed
both to capture equity in the lot and to serve as an indirect loan from
the builder to Hoffman. The goal was to open the new store by December 1.

2. The September 27 proposed financing plan

Based on Hoffman's September 11 financial statement,[32] it appeared
to Red Owl officials that, by selling the bakery building and business
and combining the proceeds with cash on hand, Hoffman would have
$26,500 in liquid assets, more than enough to make his equity contri-
bution to the franchise operation. Hoffman, as we have seen, had much
different intentions, however. He did not intend to sell the equipment
or the bakery building. Rather, he wanted to lease the building and
business to someone else and take some of the equipment to operate a
bakery in the new store. Hoffman saw the bakery business as his livelihood, available to support his wife and six children while getting
started in the new store.[33]

On September 13, acting on Lukowitz's advice, Hoffman paid the
$1,000 and exercised his option on the Chilton lot. Hoffman was eager
to do so in any event because he had heard of the possibility of an A&P
acquiring the same property for a store in Chilton. The next day, Hoffman paid off the $7,500 mortgage on the bakery building, reducing his
cash on hand in the bank to $2,500. On September 27 Lukowitz called
Hoffman and arranged for him to meet two people from the Red Owl

---

be a lot of things to be worked out?" "That's right," Hoffman replied. Record at
171.

[30] The option was subsequently extended to September 15. *Id.* at 104.

[31] Record at 100.

[32] The statement showed $10,000 cash in the bank and additional equity in
the bakery business of $16,500, consisting of the bakery building (worth
$12,000 with a $7,500 mortgage) and equipment (worth $19,500 subject to a
chattel mortgage of $7,500). *See* Exhibit 40. Apparently, this financial state-
ment was prepared at Lukowitz's request.

[33] Record at 117.

home office—Herman Carlson, the future development manager, and Walter Hall, the credit manager—at the lot in Chilton.[34] During that meeting, Hoffman gave Carlson a second financial statement which listed the bakery building as worth $12,000 and clear of liens together with cash in hand of $2,500.[35] Based on that statement, the parties prepared the first "proposed financing plan."[36] It showed Hoffman making an $18,600 equity contribution, consisting of $3,600 cash, $12,000 from the sale of the bakery building and $3,000 from the resale of the lot to the builder.[37] Also listed under "Other trade payables" was a loan from Hoffman's father-in-law of $7,500, designated as "pay interest only at 5%." Hoffman's equity interest in the bakery equipment and the bakery merchandise was indicated in a note on the proposal under "Bakery," but these assets were not part of Hoffman's proposed equity contribution for the new store. It thus appears from this first proposed plan that Red Owl assumed that the bakery would be a separate operation run by Hoffman out of the franchise store.[38]

At the end of this meeting, someone said: "There seems to be no hitch," and the parties left in an optimistic frame of mind. Several days later, Lukowitz called Hoffman, telling him to "get your money together."[39] During this phone conversation, Lukowitz reiterated that the only remaining issue was the sale of the bakery business and building (presumably to realize the $12,000 in cash as per the September 27 financing plan). While Hoffman had preferred to lease the business minus enough equipment to have a bakery in the new store, he none-

---

[34] One reason to meet at the lot was to examine the map of the site and gauge its relationship to "downtown" Chilton. Exhibit 29.

[35] Exhibit 38.

[36] *See* Exhibit 39; Record at 103–04.

[37] Hoffman's contribution to the business was designated on the statement as "Equity capital: Amount owner has to invest." Exhibit 39. Based on this first financial proposal, it appears that both Red Owl and Hoffman understood that Hoffman would put in $18,600 of his own exclusive of any borrowed funds from his father-in-law.

[38] A key question, of course, was whether Hoffman mentioned during this meeting with Carlson and Hall his understanding that $18,000 was a sufficient contribution to establish a franchise *and* his understanding that he could make this contribution partly with cash and partly with borrowed money from his father-in-law. During cross-examination Hoffman was asked, "Did you mention your $18,000 understanding to Carlson and Hall when filling out your financial statement," and he answered, "I can't recall." Record at 179.

[39] *Id.* at 230.

theless agreed to sell the business if that was a necessary condition to obtaining the franchise.

3. The November 22 proposed financing plan

On October 11, Hoffman returned to the Union State Bank and borrowed $13,500 secured by a further $6,000 chattel mortgage on the bakery equipment and a $7,500 mortgage on the bakery building.[40] Hoffman left the bank with $13,500 in cash.[41] This amount was augmented a month later when Hoffman sold the bakery building for $10,000, using $7,500 of the proceeds to retire the mortgage and retaining $2,500 in cash.[42] Thus, as of November 6, Hoffman had over $18,000 in cash equity although his net worth had declined slightly given the lower than expected sale price for the bakery building. Most of his cash ($13,500) was borrowed against his equity in the bakery equipment. Thereafter, Hoffman took a job working nights at the Elm Tree Bakery.[43]

Just before Thanksgiving, Lukowitz called to invite Hoffman to Minneapolis to iron out final details with the home office financial folks so as to get the store in operation after the first of the year. Hoffman met with Lukowitz, Carlson, Hall, and their boss, Frank Walker, in Minneapolis around November 22. At that meeting, the parties prepared a new financing proposal based on a new financial statement that Hoffman prepared and signed.[44] This new plan provided that Hoffman would contribute $12,500 in cash ($4,500 in savings plus $8,000 from the Chilton Bank secured by the bakery equipment) to-

---

[40] Exhibit 42. (There is no copy of this mortgage in the record.) The previous day, October 10, Red Owl officials had shown Hoffman a floor plan they had prepared of a proposed store in Chilton.

[41] Thus, as of October 11 Hoffman had $16,000 in cash equity. When asked on cross-examination about his timing in paying off the prior mortgage on the bakery building on September 14 and creating a new one less than one month later, Hoffman stated that he got the cash in response to Lukowitz's statement that he should get his money together in anticipation of consummating the deal. *Id.* at 182.

[42] He also guaranteed the lease to his top baker Michael Grimm at $120 per month. *Id.* at 137.

[43] *Id.* at 138. Presumably, Hoffman still had $18,000 in cash on hand at that time.

[44] This new financial statement is not in the record. But based on the financing plan that the parties then concluded it appears that Hoffman had in the interim retired most or all of the $13,500 chattel mortgage on the bakery equipment owed to the Union State Bank, thereby reducing his cash on hand to about $4,500.

gether with the bakery equipment. Because the equipment was worth $18,000 and subject to a loan of $8,000, it represented an in-kind capital contribution to the business of about $10,000.[45] In essence, the deal now proposed that the residual value of the bakery equipment (i.e., its value after the bank loan was paid off) become the major component of his contribution to the franchise. It replaced the previous plan to raise $12,000 in cash from the sale of the bakery building, an asset that Hoffman had previously listed as free from liens.

Shortly after the meeting, Hoffman received a copy of the November financing proposal in a letter from Carlson, the credit manager. In the letter, Carlson explained the changes from the previous plan: "You will find enclosed a report indicating our capital requirements. You will recall that in your visit to the office that our original thinking on this was subsequently revised in order to properly reflect the amount of equity capital that you personally have for investment."[46] The problem, in essence, was that the sale of the bakery building yielded less than was predicted and, moreover, contrary to Hoffman's initial representations, the building had been mortgaged. When it became clear that the building was not unencumbered and thus could not provide a major portion of Hoffman's equity contribution, the financing plan had to be revised. After some reflection, Hoffman agreed to this revised proposal.[47]

Throughout this period, while Red Owl was interesting in tying down Hoffman's equity contribution, Hoffman was concerned about an

---

[45] Exhibit 32. The plan called for Hoffman to contribute "equity capital" of $4,600 in cash and $17,000 in bakery equipment (now clear of liens). The plan again proposed that Hoffman would borrow $7,500 from his father-in-law, still on a "no pay, interest at 5%" basis. In addition, the "profit" on the resale of the lot was increased to $4,000, and Hoffman was to borrow an additional $8,000 from the Union State Bank in Chilton to be secured by the bakery equipment (thereby turning some of his equity in the equipment into cash). The parties must have agreed that Hoffman would use $13,500 of his cash to retire the chattel mortgage on the bakery equipment (that would leave him with about $4,500 in cash as per the proposed financing plan).

[46] Record at 144–45. This statement by Carlson reflects the realization on the part of the Red Owl financial people that Hoffman could raise $18,000 in cash equity only by committing his equipment to the enterprise. They had initially thought, based on the September 11 financial statement, that Hoffman had business equity of $28,000 ($2,500 cash + $12,000 bakery building + $14,500 equity in equipment and inventory). But the November financial statement showed business equity of only $22,100 ($4,600 cash + $17,500 bakery equipment).

[47] Record at 102.

entirely different issue. Rather than focusing on how much equity he was putting into the operation, he was focused on the amount of cash, whether encumbered or unencumbered, that he was required to "contribute." Consequently, he considered this November proposal to require an additional $6,000 in cash beyond his original $18,000 commitment.[48] He reached that conclusion by adding together the $7,500 loan from his father-in-law, plus his cash contribution of $4,600, plus the $8,000 loan from the Chilton bank secured by the bakery equipment, plus the $4,000 profit on the lot. This conclusion reflects Hoffman's basic misunderstanding of the economics of the transaction[49]; a misunderstanding that began with the first proposed financing plan, continued through the November meeting and ultimately was the proximate cause of the deal breaking down the following February.

In retrospect, the source of the misunderstanding following the November meeting seems clear. Hoffman believed he was making an additional $6,000 cash "contribution" while the Red Owl people believed that the equity Hoffman had available to contribute was $6,000 less than he had originally represented. Throughout the negotiations in Minneapolis and thereafter, Red Owl officials expressed concern that, of the $24,000 to $26,000 that Hoffman was planning to contribute, only $13,000 was equity (free cash and amounts borrowed against his equity in the bakery equipment).[50] The balance was to be borrowed unsecured from Hoffman's father-in-law and the building contractor.

4. The December financing proposal

Shortly after the November meeting, Lukowitz called Hoffman and asked to meet him at the Red Owl store in Appleton. Lukowitz had a wire from Carlson stating that they needed to secure an additional

---

[48] *Id.* at 141–44.

[49] Hoffman was making an apples and oranges comparison. The $18,000 was his equity contribution. The amount of cash he might need to successfully start up the franchise was a different issue. Red Owl was eager to have him borrow sufficient cash to avoid a cash-flow crunch in the early months. Their point to him was that he had control over this debt, and if he did not need the additional cash he could retire any or all of it. *See infra* note 80. It wasn't until the very end of the negotiations that Red Owl learned that Hoffman was constrained by his father-in-law from incurring any more debt. *See infra* text accompanying note 59. Nevertheless, Hoffman's calculation was also used by Hoffman's lawyers, accepted implicitly by defendants' counsel and by the trial judge. As a result, the fundamental misunderstanding between Red Owl officials and Hoffman was never made clear to the jury. *See infra* text accompanying note 96.

[50] Record at 223.

$2,000 for marketing and promotion of the new store. Hoffman replied, "I have to find out if I can make $2,000 more available."[51] Several days later, Hoffman talked the situation over with his wife and his father-in-law. They hit upon a solution to Hoffman's evident problems in coming up with the needed financing: Hoffman and Simon Vanden Heuvel would go into the franchise as equal partners. Vanden Heuvel would contribute $13,000 in cash and Hoffman would contribute the balance.[52]

Before this new scheme had been vetted with Lukowitz, the Red Owl home office people sent a third financing proposal in early December. This plan reflected the additional $2,000 needed for promotion. It showed Hoffman's equity contribution unchanged at $22,100 ($4,600 in cash and $17,500 in bakery equipment).[53] In order to raise additional cash to operate the store, the plan proposed an $8,000 loan from the Chilton bank secured by Hoffman's equity in the bakery equipment, a $7,500 no-pay, 5-percent-interest loan from his father-in-law, and a $6,000 cash "profit" from the resale of the Chilton lot to the builder. In short, Hoffman's cash contribution (borrowed funds plus equity) had been increased by $2,000 to $26,100, but the only change from the previous plan was to increase the "profits" from selling the lot from $4,000 to $6,000.

Shortly after receiving this proposal, Hoffman called Lukowitz and told him of the new arrangement he had made with Simon Vanden Heuvel to secure $13,000. Lukowitz replied, "This is good. I'm sure that we can go ahead at this point."[54] He then passed on this latest information to the Red Owl front office in Minneapolis. Two days later, Lukowitz called to arrange a meeting at the end of January with Carlson and Walker at the Red Owl store in Appleton. Prior to that meeting Lukowitz and Hoffman met to discuss the new arrangement in more detail. Upon learning of the terms for Vanden Heuvel's contribution, Lukowitz suggested, "Let's not go into the partnership with the front office. After it is all done, you can take your father-in-law in the way you want."[55]

---

[51] *Id.* at 145–46.

[52] *Id.* at 147.

[53] Exhibit 33.

[54] Record at 149.

[55] Record at 186. Notwithstanding his trial testimony (which we must assume that the jury believed), in deposition Hoffman was asked, "To whom in the Red Owl organization did you tell that your father-in-law had to be a partner?" Answer: "I don't know if I ever told anybody." *Id.*

5. *The January 26 financing proposal*

On January 26, 1962, Hoffman met Carlson, Walker, and Lukowitz at the Appleton store. One of the Red Owl people said, "We are ready to go forward" and showed Hoffman a final financing proposal,[56] one that addressed Red Owl's continuing concerns about approving Hoffman for a franchise: the high debt-to-equity ratio reflected in Hoffman's proposed contribution to the enterprise. The solution was to have the $13,000 loan from Simon Vanden Heuvel subordinated to general creditors.[57] Without a subordination agreement, the $13,000 (whether considered an unsecured debt or a contribution to equity) would have reduced Hoffman's equity contribution to $9,000. But with a subordination agreement in place, Hoffman's equity would remain at $22,500 and his cash position would be significantly enhanced. The additional $6,000 from Simon together with a further proposed bank loan of $2,000 would increase the cash available to fund operations from $62,500 (as reflected in the previous plan) to $70,500. This latest (and last) plan listed Hoffman's equity contribution as essentially unchanged at $22,500, consisting of $5,000 in cash and $17,500 in bakery equipment.[58]

From Hoffman's perspective, however, this latest plan required $8,000 more in borrowed funds, bringing to $34,000 the combined total of debt and equity. He had two objections to the plan. The first revealed clearly the divergence in the parties' understanding of the transaction: Hoffman felt that with the additional cash from his father-in-law and the new bank loan of $2,000 he should not be required to borrow $8,000 from the Chilton bank secured by his equity in the bakery equipment. Frank Walker, the senior Red Owl officer, attempted to reassure him that the additional $8,000 in cash to begin operations was for his benefit and was not an increase in his equity contribution. After all, Hoffman had complete control over those borrowed funds. "It's your money," Walker said, "It isn't ours." He tried again: "Joe, if after a reasonable length of time these funds aren't used, pay them back to the bank."[59] Hoffman was adamant in reply, "My father-in-law won't let me be in debt." That was the end of the meeting.

It seems plain, in retrospect, that Hoffman's real objection had to do with his personal relationship with his father-in-law, who appears to

---

[56] Exhibit 34.

[57] Red Owl had prepared a subordination agreement that was also delivered to Hoffman to be signed by his father-in-law. *See* Exhibit 46.

[58] *Id.*

[59] Record at 333.

have been a prosperous, but stern, Calvinist. Hoffman could not borrow the $8,000 from the Chilton bank because his father-in-law didn't believe in debt. He could not propose to his father-in-law that his $13,000 contribution be subordinated to creditors and treated legally as a gift because his father-in-law was sufficiently skeptical about Joe's business acumen that he wanted to have some control over his money. As a consequence, despite Lukowitz's urging, Hoffman never even asked his father-in-law to sign the proposed subordination agreement. He returned home and called Walter Hall, the development officer, in Minneapolis to complain. Hall admitted "this thing has gotten a little goofed up." But when Hoffman asked "what about a smaller store," Hall replied "It's this store or none and that's it. . . ."[60] Finally, on February 2, 1962, Hoffman wrote to Lukowitz: "After doing my utmost to put this together for 2½ years, it seems to me Red Owls' [sic] demands have gotten beyond my power to fulfill. Therefore, the only thing I can do at this time is drop the entire matter and try to make up the losses I suffered, due to your ill-advice."[61]

The Trial

Joseph Hoffman's plan to "make up" for the losses he had incurred from the failed negotiations with Red Owl officials was to consult legal counsel and ultimately to sue Red Owl and Lukowitz for damages arising out of his reliance on their representations made during the negotiation process. A year and a half later, on October 21, 1963 at 9:30 a.m., trial began in the Circuit Court of Outagamie County in the City of Appleton, Wisconsin. The presiding judge was A. W. Parnell. Representing Joseph and Shirley Hoffman was G. H. Van Hoof and John Wiley of the firm of Van Hoof & Van Hoof of Little Chute, Wisconsin. Representing the defendants, Red Owl Stores, Inc., and Edward Lukowitz, was David Fulton of the firm of Benton, Bosser, Fulton, Menn and Nehs of Appleton.[62]

The word "promise" was not uttered during the trial. The plaintiffs' theory of the case was that a representation made by the defendants on which Hoffman reasonably relied to his detriment was actionable without more. As Hoffman's attorney argued to the court following the conclusion of the trial: "It is our position that if Mr. Hoffmann acts in reliance on any representations, statements or misconduct, we don't care if it ever results in a final contract. Our position is that they are

---

[60] Record at 156.

[61] Exhibit 35.

[62] Record at 77.

then liable for damages, regardless, because they have jockeyed him out of position." In response, the court replied: "I don't think what you are saying makes legal sense—if you will pardon me. In other words, they had to make a material representation that if he would do certain things the end result would be they would give him a store in Chilton. Unless there is a *promise* all the representations in the world wouldn't make any difference. If they are dealing at arm's length, without any eventual *promise* to do anything on the part of Red Owl, it doesn't make any difference what they represented to him."[63]

Here was the big opening for Fulton, the defendants' lawyer, to press the point that there were no grounds for misrepresentation liability whether in tort or contract in the absence of a legal duty owed to the plaintiffs. In the absence of a promise conditioned on such a misrepresentation there was no duty in contract. Moreover, courts generally hold that there is no tort duty of care owed to a commercial party engaged in arm's-length negotiations.[64] Nor have courts in the United States recognized a duty to bargain in good faith, much less a duty to bargain carefully to avoid careless but nonwillful misrepresentations. Mistake, in other words, is relevant generally only if the parties have already formed a contractual relationship.[65]

But Fulton, as he had throughout the trial, chose to rest on a single argument: The negotiations were too indefinite to form a contract, and absent a contract there was no basis for liability. This might well have been true, but Fulton did not educate the court as to why it was so. Nor did he try to narrow the scope of the special verdict that permitted the jury to find liability based on innocent misrepresentations that were relied upon. Thus the issue of mutual misunderstanding—that neither party knew or had reason to know the meaning attached by the other to the representations about Hoffman's capital contribution—was not put before the jury.

In consequence, the court prepared a special verdict that took the contract question away from the jury but left them with the task of determining the following:

1. Were representations made by Red Owl officials that if Hoffman fulfilled certain conditions a deal for a franchise store would be concluded?

[63] This is the only time in the entire proceedings that the word "promise" was spoken. Record at 439–40 (emphasis added) .

[64] *See* RESTATEMENT (FIRST) OF TORTS §762 (1939).

[65] There are exceptions, most notably the construction bid cases such as Drennan v. Star Paving, 333 P.2d 757 (1958). *See* Gergen, *supra* note 6, at 1–2.

2. Did Hoffman reasonably rely on those representations?
3. Was it reasonable for Hoffman to so rely?
4. Did Hoffman fulfill all the conditions required by the terms of the negotiations?
5. What sum of money would reasonably compensate Hoffman for the sale of the Wautoma store, the bakery building, the option on the lot, moving to Neenah, and the rental of a house in Chilton?[66]

Subsequently, when instructing the jury, the court used the subjective/objective test of reasonable reliance usually reserved for fraudulent misrepresentation. Judge Parnell told the jury to determine the reasonableness of Hoffman's reliance by taking into consideration Hoffman's experience, his education, and all other circumstances. Thus the question was not whether a reasonable person would have so relied, but whether a person of like business experience, knowledge, and background acting under the same circumstances would have relied.[67]

Following the court's instructions, the jury retired at 12:06 p.m. to elect a foreman and have lunch. They returned with their verdict at 4:27 p.m., having eaten lunch and elected Abe Golden as foreman. The jury found for Hoffman on all the specific questions and fixed damages at $140 for the moving expenses, $125 for the house rental, $1,000 for the option on the lot, $2,000 for the sale of the bakery building and $16,735 for the sale of the Wautoma store. Given that these items sum to $20,000, and given the short time for deliberation, it seems plausible that the jury decided that $20,000 would be the right amount to punish Red Owl for disrespecting one of their fellow citizens and then simply designated the balance of the "damages" to losses arising from the premature sale of the Wautoma store after making specific findings on the other items. In any event, there was no evidence introduced that would have supported the $16,735 figure reached by the jury.

Judge Parnell immediately questioned whether there was any evidentiary basis for that finding and dismissed the jury with his thanks.[68] The defendants filed a motion for judgment notwithstanding the verdict on the ground that the evidence was insufficient as a mat-

---

[66] Record at 26–28.

[67] Record at 448–51.

[68] There seems more than a little irony in his final statement to the jury that "I know that it has been a long and protracted case and called for considerable patience on your part, and sacrifice and considerable effort, as is evidenced by the fact that you have been out all afternoon on the verdict." *Id.* at 457.

ter of law to support Red Owl's liability and, in the alternative, to reduce the awards for losses on the sale of the store and bakery building
to such sums as an unprejudiced jury could have awarded or, in the
alternative, to grant defendants a new trial on the issue of damages.

On March 16, 1964, Judge Parnell entered his order on the motion
for judgment. He affirmed the jury verdict in all respects save damages, in particular the claimed losses in the sale of the Wautoma store.
There he found the award of $16,735 against the weight of the evi-
dence, wholly without foundation or support and contrary to the instructions of the court. Thus he ordered a new trial on the sole issue of
damages for loss, if any, on the sale of the Wautoma inventory and fixtures. Red Owl appealed the court's decision affirming the jury verdict
to the Supreme Court of Wisconsin and Hoffman appealed that portion
of the order that reversed the verdict on damages.[69]

The Appeal

1. The appeal briefs

Red Owl's brief to the Supreme Court of Wisconsin raised three substantive issues. First, Red Owl argued there should be no recovery as a
matter of law in contract because, as found by the trial court, the
statements made by Red Owl representatives were preliminary negotiations, and any statements made during the negotiations were too
uncertain or indefinite to be the basis for finding an enforceable contract claim. Second, recovery could not be had under a theory of estoppel in pais since, under Wisconsin law, equitable estoppel can be used
only as a shield—to prevent the defendant from denying that a particular fact is true—and not as a sword to create a right of recovery that
does not exist in the first instance. Third, the plaintiffs could not recover on the basis of promissory estoppel because there were no representations definite enough to qualify as "promises" within section 90
and, in any event, plaintiffs suffered no injustice since the reason the
deal fell through was Hoffman's refusal to present the subordination
issue to his father-in-law.[70]

---

[69] Red Owl perfected its appeal to the Supreme Court of Wisconsin from the
Order on Motions after Verdict on June 25, 1964.

[70] Appellants' brief at 31–52. With respect to damages, Red Owl claimed
that the award of $16,735 was reached by merely subtracting awards for mov-
ing expenses, rent of a house in Neenah, sale of the bakery building, option on
the lot, from a gross figure of $20,000, demonstrating that the jury pulled the
figure out of the air. There was no evidence of loss of bargain in the June sale
of the grocery business and thus it was error to remand for a new trial.

In response, Hoffman's lawyers primarily rested their case, as they had at trial, on the theory of equitable estoppel. They argued that, in light of the misrepresentations of its agents, Red Owl was estopped from claiming that there was no contract.[71] They also argued for an implied-in-fact contract on the grounds that Hoffman would not have done the things he did had there not been a contract to award him the store.[72] Finally, they claimed a right to damages on the basis of promissory estoppel, simply ignoring the appellants' argument that promissory estoppel is available where there is a promise but no consideration, but is not available when there is no promise in the first place.[73]

2. The decision of the Wisconsin Supreme Court

Writing for a unanimous court, Justice Currie ignored the issue of equitable estoppel and focused exclusively on the promissory estoppel argument. The court asked, Should the doctrine of promissory estoppel as embodied in section 90 of the *Restatement of Contracts* be recognized, and, if so, is it satisfied here? The court held that this issue was squarely presented since "no other possible theory has been presented to or discovered by this court which would permit plaintiffs to recover."[74] Promissory fraud was the only other possible theory the court could imagine might cover this case, but the court held that such action would not lie absent a present intent by Red Owl not to fulfill a promise at the time it was made. The court rejected the possibility that Red Owl had made any of its "promises" in bad faith or with a present intent not to perform.

Turning then to section 90, the court endorsed and adopted the doctrine of promissory estoppel and found ample evidence of all of its elements to support the jury verdict. Indeed, the court identified a number of "promises and assurances" made by Red Owl representatives, the foremost being the promise by Lukowitz "that for the sum of

---

[71] Appellees' brief at 23.

[72] *Id.* at 19–20.

[73] With respect to the promissory estoppel claim, the appellees' brief simply quoted from *Restatement of Contracts* §90, ill. 3, that if "*A* promises *B* that if *B* will go to college and complete his course he will give him $5,000 and *B* does so: Then *A*'s promise is binding." Appellees' brief at 24.

[74] 133 N.W.2d at 273. Given that the plaintiffs' primary theory at trial and on appeal was equitable estoppel, this is a most peculiar statement, only exceeded by the following: "[T]he trial court frame[d] the special verdict on the theory of sec. 90 of the Restatement." *Id.* In fact, the word "promise" was never uttered during the trial testimony or in the court's instructions to the jury, not to mention "section 90" or "promissory estoppel."

$18,000 Red Owl would establish Hoffman in a store."[75] The court adopted Hoffman's claim that, after the store was sold and the lot purchased, the $18,000 figure was changed to $24,100, then increased to $26,100 with the assurance that the deal would go through, then Hoffman was induced to sell his bakery building on the assurance that this was the last necessary step but instead the figure was increased yet again to $34,000. Based on these findings, the court concluded that there was ample evidence to sustain the jury's findings that the promissory representations made by Red Owl were reasonably relied upon by Hoffman to his detriment.

The court then turned to the central question raised by Red Owl on appeal—that the representations made by Lukowitz were simply too uncertain and indefinite to form the basis of contract liability. Under the indefiniteness doctrine, a representation does not qualify as a promise if the undertaking is uncertain or unclear or if key material facts essential to that undertaking have not been specified. The court conceded that many factors were never agreed upon, including the design, layout, and cost of the store, who the builder would be, the price the builder would pay for the land and the resulting rental, the term of the franchise, and the renewal and purchase options. All of these considerations are what led the trial court to conclude as a matter of law that the parties' negotiations were preliminary and could not form the basis for a contract. But, the appellate court held, a promise sufficient to sustain a claim in promissory estoppel need not be the equivalent of an offer that would result in a binding contract if accepted.[76]

---

[75] This statement by the court is not supported by the record, even as it was edited for the appeal. Hoffman testified only that Lukowitz assured him that $18,000 was a sufficient amount to secure a franchise. There was no testimony that Lukowitz ever said that in return for an $18,000 contribution "he would establish Hoffman in a store."

[76] Specifically, the court held the following:

If promissory estoppel were to be limited to only those situations where the promise giving rise to the cause of action must be so definite with respect to all details that a contract would result were the promise supported by consideration, then the defendants' instant promises to Hoffman would not meet this test. However, §90 of the Restatement does not impose the requirement that the promise giving rise to the cause of action must be so comprehensive in scope as to meet the requirements of an offer that would ripen into a contract if accepted by the promisee.

133 N.W.2d at 275.

Finally, the court turned to the issue of damages, and here it affirmed the trial court's order of a new trial on the issue of damages for the premature sale of the Wautoma store. The court held that since recovery was had under section 90, Hoffman's damages should not exceed his actual reliance losses suffered by the sale, and thus the evidence did not sustain the $16,735 jury award.

The Hoffman Saga as a Cautionary Tale

Even with the facts as found by the court, grounding Red Owl's liability on a promissory estoppel theory is simply untenable as a matter of contract doctrine. Nothing in the law of contracts supports the court's legal analysis. To the contrary, the *Restatement of Contracts* has only one definition of a promise, and that definition applies equally to a promise that is the product of a bargained-for exchange and a promise for which enforcement is sought on the grounds of induced reliance.[77] The doctrine of indefiniteness holds that for a representation to qualify as a promise, it must be sufficiently clear and definite that it justifies the promisee in believing that a commitment has been made. If the terms of a manifestation of intent are uncertain or indefinite, then, by definition, it fails to qualify as a promise.[78] If neither party has made a promise, there is no claim under section 90. Rather, the parties' initial communications to each other fall in the category of unenforceable preliminary negotiations. Hoffman thus is wrong as a matter of contract doctrine.

1. Are there any theories on which liability could be based?

Some scholars have suggested that the opinion in *Hoffman* can be grounded on a duty to negotiate in good faith.[79] Putting aside the difficulties inherent in applying such a standard, there is simply no evidence of any bad faith by any of the Red Owl officials. At most Lukowitz was careless in his initial representation because he did not inquire further as to what Hoffman meant by his statement that he had about $18,000 to contribute. But, if anything, Hoffman was much more careless. Certainly, he could see by September 1961, when he was handed a proposed financing plan, that what he was to contribute was

---

[77] *See, e.g.,* RESTATEMENT (SECOND) OF CONTRACTS §§2, 90 (1979) [hereinafter RESTATEMENT] (section 2 defining a *promise* as a manifestation of an intention to be bound so made that it justifies the promisee in believing a commitment has been made, and section 90 beginning, "A *promise* . . .").

[78] RESTATEMENT §33.

[79] *See, e.g.,* Duhl, *supra* note 6, at 315–21; PATRICK ATIYAH, PROMISES, MORALS, AND LAW 80–92 (1981); Knapp, *supra* note 6; Summers, *supra* note 6.

"equity" of at least $18,000. While the proposed cash requirements for the franchise did increase over time, the equity requirements remained largely fixed and the additional proposals for cash were loans that Hoffman was free to repay if he didn't need the cash flow for his grocery business.[80]

Moreover, Red Owl's continued insistence that Hoffman make a substantial equity contribution to the franchise reflects perfectly appropriate business judgment. The risk in any franchise contract is that the interests of the parties will be misaligned and, as a consequence, the franchisee may manage its operation in a manner inconsistent with the interests of the franchisor. A widely recognized conflict that arises with excessive debt financing is that the agent may be motivated to increase the riskiness of his management of the franchise. By "putting all his eggs in one basket," the agent can gamble with the borrowed funds. If the venture is successful, all the returns in excess of the fixed debt accrue to the agent. But if the venture fails, the agent shares the loss with his creditors.[81] Red Owl, therefore, was properly concerned about avoiding this problem by working toward a jointly beneficial financing plan, one that protected their brand name from the possibility that its value would be diluted by Hoffman's risky business decisions.

Mark Gergen and others have suggested that the best theory of liability is negligent misrepresentation.[82] But there are many problems applying this theory to arm's-length bargaining contexts. Many courts don't recognize this tort at all,[83] and the *Restatement* rule requires that the party making the statement owe a duty to the plaintiff to supply correct information to him.[84] Because casual statements and contacts

---

[80] Red Owl was appropriately concerned that Hoffman have sufficient cash on hand to begin operations, since a failure of a new franchise store would adversely affect the Red Owl brand. Lukowitz testified that the proposed increase in cash reflected in the January financing plan was prompted by Red Owl's experience in opening new franchises and finding that additional cash was often needed to "get them off the ground, especially if you are new in a location." This additional cash was intended "for the protection of the operator." Record at 307.

[81] For discussion, see Robert E. Scott, *A Relational Theory of Secured Financing,* 86 Colum. L. Rev. 901, 919–22 (1986).

[82] *See, e.g.,* Gergen, *supra* note 6, at 34–36; CHARLES FRIED, CONTRACT AS PROMISE 24 (1981).

[83] *See, e.g.,* Haigh v. Matsushita Elec. Corp., 676 F. Supp. 1332 (E.D. Va. 1987) (applying Virginia law).

[84] Under *Restatement (Second) of Torts* §552, an action for negligent misrepresentation lies only against one "who in the course of his business or profes-

are prevalent in business, under the majority rule in commercial contexts, liability for negligent misrepresentation is imposed only where
the party making the statement possess unique or specialized expertise
or is in a special position of trust and confidence with the injured party
such that reliance on the negligent misrepresentation is justified.[85] It
has been specifically held, for example, that a franchisee could not
maintain an action for negligent misrepresentation where the franchisor was not in a business of supplying information.[86] Moreover, a claim
for negligent misrepresentation ordinarily cannot be based on unful-
filled promises or statements as to future events. Finally, recovery of
purely economic loss for negligent misrepresentation is available only
when there is a special relationship between the parties or when the
representation is made by one in the business of supplying information
for the guidance of others.[87]

A final theory of liability is recovery in quasi-contract for unjust enrichment. Here the argument would be that Hoffman conferred a benefit on Red Owl during the period from May through November when he
purchased and then sold his grocery store, sold the bakery building and
purchased an option on the lot in Chilton. All these actions gave Red
Owl some further indication of the kind of franchisee that Hoffman
was likely to be—was he enterprising and resourceful or was he a bit of
a doofus? Quasi-contract claims based on unjust enrichment rarely succeed, however, unless the defendant specifically and wrongfully induced the benefit. A quasi-contract claim does not lie simply because
one party benefits from the efforts or obligations of others, but instead
"it must be shown that a party was unjustly enriched in the sense that

---

sion, or in any other transaction in which he has a pecuniary interest supplies
false information for the guidance of others in their business transactions. . . ."

[85] *See, e.g.*, Eternity Global Master Fund, Ltd. v. Morgan Guar. Trust Co.,
375 F.3d 168 (2d Cir. 2004). Thus, many courts hold there is no tort of negligent misrepresentation in the vendor/purchaser context. The key to the tort is
that plaintiff must allege and prove that the defendant owes a duty to plaintiff
to communicate accurate information. Thus, plaintiff must show that defendant either was in the business of supplying information or that defendant had
a pecuniary interest in plaintiff's transaction with a third party. Continental
Leavitt Communications, Ltd. v. PaineWebber, Inc., 857 F. Supp. 1266 (N.D. Ill
1994); American Protein Corp. v. AB Volvo, 844 F.2d 56 (2d Cir. 1988).

[86] Bonfield. v. AAMCO Transmissions, Inc., 708 F. Supp. 867 (N.D. Ill.
1989).

[87] Gebrayel v. Transamerica Title Ins. Co., 888 P.2d 83 (Or. 1995); Continental Leavitt Communications, Ltd. v. PaineWebber, Inc., *supra* note 78.

the term 'unjustly' could mean illegally or unlawfully."[88] This at least puts the key question to a court: Was Hoffman induced to provide information to Red Owl by trick or was he a "mere volunteer"?

The trial transcript strongly suggests that Lukowitz was trying to mediate between Hoffman's meager capital assets and the home office's capital requirements. The facts as found by the court show only that Lukowitz was eager to secure a franchise for Hoffman, no doubt because he would earn a commission if the deal went through. The steps that he urged Hoffman to take—selling the store, buying the lot, and moving to Neenah—all seem designed to accelerate the approval process, not to induce an unbargained-for benefit for Red Owl. Under the circumstances, then, shouldn't Hoffman have been more cautious in nailing down exactly how much capital he would have to provide prior to buying the grocery store, selling the store, selling his bakery, and buying an option on a lot?

Jason Johnston has argued that Red Owl might properly be held liable if the facts showed that Red Owl had a low opinion of Hoffman's prospects as a franchisee but hid that fact from Hoffman and instead encouraged his subsequent actions to see whether—against the odds—he turned out to have better talents than they initially believed.[89] The problem with this argument is that the facts simply belie that story. The evidence shows that Red Owl officials worked hard to find a way to stretch what they discovered to be Hoffman's meager capital so as to make the franchise deal work. The series of financial proposals from September 1961 to January 1962 were motivated less by Red Owl's escalating financial requirements than by Hoffman's frequent shifting

---

[88] *See, e.g.*, First National Bank of St. Paul v. Ramier, 311 N.W.2d 502, 504 (Minn. 1981); Greg Fimon v. Kenroc Drywall Supplies, Inc., 2003 Minn. App. Lexis 311 (Minn. 2003).

[89] Johnston, *supra* note 6, 496–99 (suggesting that Red Owl should be found liable if it misrepresented its relative optimism about the deal in order to learn more about Hoffman as a potential manager). A variant of this argument is offered by Ofer Grosskopf and Barak Medina in their interesting paper, *Regulating Contract Formation: Precontractual Reliance, Sunk Costs, and Market Structure,* 39 Conn. L. Rev — (2007). They argue that the Hoffmans, being inexperienced and naïve, underappreciated the risk of failed negotiations and thus over-invested in precontractual reliance. Red Owl, as an experienced repeat player, should have been conscious of this risk and taken steps to prevent it. Holding Red Owl liable for Hoffman's reliance costs motivates it to prevent such unwarranted investment. Apart from the fact that this solution would seem to have negative activity level effects (such as chilling negotiations with prospective franchisees who are behaviorally impaired), as with Johnston's argument, the theory simply doesn't fit the facts.

of his capital. That the deal broke down is more a function of the thin margin on which Hoffman was operating than any attempt by Red Owl to disguise their pessimism about the proposed transaction.

2. What about "fundamental fairness"?

But, as others have noted, there is a highly salient aspect to the Hoffman story—the evident disparity in income, education, and business acumen between Joe Hoffman and the Red Owl corporate officers. Is *Hoffman v. Red Owl* simply a case about fundamental fairness—one where the search for a strong doctrinal justification for liability is beside the point? In Peter Linzer's words, this may be a case for "rough justice" and not for doctrinal niceties.[90] The story of the hometown "little guy" pitted against a large, impersonal, and out-of-state corporation certainly seems the best explanation for the jury verdict, but more, surely, is required from the Wisconsin Supreme Court. And, the truth is that the facts as revealed at trial simply do not support the fairness claim. Nowhere in the record, for example, is there any testimony that Lukowitz said what was attributed to him by the Wisconsin court nor were Hoffman's proposed equity contributions ever substantially increased as the court implied.

The testimony is that Hoffman said to Lukowitz and his associate at the May 1961 meeting, "Fellows, you know how much money I got— approximately $18,000. Will this put me in a bigger operation or won't it?" And Lukowitz then responded that an investment at that level "would not be a problem."[91] At most this is a representation that $18,000 of capital is enough for one to be established in a store assuming all other details are ironed out. In addition, the capital requirements for Hoffman were not increased in the manner the court suggests. As indicated earlier, Hoffman's proposed equity contribution changed from $18,600 in the first financial proposal in September to $22,100 in the second proposal in November. This change was apparently motivated by the fact that the bakery building was encumbered (contrary to Hoffman's earlier representation) and the resulting need to shift the focus of Hoffman's proposed equity contribution to the bakery equipment. Thereafter, Hoffman's equity contribution remained essentially unchanged through the third and fourth financing proposals in December and January.

To be sure, Lukowitz did make two subsequent assurances—that with the additional $2,000 in promotion "the deal would go through," and that the sale of the bakery building in November "was the last

---

[90] Linzer, *supra* note 6, at 719–20.

[91] Record at 86.

step." But these statements were all made after the September meeting between Hoffman and Carlson and Hall from the home office. By that time, Hoffman knew well that their approval and not Lukowitz's was the key to securing the franchise. Given these facts, the question is not whether Hoffman was exploited by corporate barons (Lukowitz, after all, had less education than he did).[92] The real issue was whether Hoffman's understanding of the transaction was a reasonable one and, more important, was it the only reasonable one.

At the end of the day, imposing liability for precontractual reliance because one party failed to correct the other's misunderstanding has significant costs, especially if one believes that, ordinarily, precontractual negotiations are essentially truthful. Jason Johnston has argued persuasively that such "cheap talk" should not be subject to liability in the ordinary case because delay in reaching a deal is costly to the parties and thus negotiators already have incentives to communicate useful information.[93] There may be sound reasons to accept the costs of chilling future negotiations in order to prevent exploitation of the weak by the strong, but there is scant evidence of any exploitation in the negotiations between Joseph Hoffman and the representatives of Red Owl Stores.

3. Lawyering matters: Arguments that Red Owl failed to pursue

One lesson from a close review of the *Hoffman* case is that the quality of legal argument matters. The record of the case reveals much to criticize about the way Red Owl's attorneys defended their clients.[94] In

---

[92] Lukowitz had a high school degree; Hoffman had a year of business and management courses at a local business college. Record at 78.

[93] Johnston, *supra* note 6, at 418–39.

[94] Among other dubious trial tactics, Red Owl's attorneys responded to the plaintiffs' request to call Carlson, Hall, and Walker as adverse witnesses by instructing the Red Owl home office personnel not to be present in court during the plaintiffs' case in chief. Thus, the following colloquy occurred in the presence of the jury with Van Hoof (Hoffman's attorney) and Fulton (Red Owl's attorney:

> Mr. Van Hoof: I would like to call Mr. Carlson adversely.
> Mr. Fulton: Carlson is not present.
> Mr. Van Hoof: I would like to call Mr. Hall adversely.
> Mr. Fulton: He is not present.
> Mr. Van Hoof: I would like to call Mr. Walker adversely.
> Mr. Fulton: He is not present.
> The Court: Did you make a request to have them present?
> Mr. Van Hoof: They are out of state, and I couldn't subpoena them.

Record at 344–45.

particular, they failed to raise three issues, either at trial or on appeal, that seem quite cogent given the trial testimony. First, did Lukowitz have apparent authority to make financial representations? This question is particularly important once the chronology is clear. According to Hoffman, Lukowitz made his first representation in May when he assured Hoffman that $18,000 would be a sufficient capital investment. In September, Hoffman met with Carlson and Hall, and by then he was aware that they were the parties who would negotiate the financial terms of the transaction.[95] In the interim, the only actions Hoffman plausibly took in reliance on the Lukowitz assurance were the sale of the grocery business in June and the purchase of the option on the lot in Chilton in September. But the moving expenses, the house rental in Neenah, and the sale of the bakery building all occurred subsequently. There is no testimony that either Hall or Carlson made any similar representations to Hoffman. Thus the one representation that Hoffman might reasonably assume Lukowitz was authorized to make was the initial assurance in May regarding the minimum capital requirements for a franchise, and, as suggested earlier, the parties attached different meanings to this assurance.

Second, was Hoffman's reliance reasonable? At the September meeting with Hall and Carlson, and thereafter until he broke off negotiations, Hoffman never asked the Red Owl home office people to confirm his understanding about the source of funds for his contribution or to explain what Red Owl meant by its assurance that $18,000 would be a sufficient capital investment. This silence is all the more puzzling since Hoffman saw four different financing proposals, each of which specifically listed "Equity Capital (Amount owner has to invest)" as a separate line item apart from "Loans."[96] To be sure, the reasonableness of Hoffman's reliance was a question of fact for the jury. But recall that the trial court instructed the jury on the subjective/objective test of reasonable reliance, one that required the jury to assess Hoffman's be-

---

It is hard to imagine any more powerful way in which Hoffman's attorney could have emphasized to the jury that this was a case of a native son of Wisconsin who was in a dispute with out-of-state corporate big-wigs who were too busy to even show up to hear what Hoffman had to say.

[95] RESTATEMENT (SECOND) OF AGENCY §136(1) provides that "an agent's apparent authority is terminated . . . when the principal states such a fact to the third person." Thus, the key question was whether Hall and Carlson indicated directly or indirectly to Hoffman that Lukowitz had no authority to make financial representations on behalf of Red Owl. Clearly, Hoffman had reason to know that this was so.

[96] *See* Exhibits 32, 33, 34, and 39.

havior against the standard of a person with similar education, business experience, and acumen rather than the purely objective standard of the reasonable person. This more forgiving test of reasonable behavior is properly applied to fraud, duress, and other intentional acts but not to a promissory estoppel or a negligent tort theory of the case. Thus Red Owl's attorneys had an opportunity to object to that instruction and thereby challenge the reasonableness of Hoffman's behavior on appeal.

Third, and most important, the transcript makes clear that the parties never had a mutual understanding about the meaning of the statement, "I have approximately $18,000—will this put me in a bigger operation or won't it?" The Red Owl representatives clearly meant that Hoffman would have to contribute equity of at least that amount, and Hoffman clearly was focusing on how much cash he would put into the transaction, whether borrowed or not. Who is responsible for Hoffman's misunderstanding about the assurance that $18,000 of capital would be sufficient? The rule in contract negotiations is that each party is responsible for clarifying his understanding of the meaning the other attaches to ambiguous words and phrases, and this rule would strongly argue against liability in this case.[97] While the appellants' brief does point out that this ambiguity was unresolved, Red Owl's attorneys failed to tie this apparent misunderstanding to any legal conclusion, and they raised the point only to show that the negotiations were ongoing and indefinite.

One shouldn't be too hard on the attorneys for Red Owl, however. From their perspective there was no theory on which liability could properly be based as the law existed at the time. There was no justifiable claim for breach of a bargain contract because the representations were too indefinite to be a promissory commitment. For the same reason, liability could not properly be based on promissory estoppel. Equitable estoppel was inappropriate under Wisconsin law as it could not be used to create a right where none previously existed. And there was then no cause of action in Wisconsin for negligent misrepresentation. Where Red Owl's lawyers failed, from the outset, was to present their clients' behavior and actions in a reasonable and defensible light. They could and should have elicited testimony about how hard everyone worked to make the negotiations succeed, and how it came to naught

---

[97] RESTATEMENT (SECOND) OF CONTRACTS §20(2) provides, "There is no manifestation of mutual assent to an exchange if the parties attach materially different meanings to their manifestations and (a) neither party knows or has reason to know the meaning attached by the other; or each party knows or has reason to know the meaning attached by the other."

ultimately because of Hoffman's personal constraints: He needed Simon Vanden Heuvel's money to make the deal work and yet those funds came with strings attached that ultimately undermined the deal.

4. *Epilogue*

How was this dispute resolved and what happened to Joseph Hoffman? Professor Stewart Macaulay and his colleagues report that the parties settled the case for $10,600. Of that sum, $4,000 went for attorney's fees, and the Hoffmans retained the balance. Joseph Hoffman, meanwhile, became a very successful insurance salesman, wining several awards for sales volume. He and his family moved to Milwaukee, where he rose through the ranks of the Metropolitan Life Insurance Company to become district manager. Thereafter, he was transferred to Indiana and remained with the company in a managerial capacity.[98] Finally, why was Hoffman so restless and eager to escape the bakery business in the first place? Grant Gilmore reported some years ago that Hoffman's motivations may have been largely independent of Red Owl's representations: The poor fellow, he told me, was allergic to bread!

Whither the Law of Preliminary Negotiations and Preliminary Agreements?

How do contemporary American courts actually treat reliance investments made before the parties have written a complete contract? Alan Schwartz and I report the results of a study of recent litigation in a forthcoming article.[99] We began with a sample of 108 cases litigated between 1999 and 2003.[100] Thirty of the cases raised the issue of reliance in the context of ongoing negotiations. The underlying question in each case was whether the plaintiff could recover reliance costs if the parties had not yet reached agreement. The courts denied liability, whether premised on promissory estoppel, quantum meruit, or negligent misrepresentation, in 87 percent of these preliminary negotiation cases. The case data show that, absent intentional misrepresentation

---

[98] I MACAULAY, KIDWELL & WHITFORD, *supra* note 5, at 403–04.

[99] Alan Schwartz & Robert E. Scott, *Precontractual Liability,* 120 Harv. L. Rev. — (2007).

[100] We examined all public databases for preliminary negotiation and preliminary agreement cases proceeding under the following theories of liability: promissory estoppel, quantum meruit, implied contract, definiteness, and intent to be bound. The final sample of 108 relevant cases represented twenty-nine state jurisdictions, nineteen federal district courts, and seven federal courts of appeal.

or deceit, there is generally no liability for reliance investments made during the negotiation process.[101]

In sum, courts will not grant recovery for "early reliance" unless the parties, by agreeing on something significant, have indicated their intention to be bound. Put more directly, the cases do not revolve around preliminary negotiations but rather around preliminary agreements. Thus, for example, in the remaining 78 cases in our sample, the parties had agreed on at least some material terms. In 29 cases, the court denied recovery, even though the parties had reached agreement on some (or even most) terms, because the parties had indicated, either expressly or by implication, that they did not yet intend to be legally bound. In 37 cases, the court held that the parties had made a complete contract, even though they contemplated a further memorialization of terms, because the evidence showed that the formal writing was not essential. Finally, and most interesting, in 12 cases involving "agreements to agree," the court found a binding preliminary agreement to negotiate further in good faith. These latter cases are interesting because they are the forefront of an emerging rule governing preliminary agreements.

The common law has historically had great difficulty with preliminary agreements that expressed a mutual commitment on agreed terms but where significant additional terms remained to be negotiated. Typically, parties have agreed to negotiate further over the remaining terms. These agreements to agree confront the indefiniteness doctrine head-on. Until recently, courts have held consistently that such agreements to agree were unenforceable under the common law of contracts so long as any essential term was open to negotiation.[102] The cases in our sample thus reflect a major shift in doctrine involving agreements to agree where key terms remain unresolved. The modern framework for determining intent in agreements to agree (as well as cases dealing with the timing of enforcement) was first proposed by Judge Pierre Leval in *Teachers Insurance and Annuity Association of*

---

[101] "It is fundamental to contract law that mere participation in negotiations and discussions does not create a binding obligation, even if agreement is reached on all disputed terms. More is needed than agreement on each detail, which is over all agreement to enter into the binding contract." Teachers Insurance & Annuity Association v. Tribune, 670 F. Supp. 491, 497 (S.D.N.Y. 1987). *See also* Reprosystem, BV v. SCM Corp., 727 F.2d 257 (2d Cir. 1984).

[102] SCOTT & KRAUS, *supra* note 5, at 34–44, 322–25. Agreements to agree on price in sales contracts are enforceable under the Uniform Commercial Code if the parties evidence an intention to be bound. *See* UCC §2-305(1)(b).

America v. Tribune.[103] The Leval framework has subsequently been adopted by the Second Circuit[104] and is now followed in at least thirteen states, sixteen federal district courts, and seven federal circuits.[105] The framework sets out a new default rule for cases where the parties contemplate further negotiations. This rule relaxes the knife-edge character of the common law under which agreements are either fully enforceable or not enforceable at all.[106]

Leval's framework relies on two distinct categories of preliminary agreements that will have binding force. The first (Type I) is a fully binding preliminary agreement. Here the parties agree on all the terms that require negotiation (including whether to be bound) but agree to memorialize their agreement in a more formal document. A Type I agreement binds both sides to their ultimate contractual objective just as if it were a formalized agreement, since the signing of a more elaborate contract is seen as only a formality. Thus either party may demand performance of the transaction even though the parties fail to produce the more elaborate documentation of their agreement.[107]

The second and more interesting type of preliminary agreement (Type II) is a binding preliminary commitment that is created when the parties have reached agreement on certain major terms of the deal but leave other terms open for further negotiation. The parties to such an understanding "accept a mutual commitment to negotiate together in good faith in an effort to reach final agreement."[108] Neither party, however, has a right to demand performance of the transaction. Rather they have a legal obligation to attempt to negotiate the open issues in good faith within the agreed framework. If a final contract is not agreed upon, the parties may abandon the transaction. Our sample shows that the enforcement of these binding preliminary agreements is now well accepted. Indeed, a federal court recently declared the enforcement of such agreements as "the modern trend in contract law."[109]

---

[103] 670 F. Supp. 491 (1987).

[104] Adjustrite Systems, Inc. v. GASB Business Services, Inc., 145 F.3d 543, 547–48 (2d Cir. 1998).

[105] Schwartz & Scott, *supra* note 99, at ——.

[106] 145 F.3d. at 548.

[107] *Id.*; Gorodensky v. Mitsubishi Pulp Sales (MC), Inc., 92 F. Supp. 2d 249, 254–55 (S.D.N.Y. 2000).

[108] 670 F. Supp. at 498.

[109] Beazer Homes Corp. v. VMIF/Anden Southbridge Venture, 235 F. Supp. 2d 485, 498 (E.D. Va. 2002).

The preceding discussion demonstrates that scholars interested in commercial contracting should shift their focus from the largely irrelevant issue of precontractual reliance to the fundamental questions raised by the enforcement of these preliminary agreements. The emerging rule requires courts to resolve two key questions: When have the parties reached "an agreement" sufficient to impose a duty to negotiate in good faith? And what behavior constitutes a breach of that duty? The current framework fails to provide much guidance in answering these questions.[110]

Indeed, we can't answer the legal questions until we first understand better the commercial behavior that has generated this litigation. The sheer volume of litigation over these preliminary agreements exposes a deep puzzle. Parties often write fully binding contracts before they invest in reliance. And when they need to invest early prior to final contract, they can (and do) contract directly on reliance. Yet these parties invest prior to final contract and they fail to contract specifically on reliance. Why do parties put themselves in this situation? And, finally, when negotiations break down and one party exits, when would the other party have a reasonable expectation of compensation absent an explicit promise to reimburse reliance expenditures? Schwartz and Scott provide one answer to this question,[111] but the academic debate over the law of preliminary agreements is only just beginning. The delay in understanding this important and heretofore largely ignored area of commercial law is attributable, at least in part, to the myth of precontractual reliance and the unfortunate case of *Hoffman v. Red Owl Stores, Inc.*

---

[110] The multi-factored character of the Leval test confines the court's discretion more than a broad standard based on intent. But so long as the courts do not attach weights to the factors or otherwise specify the relationship between them, the factors may point in different directions and thus the test will lack transparency.

[111] Schwartz and Scott argue that the duty to bargain in good faith arises where one party promises to make a simultaneous investment prior to negotiating the remaining terms and thereafter delays its investment strategically. Under those circumstances, they argue that the party who invested first should be entitled to recover its reliance costs and that a failure by the delaying party to bargain over the amount of those costs would qualify as a breach of the duty. Schwartz & Scott, *supra* note 99, at —.

4

Richard A. Epstein[*]

ProCD v. Zeidenberg:
Do Doctrine and Function Mix?

Background of the Case

The purpose of this essay is to recount with some particularity the philosophical, economic, and legal issues raised in one of the most important contract cases of the past generation. *ProCD v. Zeidenberg* explores in a new technological context two critical and recurrent issues of contract law: how the formal rules of offer and acceptance apply to shrinkwrap and clickwrap transactions, and whether an otherwise valid contractual provision is preempted by federal law.[1] The first issue

[*] James Parker Hall Distinguished Service Professor of Law, The University of Chicago; Peter and Kirsten Bedford Senior Fellow, The Hoover Institution. In the interests of full disclosure, I should mention that I had written, as a consultant for the Digital Commerce Coalition, a letter dated September 11, 2000, responding to the Federal Trade Commission's request for public comment regarding its High-Tech Warranty Project, extensive portions of which have been incorporated into an article on the UCITA, Richard A. Epstein, *Contract, Not Regulation: UCITA and High-Tech Consumers Meet Their Consumer Protection Critics, in* CONSUMER PROTECTION IN THE AGE OF THE "INFORMATION ECONOMY" 205 (Jane K. Winn ed., forthcoming 2006). I also wrote two letters in defense of the UCITA approach to the American Bar Association in January 2003. The views in this paper are my own. My thanks to David Strandness, Stanford Law School, Class of 2007, for his outstanding research assistance.

[1] ProCD, Inc. v. Zeidenberg, 908 F. Supp. 640 (W.D. Wis. 1996), rev'd and remanded, 86 F.3d 1447 (7th Cir. 1996). Since the two cases have the same name I shall reference them as *Crabb* and *Easterbrook*, after the judges who wrote the trial court and appellate decisions.

concerns the application of the perennial rules of offer and acceptance to the brave new world of computer software. It conveniently breaks into two parts. The initial inquiry is whether two parties have entered into any agreement at all. Then if it is established that the parties made some agreement, which terms proposed by either side are included or excluded? The particular contracts involved in *ProCD* were formed between the "seller" of computer software and the ultimate "buyer," who purchased the software package through a retailer who was conveniently allowed to drop out of the picture.[2] At issue in this case was how the rules of offer and acceptance, as captured in the Uniform Commercial Code, apply to shrinkwrap contracts where the seller seeks to impose restrictions on how particular products may be used.

The second question in *ProCD* arises only if the plaintiff overcomes the initial hurdle and persuades a court that the parties have indeed entered into an agreement that contains the seller's desired provisions. Phase two asks what types of substantive limitations the vendor may place on its product use that are consistent with public policy. More concretely, does the copyright law of the United States place any federal limits on the use restrictions that the software seller may impose on its buyer with respect to the data that has been transferred (or licensed) to the buyer? The issue is technically described as one of federal preemption: Does the command of a valid federal statute block, expressly or by implication, the use of certain contractual terms otherwise allowable under state law?

ProCD raises both issues in vivid fashion because it is twice blessed by two strong opinions that point in opposite directions. Judge Barbara B. Crabb of the Western District of Wisconsin held that Zeidenberg had purchased the software free of ProCD's effort to restrict his use of the transmitted data. Judge Frank H. Easterbrook, writing for himself and Judges John L. Coffey and Joel M. Flaum, ruled four-square for the plaintiff on both the contract interpretation and the copyright preemption issues. The two contrasting opinions reflect a profound difference in the role economic analysis plays in influencing the legal analysis. That difference is encapsulated in the distinction between doctrine versus function: Judge Crabb is the faithful doctrinalist and Judge Easterbrook the ardent functionalist.

---

[2] For how the retailer might be brought back in, see *infra* text accompanying notes 46–48.

Before getting too far ahead of the story, however, it is important to recall the undisputed facts of the case.[3] That innocent-sounding task is fraught with hidden obstacles because Judges Crabb and Easterbrook had profound differences as to which facts really mattered and why. Both judges noted that ProCD, the plaintiff, was a software vendor who had compiled on its Select Phone™ CD-ROM software program a single database containing comprehensive information about some 95 million phone numbers drawn from 3,000 separate telephone directories. The data collected contained more information than is normally found in phone books. In addition to the usual names and addresses, it offered nine-digit zip codes and various industrial codes. The purchasers of Select Phone™ could sort the information by category for use in organizing mailings, research, and other applications. This extensive compilation of data was treated throughout the case as falling outside the scope of copyright protection because it did not have what the Supreme Court termed in *Feist Publications, Inc. v. Rural Telephone Service Co.*[4] the minimum level of "originality" to receive copyright protection.[5] In its view, the compilation of names, addresses, and places was just raw information that others could copy at will on the ground that "sweat of the brow" information did not receive copyright protection.[6] That information, however, did not come cheap, but cost ProCD over $10 million to compile, and more for regular updates needed to reflect the constant shifts in population and phone usage. This data package was accompanied by a copyrighted program that allowed the buyer to download this data onto his or her computer.

The defendants in this case were Matthew Zeidenberg, then a graduate student in computer sciences at the University of Wisconsin, Madison, after studying undergraduate physics at Harvard, and his solely owned corporation, Silken Mountain Web Services. (The differences between Zeidenberg and his corporation don't matter, and so will not be mentioned further.) Zeidenberg did not come to this litigation by

---

[3] For these facts, see *Crabb*, 908 F. Supp. at 644–46, and *Easterbrook*, 86 F.3d at 1449–50.

[4] 499 U.S. 340 (1991).

[5] In fact, Judge Easterbrook subsequently opted for a narrow reading of *Feist* in *American Dental Association v. Delta Dental Plans Association*, 126 F.3d 977 (7th Cir. 1997) (holding copyrightable the ADA's taxonomy of dental procedures, by number, long and short description).

[6] 499 U.S. at 359–60.

mere happenstance.[7] Rather, he originally purchased the Select Pho-
ne™ program from a local retailer to do work in a voter registration
program, because it allowed him to download the names, phone numbers, and addresses of everyone within a particular zip code. He later
observed that he had been drawn to the program because ProCD had
advertised "that there are no limits on how many records you could
download from the CD."[8] Once his voting drive was over, he hatched a
scheme (which never proved profitable) to place the ProCD listings on
the Internet from which he hoped to make money by selling banner
advertising.[9] In a subsequent interview, he made it clear that he came
up with the idea of posting the phone numbers online after he had read
Feist, a case that had been discussed in Select Phone's™ user man-
ual.[10] Not content with his own reading of the case law, he consulted
with John Kidwell, a professor of law at the University of Wisconsin, to
learn about the legality of his proposed Internet posting in light of the
opening in the copyright law that *Feist* created—a vivid reminder of
how individual actors respond to the incentives created by legal rules
on property rights. Kidwell told him, with partial omniscience, "Yeah,
you're probably legally in the clear, but you'll definitely be sued."[11] Zeidenberg used ProCD's copyrighted program to download the data onto
his personal computer, and then made the data available to the world
by placing it on an Internet host computer. The lawsuit was commenced when ProCD got wind of his venture after it had been made
public.

The Select Phone™ boxes did not set out all the terms on which the
package was sold. But it did point in small print (a phrase that Judge
Crabb pointedly used,[12] but that Judge Easterbrook omitted) that the
transaction was made conditional on terms that were contained in the
user guide inside the box. The user guide included a "Single User License Agreement," which told the user that he did not have outright
ownership of the listings supplied to him, but was authorized only as a

---

[7] Zeidenberg offered his thoughts about the case in an interview with William Whitford, Emeritus Professor of Law at the University of Wisconsin.
Freedom from Contract Symposium: Appendix, ProCD v. Zeidenberg *in Context,* 2004 Wis. L. Rev. 821.

[8] *Id.* at 822.

[9] *Id.* at 823–24.

[10] *Id.* at 823.

[11] *Id.* at 824.

[12] *See Crabb,* 908 F. Supp. at 645.

licensee to use that information in ways consistent with his license.[13] Software vendors call these "end-user licenses," but the common term for them is shrinkwrap licenses, which refers to the fact that they can be accessed only after the shrinkwrap, which protects the package before use, is removed. (The equivalent for downloaded programs is a "clickwrap" license.) Once installed, the computer program spreads across the opening screen a notice that hammers home the point that the licensed program could be used only in accordance with the limitations found in the Single User Agreement. In some instances (much less common today), the licenses state that they take effect the instant the shrinkwrap is removed, but ProCD took a more cautious provision that left the user an escape hatch after booting up the program:

> Please read this license carefully before using the software or accessing the listings contained on the discs. By using the discs and the listings licensed to you, you agree to be bound by the terms of this License. If you do not agree to the terms of this License, promptly return all copies of the software, listings that may have been exported, the discs and the User Guide to the place where you obtained it.[14]

The key provision of the license at issue here reads as follows:

> [Y]ou will not make the Software or the Listings in whole or in part available to any other user in any networked or time-shared environment, or transfer the Listings in whole or in part to any computer other than the computer used to access the Listings.[15]

Both parties agreed that Zeidenberg did not know of this particular restriction when he made his initial box purchase in late 1994. Nonetheless, it was agreed that he was "aware" of the restriction before he used the program to download the listings onto the Internet. Zeidenberg also purchased two upgraded versions of ProCD in March and April 1995, both of which contained the same constellation of notifica-

---

[13] *Id.* at 644.

[14] *Id.*

[15] *Id.* at 645. This provision is perfectly standard in most software contracts. See, for a similar provision, Vault Corp. v. Quaid Software Ltd., 847 F.2d 255, 257 n.2 (5th Cir. 1988), which reads, "You [the user] may not transfer, sublicense, rent, lease, convey, copy, modify, translate, convert to another programming language, decompile or disassemble the Licensed Software for any purpose without Vault's prior written consent."

tion on the box, user guide, and computer program, of which Zeidenberg was again aware when he put the upgraded programs into use.[16]

It is instructive to note that Judge Easterbrook did not trouble himself with setting out either of these two license provisions quoted by Judge Crabb. His judicial economy was justified because the disputed terms in ProCD, like contractual provisions subject to litigation, did not raise any devilish issues of contractual interpretation: The clause said what it meant, and meant what it said. It was therefore rightly stipulated by both sides that Zeidenberg was in violation of this clause if it were a valid portion of the entire contract, but that the result was otherwise if the clause had not been incorporated into the agreement. The issue thus quickly came to a head when ProCD, through the distinguished Boston firm of Hale & Dorr,[17] demanded that Zeidenberg cease making any unauthorized use of the program. It's clear why the plaintiff resorted to heavy artillery from its opening salvo. If either of the defendants' arguments worked in this case, then the restrictions on use would hold in few if any cases. On the other side, Zeidenberg cared about only his case, not about the fate of an industry, so for him the stakes were lower. He was represented chiefly by David Austin, a recent graduate of Boston's Northeastern Law School trying his first case after passing the Wisconsin Bar.[18] Notwithstanding the evident disparity in firepower, Zeidenberg stuck to his guns and insisted that the restriction on networked uses was not part of the contract. ProCD quickly obtained a preliminary injunction, for Judge Crabb rightly thought that "its entrepreneurial effort"[19] was entitled to at least that much protection. Less than four months later, in January 1996, Judge Crabb wrote an exhaustive opinion before granting summary judgment for the defendants on both their grounds. Judge Easterbrook matched her speed by reversing her judgment on both grounds, with orders to enter the injunction in June 1996.

More important, for our purposes, this complete flip-over represented a vast difference in world view, which is reflected in how the two decisions were organized. Judge Crabb discussed the copyright preemption question first and the contract question second. Let's turn first to the contract formation issue and then to the copyright issue.

---

[16] *Crabb*, 908 F. Supp. at 645.

[17] The point was not mentioned in the decision but can be found in Zeidenberg's account, *Freedom from Contract, supra* note 7, at 829. The firm had a partner, senior associate, and junior associate on the case.

[18] *Id.* at 827.

[19] *Crabb*, 908 F. Supp. at 646.

Judge Crabb's View of Contract Formation

Judge Crabb's view of the contract formation issue was shaped in part by her initial conclusion that *Feist* showed that the current copyright law did not respond to the "equitable" claim that the compilers of databases had for legal protection. In her view, the Supreme Court left the matter of further database protection to Congress, and not to lower courts. Thinking globally, she viewed ProCD's contract claim as an unwise attempt to use shrinkwrap licenses to circumvent the limitations of the copyright law. The contract and the copyright, of course, do not cover identical domains, because shrinkwrap licenses contain other clauses, such as arbitration requirements or limitations on consequential damages, that the copyright laws leave untouched. But the overlap between the contract and copyright remains undeniable.

At this point, Judge Crabb's view of these shrinkwrap provisions was heavily influenced by an article written by Professor Mark Lemley,[20] which took a critical view of shrinkwrap licenses, in Judge Crabb's words "because the typical software transaction does not involve bargained agreements concerning use limitations, but a purchase made by a computer user at a retail store or through the mail, with little discussion or bargaining between the producer and the user."[21] Professor Lemley and Judge Crabb's implicit image of a prototypical contract is a dickered agreement between the two sides where all possible terms are in play; shrinkwrap agreements fall well short of this ideal because of the lack of opportunity for real bargaining.

This initial attitude then sets the stage for the more detailed arguments that followed. The first of these addressed the characterization question mentioned above: Do these shrinkwrap transactions fall into the category of sales or of licenses?[22] In one sense, the initial query is why ask this question at all. One naïve view is that matters of classification don't count so long as the parties are clear as to what their obligations are. So long as the parties know what is required of them, what difference does it make what these obligations are called? Yet in a profound sense, this attitude of studied indifference overlooks the regula-

---

[20] Mark A. Lemley, *Intellectual Property and Shrinkwrap Licenses*, 68 S. Cal. L. Rev. 1239, 1241 (1995).

[21]*Crabb*, 908 F. Supp. at 650; *see also* Lemley, *supra* note 20, at 1248–49 ("Blackletter contract law sets out three predicates to the formation of a contract: offer, acceptance, and consideration. Behind these requirements is the overarching notion of a bargain between the parties. . . . But where is the bargain in a standard form shrinkwrap license that is not even signed by the party against whom it will be enforced?").

[22] *Crabb*, 908 F. Supp. at 650–51.

tory superstructure in the law of contracts. More specifically, remember that sales are governed by the Uniform Commercial Code while licenses fall outside its scope. If therefore this transaction is a sale, all the rules on offer and acceptance that are adopted by the Code come into play. If, however, the transaction is a license, then the rules of offer and acceptance at common law govern. Since the UCC contains a number of distinctive provisions on contract formation, the choice of boxes really matters.[23]

How then did Judge Crabb decide this characterization question? As is common on matters of this sort, she drew a mental picture of a paradigmatic sale and license transaction, and then asked whether the disputed transaction is more analogous to one rather than the other. That task is more difficult than one might imagine because both sales and licenses are enormous fields in which the variation within areas is as great as the variation across areas. In patents and copyrights, for example, licensing by an owner is much more typical than a sale, although both are possible. Software is not quite either, but close enough that the license analogy could not be ignored, especially since that term is used in the disputed agreements. Nonetheless, Judge Crabb argued for the sale transaction because "purchasers of mass market software do not make periodic payments but instead pay a single purchase price, the software company does not retain title for the purpose of a security interest and no set expiration date exists for the 'licensed' right."[24]

Unfortunately, the commercial world is not quite that dichotomous. Although most sales are typically made for a lump sum payment, installment sales are also common. On the other side, licenses may feature lump sum payments as well as periodic ones. Of course, a software company doesn't hold a security interest in the software because there is no unpaid debt after purchase; but that is also true of most sales as

---

[23] *See, e.g.*, UCC §2-207 Additional Terms in Acceptance or Confirmation, which departs from the mirror-image rule of offer and acceptance used at common law.

[24] *Crabb*, 908 F. Supp. at 651 (citing Gary W. Hamilton & Jeffrey C. Hood, *The Shrink-Wrap License—Is It Really Necessary?* 10 Computer L. 16 (1993)). Judge Crabb also explains that most courts have applied the UCC to mass market software transactions, 908 F. Supp. at 650 (citing Lemley, *supra* note 20, at 1244 n.23 (citing numerous federal and state law cases)), and that most scholars agree that the UCC should apply to such transactions, 908 F. Supp. at 651 (citing Bonna Lynn Horovitz, Note, *Computer Software as a Good Under the Uniform Commercial Code: Taking a Byte out of the Intangibility Myth*, 65 B.U. L. Rev. 129 (1985); Lemley, *supra* note 20, at 1244 n.23).

well. From Roman times onward, some perpetual leases, for example, remain in force so long as an annual fee has been paid, often to evade state restrictions against the outright sale of land.[25] For all it mattered, ProCD could easily have a term demanding the return of the software after ten years, knowing full well that the product would have been worthless at that time. Once the categories start to matter, parties will seek to guide their contract into their preferred box.

Once Judge Crabb classified this transaction as a sale of goods covered by the UCC, she applied its rules of contract formation to the exclusion of the common law. Under §2-206, the offer is made when the retailer places Select Phone™ on the shelf, which is in turn accepted when Zeidenberg took possession of the package and paid the purchase price.[26] The contract was therefore complete at that time, and the only question was whether it included any of those terms found inside the box that were not apparent on its cover, or had not been mentioned by the retailer during the course of the sale transaction. Finding that the small print that referred to terms not immediately in evidence, Judge Crabb concluded that the contract was complete without them. The terms contained inside the package were offers for a contract modification that came too late, and were in any event not accepted.[27]

Her view comported with earlier cases on the subject. In *Step-Saver Data Systems, Inc. v. Wyse Technology*,[28] the disputed terms were only known to the buyer after the package was opened, which was held too

---

[25] *See, e.g.,* FRANCIS DE ZULUETA, THE INSTITUTES OF GAIUS 145 (Clarendon Press 1946).

[26] *Crabb*, 908 F. Supp. at 651–52. "Under §2-206, the placement of product such as Select Phone™ on a store shelf constitutes an offer." By whom? *See infra* text accompanying notes 46–48; *see also* UCC §2-206:

Offer and Acceptance in Formation of Contract

  (1) Unless otherwise unambiguously indicated by the language or circumstances

     (a) an offer to make a contract shall be construed as inviting acceptance in any manner and by any medium reasonable in the circumstances.

UCC §2-204:

  A contract for the sale of goods may be made in any manner sufficient to show agreement, including conduct by both parties which recognizes the existence of such a contract.

[27] *Crabb*, 908 F. Supp. at 654–55. *See* UCC §2-209, dealing with modification, rescission, and waiver.

[28] 939 F.2d 91 (3d Cir. 1991).

late, so the terms were not part of the contract. In *Arizona Retail Systems, Inc. v. Software Link, Inc.*[29] those terms were "visible" on the outside of the software envelope and hence bound the person who thereafter opened it. The decisive line of inquiry had to do with the level of notice on receipt of the package. Each purchase was evaluated on its own, wholly apart from any ongoing course of dealing of which it was a part. The early date of contract formation thus worked systematically in favor of the buyers in this case. But at no point did she treat the limitations on transfer as inconsistent with public policy, for so long as early and prompt notification was given, it was as binding as any other restriction.

Yet recall that Zeidenberg made three separate purchases. Does he therefore have knowledge before opening the package the last two times? In summarizing a passage from *Step-Saver*, Judge Crabb stated "exposure to proposed terms in previous transactions did not change the fact that these terms were not agreed to at the time of subsequent contract formations."[30] She then expressed her own uneasiness on the matter as follows:

> The decision on this issue is a close call. Defendants may have known the exact terms of the user agreement at the time of their second and third purchases of Select Phone™. In that case, I would not find it inherently "unjust," as did the court in *Step-Saver*, to hold a party to the terms a seller incorporates into a standard form contract. However, I would agree with that court that it is unwise to hold a buyer to those terms when software companies are free to change the terms of their shrinkwrap licenses between initial and later versions of their products. Like any other parties to a contract, computer users should be given the opportunity to review the terms to which they will be bound each and every time they contract. Although not all users will read the terms anew each time under such circumstances, it does not follow that they should not be given this opportunity. Defendants cannot be held to the user agreement included with the second and third copies of Select Phone™ they purchased merely because they were aware of the terms included with the initial version. Each software purchase creates a new contract. Computer users should be given a fresh

---

[29] 831 F. Supp. 759 (D. Ariz. 1993).

[30] *Crabb*, 908 F. Supp. at 654 (citing *Step-Saver*, 939 F.2d at 104).

opportunity to review any terms to which those contracts will bind them.[31]

Judge Easterbrook's View of Contract Formation

In issuing her judgment, Judge Crabb paid little attention to two important facts. First, the disputed provision is perfectly standard and does not in fact vary from one transaction to another. Second, there are no recorded instances in which any potential software purchaser has been ever able to obtain a waiver of any of the restrictions found in these agreements, including the use limitation at issue in *ProCD*.

To Judge Easterbrook, those two points shaped his approach to the case. His functional view of the law of contract is that it allows bargains by which both parties are able to improve their economic position. It therefore seems odd that any body of contract doctrine, either at common law or under the UCC, should adopt a version of the contract that does not appear to satisfy that condition of mutual gain. So Easterbrook writes a mini law review article on equitable issues that caused Judge Crabb some minor discomfort. As one of the leading members of the Chicago School of Law and Economics, his purpose is to explain why the deal that ProCD envisions makes economic sense, while that which Zeidenberg champions does not. Accordingly, he starts out with an examination of the role of price discrimination in product markets.[32]

It should be no surprise that the words "price discrimination" were never used in either Judge Crabb's opinion nor in Professor Lemley's article on which she so heavily relied. To set up that discussion, Easterbrook points to one undisputed fact about ProCD's business plan that was not mentioned below. "ProCD decided to engage in price discrimination, selling its database to the general public for personal use at a low price (approximately $150 for the set of five discs) while selling information to the trade for a higher price."[33]

Easterbrook raises this point to show that Judge Crabb's view of contract law makes the software market unsustainable in the long run. Easterbrook thus first explains the well-known advantages of price discrimination. First look at the demand side. Like many vendors, ProCD operated in a market in which some buyers make extensive use of its property, for which they will pay a proportionately handsome sum. Those individuals who use it for limited purposes are not pre-

---

[31] 908 F. Supp. at 654–55.

[32] *Easterbrook*, 86 F.3d at 1449–50.

[33] *Id.* at 1449.

pared to pay the same large fees as these high demanders. Next look at the supply side. Select Phone™ cost huge sums to develop in the first instance. Nonetheless each additional unit of the product can be supplied at close to zero marginal cost. Faced with a pattern of high fixed and low marginal costs, the firm needs to do two things at once. First, it must find a way to recover the high fixed costs of the initial production (which for this purpose includes updates of the original database that are not sensitive to the usage levels of individual customers). Yet at the same time it would like to reach as many potential purchasers for its products as possible.

As Easterbrook notes, it is not possible to achieve both these goals simultaneously if ProCD is constrained to charge a uniform price to all potential users. That single price could be set at any one of three levels, all of which are unsatisfactory. The first pricing strategy sets the uniform sale price low enough to reach all the casual product users. The problem is that high level of market penetration comes at a high revenue loss, which makes it unlikely that ProCD could recover either its initial $10 million investment or its updating fees. The second pricing strategy abandons the low end of the market and sells exclusively to high-volume users at high prices. That strategy might allow it to recover its fixed costs, but it carries with it two serious weaknesses from a social point of view. First, any additional revenue from low-intensity users could make the difference between a profitable and a failing venture, so that limiting the seller to high-intensity customers reduces the likelihood that the venture will get off the ground in the first place. Second, that strategy, even if successful, has the unfortunate side effect of precluding all of ProCD's low-intensity users who were prepared to pay $150 for the program, but not the headier sums demanded from high-intensity users. In desperation, a third strategy allows the firm to charge a price midway between the ideal price for high- and low-intensity users. But this Solomonic solution may well yield the worst of both worlds. It could keep the high demanders but reduce the revenue obtained from them, without letting the lower demanders back into the market.

As Easterbrook well recognized, this simplified model assumes for convenience that all users are grouped into these two classes, when in practice ProCD is much more likely to find a continuum of demand for its programs. Ideally, if ProCD knew the reservation price for each potential user—that is, if it knew the maximum that each party was prepared to pay—it could abandon the simple high-low strategy and charge each potential buyer one penny less than the highest amount it was prepared to pay. But that information is denied to us all, so ProCD did the next best thing (i.e., found a "second-best" solution) and sorted its buyers into two or more classes: sales to the trade at a high price;

sales to individuals at a lower price. That common distinction is, for
example, often used in product warranties, where the ordinary home-
owners receive warranty protection for their appliances only if they do
not turn them to commercial use.[34] Once ProCD breaks down the market into two broad categories, it should increase the likelihood that it
will both recover its fixed costs and reach the broadest possible segment of the market. As this contracting strategy has no negative external effects on third parties, it works a Pareto improvement: The
ProCD contracting scheme leaves everyone better off—block its inno-
vative contracting system and social welfare falls.

It's just at this point that the anti-networking provision plays a crucial role. This clause prevents anyone who purchases ProCD's software
program for personal use from using it for the trade. Only by shutting
down such activity could it maintain the two-part pricing schedule so
critical to its success. Read that clause out of the deal, and then we are
back to the unhappy world of a single price for all users.

Now the atmospherics of the case change. In a subsequent interview, Matt Zeidenberg projected himself a folk hero in this "David versus Goliath" story.[35] But under Easterbrook's price-discrimination
story, his conduct poses a mortal threat to all potential low-intensity
users of the product, by forcing ProCD to abandon that segment of the
market, assuming that it stays in the market at all. At this point, the
contract analysis has a different form of urgency, which is to make
sure that efficient contractual provisions are not routinely left on the
cutting room floor.

So Judge Easterbrook then turns his attention to the process of contract formation, where, informed by his analysis of price discrimination, he goes in the opposite direction from Judge Crabb. Right off the
bat, he announces that he does not care whether this transaction is a
sale or a license, and thus is happy to examine the transaction under
the UCC with a different set of eyes.[36] His view is to find low-cost solutions that get to optimal contracts. Recall that Judge Crabb stressed
that a key element of a successful commercial transaction is the pres-

---

[34] *See* George L. Priest, *A Theory of the Consumer Product Warranty*, 90
Yale L.J. 1297 (1981).

[35] *Freedom from Contract, supra* note 7, at 829 (Zeidenberg describing the
lawsuit as a heroic battle between David and Goliath). That characterization is
contested by academics sympathetic to *ProCD. See, e.g.,* James J. White, *Contracting Under Amended 2-207*, 2004 Wis. L. Rev. 723, 741 (while writing in
the *Wisconsin Symposium on Freedom from Contract*, called Matthew Zeidenberg "a naughty fellow who should have his hands slapped.").

[36] *Easterbrook*, 86 F.3d at 1450.

ence of real bargaining over terms, or at least the opportunity to bargain over terms between the parties. Professor Lemley had made the same point earlier: "In the prototypical contract, where the parties meet face to face and discuss the terms before coming to an agreement, the bargain is obvious. But where is the bargain in a standard form shrinkwrap license that is not even signed by the party against whom it will be enforced?"[37]

Judge Easterbrook, rightly, rejects this position for its deep theoretical confusion about the relationship of contracting to contract. The key point here has to do with the role of transaction costs in economic affairs. The Crabb/Lemley position takes the view that actual negotiation is a sign of market health. But Judge Easterbrook, who writes very much in the transaction cost tradition of Ronald Coase,[38] takes the diametrically opposite position; bargains are good because of the mutual gains they generate, but bargaining is a necessary evil whose costs invariably erode the mutual gains that make voluntary bargains the key driver of social progress. We want to maximize bargains, and one way to do that is to get rid of costly bargaining that follows when contract rules are indefinite.

To see why, it is worth noting that voluntary markets that approach perfect competition—with multiple buyers and sellers, and fungible markets—display little or no bargaining of either price or terms—and a high volume of bargains. No one thinks that ordinary bulk purchases of foodstuffs done at low prices in a supermarket are suspect because the checkout clerk is purposefully denied any authority to alter the price or terms of sale. Precisely because these goods are sold in mass markets, individual bargaining is not a sustainable strategy when speed is of the essence for high-volume transactions. No one wants to stand in line behind the asocial customer who has a hankering to bargain over prices. Successful firms will not tolerate such behavior for the administrative breakdown it signals, for the loss of control that it has over its internal operations, and for the massive customer resentment it spawns. Using nonnegotiable terms and uniform (low) prices shores up the customer base by allowing uninformed consumers to piggyback on their more knowledgeable compatriots. Of course, all the world is not a checkout line, so with nonfungible assets, such as the sales of homes and businesses, costly bargaining over price and terms is inescapable. But mass marketing avoids these hassles—at least if

---

[37] Lemley, *supra* note 20, at 1248–49.

[38] See, yet again, Ronald H. Coase, *The Problem of Social Cost*, 3 J.L. & Econ. 1 (1960).

the integrity of its contract structure is observed. What Crabb and
Lemley see as a sign of contract health is in many instances a social
cancer.

Armed with this perspective, Judge Easterbrook has a very different
take on the view of the UCC that requires all terms to be visible to be
part of the contract:

> But why would Wisconsin fetter the parties' choice in this way?
> Vendors can put the entire terms of a contract on the outside of
> a box only by using microscopic type, removing other informa-
> tion that buyers might find more useful (such as what the soft-
> ware does, and on which computers it works), or both. The
> "Read Me" file included with most software, describing system
> requirements and potential incompatibilities, may be equiva-
> lent to ten pages of type; warranties and license restrictions
> take still more space. Notice on the outside, terms on the in-
> side, and a right to return the software for a refund if the terms
> are unacceptable (a right that the license expressly extends),
> may be a means of doing business valuable to buyers and sell-
> ers alike.[39]

The differences in attitude should be crystal clear. Judge Crabb
thought that insisting that all relevant terms be visible on the box
struck a blow for consumer freedom. Judge Easterbrook treats such a
requirement in the opposite fashion, as a restraint (or fetter) on freedom of contract. As with all such restraints, these operate to the disadvantage of both seller and purchaser by reducing the gains from trade.
In this case, the hidden costs derive from the scarcity of high rental
space on the box top. By analogy, modern real estate developers commonly place commercial businesses on the ground floor and residential
homes up top, with offices sandwiched in between. They want places
that serve high traffic to have easy access to the customer base. Merchants operate in exactly the same way, by accentuating the positive.
They know that customers think first of what products are intended to
do, not what legal restrictions are placed upon their use. If the law required them to place second-order warnings on the box, then it necessarily displaces the kind of information that consumers are likely to
find more useful, especially for the 99-plus percent of consumers who
are happy to play by the seller's rules. Cluttered boxtops reduce consumer awareness of the positive product feature: They must therefore
be offset by more advertisement, which raises cost and thus shrinks

---

[39] *Easterbrook*, 86 F.3d at 1450–51.

demand. Easterbrook is right to point out the consumer harm that flows from ostensibly pro-consumer rules.

The question then arises what should be done. In many ordinary sales contracts, it is tolerable to keep the traditional rule that the contract is formed when the product is purchased at the store. It is not as though the green grocer is determined to contract out of a warranty of merchantable quality. But with software, which is an information good, the contracts for sale are more complicated because of how easy it is to share that information with others in ways that defeat any socially valuable scheme of price discrimination.

At this point, it is critical to deviate from the traditional doctrinal rule that holds contract complete at the time of sale, because it disrupts the orderly pattern of exchanges that markets have found to deal with high-information goods. The great vice of the Crabb position is that it embraces a default rule of contract formation that flies in the face of the traditional and sensible practices long used by industries to flog their software. That view overlooks the transaction nightmare it spawns, and proceeds as if there were no reputational constraints that serve as a bulwark against sharp practices. Judge Crabb should have followed her equitable instincts in this case, because the true spoiler of the situation was not ProCD, but Zeidenberg. Accordingly, when Easterbrook reads §2-204, his functional instincts lead him to come out the exact opposite way from Judge Crabb:

> A vendor, as master of the offer, may invite acceptance by conduct, and may propose limitations on the kind of conduct that constitutes acceptance. A buyer may accept by performing the acts the vendor proposes to treat as acceptance. And that is what happened. ProCD proposed a contract that a buyer would accept by using the software after having an opportunity to read the license at leisure. This Zeidenberg did. He had no choice, because the software splashed the license on the screen and would not let him proceed without indicating acceptance. So although the district judge was right to say that a contract can be, and often is, formed simply by paying the price and walking out of the store, the UCC permits contracts to be formed in other ways. ProCD proposed such a different way, and without protest Zeidenberg agreed.[40]

The Easterbrook analysis of delayed acceptance thus solves the central problem with shrinkwrap contracts, by allowing for the incorporation of the critical terms that are revealed only after the package is

---

[40] *Id.* at 1452.

opened or the product is installed. As such, it represents an enormous advance over Judge Crabb's view, which, by placing the time of contracting earlier, knocks out the entire set of terms that is so essential to the business bargain. But function alone does not carry the day. Doctrinal issues always rear their ugly heads. Postponing contract until the later time creates fresh problems, ones that Easterbrook does not discuss, because now there is no agreement between the parties to cover any events that occur between the time of sale and the moment the package is opened or installed. Thus suppose that the software package were lost or damaged before it was opened. If the contract had been complete at the time of sale, as Judge Crabb had found, then the risk of loss passes to the buyer. But if the contract is complete only when the box is opened, then how should the contract allocate the risk of loss? At that point, the status of the box remains unclear, and the not-yet buyer could argue that he or she was only a bailee of the goods who did not bear the risk of loss in the absence of negligence in caring for the goods.

More generally, sound commercial relations make it desirable to push the time of contract forward, not backward, so that the agreement can cover all aspects of the transaction once any part payment or performance has occurred. For example, the great case of *Carlill v. Carbolic Smoke Ball* allowed the buyer of the smoke ball to claim the £100 reward when she caught influenza after she used the smoke ball.[41] The English Court of Appeal treated the use of the smoke ball in accordance with its terms as an acceptance by conduct, in line with the Easterbrook opinion. But that solution, which got Mrs. Carlill £100, had a systematic failing insofar as its belated contract did not govern relationships before it was accepted, i.e., after the sale and before the course of treatment had been completed. That left open the question of whether Carbolic could "revoke" its offer in that interim period, after use had been started but before it was completed. Since there is no good commercial reason to allow Carbolic that bit of contractual opportunism, the long-standing legal solution implies a subsidiary term or agreement to keep the principal undertaking open until the buyer had a chance to complete the prescribed course of treatment. Moving the contract forward to the time of sale has the advantage of letting it govern the usual portions of the business, e.g., risk of loss, for which no special rules are needed. Hence it is possible to combine the best of Easterbrook's relentless functionalism with Judge Crabb's unyielding formalism. The initial contract is complete on sale, but it contains an

---

[41] *See* Carlill v. Carbolic Smoke Ball Co., [1893] 1 Q.B. 256 (C.A. 1893) (Bowen, L.J., Lindley L.J & Smith, L.J.).

implicit option to allow the buyer to back out of the deal once he or she examines the terms—an option that is almost never likely to be exercised. That solution is parallel to the one that eventually prevailed in dealing with the transaction in *Carlill*. Thus *Restatement (Second) of Contracts* §45[42] treats the original promise as containing an implicit option that allows the offeree a clear opportunity to finish an engagement that he has started before any revocation was made.[43] And there is little doubt that the response to this particular problem was one of the driving forces to the adoption of the offer and acceptance rules in the Uniform Commercial Code.[44]

Both this option view and Judge Easterbrook's deferred acceptance solve the big problem of getting the full range of terms into the contract. But patching the big hole still leaves a smaller one to plug. What should be done when, against all odds, the buyer decides to leave that take-it-or-leave-it offer? The contract in *ProCD* suggests only that the buyer return the product to the dealer from which it was purchased. It does not say in so many words that he is entitled to his money back, although that is certainly the initial correct response in cases of this sort. The only complication that could arise is if it is possible to unlock the contents of the CD, bypassing the lockout devices intended to prevent use of the product. But in general, the right response is that the original seller is duty bound to take back the CD so long as it is in undamaged condition, even if it is no longer in the original container.

The actual contract in ProCD did not quite hit the nail on the head because it did not flat out say that ProCD would take back the software if the buyer decided to reject the terms. It said only to return the box "to the place where you obtained it," without naming the retailer.[45] In fact this conscious evasion adds some notable complications into the

---

[42] §45. Option Contract Created by Part Performance of Tender

    (1)   Where an offer invites an offeree to accept by rendering a performance and does not invite a promissory acceptance, an option contract is created when the offeree begins the invited performance or tenders a part of it.

    (2)   The offeror's duty of performance under any option contract so created is conditional on completion or tender of the invited performance in accordance with the terms of the offer.

[43] For variations on this theme, see Clarke B. Whittier, *The Restatement of Contracts and Mutual Assent*, 17 Cal. L. Rev. 441, 450 (1928–29).

[44] *See* FRIEDRICH KESSLER & GRANT GILMORE, CONTRACTS: CASES AND MATERIALS 291 (2d ed. 1970) (referring to UCC §2-206).

[45] *Crabb*, 908 F. Supp. at 644.

analysis that both Judges Crabb and Easterbrook finessed by proceeding as if ProCD and Zeidenberg had made a contract. Yet that description seems falsified by the simple observation that "[i]n later 1994, defendant Zeidenberg purchased a copy of Select Phone™ at a local retail store."[46] (Note how Judge Crabb uses the word "at" rather than "from," which carries a somewhat different connotation.) But now return to the language of reasonable expectations that dominates the UCC. It is hard to think that Zeidenberg thought he purchased the box from ProCD, and ProCD's return statement makes it appear as though the retailer is responsible for deciding whether to offer a refund. But if ProCD has not entered into any contract with Zeidenberg, then where does it get the right to enforce any limitations against transfer? The privity limitation states that only parties to a contract can have rights under it. That principle has long bedeviled the law of torts and now comes back with a vengeance.

Recall a famous observation of Judge Cardozo in *MacPherson v. Buick Motor Co.*: "The dealer was indeed the one person of whom it might be said with some approach to certainty that by him the car would not be used. Yet the defendant would have us say that he was the one person whom it was under a legal duty to protect. The law does not lead us to so inconsequent a conclusion."[47] So here, the party that has the real stake in the reuse of this program is ProCD, so it would be odd to say that the only contractual action belongs to the retailer, who has neither the expertise nor interest to sue. One could try to think of ProCD as having received some assignment of the seller's interest, which would be very odd if the additional terms were not part of the retail contract.

In fact, we should all be relieved that no one sought to open this can of worms, because it allowed the real confrontation to emerge. But there is an important object lesson here, in which some network of contracts (at least three) is needed to link the three parties of this transaction together: retailer–customer, customer–manufacturer, and manufacturer–retailer. It may well be that the best solution is for ProCD to promise its buyers that they can make returns of the unused application to the retailer from whom the purchase was made. It also seems appropriate for ProCD to guarantee its retailers that they will receive their money back for any returns as well. The web of contracts is not easy to develop explicitly on a piecemeal basis, so it makes sense for everyone to drop the retailer out of the picture. Ironically this is easier

---

[46] *Id.* at 645.

[47] 111 N.E. 1050, 1051 (N.Y. 1916).

under the Roman Law, which places the emphasis on agreement, and less on offer and acceptance.[48] But somehow the law has to find a way to allow the real party in interest to seek its injunctive relief precisely because the privity limitation does a bad job in getting matters right.[49] No one said that the contract law of offer and acceptance had to be easy. It isn't.

Copyright Preemption

The second of the two contract issues in *ProCD* is at a conceptual level far removed from the nitty-gritty of offer and acceptance. Now the field of combat changes. Here it is assumed that the parties have entered into a transaction that meets all the requirements for a valid contract under state law on the terms that ProCD sought, including the prohibition against the use of its files for commercial purposes. Now the question is whether the copyright law trumps the contract law under the doctrine of preemption. The basic doctrine of preemption stems from the Supremacy Clause of the United States Constitution, which provides that "[t]his Constitution, and the Law of the United States which shall be made in Pursuance thereof; and all Treaties made, or which shall be made, under the Authority of the United States, shall be the supreme Law of the Land; and the Judges in every State shall be bound thereby, any Thing in the Constitution or the Laws of Any State to the Contrary notwithstanding."[50] The substantive message from this clause is that any lowly federal law trumps any state law that operates to the contrary. State judges are expressly bound to follow the federal law. It is assumed that the federal judges are not exempt from this provision, but that they would do so in any event, given that their natural loyalties lie within the federal system.

---

[48] *See* James Gordley, *Enforcing Promises*, 83 Cal. L. Rev. 547, 562 (1995).

[49] A similar solution was adopted in the early law of product liability with goods sold in sealed containers, where the action for any dangerous condition placed in the product (slivers of tin in the tuna can) was brought against the manufacturer, and not the retailer. *See, e.g.*, Richenbacher v. California Packing Corp., 145 N.E. 281 (Mass. 1924) (heavy gray glass in spinach can). The modern law that allows the action against the retailer who acts as a mere conduit, *see* Vandermark v. Ford Motor Co., 391 P.2d 168 (Cal. 1964), creates additional problems by bringing in a third party that complicates the litigation (in ways that are of direct relevance to civil procedure classes, given that an out-of-state manufacturer cannot remove to federal court if the plaintiff joins in an in-state retailer).

[50] U.S. CONST. art. VI, cl. 2.

There is little question that the doctrine of preemption has become more important in the past generation. State courts are constantly inventing new substantive doctrines at the same time that Congress has continued to multiply federal laws. Thirty or forty years ago it was possible for any torts or contracts law to remain blissfully ignorant of the ins-and-outs of preemption, but today preemption has figured constantly in what used to be thought of as "private" disputes. *ProCD* is no exception to this general rule. In this particular situation the modern copyright law has this to say on the question of preemption.

Section 301(a) of the Copyright Act reads:

a) On and after January 1, 1978, all legal or equitable rights that are equivalent to any of the exclusive rights within the general scope of copyright as specified by section 106 in works of authorship that are fixed in a tangible medium of expression and come within the subject matter of copyright as specified by sections 102 and 103, whether created before or after that date and whether published or unpublished, are governed exclusively by this title. Thereafter, no person is entitled to any such right or equivalent right in any such work under the common law or statutes of any State.

To flesh out this picture, section 102 offers copyright protection to a list of original works that include literary, musical, dramatic compositions, as well as pantomimes, choreographs, pictures, motion pictures, and other works. More to the point here, section 103 covers compilations and derivative works. Having stated this background Judge Crabb accordingly held that preemption occurred if two conditions are satisfied: "1) the work in which the state law right is asserted comes within the 'subject matter' of copyright, as specified in 17 U.S.C. §§102 or 103; and 2) the state law right asserted is equivalent to any of the rights specified in 17 U.S.C. §106."[51]

The first of these two questions raises a conundrum that is common to many claims of federal preemption. The *Feist* decision held that sweat-of-the-brow databases were not sufficiently original to receive protection under the copyright law.[52] So the question is how can a database that flunks database protection "come within the subject matter" of copyright law? Why, in other words, is it appropriate to count near misses as hits? The answer to this question lies in the nuances of federal preemption law. The most obvious cases of preemption arise

---

[51] *Crabb*, 908 F. Supp. at 656.

[52] 499 U.S. at 359–60.

when the state law commands what the federal law prohibits. But the scope of preemption goes one step further to cover situations where the federal law "occupies the field." One illustration of field occupation arises if some state tried to protect copyrights for ten years longer than the Copyright Act. There is no logical contradiction between the longer term that state law desires and the shorter federal term. Nonetheless, the uniform view is that the Copyright Act was intended to introduce "a delicate balance" between works that were privately owned and those that fall into the public domain.[53] That decision reflects a judgment as to the need to create copyrighted works in the first instance, and the need to secure their wide dissemination. The longer term upsets that congressional balance, and hence is preempted.

The matter of field occupation can arise in other cases. Both Judge Crabb and Easterbrook relied on *Baltimore Orioles, Inc. v. Major League Baseball Players Association*.[54] There the players association challenged the claim of major league baseball teams that they held the exclusive rights to all televised performances of major league baseball games under the copyright law. The players' argument was first that their performances on the field lacked the creativity to meet the originality requirement of the copyright law, and second that they enjoyed rights of publicity—the use of name or likeness for commercial purposes—under state law.[55] As was held in *Baltimore Orioles*, "[a]s long as a work fits within one of the general subject matter categories of section 102 and 103, . . . [section 301(a)] prevents the States from protecting it even if it fails to achieve Federal copyright because it is too minimal or lacking in originality to qualify."[56] That describes ProCD's

---

[53] *See, e.g., Crabb*, 908 F. Supp. at 658.

[54] 805 F.2d 663, 676 (7th Cir. 1986).

[55] *See* RESTATEMENT (SECOND) OF TORTS: APPROPRIATION OF NAME OR LIKENESS §652C (1977) ("One who appropriates to his own use or benefit the name or likeness of another is subject to liability to the other for invasion of his privacy.").

The right of publicity is the more common modern name for the tort. The common law right of publicity cause of action "may be pleaded by alleging (1) the defendant's use of the plaintiff's identity; (2) the appropriation of plaintiff's name or likeness to defendant's advantage, commercially or otherwise; (3) lack of consent; and (4) resulting injury." White v. Samsung Electronics America, Inc., 971 F.2d 1395, 1397 (9th Cir. 1992) (quoting Eastwood v. Superior Court, 198 Cal. Rptr. 342, 347 (Ct. App. 1983) (citing WILLIAM L. PROSSER, LAW OF TORTS §117, at 804–07 (4th ed. 1971))).

[56] *Crabb*, 908 F. Supp. at 656 (quoting 805 F.2d at 676 (citing H.R. REP. NO. 94-1476, at 51 (1976), *as reprinted in* 1976 U.S.C.C.A.N. 5659, 5747))).

database to a T. Judge Easterbrook did not take issue with any element of her analysis.

The second element of the argument proved, however, to be more
controversial because it deals with the vexed relationship of property
and contract more generally. What rights then are to be regarded as
"equivalent" to the exclusive rights under the copyright law? As far as
Judge Crabb was concerned, this contract was suspect because it
sought to circumvent the limitations of the copyright law. "Plaintiff
argues that the contractual restriction imposed in its user agreement
established an 'extra element' that makes its breach of contract claim
different from its copyright infringement claim but, in reality, its
breach of contract claim is nothing more than an effort to prevent defendants from copying and distributing its data, exactly what it sought
to bar defendants from doing under copyright law."[57]

But Judge Crabb does not claim that copyright law blocks all contracts over materials that fall near or within its protection. Thus it
would be absurd to argue that copyright law would have shielded
ProCD from suit if it had refused to pay its employees for compiling its
database, or conversely, that the employees could in turn just refuse to
turn over data from its database because it was not entitled to copyright protection. Both those results would massively disrupt routine
business transactions that are wholly consistent with the basic objectives of the copyright law. Any such holding would also call into question the ability of individuals to make contracts with respect to trade
secrets, which often cover databases that do not receive copyright protection. Yet the Supreme Court has long held that state trade-secret
law extends to intellectual property that receives neither copyright nor
patent protection, and it allows parties to freely license trade secrets
for use by others.[58]

Having set up her test, however, Judge Crabb was obliged to sort
through the cases to decide which causes of action are so collateral to
copyright law that they are not preempted by it. Thus in *Harper &
Row Publishers, Inc. v. Nation Enterprises*,[59] Harper & Row sued for
conversion and tortious interference of contract rights when the *Nation*
published substantial portions of Gerald Ford's memoirs in its magazine. The claims in question here were duplicative of the copyright
claims and hence were preempted by federal law. Subsequently, the

---

[57] 908 F. Supp. at 657.

[58] Kewanee Oil Co. v. Bicron Corp., 416 U.S. 470 (1974).

[59] 723 F.2d 195, 201 (2d Cir. 1983), rev'd on other grounds, 471 U.S. 539
(1985).

Supreme Court found, as the court of appeals did not, that the *Nation* did not make out the fair use defense under the copyright law. Since the misappropriation and conversion claims were brought against strangers, these were of the type of state law claims that the copyright law preempted when it occupied the field.[60]

On the other side of the ledger, in *Acorn Structures, Inc. v. Swantz*,[61] the court held that the copyright law did not block a corporation from suing an architect to whom it had sold plans from turning them to an unauthorized use. Similarly, in *Taquino v. Teledyne Monarch Rubber*,[62] the plaintiff was not preempted when he sued to enforce a covenant not to compete against the defendant, who sought to compete on the strength of the information it had acquired by contract. In *National Car Rental Systems, Inc. v. Computer Associates International Inc.*,[63] the court held that copyright did not preempt contract law when a licensor sought to restrain the use of the database for third persons when the license permitted its use only for internal purposes.

The question then arises how to read these precedents. Judge Crabb opted to read them narrowly.

> To the extent that *National Car Rental*, *Taquino*, [and other cases] support the proposition that a copyright infringement claim is not equivalent to a contract claim merely because the contract claim requires a plaintiff to show the additional element of breach, I disagree respectfully with their conclusions. Contracts that seek to protect reproduction and distribution rights step into territory already covered by copyright law. It would alter the "delicate balance" of copyright law to allow parties to avoid copyright law by contracting around it.[64]

In order to assess this claim, first recognize that there is no question that the protections that ProCD received under its contract were greater than those that were allowed under the copyright law generally. As Professor Lemley has carefully explained, particular contracts (though not necessarily the one involved in ProCD) often impose more extensive restrictions on the licensee (precisely because he is not a buyer) that go beyond those under the copyright law.[65] The copyright

---

[60] *Harper & Row*, 471 U.S. at 569.

[61] 846 F.2d 923, 926 (4th Cir. 1988).

[62] 893 F.2d 1488, 1501 (5th Cir. 1990).

[63] 991 F.2d 426, 433 (8th Cir. 1993).

[64] *Crabb*, 908 F. Supp. at 658.

[65] Lemley, *supra* note 20, at 1245–48.

law, under the "first sale" doctrine, routinely allows any individual to sell or give away its copy of the work without the permission of its owner.[66] The Copyright Act in general allows parties to make archival copies of their work, which contracts could also restrict.[67] Moreover, the particular license could prevent the licensee from decompiling or disassembling the database supplied for its own use, which thereby denies it the right to "reverse engineer" intellectual property, a right that as a general matter is preserved under, for example, the law of trade secrets.[68] And of course, in this instance the prohibition against networking prevented Zeidenberg from deploying the database for commercial use.

In light of this background, Judge Crabb held that the copyright law preempted the contract right of action so long as its sole intention was to impose protections that the licensor would not otherwise have against the licensee under the Copyright Act.[69] It was on this point that Judge Easterbrook parted company with her, based on his economic understanding of the issues. He saw no need to draw fine distinctions between those contract provisions that survive the copyright law and those that do not. For him, the root difference is much more fundamental. Contracts create rights that are good between parties, while the copyright law gives the copyright holder rights good against the world:

> Rights "equivalent to any of the exclusive rights within the general scope of copyright" are rights established by law— rights that restrict the options of persons who are strangers to the author. Copyright law forbids duplication, public performance, and so on, unless the person wishing to copy or perform the work gets permission; silence means a ban on copying. A copyright is a right against the world. Contracts, by contrast, generally affect only their parties; strangers may do as they please, so contracts do not create "exclusive rights."[70]

The points raised here deserves some explication. The first point to note is that all property rules, including those for copyright and other forms of intellectual property, establish legal relations between one person—the owner—and the rest of the world. If the law did not create these rules, then only the law of contract could be used to organize

---

[66] 17 U.S.C. §109(b)(1) (2000); Lemley, *supra* note 20, at 1246 & n.28.

[67] §117; Lemley, *supra* note 20, at 1246 & n.29.

[68] Lemley, *supra* note 20, at 1247 & n.31.

[69] *Crabb*, 908 F. Supp. at 658–59.

[70] *Easterbrook*, 86 F.3d at 1454.

these relationships. But note how feeble contract law is for that task. No owner could work out relationships with the rest of the world, one person at a time. Any owner who organized a separate peace with 99-plus percent of the population would gain nothing so long as a tiny handful of people remained free to enter his land or to copy his original works. Only a strong legal rule can create property rights.

But what rights? In general, a viable system of property rights has to start with two critical features. First, it can demand only forbearance from others, not cooperation. For land, outsiders have to keep off to respect the owner's exclusive rights of possession. For copyrights, outsiders cannot reproduce these works at their free will and pleasure. Infringement is the intellectual property analog to trespass. Any effort, however, to enlist the cooperation and support of nonowners is doomed to failure in either sphere. No general law could require everyone (or anyone) to plow the fields of any one of a million farmers, or to publish ads for any one of a million authors. Forbearance, in contrast, is easily "scalable" in that it is as easy to forbear from entering the land of millions as it is from entering the land of one person. But contract duties are not scalable. It is not as easy to work for a million employers as for one.

Of course, the duty of forbearance, while universal, is not an absolute one. The strangers who cannot be conscripted to serve an owner may in limited conditions of necessity use the property of others. The law of necessity for land[71] and the law of fair use for copyright both set out circumstances in which a breach in the wall of exclusion helps improve overall welfare. People can enter land to save their own lives, even if they may have to compensate the owner thereafter. And similar conceptions of necessity sometime allow individuals to use copyright material of another in order to secure interoperability of computer programs.[72] These exceptions are quite narrow in most cases, and need not be discussed here. Zeidenberg had no credible claim to fair use under any applicable copyright law.

We can, therefore, put aside the narrow claims of privilege for using property of another. The real question here is whether the "delicate balance" that the land law creates with farms and houses or the copyright law creates with literary works and databases should be impervious to alteration by voluntary contract. The emphatic answer is no,

---

[71] *See, e.g.*, Vincent v. Lake Erie Transportation Co., 124 N.W. 221 (Minn. 1910) (duty to pay damages for entries under necessity); Ploof v. Putnam, 71 A. 188 (Vt. 1908) (privilege to enter to preserve life or limb).

[72] 17 U.S.C. §1201(f) (2000) (governing interoperability).

because the basic dynamic is wholly different from that involved in the initial creation of any system of property rights. Once the positive law sets an owner's basic rights against the rest of the world, why stop the owner from entering into a particular transaction with a designated outsider? Against the backdrop of secure property rights, owner and outsider can strike a bargain that improves the position of both. That happens when workers are hired to plow land or to build houses. It happens when an owner lets someone else enter his property, while barring others from entering the premises as well. Yet if the landowner were told that it could not prevent the licensee from transferring his rights to others, then the whole deal might come falling down.[73]

The same logic applies to copyrights, or for that matter to all forms of intellectual property. The delicate balance that the law creates makes perfect sense between strangers. But any copyright holder has private information about the value of his copyrighted work that the legal system could never hope to duplicate. If he wants to license it to a third person, then why prohibit this transaction, which works to the benefit of both parties? What distinguishes the ability to prevent unauthorized use of architectural plans in *Acorn*, or its use for third parties in *National Car Rental,* from the unauthorized use in *ProCD*? In all these voluntary transactions, the copyright holder does not take advantage of his buyer or licensee by stealth or coercion. That increased resource level creates positive externalities for third persons who now have increased opportunities for trade. The right approach always allows owners to individuate their rights with particular persons. This position does not only apply to copyrights but covers all form of property, including trade secrets. There is no question that the holder of a trade secret cannot prevent its independent discovery by a stranger. But it is quite a different matter if the seller of a product that embod-

---

[73] *Cf.* Tulk v. Moxhay, (1843–1860) All Eng.Rep. 9 (L.C.). The defendant bought a plot of land from a seller, and the land contained a covenant from the original owner (whose remaining land was adjacent to the plot in question) requiring that it be used only for a "square garden." The defendant refused to follow the covenant, and the lower court granted the owner of the adjacent land an injunction. The Lord Cottenham, L.C., upheld the injunction, explaining that "[i]t is . . . contended, not that the vendee could violate that contract, but that he might sell the piece of land, and that the purchaser from him might violate it without this court having any power to interfere. If that were so, it would be impossible for an owner of land to sell part of it without incurring the risk of rendering what he retains worthless. . . . [N]othing could be more inequitable than that the original purchaser should be able to sell the property the next day for a greater price, in consideration of the assignee being allowed to escape from the liability which he had undertaken."

ies a trade secret requires by contract the buyer not to reverse engineer that product. The contract provision here encourages the voluntary dissemination of useful products and should be enforced, as it usually is.[74] In all these cases, the key function of property rights is to create the baseline from which voluntary transactions can take place. It is not, as Judge Crabb assumed, to block further voluntary transactions.

In the end, a broad intellectual gulf separates Judge Crabb from Judge Easterbrook. She looks at these voluntary transactions with deep suspicion, as if they were a deviation from some grand copyright scheme. Contract is thus a dubious end run around property. Judge Easterbrook follows the economic model and sees voluntary contracts as improving social welfare by voluntary exchange. He rightly understands that the Copyright Act prevents the states from creating new or different property rights among strangers. He is equally correct to deny that copyright law prevents the creation of new and different property right by contracts. Once again his sure sense of the economic function of property and contract rights leads him to a result that is easy to miss on a traditional doctrinal approach.

Epilogue

ProCD has both its personal and institutional significance. As to the immediate parties, ProCD was acquired by a firm called Acxiom in April 1996 for about $47 million in stock.[75] One month later, the decision in *ProCD* came down, and ironically Acxiom's stock dropped two points, from 34 to 32, on the news.[76] The impact on Matthew Zeidenberg is captured by his own assessment of the overall situation, which encapsulated his view of law and economics generally:

> [C]oming into this as a sort of a naïve person who'd never been involved in a lawsuit before, I really expected a lot more consistency in the law. . . I researched what the law was, and I went into court and I expected to get what I got from Barbara Crabb. And then when I got to Judge Easterbrook, I had no idea about, you know, the Olin Foundation and "law and economics" and the Chicago School and Judges Easterbrook and Posner and this whole thing; you know I had no idea that this kind of thing could happen. I was just totally blown away.[77]

---

[74] *See, e.g.*, Davidson & Associates v. Jung, 422 F.3d 630 (8th Cir. 2005).

[75] *Acxiom Stock Up on Deal*, N.Y. Times, Apr. 10, 1996, at D4.

[76] Eric Convey, *Danvers Firm Wins Court Battle*, Boston Herald, June 25, 1996.

[77]*Freedom from Contract, supra* note 7, at 835–36.

And so he was in both senses of that term. In the end, however, it is the institutional dimension of *ProCD* that will count the most. *ProCD* raises issues of utmost importance of the question of contract formation on the one hand and the relationship between property and contract rights on the other. From what I have suggested, on intellectual grounds Judge Easterbrook's decision should have put both matters to rest. Yet for most judges and lawyers, his economic method meshes uneasily with traditional doctrinal analysis and often is thought to possess some sinister overtones to boot. Judge Easterbrook's view has continued to prevail on the copyright preemption question. It is now well settled that preemption does cover state law efforts to give additional protection against the world for works that Congress has decided to leave in the public domain.[78] Yet it has been uniformly held that the copyright law does not preempt any breach-of-contract claims, including those that prevent reverse engineering[79]—a result that is often defended on explicit freedom-of-contract grounds.[80] Ironically, some courts impose an odd qualification on this rule by insisting that a given contract provision does not supply that magical "extra element," if the rights so created are only duplicative of the copyright law. Preemption requires that the contract offer some protection that the copyright law does not supply.[81] Many states have adopted the formulation that the preemption does not apply because the contract action rests on an "extra element" found in the agreement that the copyright law does not independently require,"[82] a verbal formulation that Easterbrook and

---

[78] *See, e.g.*, Lipscher v. LRP Publications, Inc., 266 F.3d 1305, 1311 (11th Cir. 2001) (citing *Easterbrook,* 96 F.3d at 1453).

[79] *See* Bowers v. Baystate Technologies, 320 F.3d 1317 (Fed. Cir. 2003) ("Indeed, most courts to examine this issue have found that the Copyright Act does not preempt contractual constraints on copyrighted articles."); *see also* Logicom Inclusive, Inc. v. W.P. Stewart & Co., No. 04 Civ. 0604(CSH), 2004 WL 1781009, *18 (S.D.N.Y. Aug. 10, 2004).

[80] *Bowers,* 320 F.3d at 1324.

[81] *See, e.g.*, Green v. Hendrickson Publishers, Inc., 770 N.E.2d 784, 789–90 (Ind. 2002); Selby v. New Line Cinema Corp., 96 F. Supp. 2d 1053, 1060 (C.D. Cal. 2000).

[82] Under the extra element test, the Copyright Act does not preempt any state cause of action if it "requires an extra element, beyond mere copying, preparation of derivative works, performance, distribution, or display." *Bowers,* 320 F.3d at 1324 (citing Data General Corp. v. Grumman Systems Support Corp., 36 F.3d 1147, 1164 (1st Cir. 1994)).

the Seventh Circuit have not expressly adopted, but without any change in the result.[83]

In contrast, with the relatively uniform response to the preemption question, the offer and acceptance issue has been fraught with controversy as freedom of contract becomes a suspect category in, of all places, contract law. There are a number of cases that have accepted Easterbrook's position under one guise or another, by allowing a seller (or licensee) to propose terms that a buyer accepts only after using or keeping the product given a prior opportunity to review its terms.[84] At the same time, some cases have continued to follow the position of Judge Crabb below,[85] which is consistent with scholarly and practitioner articles that have been harshly critical of the Easterbrook analysis.[86]

---

[83] *See, e.g.*, Pritikin v. Liberation Publications, Inc., 83 F. Supp. 2d 920, 922 (N.D. Ill. 1999) ("The Seventh Circuit has not expressly adopted the 'extra element' test[;] [h]owever, the Seventh Circuit's approach would appear to lead to similar results.").

[84] *E.g.*, Hill v. Gateway 2000, Inc., 105 F.3d 1147 (7th Cir. 1997) (another Easterbrook decision); M.A. Mortenson Co. v. Timberline Software Corp., 998 P.2d 305 (Wash. 2000) (incorporating internal terms even when the original order form did not mention the embedded terms); Brower v. Gateway 2000, Inc., 676 N.Y.S.2d 569, 570 (App. Div. 1998); Levy v. Gateway 2000, Inc., 33 UCC Rep. Serv. 2d 1060, 1062 (N.Y. Sup. Ct. 1997); *see also* I. Lan Systems, Inc. v. Netscout Service Level Corp, 183 F. Supp. 2d 328 (D. Mass. 2002), which reached the same conclusion under the combined application of UCC §2-204 and UCC §2-207.

[85] Klocek v. Gateway, Inc., 104 F. Supp. 2d 1332 (D. Kan. 2000); Litra v. Gateway, Inc., 734 N.Y.S.2d 389, 396 (N.Y. Civ. Ct. 2001); Softman Products Co., LLC v. Adobe Systems, Inc., 171 F. Supp. 2d 1075 (C.D. Cal. 2001), where the court held the license invalid because of a lack of adequate notice and the absence of a clear opportunity to manifest consent to the terms of the license. Unlike *ProCD*, the licensee had resold unopened software in violation of the license agreement. Yet the licensee had never viewed the relevant license term because it was located inside the unopened software. There have been a number of other cases that have followed a similar approach. *See* Specht v. Netscape, 306 F.3d 17 (2d Cir. 2002); Defontes v. Dell Computers Corp., 2004 WL 253560 (R.I. Super. Ct. Jan. 29, 2004) (unpublished opinion).

[86] *See Klocek,* 104 F. Supp. 2d at 1339 n.9, which summarized this literature as follows:

> Legal commentators have criticized the reasoning of the Seventh Circuit in this regard. *See, e.g.*, Jean R. Sternlight, *Gateway Widens Doorway to Imposing Unfair Binding Arbitration on Consumers*, Fla. Bar J., Nov. 1997, at 8, 10–12 (outcome in *Gateway* is questionable

The largest battle over *ProCD* has not involved the case law, but has centered around the subsequent efforts of the National Conference of Commissioners on Uniform State Laws to address these issues in the Uniform Computer Information Transactions Act (UCITA), which is every bit as long and convoluted as the UCC.[87] UCITA is widely and correctly perceived as more sympathetic to the views of Judge Easterbrook than to those of Judge Crabb. UCITA formulates explicit rules to deal with mass-market licenses used in mass-market transactions, which cover end-user or shrinkwrap licenses.[88] UCITA allows these transactions to take before their full terms are disclosed, provided that the putative licensee is allowed to return the software after inspection of the terms and receive reimbursement for reasonable expenses.[89]

UCITA has been adopted in a few states but has met with fierce resistance everywhere. Its opponents have formed an anti-UCITA lobbying organization, AFFECT, or Americans for Fair Electronic Commerce Transactions.[90] A debate over UCITA was the major dispute at the

---

on federal statutory, common law and constitutional grounds and as a matter of contract law and is unwise as a matter of policy because it unreasonably shifts to consumers search cost of ascertaining existence of arbitration clause and return cost to avoid such clause); Thomas J. McCarthy et al., *Survey: Uniform Commercial Code*, 53 Bus. Law. 1461, 1465–66 (Seventh Circuit finding that UCC §2-207 did not apply is inconsistent with official comment); Batya Goodman, *Honey, I Shrink-Wrapped the Consumer: The Shrinkwrap Agreement as an Adhesion Contract*, 21 Cardozo L. Rev. 319, 344–52 (Seventh Circuit failed to consider principles of adhesion contracts); Jeremy Senderowicz, *Consumer Arbitration and Freedom of Contract: A Proposal to Facilitate Consumers' Informed Consent to Arbitration Clauses in Form Contracts*, 32 Colum. J.L. & Soc. Probs. 275, 296–99 (judiciary (in multiple decisions, including *Hill*) has ignored issue of consumer consent to an arbitration clause).

[87] The drafts are at http://www.law.upenn.edu/bll/ulc/ulc.htm#ucita, the official site for the National Conference of Commissioners on Uniform State Laws.

[88] For the definitions, see UCITA §102(43) & (44). Section 102 has sixty-five definitional provisions.

[89] UCITA §209(2)(b) & (c).

[90] Found at http://www.ucita.com, in a Web-based masterstroke, AFFECT has occupied for its Web address the UCITA name. It is the first place that anyone would go to find information about UCITA, and it is firmly in the hands of its opponents. For a list of anti-UCITA publications, see http://www.badsoftware.com/uccindex.htm. For one such article, see Jean Braucher, *Amended Article 2 and the Decision to Trust the Courts: The Case*

American Bar Association 2003 meetings, and the House of Delegates was asked to back the ABA UCITA Standby Committee's May 29, 2002, report, which had supported the adoption of UCITA.[91] In the face of opposition, the matter was withdrawn before it could receive an up-or-down vote of the House of Delegates. In January 2003 I wrote a letter on behalf of UCITA that was sent to every member of the House of Delegates.[92] Thomas E. Workman of the Association of Life Insurance Counsel wrote in response:

> Professor Richard Epstein lauds UCITA's "freedom of contract" philosophy. We find confusing Professor Epstein's apparent view that delayed boilerplate language, not available to customers when they make software acquisition decisions, represents freedom of contract to anyone but the drafter—namely the software manufacturer. As members of the life insurance industry, we are, of course, familiar with standard form agreements. Most of our contracts, however, include mandated terms and exclude prohibited terms. Moreover, we may not use contract forms in a state until they are approved by the state insurance regulator. The insurance laws that impose these requirements were enacted in recognition of the importance of

---

Against Enforcing Delayed Mass-Market Terms, Especially for Software, 2004 Wis. L. Rev. 753.

For my defense of UCITA against its many critics, see *supra* note *, which deals more with why it is important to allow software vendors to contract out of liability for consequential damages for economic losses, which is allowed under UCITA §803(d):

> d)   Consequential damages and incidental damages may be excluded or limited by agreement unless the exclusion or limitation is unconscionable. Exclusion or limitation of consequential damages for personal injury in a consumer contract for a computer program that is subject to this [Act] and is contained in consumer goods is prima facie unconscionable, but exclusion or limitation of damages for a commercial loss is not unconscionable.

For my general views on this topic, see Richard A. Epstein, *Consequential Damages in the Law of Contract*, 18 J. Legal Stud. 105 (1989).

[91] UCITA STANDBY COMMITTEE, AMERICAN BAR ASSOCIATION, REPORT TO CONFERENCE AND RESPONSE TO CONCERNS EXPRESSED IN ABA WORKING GROUP REPORT (May 29, 2002).

[92] Letter from Professor Richard Epstein to American Bar Association House of Delegates (Jan. 15, 2003), *available at* http://www.nccusl.org/ nccusl/ucita/ucita/Epstein_UCITA.pdf (last visited Jan. 11, 2006).

insurance in commerce and the uneven bargaining power of the parties.[93]

It was a set of charges that I could not let pass in silence:

Mr. Workman is wrong to think that there is some vice in having "delayed boilerplate language, not available to customers when they make their software acquisition decisions." At first I was at a complete loss as to what he might be thinking. I can think of nothing in sections 201 to 207 of the draft that lead to any untoward results. Nor does Mr. Workman point to the section or language of UCITA that he finds offensive, but artfully writes as though buyers are bound by contract before they know the terms of their agreement, or have the opportunity to learn of them. But that of course is not what he says when you read him a second time. Rather he uses the muddy expression "software acquisition" to conceal what is at stake here. The acquisition decision to which he refers is the placement of an order for software. That order however does not become a contract because UCITA itself requires that individual consumers have an opportunity to review the terms before the acceptance takes place, and may return the goods free of charge if they do not like them afterwards.[94]

So the beat goes on! And you thought that offer and acceptance was a dull subject!

---

[93] Letter from Thomas E. Workman, President and Chief Executive Officer, Association of Life Insurance Counsel, to American Bar Association House of Delegates: Response to Letter of Professor Richard Epstein (Jan. 27, 2003) (on file with author).

[94] Letter from Professor Richard Epstein to American Bar Association House of Delegates: Response to Letter of Thomas E. Workman (Jan. 29, 2003), which is available at http://www.nccusl.org/nccusl/ucita/EpsteinWorkman_response.pdf (last visited Jan. 11, 2006).

5

Carol Sanger*

Developing Markets in Baby-making: *In the Matter of Baby M*

Introduction

In the spring of 1985, the fortunes of two ordinary New Jersey couples, Richard and Mary Beth Whitehead and William and Elizabeth Stern, became profoundly and quite publicly entangled. The Whiteheads, a working-class couple from Brick Township, had been married for twelve years. They had met in Mary Beth's brother's luncheonette, where Richard (Rick) was a regular patron and Mary Beth a teenage waitress. Their early life together had been somewhat rough and tumble—frequent moves, a marital separation, a spell on welfare—but by the early 1980s, their circumstances had improved. Rick had a steady job as a garbage truck driver; the couple now owned a house, if heavily mortgaged. The Whiteheads also had two much-loved children, a son, Ryan, born in 1974 and a daughter, Tuesday, born a year later, and in this regard they were content. Shortly after Tuesday's birth, they had decided that their family was perfect and complete; to keep it that way, and with eighteen-year-old Mary Beth's approval, Rick had a vasectomy.

The Sterns, married only a year less than the Whiteheads, had met and married while graduate students at the University of Michigan. The couple had decided to postpone their family until Betsy had completed her medical training, when they would be more financially se-

---

* Barbara Aronstein Black Professor of Law, Columbia Law School. Reprinted with permission from the *Harvard Journal of Law & Gender*, Vol. 30 (2007).

cure.[1] In 1985, after Betsy finished her residency, the Sterns moved
from an apartment in the Bronx to the pleasant bedroom community of
Tenafly.[2] The location eased their daily commute to New York City,
where Betsy worked as a pediatric oncologist and Bill as a medical re-
searcher. Although in almost every respect the Sterns appeared to live
a comfortable, satisfying life, something was missing. Due to a medical
condition, Betsy was unable to have children, and the couple felt this
deprivation most painfully. They had briefly considered adopting but
waiting lists for infants were long. Moreover, as the only child of Jewish parents who had survived the Holocaust, Bill specially longed for a
biological child of his own.[3]

The complementarity of desire, ability, and resources between the
Whiteheads and the Sterns led to an interesting agreement between
the two couples. Mary Beth agreed to be artificially inseminated with
Bill's sperm and, if she became pregnant, to give the baby to the Sterns
to raise as theirs in an arrangement known generally as traditional
surrogacy. For their part, the Sterns agreed to pay Mary Beth
$10,000.[4] The deal was arranged by the Infertility Center of New York
(ICNY), opened in 1981 by a Michigan attorney, Noel Keane.

For the next several months, Bill and Mary Beth met up at the
Vince Lombardi Rest Stop on the New Jersey Turnpike to drive together into New York City for the inseminations.[5] Six months and
eleven inseminations later, Mary Beth conceived and on March 27,
1986, the infant soon to be known around the world as Baby M was
born.

---

[1] Testimony of William Stern, 1 BABY M CASE: THE COMPLETE TRIAL TRAN-
SCRIPTS 61–62 (1988) (Direct); Testimony of Elizabeth Stern, 1 Trial Transcripts 53 (Direct).

[2] "Fine schools, quality housing, recreational facilities, parks and wood-
lands, good cultural programs, diverse houses of worship, and quality borough
services all help to attract newcomers to and keep older residents in this historic town and help to maintain a small town feeling." The Borough of Tenafly,
NJ, http://www.tenaflynj.org/content/52/default.aspx

[3] Susan Edelman, *The Parents Behind the Baby M Tug of War—A Father
Fighting to Keep His Only Blood Relative*, The Record (Hackensack, N.J.), Sept.
9, 1986.

[4] The $10,000 was placed in escrow with the ICNY, payable when Mary
Beth surrendered the baby to Bill. Under the terms of the agreement, if Mary
Beth miscarried before the fifth month of pregnancy, she would receive no
compensation except for the medical expenses. If she miscarried after the fifth
month, she was to receive $1,000.

[5] Testimony of William Stern, 1 Trial Transcripts 120–26 (Direct).

This is where the seemingly happy match between the Sterns and the Whiteheads came to an end. Within days of the birth, Mary Beth was overcome with love for little Sarah (the name she had put on the baby's birth certificate), and she refused to let the Sterns keep her. Weeks of desperate negotiations followed, as Betsy and Bill implored Mary Beth to keep her promise and Mary Beth became more fervently determined to keep her baby, threatening suicide if she could not. In early May, the Sterns sued to have the agreement enforced, and, following an ex parte hearing to determine the temporary custody of the baby, Judge Harvey Sorkow of the Bergen County Court ordered that little Melissa (the Sterns' name for the baby) be turned over to them. The Whiteheads fled to Florida but were eventually found by private detectives. In a dramatic confrontation (related to the press in great detail by Mary Beth's mother), the police took Baby M, who was finally delivered into the physical custody of the Sterns.[6]

The case that followed can easily be called the custody trial of the twentieth century.[7] Every aspect of the six-week trial—from Tuesday's tears to Betsy's (real) hair color to expert testimony on the best way to play patty cake—was covered in depth and worldwide, as was the trial court's decision ordering specific performance of the contract and awarding the Sterns custody of the baby. The case remained in the news during Mary Beth's appeal to the New Jersey Supreme Court, as paparazzi snapped away at Mary Beth arriving for her weekly supervised visitation and as partisans on both sides prepared amici briefs and battled it out on op-ed pages nationwide. On February 3, 1988, the New Jersey Supreme Court reversed the trial court decision, declaring that under New Jersey law, surrogacy contracts were "illegal and possibly criminal."[8] Although it declared the surrogacy contract was void, the Court awarded custody of the baby to the Sterns, no longer as a matter of contract enforcement but applying the "best interest of the child" standard used generally in contested custody cases between parents. It then remanded the case for a determination regarding the scope of Mary Beth's visitation.[9]

---

[6] Bob Port & Stephen Hegarty, *Surrogate Mom in Pasco, N.J. Couple Fight over "Baby M,"* St. Petersburg Times, Aug. 1, 1986.

[7] For the nineteenth-century contender, see MICHAEL GROSSBERG, A JUDGMENT FOR SOLOMON: THE D'HAUTEVILLE CASE AND LEGAL EXPERIENCE IN ANTEBELLUM AMERICA (1996).

[8] 537 A.2d 1227 (N.J. 1988).

[9] In granting Mary Beth liberal visitation, the lower court gently chided both sets of parents: "Mary Beth Whitehead Gould must accept and understand that Melissa is not Sarah and that her father and stepmother will be her

The case provoked philosophical debate, political organizing, and legislative action as ethicists, feminists, theologians, lawmakers, and area men and women weighed in on surrogacy's moral, legal, and practical significance. *Baby M* set the stage for debates about the commodification of children, women's reproductive autonomy, and the meaning of family in an era of technological possibilities,[10] concerns now directed at the ever more sophisticated forms of assisted reproduction that have come into being since 1985.

In this essay I want to explore the *Baby M* case from a different, less philosophical perspective. The question I pose is simply this: How did the Sterns and the Whiteheads find one another in the first place? After all, aside from their New Jersey location (and a shared fondness for Bruce Springsteen?), the two couples had little in common.[11] Mary Beth was a high school dropout; Betsy had a Ph.D. and an M.D. from Michigan. Rick was a Vietnam vet fighting an ongoing battle with unemployment and alcoholism; Bill led what close friends called "a quiet, industrious life."[12] The Whiteheads and the Sterns didn't travel in the same social, employment, or consumer circles. How was it then that these two couples, strangers to each other with nothing in common but complementary desires, were able to connect and to reach a deal regarding the most intimate of arrangements: insemination, pregnancy, and parenthood? To put the question another way: How did a market for baby-making get going in New Jersey in the mid-1980s?

---

parental-role models and provide the day-to-day, parent-child interaction which will largely determine what kind of person Melissa will become . . . . William and Elizabeth Stern must accept and understand that Melissa will develop a different and special relationship with her mother, stepfather, siblings, and extended family, and that these relationships need not diminish their parent-child relationship with Melissa." 542 A.2d 52, 54 (N.J. Super. Ct. Ch. Div. 1988).

[10] See MARGARET JANE RADIN, CONTESTED COMMODITIES: THE TROUBLE WITH TRADE IN SEX, CHILDREN, BODY PARTS, AND OTHER THINGS (2001); ELIZABETH ANDERSON, VALUE IN ETHICS AND IN ECONOMICS (1993); Debra Satz, *Markets in Women's Reproductive Labor*, 21 Phil. & Pub. Affairs 107 (1992); MICHAEL SANDEL, THE MORAL LIMITS OF MARKETS: WHAT MONEY CAN'T BUY (1988).

[11] Although high school does not always predict future achievement, the graduating high school yearbooks of Rick, Bill, and Betsy offer a few clues. Bill was in the Latin Club, Library Staff, Spelunking Club, Chess Club, and United Nations Committee. Betsy's high school career is captured by the motto underneath her senior picture: "An accomplished girl is a girl worth knowing." Rick has a nice picture but apparently never joined a single club.

[12] Edelman, *supra* note 3 ("[The Sterns] don't smoke, they don't use drugs, they don't drink. They're so blah.").

In asking this, I put aside the question of whether there *should* be such a market as well as the question of what exactly surrogacy sells: the baby itself, the mother's reproductive services, or the mother's parental rights. I simply want to look at the market that did in fact exist and ask how it came about.

Markets

Before going further, we should stop to ask, just what is a market? The question may be a soft pitch for some, but because we are dealing with an unprecedented kind of transaction, at least circa 1985, it is worth starting from first principles. Economist John McMillan explains that a market for something exists if there are people who want to buy it and others who want to sell.[13] A market then is simply a network in which buyers and sellers interact to exchange goods or services for money. The market itself is the place where the trade occurs. It can be a physical place, like Wal-Mart or Wall Street, or it can exist in the ether, like eBay.

It is crucial to a market transaction that the parties to the trade, constrained as they may be by their own resources and by the rules of the marketplace, are nevertheless acting voluntarily.[14] They may not be happy with their overall situation, but under the circumstances each is happier in the exchange and wants to make the deal. At least at the time of the transaction, each is happier with what they are getting than with what they are giving up. This is how markets create value. Without a market people may wish they could make a trade but they can't. They are stuck with what they have. On the other hand, once a market brings an array of buyers and sellers together, there is no telling what they might exchange with one another.

Because trades produce gains, people are "relentless in finding ways to realize them"; as McMillan puts it, "markets have a way of breaking out."[15] They spring up in what might seem unlikely places, such as prisons or playgrounds, and they spring up in relation to new and imaginative ventures, like tanning or iPods. Some markets are carefully planned. Readers may remember seeing billboards a few years back of hipsters in silhouette somehow dancing to their own music through strange white earphones, and wondering just what product was being advertised. Other markets develop spontaneously: Consider the market in bootleg liquor that sprang up almost overnight during

---

[13] JOHN MCMILLAN, REINVENTING THE BAZAAR: A NATURAL HISTORY OF MARKETS 5 (2002).

[14] *Id*. at 6.

[15] *Id*. at 16.

Prohibition or the market in rationed goods during the Second World War.

Of course, the development of a market is never *entirely* spontaneous. There must be a mix of background conditions that make a particular trade both desirable and possible. There must be buyers who want the product, whether because it is the kind of thing people always want, like food, or because some have learned to want it, as with iPods. There must also be sellers willing to provide the goods or services, and the parties must be able to find one another and to agree on terms. These are some of the basics necessary for market formation.

This essay situates *Baby M* within the economic framework of a developing market. To be sure, commercial surrogacy—conception as economic exchange—is now big business worldwide.[16] I return here, however, to its origins. I argue that the market for surrogacy in the mid-1980s resulted from the intersection of four distinct factors that did not exist or would not have combined in just the same way ten years earlier or ten years later. The four factors are these: cultural attitudes toward parenthood and toward maternity, the state of reproductive technologies, the absence of controlling law, and the entrepreneurial intervention of intermediaries.

It is the last of these that may explain why the match between Baby M's parents proved such a disaster. This is certainly how the New Jersey Supreme Court sized things up. After describing the Sterns' childless plight and Mary Beth's desire to help, the court disapprovingly observed that "[t]he situation is ripe for the entry of the middleman who will bring some equilibrium into the market by increasing the supply through the use of money."[17] This is, of course, the very essence and point of intermediation. Middlemen everywhere, to use the court's words, are "propelled by profit." Nonetheless, the court made clear that "[w]hatever idealism may have motivated" the Sterns or the Whiteheads, middlemen had no business arranging a sale of this sort: "In New Jersey the surrogate mother's agreement to sell her child is void."[18] I suggest, however, that the problem that gave rise to *Baby M*—the mother's refusal to comply—arose not because intermediaries were *involved* but because they performed the job badly.

---

[16] The fertility business now generates over $3 billion a year in the United States alone. DEBORA L. SPAR, THE BABY BUSINESS: HOW MONEY, SCIENCE, AND POLITICS DRIVE THE COMMERCE OF CONCEPTION 3 (2006).

[17] 537 A.2d at 1249.

[18] *Id.*

The Desire for Children: Infertility

For a market in babies (or baby-making) to exist, babies must be something people affirmatively want and are willing to trade for.[19] The first part of the proposition may seem self-evidently true: Of course people want babies! While offspring might once have been desired for their contributions to the household economy or to secure care in one's dotage,[20] motivations for parenthood today, at least in the United States, have less to do with finances than with personal satisfaction.[21] Having children is understood as fun, a source of emotional fulfillment, a good reason to browse the Pottery Barn Kids catalogue.[22] For many people, having children makes life worth living. As the wife of one surrogate-seeking couple put it, "You participate in life in a different way when you have children."[23] The desire for *biological* children is particularly intense. While anthropologists point out "the centrality of biogenetic relatedness in Euro-American Kinship ideology,"[24] the simple

---

[19] For an early and important argument defending a legal market in babies for adoption, see Elisabeth M. Landes & Richard A. Posner, *The Economics of the Baby Shortage*, 7 J. Legal Stud. 323 (1978) (explaining how a market would increase the welfare of babies, birth mothers, childless couples, and taxpayers).

[20] In this regard, people did *not* always want babies. Babies need care and feeding and even then they might die and be of no economic use. In earlier times then, children were a more proven commodity; children, not babies, therefore commanded a price. See Mark Ramseyer, *The Market for Children: The Evidence from Early Japan*, 11 J.L. Econ. & Org. 127 (1995).

[21] The Gallup Poll, Vol. 55, No. 5, June 4, 1990.

[22] *See* Carol Sanger, *M Is for the Many Things*, 1 S. Cal. Rev. L. & Women's Stud. 15, 48–49 (1992) (observing that people want children for a range of reasons: to keep a marriage together; to meet social, spousal, or parental expectations; and to pass on the family name, genes, or silver). An expert witness testified that for Bill Stern, "the goal of maintaining the genetic family line was a chance to ward off existential loneliness"; Michelle Harrison, *Social Construction of Mary Beth Whitehead*, 1 Gender & Soc'y 300 (1987) (quoting Brodzinski deposition).

[23] *Baby Brokers Advertise "Wombs to Rent,"* Detroit Free Press, Sept. 20, 1989.

[24] Helena Ragone, *Chasing the Blood Tie*, 23 Am. Ethnologist 352, 355 (1996). This assumed preference for biological children was reflected in a range of adoption practices and protocols. Until fairly recently, adoptive couples had to prove their infertility; agencies feared adopted children might become second stringers if the parents later produced their own biological children. JUDITH S. MODELL, KINSHIP WITH STRANGERS: ADOPTION AND INTERPRETATIONS OF KINSHIP IN AMERICAN CULTURE (1994). Indeed, until the advent of open adoption in the 1990s, the very point of adoption was to simulate biological parenthood all the

idea of wanting one's own children is familiar, a commonplace and widely held aspiration.

But the more pertinent question for this inquiry is not why people desire children, but how they feel and what they do when they cannot have them in the ordinary course. What is the social and affective significance of infertility? Not surprisingly, the answer depends in great part on cultural attitudes toward childbearing: the greater the social or personal significance of being a parent, the greater the stigma and the harder the blow of childlessness. After all, at various points in time, "the meaning of parenthood has encompassed moral and civic obligation, marital and sexual success, personal maturity and normality."[25] Attitudes and responses to childlessness therefore change over time; looking just at the second half of the twentieth century, they seem to change almost by the decade. For example, as historian Elaine Tyler May has explained, the "baby boom" of the 1950s resulted not only from postwar prosperity but from a profound change in the national political culture: "The ideology of domesticity, focused on the nuclear family with children, came to embody the hope for the future of the nation and the ultimate achievement of happiness and personal satisfaction for its citizens."[26] Parenthood in the 1950s conferred not only full adult status, but also evidence of socially sanctioned heterosexuality and patriotic citizenship.[27]

This new "procreative consensus" had profound consequences for childless couples who in earlier periods might have mourned the absence of children but would have been less marginalized socially.[28] In the 1950s, infertility, especially for women, became deeply stigmatizing: a source of pity and a marker of biological failure (at best) and psy-

---

way down: Parents were counseled to keep the adoption secret; new replacement birth certificates were issued naming the adoptive mother as the birth mother.

[25] *See* JAN VERVEERS, CHILDLESS BY CHOICE 3–6 (1980).

[26] ELAINE TYLER MAY, BARREN IN THE PROMISED LAND: CHILDLESS AMERICANS AND THE PURSUIT OF HAPPINESS 129 (1995). *See also* ELAINE TYLER MAY, HOMEWARD BOUND: AMERICAN FAMILIES IN THE COLD WAR ERA 162–82 (1988).

[27] *See* MAY, BARREN IN THE PROMISED LAND, *supra* note 26, at 199–203.

[28] Movie stars offer some insights into the status of childlessness. Mary Pickford and Douglas Fairbanks (Google them!) had no children yet reigned as America's most glamorous couple. *See* MAY, BARREN IN THE PROMISED LAND, *supra* note 26, at 88. Today it is hard to buy anything without being regaled at the cash register with cover shots of some celebrity's latest.

chological deviance (at worst).[29] With few successful medical interventions, adoption became an acceptable and more popular method of acquiring children. Childless couples mimicked biological parenthood by adopting children who, under prevailing practices, were often matched by physical characteristics, enabling the adoptive parents to "pass" as natural parents.

The 1960s and early 1970s wrought a dynamic series of changes in cultural attitudes toward parenthood. "The pill" was invented, marketed, and used; contraception and abortion became legal. By the mid-1970s, a new procreative ethos had taken hold. Having children was no longer a matter of luck or fate but a decision that women had begun to make for themselves for the first time in history. Women's Liberation—and the beginning of sex equality in education and employment—had arrived, and what many women seemed to want to liberate themselves from was families. Motherhood could be postponed! Graduate school beckoned! Being "child-*free*" (as opposed to child*less*) was no longer necessarily a tragedy but, as the zero population growth movement reminded everyone, a socially responsible "life-style choice."[30] During this period, at least within educated upper-middle-class circles, *mothers* and not the childless were regarded with pity.

Then came the 1980s, with its renewed focus on the family. Parenthood was now imbued with the satisfactions of capitalism. According to the prevailing ethos, working hard and delaying gratification were understood to produce certain rewards: leisure, consumer goods, and a fulfilling private life in which children played a central role.[31] Movies captured the Zeitgeist. As one critic observed, "Men and women do not fall in love with each other in the movies anymore. They fall in love with babies. Babies are the new lovers—unpredictable, uncontrollable, impossible and irresistible."[32] As this new pro-natalism took hold, many women began to rethink their earlier, perhaps too hasty rejection of maternity. In addition, biological clocks started going off. Journalist Anne Taylor Fleming described her merciless, decades-long

---

[29] For an excellent discussion, see Margarete Sandelowski, *Failures of Volition: Female Agency and Infertility in Historical Perspective*, 15 SIGNS 475, 495 (1990).

[30] To be sure, childlessness was not a universal preference during this period; many women wanted to become mothers and were distraught when they could not. Margarete Sandelowski, *Fault Lines: Infertility and Imperiled Sisterhood*, 16 Feminist Stud. 33 (1990).

[31] MAY, BARREN IN THE PROMISED LAND, *supra* note 26, at 212.

[32] Delia Ephron, *In this Year's Movies Baby Knows Best*, N.Y. Times, Mar. 13, 1988, A&L, at 1.

quest to reproduce after having put it off to do other satisfying things: "babyless baby boomers," fast approaching age forty, became concerned with "cheating fate and getting our hands on an embryo, a baby, a life."[33] To be clear, in providing this quick historical snapshot my claim is not that the desire to have children is entirely or even primarily socially constructed. Infertility is a shattering diagnosis.[34] I am suggesting, however, that cultural attitudes regarding the meaning of parenthood, when combined with technologies that offer even the *chance* of biological parenthood, have made childlessness (and even adoption) less acceptable and that this in turn has important implications for the market demand for baby-making.

It is here that we meet up with Betsy Stern, who, at age forty-one, discovered she could not easily have children, and with Mary Beth Whitehead, age twenty-six, who was happy to have more.

The Desire for Children: Fertility

A market in surrogacy requires not only "buyers" who want babies but also suppliers who are willing to produce and part with them. This requires a more cabined and narrowly defined desire for babies: one that focuses on child*bearing* rather than child*raising*. Women who become surrogates accept—indeed, they seek out—what we might characterize as a partial or temporary form of motherhood: conception, pregnancy, and labor.[35] Moreover, they agree to do this for money. The agreement in *Baby M* was not what is sometimes called "altruistic surrogacy," as when one sister carries a baby for another purely for love. Mary Beth Whitehead was to receive $10,000. There is (or was) something deeply unsettling about this. Giving up one's child for profit suggests a form of maternity that is not only crimped but crass. It goes against everything that selfless American motherhood stands for. How then can a market for surrogacy take hold if the mother's participation, and to some extent the couple's, goes so violently against the cultural grain?[36]

---

[33] Anne Taylor Fleming, Motherhood Deferred 13–14 (1994).

[34] See, for example, the materials on coping with infertility offered by Resolve: The National Infertility Association at http://www.resolve.org.

[35] The deliberate "seeking out" distinguishes surrogacy from adoption. Unlike already pregnant women who place children for adoption, surrogate mothers affirmatively choose pregnancy for the very purpose of giving the baby to others to raise.

[36] I recognize that the social consensus on anything—including what one may buy—is seldom perfectly shared in a society. This explains why black

The answer is that for the participants, surrogacy is anchored (or at least moored) in acceptable pro-natalist ideology. Surrogate mothers are deeply invested in maternity: their own and that bestowed upon the couple. One surrogate explained it simply: "I'm a kind of mommy person and having a child is the single most wonderful thing I've done. . . . Nine months of my life is not that much to give to a couple."[37] Study after study reveals that women become surrogates for a combination of three reasons: they like being pregnant; they want the money; and despite the fact of payment, they regard having a baby for a childless couple as a gift—a blessing—of the highest order.[38] The first of these is not so hard to understand, even for those who have not had the pleasure. Pregnancy is for some women a deeply satisfying experience, both physically and socially. It often bestows an enhanced public status: Strangers smile at pregnant women and sometimes give them their seat on a bus.

But exactly because pregnancy is a public status,[39] the mother must have a story—an explanatory ideology—for herself and a morally acceptable explanation for her family and friends about what happened to the baby after the nine months has passed. The explanation is a complex blend of altruism and gain. The compatibility of the two is not so unfamiliar. People regularly take salaried jobs even though the primary motivation is not monetary: consider public school teachers or public interest lawyers. Thus despite the money, surrogate mothers conceptualize the transaction as a gift to the couple. As one surrogate mother explained, "Yes, this helped me financially but what I got out of

---

markets—whether in liquor or rationed goods or babies—arise when a transaction is forbidden. This inevitability has led many jurisdictions to regulate rather than to prohibit various socially disputed forms of commercial exchange. *See generally* MICHELLE GODWIN, BLACK MARKETS (2005).

[37] David Gelman & Daniel Shapiro, *Infertility: Babies by Contract*, Newsweek, Nov. 4, 1985. When she explained to her own husband that she intended to sign on as a surrogate, his response was, "Have you gone crackers or something?"

[38] Another reason given by some 10 percent of surrogates is the desire to compensate for an earlier reproductive loss such as an abortion or having placed a child for adoption. Hilary Hanafin, *Surrogate Parenting: Reassessing Human Bonding,* Center for Surrogate Parenting, Inc. & Egg Donation, Inc., *available at* http://www.creatingfamilies.com/hanafin.html. Philip J. Parker, *Motivation of Surrogate Mothers: Initial Findings,* 140 Am. J. Psychiatry 117 (1983).

[39] For a discussion of the rare but unhappy instances of concealed pregnancies, see Carol Sanger, *Infant Safe Haven Laws: Legislating in the Culture of Life*, 106 Colum. L. Rev. 753 (2006).

it was worth so much more than just the money."[40] Infertility centers capitalize on this understanding. Response levels increased dramatically when one agency changed the wording of its advertising copy from "Help an Infertile Couple" to "Give the Gift of Life," even though the payment scheme stayed the same.[41] As one mother put it, "What's 10,000 bucks? You can't even buy a car. My father would have given me the money *not* to do it."[42] I will say more about the price shortly, but for now, I want simply to underscore the way in which the ideology of reproductive altruism makes surrogacy possible. Although the exchange has a price, providing parenthood to the infertile—giving someone a baby—is regarded as a price beyond rubies and it is this characterization that surrogate mothers hang on to and with which most receiving couples agree.[43] There is, you might say, a market for altruism.

Surrogacy draws on maternal values in another way: It enables women to take care of their own children throughout the pregnancy, thus enhancing their existing status as mothers.[44] As Mary Beth Whitehead explained, the deal with the Sterns was, like other jobs she had taken (except maybe go-go dancing in her sister's bar), a way of increasing the family income "without taking me away from my children."[45] In this way surrogacy uniquely combines the preference of

---

[40] Resolve Fact Sheet 56 (Surrogacy), http://www.resolve.org. Not all surrogates (or at least not all of their boyfriends) are into altruism. One young man who had accompanied his girlfriend to Keane's Michigan offices stated quite clearly: "[T]he baby means absolutely nothing. It's like watching someone's car for nine months. We're in it for the money; it's a business. That's the way we look at it." Anne Taylor Fleming, *Our Fascination with Baby M*, N.Y. Times Magazine, March 29, 1987.

[41] *See* Ragone, *supra* note 24, at 355.

[42] *Id.*

[43] *Id.* at 356 (reporting that most couples believe that money is "never sufficient to repay the debt they have incurred").

[44] Surrogacy programs now require surrogates either to be mothers or to have experienced pregnancy and childbirth in order for them to more fully appreciate the nature of their decision.

[45] MARY BETH WHITEHEAD, A MOTHER'S STORY: THE TRUTH ABOUT THE BABY M CASE 80 (1989) (with Loretta Schwartz-Nobel). Whitehead also believed that providing another couple with a baby might in some sort of karmic way help her own infertile sister become pregnant. In addition, the money surrogates earn is always used for *family* needs and expenses, and rarely spent on the mother herself. This may serve to pay children and spouse back for the costs that the pregnancy imposes on them. Consider, for example, that the surrogate

some women to be traditional stay-at-home moms while engaging in paid labor at the same time.[46] It recognizes the value of reproductive work of women who, in the never-ending schism between career and home, often feel undervalued. Popular culture played its part in "widening the gulf between women with children and women who wanted them by telegraphing to the less blessed endless pictures of us allegedly liberated hussies abstaining from motherhood and running marathons."[47] On this score, surrogacy may produce at least the appearance of some social leveling: the surrogates' fertility makes up for "perceived, if unacknowledged, economic differences" between the surrogate and the commissioning couple.[48]

In sum, we seem to have the essential ingredients for market exchange: willing couples who want to raise genetically related children and fertile women willing to produce them.[49]

---

and her partner must abstain from sex during the entire fertilization process. This is an externality worth thinking through.

[46] Not all surrogates stay at home. In a study of forty-one women recruited by Noel Keane between 1981 and 1985, nearly a third kept their regular jobs during their pregnancies. Nancy E. Reame & Philip J. Parker, *Surrogate Pregnancy: Clinical Features of Forty-four Cases*, 162 Am. J. Obstetrics & Gynecology 1220, 1221 (1990). On the appeal to mothers of working at home, see Eileen Boris, *Homework and Women's Rights: The Case of the Vermont Knitters, 1980–1985*, 13 SIGNS 98 (1987).

[47] FLEMING, *supra* note 33, at 181.

[48] Ragone, *supra* note 24, at 358.

[49] Throughout this discussion I have discussed surrogacy as an arrangement with the couple on one hand and the surrogate on the other. In fact, the relational dynamics are more complicated and involve at least three other pairings. To begin, commissioning husbands and wives may not come to the surrogacy decision with equal enthusiasm. Certainly a traditional surrogate is the *husband's* best option for a genetically related child, but little work has been done on the gender dynamics of reproductive desire. Would wives be as or more satisfied with adoption, for example, than with a child that is related only to the husband? Surrogacy also requires negotiation and understanding between the surrogate and her husband or partner. After all, he is, like Richard Whitehead, involved legally, practically, and to some extent emotionally in the arrangement. Finally, the relationship between the surrogate and husband of the commissioning couple is also complex. As Ragone points out, reproduction is usually associated with sex yet in surrogacy the mother of the husband's child is not his sexual partner. One consequence of this somewhat awkward intimacy seems to be that a closer relationship develops between the *wife* and the surrogate than between the husband and the surrogate. After fertilization, his social role is de-emphasized. *See* Ragone, *supra* note 24, at 359–61.

Technology

The market for surrogacy in 1985 was also determined by the state of reproductive technology. Nontechnological surrogacy—a woman bearing a child for a childless couple—had been around for ages. Several infertile biblical wives (Rachel, Sarah) commanded their husbands to "go in unto" their maids (Bilhah, Hagar) in order to beget children and build a family. By the mid-twentieth century, the mechanics of surrogacy had changed. Artificial insemination meant that husbands no longer had to "go in unto" anyone: "arm's length conception" was now available.[50] If the husband was the infertile partner, wives could be inseminated with donor sperm and, at least in the pre-DNA days of the early 1980s, no one in or outside the family need be the wiser.[51] The situation was more complicated and less private in the case of female infertility: The production of a child using the husband's sperm necessarily involved the participation of another woman.

If Betsy Stern had discovered her infertility ten years earlier, adoption would have been the couple's sole route to parenthood. Ten years later, there was an expanded set of options. The Sterns would probably have attempted a combination of in-vitro fertilization (mixing Betsy's eggs with Bill's sperm in a petri dish) and gestational surrogacy (implanting the resulting embryo into another woman who would then carry and deliver the baby).[52] Today, 95 percent of all surrogacy arrangements are for gestational surrogacy,[53] and the Sterns considered

---

[50] *See* SPAR, *supra* note 16, at 73.

[51] As one mother who conceived via artificial insemination explained, "We won't tell [our daughter]—or our friends or family—because there's no way she can find that father. It is our secret; it will go with us to the grave." Anne Taylor Fleming, *New Frontiers in Conception*, N.Y. Times Magazine, July 20, 1980.

[52] Betsy's age—forty-one in 1985—and the viability of her eggs would have been the primary complication. Age has limited the availability of surrogacy as a remedy for negligence. In an English case, Briody v. St Helens & Knowsley Area Health Authority, [2002] 2 W.L.R. 394, [2001] 2 F.L.R. 1094, (2001), the plaintiff successfully sued her physician whose negligence caused her to have a hysterectomy. The court refused to award her the costs of hiring a traditional surrogate. The plaintiff's age made it unlikely that she would have succeeded with in-vitro fertilization using her own eggs and a gestational surrogate. Traditional surrogacy—artificially inseminating a younger woman who would carry the baby to term—would therefore put the plaintiff in a better position than she would have been in.

[53] Indeed, 30 percent of surrogacy agencies in the United States now offer only gestational surrogacy. Mhairi Galbraith, Hugh V. McLachlan & J. Kim Swales, *Commercial Agencies and Surrogate Motherhood: A Transaction Cost Approach*, 13 Health Care Analysis 11 (2005).

it even then. But as Bill testified, "at that time nobody in this country was doing it, it was strictly experimental."[54] If in 1985 Bill Stern wanted to transmit Stern genes to the next generation, he needed a fully integrated surrogate. He needed a Mary Beth Whitehead.

The State of the Law

Law plays a crucial role in market development in several regards. In the first instance, it provides a system of property rights against which exchanges take place. People want to know with certainty what is theirs to sell and what interests they acquire when they buy something.[55] In the area of reproductive commerce, however, the question of whether or the extent to which babies, sperm and eggs, or frozen embryos are property is complicated and only partially resolved. Still, even without a definitive property regime, the law can still clarify the legal relationships that result from the various procreative arrangements, and in this way influence market development. Artificial insemination (AI) provides a good example. Although by the mid-1950s AI was easy to accomplish technologically, few doctors offered it as a treatment for infertility because of its murky legal status; a few early cases had held that a child born through AI was the product of adultery.[56] Once the law regarding paternity was settled—statutes now generally provide that a child born to a wife using donor sperm is legally the child of the married couple and not of the sperm donor[57]—the market for sperm and insemination services took off.

While property rights create the background incentives, contract

---

[54] Testimony of William Stern, 1 Trial Transcripts 82–83. The technical problem was that although researchers could retrieve eggs during ovulation, they were unable to sustain the eggs in vitro awaiting fertilization. *See* SPAR, *supra* note 16, at 21–25.

[55] *See* JAMES M. BUCHANAN, THE LIMITS OF LIBERTY: BETWEEN ANARCHY AND LEVIATHAN 17–23 (1975); Douglass C. North, *Institutions,* 5 J. Econ. Persp., Winter 1991, at 97; Harry Scheiber, *Regulation, Property Rights, and the Definition of the Market,* 41 J. Econ. Hist. 103 (1981).

[56] *See* Gaia Bernstein, *The Socio-legal Acceptance of New Technologies: A Close Look at Artificial Insemination,* 77 Wash. L. Rev. 1035 (2002); *see also Note,* 1982 B.Y.U. L. Rev. 935.

[57] The child is legally the couple's so long as the husband agreed to the insemination. This explains why Richard Whitehead, the husband of an inseminated wife, was asked to sign a "Statement of Non-consent" as part of the overall agreement: "I, Richard Whitehead . . . recognize that by refusing to consent to the insemination, I cannot legally be declared or considered to be the legal father of any child conceived thereby." Exhibit G, 6 Trial Transcripts.

law stabilizes markets by clarifying when agreements or particular terms in agreements are enforceable. Parties are more likely to enter into deals if they know that the law will compel performance, or at least compensate its breach. The inability to enforce a contract because it is illegal or violates public policy is likely to thwart the development of new markets and shut down existing ones (or drive them underground into "black markets" with their many associated inefficiencies). When the law is clear on enforceability, people gain confidence and business picks up. California surrogacy firms now regularly advertise that state's receptivity to contractual reproductive arrangements: "Infertile couples around the world have found California to be a favorable legal forum. . . . Prospective parents, surrogates, and egg donors can be reasonably certain that their intentions, as expressed by their agreement, will be upheld in California."

In contrast, the legal status of surrogacy in New Jersey before the *Baby M* decision was up for grabs. Unlike Michigan, where in 1981 a judge had ruled that paying surrogates violated the state's prohibition on baby-selling,[58] there were no adverse judicial opinions or statutory bans in New York or New Jersey. Indeed, the Michigan ruling was exactly why Noel Keane, the person who brought the Sterns and the Whiteheads together, had opened an East Coast office in the first place.[59] As he later commented, "if the point of the [Michigan] law was to . . . stop surrogate parenting in its tracks, . . . it has fallen on its face."[60] Keane was acutely aware of the legal vacuum in which he operated, and he made sure that the couples who used his services understood that they bore the risk of this indeterminacy. The ICNY contract with Bill Stern stated clearly that "ICNY makes no representations or warranties with respect to matters of law or the legality of surrogate parenting."[61]

There is, however, one way in which the implications of an agreeable legal regime play out differently in a market for surrogacy than with many other enterprises. Unlike, say, corporations, where a firm can incorporate in Delaware but conduct its business wherever it is

---

[58] *See* Doe v. Kelley, No. 78 815 531 CZ (Wayne County Cir. Ct. Jan. 28, 1980) (cited in NOEL KEANE, THE SURROGATE MOTHER 336 (1981) (with Dennis Breo)).

[59] Nadine Brozan, *Surrogate Mothers: Problems and Goals*, N.Y. Times, Feb. 27, 1984, at C12.

[60] Saundry Torry, *Wrestling with Surrogate Motherhood*, Wash. Post, Feb. 12, 1989.

[61] Stern-ICNY Contract.

really located, the relational aspects of a commissioned pregnancy make physical proximity between the parties more important. Close relationships between the surrogate and the couple, especially the wife, are common; the satisfactions of this relationship to the surrogate are one reason why the agreements so rarely implode. "Distanced surrogacy" is certainly possible, but may increase the likelihood of breach by the lonely surrogate whose loyalties may attach to the baby rather than the couple.[62]

The Role of Intermediaries

Many buyers and sellers deal with one another without the efforts or interventions of middlemen. Verizon runs an ad offering 200 extra minutes; if consumers are interested, they contact Verizon. Similarly, if you want to sell your car, you might put a "For Sale" sign on a side window and wait to see who gives you a call. On the other hand, you could sell your car to a car dealer (probably for less), get the cash, and be done with it. This has advantages for you and for buyers who want a car like yours and are more likely to find it at the dealer's than in your driveway.

Middlemen or intermediaries operate across a huge range of consumer, commercial, and financial markets; indeed, intermediation activities comprise at least one-quarter of the gross domestic product.[63] Some, like the car dealer and most retailers and wholesalers, buy the goods for resale. Others, like real estate agents or dating services, act strictly as matchmakers, connecting parties who then contract directly with one another.[64] Without intermediaries, mutually beneficial deals may be lost because buyers and sellers will not be able to find one another or to strike a deal.[65] Middlemen take advantage of the lack or imbalance (the "asymmetries") of information that would-be trading partners have about one another, about the product, or about other aspects of the market. They save parties the time, effort and money ("search costs") that it would otherwise take to find the right trading partner (someone who has what you want on acceptable terms). Intermediaries reduce transaction costs and, at the same time, earn a profit

---

[62] The global outsourcing of surrogacy, especially now that gestational surrogacy is the norm, has interesting market (and regulatory) implications.

[63] Daniel F. Spulber, *Market Microstructure and Intermediation*, 10 J. Econ. Persp., Summer 1996, at 137.

[64] *See* Abdullah Yavas, *Marketmakers versus Matchmakers*, 2 J. Fin. Mediation 33 (1992).

[65] *See* McMILLAN, *supra* note 13, at 45.

for themselves.[66] They make money ("capture some of the gains of the trade") by improving the likelihood a trade will take place.

In addition to matching, intermediaries perform other functions designed to smooth the way to a deal. These include seeking out suppliers, finding and encouraging buyers, helping set prices and terms, and sometimes monitoring performance.[67] They inform buyers and sellers on the state of the market, enabling them to form reasonable expectations. Here too intermediaries bridge informational asymmetries: "When the characteristics of buyers and sellers are unobservable, intermediaries market information and provide guaranties for market quality. When the actions of buyers and sellers are costly to observe, intermediaries provide monitoring and contracting services."[68] By providing these various coordination functions—helping buyers and sellers meet and transact—intermediaries create and operate markets.

With all this in mind, let us turn to the middleman responsible for much of what transpired in *Baby M.* I want to focus on how three intermediation functions—searching and matching, price setting, and quality control—played out in the transaction that enveloped the Whiteheads and the Sterns.

Enter Noel Keane

Although he described himself, with mock disparagement, as "the East Dearborn kid who wasn't smart enough for college,"[69] by the early 1980s, attorney Noel Keane was described by just about everyone else as "the undisputed father of surrogate motherhood."[70] The most prominent of the handful of early lawyers and doctors offering surrogacy services, Keane was regarded as "a pioneer." An early press piece in the *New York Times* reported that Keane "[r]evolutionized the production of babies just as surely as that earlier son of Dearborn, Henry Ford, revolutionized the production of automobiles."[71] Keane explained his passion for surrogacy in terms of religion and compassion. Affirming

---

[66] Spulber, *supra* note 63, at 147.

[67] *Id.* at 135.

[68] *Id.* at 136. Consider rental agencies that supervise properties, monitor tenants, and sometimes collect rents for landlords.

[69] *See* KEANE, *supra* note 58, at 126.

[70] James S. Kunen, *Childless Couples Seeking Surrogate Mothers Call Michigan Lawyer Noel Keane—He Delivers*, N.Y. Times, March 30, 1987. By 1987, Keane had arranged one-third of the 500 or so births resulting from commissioned pregnancies nationwide.

[71] *Id.*

his strong Catholic faith, Keane explained that he was "making my stand on the side of people who want to create life."[72] "If you have not been there, if you have not wanted children or had no problem in having your own, then you cannot presume to know what drives these childless people. I believe in surrogate motherhood because I believe there are thousands of people who want it and need it, including the surrogate mothers. I intend to help them."[73] When asked how he responded to criticism of surrogacy, he replied, "Who gives a s—? That's my response."[74]

Keane had arranged his first surrogacy contract in 1976 after a childless couple asked his help in finding a woman to bear the child they so desperately wanted. Moved by their plight and intrigued by occasional news reports of similar arrangements here and there around the country, Keane agreed. Finding such a woman was no small challenge. Surrogacy was neither a household word nor a familiar (let alone acceptable) practice. As in other types of new markets, would-be suppliers were not readily identifiable; indeed, most women, unaware of a market in pregnancy, would not have identified themselves as potential suppliers. (Think about how eBay made you realize there was stuff in your closet someone would actually buy just as it lured you into bidding on things you never knew you wanted.) To stir up business, Keane had to get the word out. His initial efforts fell flat. The classified sections of the *Detroit Free Press* and the *Detroit News* rejected Keane's advertisement soliciting surrogates outright.[75] Keane then turned to local college papers, which were less fussy and took the ad (and his $20).

Here things began to pick up. An inquisitive local reporter saw Keane's futuristic-sounding ad—"Childless husband with infertile wife wants female donor for test-tube baby"—in the *Michigan Daily* and arranged to meet with Keane. The interview was featured on the front

---

[72] This is not the view of the Catholic Church.

[73] KEANE, *supra* note 58, at 24.

[74] *Id.*

[75] A decade later, there was still reluctance to accept surrogacy ads. An Indiana lawyer submitted seeking-surrogate advertisements to 155 newspapers in 1987; 20 were accepted. *Baby Brokers Advertise for "Wombs to Rent,"* Detroit Free Press, Sept. 20, 1989. Some brokers found success with small shopper newspapers and city arts publications. Others were more inventive: a Texas firm put flyers on thousands of car windshields in a Houston parking lot, and a Kentucky broker made up T-shirts that read, "Babies by Levin." *Id.* Levin now uses the slogan for his Web site; *see* http://www.babies-by-levin.com/spa_google.htm.

page of the *Ann Arbor News*, complete with a photo of the couple in silhouette and Keane looking professorial in wire-rimmed glasses. The story was picked up by the Associated Press and published nationwide. Publicity snowballed as Keane granted more print and radio interviews and made the first of his five appearances on the *Phil Donahue Show*, an early and extremely popular daytime talk show.

Keane grasped the situation well. As he explained in his memoir, "I went on shows like *Donahue* for a simple reason. Other than placing classified ads, the only effective way of finding surrogate mothers was through television and news articles. The true fathers of the surrogate motherhood story, perhaps are the *Phil Donahue Show* and *People Magazine*."[76] Applications from women seeking to be surrogates began to roll in.[77] Mary Beth Whitehead learned of surrogacy through a Keane advertisement in the local *Asbury Park Press*, though by this time the price was fixed and the test-tube baby language had been replaced by more familiar vocabulary:

> SURROGATE MOTHER WANTED. Couple unable to have children willing to pay $10,000 fee and expenses to woman to carry husband's child. Conception by artificial insemination. All replies strictly confidential.[78]

Keane's advertising strategy not only produced surrogate mothers. The publicity introduced—normalized—the idea of surrogacy to childless couples as well. Regularizing surrogacy, an enterprise that certainly at the beginning "skat[ed] on the thin edge of acceptability,"[79]

---

[76] KEANE, *supra* note 58, at 173–74. Over time, Keane's advertising became more directed as niche surrogacy markets developed. In the early 1990s, Keane ran ads in Korean language newspapers in order to find Asian-American women for insemination by Japanese husbands: "[The women] don't have to be Japanese-American. We're only looking for the Asian quality, particularly the eyes." *See* Mark Alpert, *New U.S. Export to Japan: Babies*, Fortune, Aug. 10, 1992. Fees for the service were approximately $75,000 (excluding airfare).

[77] The campus ads alone produced more than 200 responses from women seeking fees that ranged from $200 to $10,000. *Hiring Mothers*, Time, June 5, 1978.

[78] 525 A.2d at 1162.

[79] Deborah L. Spar, *For Love or Money: The Political Economy of Commercial Surrogacy*, 12 Rev. Int'l Pol. Econ. 287, 289 (2005). Spar observes that because of its uncertain legal status, traditional surrogacy remained relatively rare throughout the 1980s—only a hundred matches in 1988. She characterizes surrogacy agreements as "the fodder for talk shows, perhaps, but not the makings of a market." *Id.* at 295. My argument is that the talk shows themselves contributed significantly to the makings of the market.

Keane became the go-to guy for couples yearning for a child who could be (at least half) genetically their own. Baby M's own father, William Stern, got the idea after seeing an ad seeking surrogates in a New York newspaper and remembering Keane's earlier television appearance.[80] After sending for brochures from a few infertility centers, Betsy and Bill Stern settled on the ICNY.

The surrogate-selection process worked as follows. Women applied to Keane for acceptance as potential surrogates; he called them "hosts" in the early days. Acceptance was conditioned on what Keane himself later characterized as a "minimal pre-sign-up screening."[81] After they filled out a questionnaire detailing such factors as health, education, maternal status, and income, an in-house psychologist interviewed selected applicants in person to evaluate their ability to consent to a surrogacy arrangement. If the psychologist determined that the woman was able to give informed consent to participating in a surrogacy arrangement, she was accepted into the program. She was then eligible for selection by couples, themselves unscreened, seeking surrogates. In Keane's Michigan office, prospective parents and would-be surrogates met on Saturday mornings in something close to reproductive speed-dating: each couple was assigned a private office through which surrogates would rotate. "On the heels of the surrogates, Noel Keane or his female assistant, would slip quietly in to confer with the couples to see if any matches were in the offing."[82] In New York, couples similarly sifted through albums of candidates; ICNY would then set up meetings between couples and selected candidates.[83] Although still headquartered in Dearborn, Keane traveled regularly to New York to meet with couples, though he never met the Sterns. Once the couple had chosen a surrogate, Keane then arranged for her to see a psychologist and a lawyer and for the doctors who were to perform the inseminations. As the Sixth Circuit Court of Appeals later noted, "Keane operated both as a lawyer for the contracting father and as the manager of a business."[84]

---

[80] Testimony of William Stern, 1 Trial Transcripts 80 (Direct).

[81] KEANE, *supra* note 58, at 20 (admitting that "some people were allowed to be surrogate mothers who upon hindsight might better have been rejected").

[82] Fleming, *supra* note 40.

[83] Keane's leading competitor, Dr. Richard M. Levin of Kentucky, did not permit the surrogates and couples to meet one another. Selection was made solely on the basis of written information. *See* Note, *In Defense of Surrogate Parenting: A Critical Analysis of the Recent Kentucky Experience*, 69 Ky. L.J. 877, 882–83 (1980–81).

[84] Stiver v. Parker, 975 F.2d 261, 265 (1992).

Mary Beth had not been the Sterns' first choice. After reading through the 300 applications on file at the ICNY, they had found a woman who seemed terrific. However, as Betsy testified at trial, on the day of their scheduled appointment, "the pipes in her house burst and she cancelled."[85] Only then did ICNY mention Mary Beth Whitehead: a "woman who had been working with another couple, a very highly motivated person [who] wanted to do this in the worst way and would do it for anybody so long as he had a viable sperm count."[86] Impressed with the statement of motivation on her application—"Knowing that I can give the most loving gift of happiness to an unfortunate couple plus the financial benefit to my family would be a rewarding experience"[87]— Bill and Betsy arranged to meet Rick and Mary Beth at a restaurant in New Brunswick. The meeting went well and after an hour the Sterns decided that "she was like too good to be true and we didn't want to give her up and so we agreed."[88]

Several factors made Mary Beth particularly appealing. Because she had worked with another couple for eight months, the Sterns figured she knew what surrogacy was about and was unlikely to "show up on our doorstep."[89] Moreover, Rick's vasectomy seemed a clear indication that "the Whiteheads really didn't want any more children." Bill testified that "Rick, in fact, said if Mary Beth wanted to keep the kid, he'd walk right out on her."[90] The deal informally agreed to, ICNY then drew up the formal documents; as Betsy recalled, everything was "straightforward and simple and [ICNY] would take care of everything for us."[91] On February 6, 1985, everyone signed.

On February 6, the Sterns also paid ICNY its $7,500 fee and put $10,000 in escrow for Mary Beth. Neither price was negotiated but rather both were set by ICNY. As with other issues on which there are informational asymmetries, intermediaries often smooth the way by helping establish prices. As with searching, agreeing on a price is time

---

[85] Testimony of Elizabeth Stern, 1 Trial Transcripts 83 (Direct).

[86] Testimony of William Stern, 1 Trial Transcripts 105 (Direct). After eight frustrating months of unsuccessful inseminations with Mary Beth's first couple, the husband was finally tested and found to have a low (unviable) sperm count.

[87] Testimony of William Stern, 1 Trial Transcripts 91 (Direct).

[88] *Id.* at 119.

[89] Testimony of William Stern, 1 Trial Transcripts 120–21 (Direct). As Bill testified, "she's got to know what she's been doing for all those eight months."

[90] Testimony of Elizabeth Stern, 1 Trial Transcripts 118–19 (Direct).

[91] Testimony of William Stern, 1 Trial Transcripts 92 (Direct).

consuming and also something of a gamble, particularly in a market where parties have little idea about the market value of the exchange and where there are few repeat players: most couples engage with surrogacy just once in their lives. Again, the middleman—here ICNY—extracts a surplus in exchange for shortening the period that buyers and sellers have to wait for a transaction.[92]

It is important to remember that a brokered deal involves *two* prices: the broker's own fee and the amount exchanged between the parties. The middleman's markup often "depends positively on the rate of impatience."[93] This explains why the fee to surrogacy brokers is so high, often close to or equal that paid to the surrogate. Commissioning couples are frustrated with their inability to produce a child *before* they enter the market—indeed, that frustration is what has driven them into the market in the first place. Their first preference would have been to proceed the old-fashioned way. They have to wait nearly a year (if things go well) even after they have contracted with the surrogate. Surrogacy brokers further shorten the entire waiting period by having a good supply of surrogates on hand.

Setting the second price—the one between the couple and the surrogate—is complicated because the exchange is emotionally laden on both sides and in ways that pull in opposite directions. Childless couples with means (and sometimes couples without) are often willing to pay anything: "We'd sell the car, the house even, if it comes to it. . . . There is nothing I wouldn't give up if it meant we could have a child."[94] At the same time, the fees paid to surrogates themselves are fairly low. As Mary Beth later pointed out, her $10,000 would have cashed out at $1.47 an hour.[95] The price (as well as the fact of payment discussed earlier) appears to be mediated by the mother's belief in the value—the nobility—of her service. Although surrogates want to be paid, they do not want to appear (and in general are not) mercenary. The reconciliation of payment and altruism—a kind of seller schizophrenia—is managed by keeping the price relatively low. The money signals that their labor has value; the modest sum underscores the essence of the deal as

---

[92] Ariel Rubenstein & Asher Wolinksy, *Middlemen*, 102 Q.J. Econ. 581 (1987).

[93] *Id.* at 591.

[94] JUDITH LASKER & SUSAN BORG, IN SEARCH OF PARENTHOOD: COPING WITH INFERTILITY AND HIGH-TECH CONCEPTION 11 (1987).

[95] *Whitehead's Appeal Says She Wasn't Paid Minimum Wage*, St. Petersburg Times, April 15, 1987, at A1.

a gift transaction.[96]

Things Fall Apart

In thinking about what went wrong in this case, it is easy to say, as many did, that Mary Beth was a scoundrel,[97] or alternatively, that in refusing to surrender Baby M, she finally came to her senses and exposed surrogacy for what it is. The question of "what surrogacy is" in any moral sense remains a hard one. For some, the very facts of the case—the wealth disparity between the couples, the literal tug-of-war over an infant—sufficiently indict the enterprise. But I want to stick with the game plan, accept the market, and return our attention to the role of the middleman in all of this.

In addition to searching, matching, and pricing services, there is another reason why parties turn to intermediaries and pay their fees. Brokers also provide parties with some level of assurance about the quality of the deal.[98] They know more about customer characteristics and about product features than novice, one-time transactors who are far less able to efficiently investigate such things themselves.[99] Some assurances, like warranties, attract parties because they are explicit; consider the Saturn. In other cases, the broker's general reputation

---

[96] In economic terms, the low fee acts as a "utility bribe" stimulating participation by fertile women who rightly believe their work has value (hence deserving of some payment) but who would withdraw from the market if the payment were so high as to overshadow the altruistic component. *See* Gillian Hewitson, *The Market for Surrogate Mother Contracts*, 73 Econ. Rec. 212, 222 (1997). Another way to look at the relatively low fee is as a screening mechanism. By offering a price that is not too high, middlemen screen out women so focused on money that they might be willing to engage in after-birth holdups or in undesirable behavior during the pregnancy. For the social meaning of payment, especially among intimates, see VIVIANA ZELIZER, THE PURCHASE OF INTIMACY (2005); VIVIANA ZELIZER, THE SOCIAL MEANING OF MONEY (1994).

[97] The trial court said much worse. In granting custody to the Sterns and terminating Mary Beth's parental rights, Judge Sorkow found that Mary Beth was "unreliable in so far as her promise is concerned . . . manipulative, impulsive and exploitive. She is also, for the most part, untruthful. . . . Her lack of candor makes her a poor candidate to report to the child in an age appropriate manner and time, the facts of the child's origin. She is a woman without empathy." 525 A.2d 1128, 1170 (N.J. Super. Ct. Ch. Div. 1987). *See also Polls Show Most in U.S. Back Baby M. Ruling*, N.Y. Times, Apr. 12, 1987 (reporting that after the trial court decision, 69 percent of the public agreed that surrogate mothers should be required to abide by their agreements).

[98] Spulber, *supra* note 63, at 147–148.

[99] *See* Gary Biglaiser, *Middlemen as Experts*, 24 Rand J. Econ. 212 (1993).

draws business. A good example from the world of reproduction are Danish sperm banks, which became known worldwide for providing a superior product ("the Danish stuff").[100] Their reputation grew for several reasons: Danish sperm banks require men selling their sperm to undergo unusually rigorous testing and evaluation; the banks resell only to doctors; and Danish law requires strict anonymity. These are attractive features to both buyers and sellers concerned with quality now[101] and privacy down the road.[102]

Exactly what assurances does a *surrogacy* broker provide? Other than providing an array of approved candidates from which couples themselves selected a trading partner, Noel Keane's answer was, "almost none." The ICNY contract with William Stern was absolutely clear about this:

> It is expressly understood that ICNY does not guarantee or warrant that the "surrogate mother" will in fact conceive a child; nor . . . that if a child is conceived, it will be a healthy child; nor [that] the "surrogate mother" . . . will comply with the terms and provisions of the separate agreement entered into between herself and the Natural Father, including but not limited to the "surrogate mother's" refusal to surrender custody of the child upon birth.[103]

Keane disclaimed any liability for whatever did or did not transpire once the parties had made their match and left ICNY.

But Keane could not have become the king of surrogacy if his clients were regularly frustrated in their quest for a baby. His reputation depended on the fertility and the fidelity of his candidates, and most Keane clients *were* satisfied.[104] Before Mary Beth's refusal, only three

---

[100] SPAR, *supra* note 16, at 38–39. The leader, Cryos International Sperm Bank, ships to fifty countries.

[101] *See* Rabin Schatz, *40 Sperm Donors Not Tested*, Newsday, July 15, 1993 (reporting that husband donors were not tested for hepatitis, HIV, gonorrhea, or syphilis before surrogates were inseminated). The donors were all clients of Idant, Noel Keane's insemination service.

[102] *See* SPAR, *supra* note 16, at 38–39.

[103] Stern-ICNY Contract.

[104] For an exception, see Stiver v. Parker, 975 F.2d 261 (6th Cir. 1992), in which a surrogate mother was inseminated with the untested sperm of a Keane client. Both she and the fetus contracted a sexually transmitted disease and the baby was born with severe birth anomalies. The case was particularly complicated in that the child proved not to be the genetic child of the sperm donor but of the surrogate's husband. The court held that Keane, "the surrogacy

other Keane deals had fallen through because the birth mother changed her mind; none received much notice, in part because none was litigated. For Keane, such disrupted deals were something to be expected in the intense world of surrogacy: "We are dealing with human beings with emotions, which makes it impossible to get to zero."[105]

But Mary Beth's behavior was not quite, as Keane later described it, an "unavoidable aberration." ICNY had information about Mary Beth that might well have given the Sterns—and the Whiteheads—pause had it been disclosed. After interviewing Mary Beth for an hour and a half, Keane's New York psychologist, Dr. Joan Einwohner, observed that although "[Ms. Whitehead] does not want to rear more children now that her own are in school . . . , she expects to have strong feelings about giving up the baby at the end."[106] Einwohner explained further that she had "some concern about [Whitehead's] tendency to deny feelings and think it would be important to explore with her in somewhat more depth whether she will be able to relinquish the child at the end." She then concluded her page-and-a-half report: "Except for the above reservations, Ms. Whitehead is recommended as an appropriate candidate for being a surrogate volunteer."[107] The Einwohner report was not shown to or discussed with Mary Beth, who recalled that "they just told me I had passed."[108] When it was uncovered during the litigation, Mary Beth sued Keane and the ICNY for negligence and fraud for failing to properly caution her about the difficulties they knew she might encounter in giving up a baby.[109] The Sterns had also never seen the

---

business designer and broker, and the other defendant professionals who profited from the program, owed affirmative duties" to [both the surrogate and the sperm donor], the surrogacy program beneficiaries." *Id.* at 268.

[105] Jane Gross, *Fears Ease over Contracts for Babies*, N.Y. Times, Apr. 2, 1987.

[106] Einwohner Report, April 26, 1984.

[107] *Id.* Einwohner further noted that "[i]t would be very important to [Ms. Whitehead] to have the emotional support of the adoptive parents during pregnancy and birth and a friendly relationship with them." This never happened. By the eighth month, Mary Beth resented Betsy's making suggestions regarding Mary Beth's health matters and requiring her to undergo amniocentesis, a diagnostic procedure rarely performed on twenty-six-year-old pregnant women.

[108] The evaluation was conducted in 1984 when Mary Beth first registered with ICNY. After the contract with couple number one fell through, no additional evaluation was made.

[109] The suit was later settled for some $30,000. Guy Sterling, *Surrogate Mom Sues Infertility Center for Fraud*, N.Y. Times, Oct. 15, 1986. Mary Beth also sued the gynecologist who performed the insemination, alleging that she

report; Bill explained at trial that he relied on ICNY's expertise, "on the fact that they said she was tested and approved."[110]

A second piece of undisclosed information also left Mary Beth feeling burned; she insisted it would have been a complete deal breaker had she only known. The issue concerned Betsy Stern's infertility. The contract between Mary Beth and Bill stated that "[t]he only reason for this contract is to enable William Stern and his infertile wife to have a child which is biologically related to William Stern." Similarly, a Declaration of Intent, required by ICNY for the February 6 closing and copied out in longhand by Mary Beth, stated that "I understand that the child to be conceived by me is being done so only because the wife of William Stern, natural father, is unable to bear a child."[111] In light of the contract references to infertility and inability, the ICNY ad, and the very name "Infertility Center of New York," Mary Beth believed that the Sterns could not have children of their own. Indeed, on one of the insemination commutes into the city, Mary Beth ventured to ask Bill outright what was wrong with Betsy; "[h]e told me that if Betsy was to have a child that she wouldn't live through it."[112]

But this was not quite the case. Bill and Betsy had never tried to conceive a child together, because in the early 1980s Betsy had diagnosed herself as having multiple sclerosis and, after talking to a few colleagues, concluded that a pregnancy would seriously endanger her health. The Sterns had left blank the question on an ICNY form regarding fertility status but in any event Keane's position had always been that why couples sought him out was none of his business. He accepted couples and sometimes individual clients without regard to marital status or medical history. At the trial, days of expert testimony were devoted to the question whether Betsy Stern was either infertile (incapable of conceiving) or unable to bear a child (incapable of sustaining a pregnancy). In the end, the New Jersey Supreme Court found that at the time the deal was reached, "[Betsy's] anxiety appears to have exceeded the actual risk, which current medical authorities as-

---

"showed a lack of care in determining whether Mrs. Whitehead was appropriate for a surrogacy relationship." This claim also settled out of court. Ron Hollander, *Mary Beth Settles Suit with Doctor, Attorney*, The Record (Hackensack, N.J.), July 12, 1987, at A8.

[110] Testimony of William Stern, 1 Trial Transcripts 49 (Cross by Cassidy). The Sterns, perhaps because of the disclaimer and perhaps because they won custody of the baby and simply wanted to move on with their lives, did not sue.

[111] Iver Peterson, *Baby M and Controversy over Fertility*, N.Y. Times, Jan. 31, 1987.

[112] Testimony of Mary Beth Whitehead, 1 Trial Transcripts 65 (Direct).

sess as minimal."[113] Nonetheless, the court concluded that "[b]ased on the perceived risk, the Sterns [reasonably] decided to forego having their own children."[114]

At trial, the dispute over Betsy's fertility served two purposes. The first was to tar Dr. Stern with careerist responsibility for her own fix. Mary Beth's lawyer, Harold Cassidy, threw down the gauntlet in his opening statement: "[T]he only reason that the Sterns did not attempt to conceive a child was . . . because Mrs. Stern had a career that had to be advanced."[115] Throughout the trial, Cassidy worked to portray Betsy as just "one more whiny boomer who forgot to have a baby," to borrow Anne Taylor Fleming's stinging phrase.[116] Mary Beth underscored the point: "Betsy valued her career with the same intensity that I valued motherhood."[117] The apparent complementarity that had brought the two women together in the first place transformed itself into the very reason the deal should not be enforced: Betsy Stern didn't deserve custody of the baby because she didn't want a child badly enough. She had not been willing to take a risk for motherhood.[118]

If the first purpose of the fertility testimony was to cast doubt on Betsy's maternal commitment, the second was to defend against Mary Beth's breach. Cassidy argued that the Sterns and the ICNY had misrepresented Betsy's ability to reproduce. Mary Beth was not in the business of having babies for couples who could jolly well have their own. She wasn't interested in "iffy" infertility but in *desperate* infertil-

---

[113] 537 A.2d at 1236.

[114] *Id.*

[115] Cassidy Opening Statement, 1 Trial Transcripts 29.

[116] FLEMING, *supra* note 33, at 35.

[117] WHITEHEAD, *supra* note 45, at 92. Once things went south, Mary Beth revealed many grudges and sources of dissatisfaction, including the size of the plant the Sterns brought when they visited her in the hospital ("the dinkiest"). She regularly referred to Mr. Stern as a Mr. Sperm and also raised questions about Stern's professed concerns regarding his Jewish heritage. As Mary Beth pointed out, Stern had married a Methodist, chosen a Catholic surrogate, and was planning to raise the baby Unitarian. Who knows why the Sterns did not seek a Jewish surrogate? Demographic studies suggest there are almost no Jewish surrogates; this may or may not have something to do with their choice. *See* Itabari Njeri, *Surrogate Motherhood: A Practice That's Still Undergoing Birth Pangs*, L.A. Times, Mar. 22, 1987, at 1.

[118] Cassidy linked Betsy's reproductive status to the Sterns' alleged neglect of Dr. Einwohner's report: "Mrs. Stern did not read a psychological report because Mrs. Stern thought her career too important to bear her own children." *See* 1 Trial Transcripts 29.

ity: *That* was the object of her altruism.[119]

Because the court held the contract void on public policy grounds (no baby-selling in New Jersey), it did not resolve the issue of fraud or misrepresentation. Nonetheless, from the perspective of market development and intermediation, the issue of disclosure as related to broker reputation raises two interesting questions. First, *should* ICNY have uncovered and revealed Betsy's medical history? In most commercial transactions, people do not usually care what brings the other party to the table. You may want to buy my car because you have no car or because you have three and hanker for a fourth. The used car dealer may affect an interest in this but is usually indifferent about the parties' background motivations.

Surrogacy presents a somewhat different proposition. Women act as surrogates in part because they want to perform a service for couples who are uniquely needy. Surrogates may be telling themselves fairy tales, as one critic contends,[120] but putting charges of false consciousness aside, the role of altruism in this decision to act as a surrogate seems undeniable. The value and meaning of this work diminishes if the couple was simply risk-averse or too busy to have their own baby. Under such circumstances, the good will and the bodies of surrogates seem exploited, even to the surrogate. In a sense, ascertaining the fertility status of the couple might be viewed like a background finance report or a pre-approved mortgage. The seller wants to know whether the buyer has (or in this case doesn't have) the means.

Indeed, before agreeing to bear a child, the surrogate mother might want to know more than the couple's fertility status. She might want to know—or be able to count on—the fact that the couple are likely to be good parents to her child. In a 1997 Pennsylvania case, Keane's client, a single man, killed the baby he had fathered with the surrogate when it was only a month old. He was charged with murder. In a negligence

---

[119] "Child bearing would have been an inconvenience for Mrs. Stern. Infertility was a lie. Inconvenience was the truth." WHITEHEAD, *supra* note 45, at 157. Brokers might similarly inquire about the commissioning couple's fertility; recall that Mary Beth underwent eight months of insemination with an untested sterile husband.

[120] Describing the comforting myth or "modern fairy tale that babies can properly be viewed as a consumer product for those with money to purchase them, and that by permitting this transaction, we will all live happily ever after." George J. Annas, *Fairy Tales Surrogate Mothers Tell, in* SURROGATE MOTHERHOOD: POLITICS AND PRIVACY 43 (Larry Gostin ed., 1990). For Annas, surrogacy is nothing more than "a method to obtain children genetically related to white males by exploiting poor women." *Id.*

suit brought by the mother against Keane, the court held that because
of the nature of the Infertility Center of America's (ICA's) business—"a
business operating for the sole purpose of organizing and supervising
the very delicate process of creating a child"—that a "special relationship" existed between the ICA and its "client-participants."[121]

The second question about disclosure concerns Keane's reputation.
The ICNY knew that Mary Beth might not go through with the deal
and that the Sterns had not answered the question on their questionnaire about Betsy's infertility. All this came out at trial and in the
press. Why then, in light of ICNY's seemingly shoddy performance, did
the *Baby M* case bring Keane additional acclaim and business? Justice
Robert N. Wilentz's decision was meant to close down commercial surrogacy, not cause Noel Keane to install more phone lines. Should not
the market have worked so that other, more careful surrogacy brokers
emerged to displace Keane?

There are several possible answers. It may be that the surrogacy
market was so new and beguiling that consumers paid more attention
to its possibilities than to one case of failure, featuring a surrogate
who, however sympathetic to some, was also somewhat nutty. Mary
Beth had, after all, threatened to kill herself and the baby and threatened to claim that Bill Stern had abused Tuesday.[122] After all, only a
handful of the hundreds of traditional surrogacy agreements brokered
in the United States since Noel Keane wrote the first some thirty years
ago have resulted in litigation. It would therefore seem that the market for commercial surrogacy works well, with satisfied customers on
both ends of the deal and the middleman doing quite well in the middle. It may also be that the desire for a child is so consuming that in
the market for baby-making, normal consumer skills and concerns do
not operate normally.[123]

Of course, that Keane continued to do well does not mean he did not
lose market share. Other surrogacy brokers had higher admission criteria for surrogates, and some couples may well have gone elsewhere;
we cannot know for sure. In addition, technological advances were fast

---

[121] *See* Huddleston v. Infertility Clinic of America, 700 A.2d 453 (Pa. Sup.
Ct. 1997). The court held that the duty was owed "most especially [to] the child
which the surrogacy undertaking creates." *Id.* at 460.

[122] Mary Beth also declared that despite his vasectomy, Rick was the baby's
biological father. A court-ordered paternity test put a quick stop to the claim.

[123] As Spar observes, fertility doctors confront a "statistical and moral conundrum": There are few incentives to stopping treatment; the patient wants
to keep trying, the state has no guidelines, and the doctor profits from providing because there is the possibility of success. SPAR, *supra* note 16, at 53–57.

leaving traditional surrogacy in their wake. Within a very few years, the demand for traditional surrogacy had been replaced almost entirely by the demand for gestational surrogacy, and the new technology brought in new competitors. The Internet also changed how everyone does business. It is now quite easy to find surrogacy brokers on-line and to compare their services, prices, and results.

Conclusion

In removing surrogacy from the realm of permissible commercial activity in New Jersey, Justice Wilentz focused on what he saw as the pernicious role of the middleman. By taking money out of the equation, entrepreneurs would have to go elsewhere to extract surplus from trades like this, and that is certainly what happened. Surrogacy brokers decamped to jurisdictions where surrogacy was permitted or to those still in legal limbo, as New Jersey had been. But *Baby M* had revealed surrogacy's potential for heartbreak—or, as many contended, heartbreak's inevitability—and many state legislatures took note.[124] Some banned commercial surrogacy outright; others were content to make surrogacy contracts legal but unenforceable. And in many jurisdictions, brokers have come in for special mention. Some states, such as Colorado, ban payment to the mothers but permit it to the broker. Others, such as the United Kingdom, permit payment to the mother but completely ban the broker. It is an offense in the United Kingdom to negotiate a commercial deal or even to advertise for a volunteer surrogate.[125] Where surrogacy is legal, as in California, it appears to thrive.[126] With this array of options, couples can now decide whether to follow the law of their own state or country, or to forum shop in the global market of reproductive tourism.

And what became of the players in the case?

Bill and Betsy Stern remained in Tenafly with Melissa and have granted no interviews since the decision was handed down. Tenafly seems to have protected the Stern family in their desire for privacy. As

---

[124] *See Appendix II, Status of State Legislation Proposed or Enacted Through Oct. 5, 1988, in* SURROGATE MOTHERHOOD, *supra* note 120, at 261.

[125] Surrogacy Arrangements, Act of 1985.

[126] A recent study comparing agencies in Colorado and California concluded that commercial brokers provided substantially more services to the mother and the couple than uncompensated brokers. The study also found no evidence that commercial agencies increased the exploitation of women by paying them but rather that the agencies screened out women who were particularly needy precisely to make sure they were not doing it for the money alone. *See* Galbraith, McLachlan & Swales, *supra* note 53.

one "Tenafly native" told a reporter looking for a story on Melissa's thirteenth birthday, "Bringing up this child's past will only hurt her in the long run. . . . Nobody wants to revisit the pain and suffering surrounding the case. Nobody. And in this town, everyone knows everybody."[127]

Mary Beth, now Mary Beth Whitehead Gould, lives in Bayport, Long Island, with her second husband, Dean Gould, whom she met on vacation while recuperating from the trial.[128] As she wrote in her 1989 memoir, "the purpose of my life was to have children," and she has had five: Ryan and Tuesday with Rick, "Sassy" (her nickname for Melissa), and Austin and Morgan with Dean.[129] Mary Beth's views about surrogacy have changed. Interviewed in 1999 with other notables for *People* magazine's twenty-fifth anniversary issue, she explained, "I look at people who are infertile in a totally different light. I feel sorry for people who can't see too. That doesn't mean I am going to take out an eye and give it to them."[130]

Although the Whiteheads were already divorced, Rick remained part of the celebration when the Supreme Court reversed the trial court, reinstating Mary Beth's maternal rights and granting her visitation. In 1988, however, he moved to Florida near his mother and brothers. Rick worked as a cement truck driver for Mid Coast Concrete, retired in 1994, and died in a hospice on November 28, 2001.[131]

Noel Keane continued his practice until his death of cancer at age fifty-eight in 1997. He had arranged more than 600 births since the first couple walked in twenty years earlier. ICNY stopped doing busi-

---

[127] Cori Anne Natoli, *Baby M, Away from Spotlight, Turns 13*, The Record (Hackensack, N.J.), March 28, 1999.

[128] Mary Beth became pregnant while the case was on appeal to the New Jersey Supreme Court. Her pregnancy, divorce from Rick, and remarriage to Dean two weeks later were all much reported in the press. Robert Hanley, *Whiteheads Divorce and Cite Battle for Baby M, Not Pregnancy as Cause*, N.Y. Times, Nov. 13, 1987. Mary Beth's attorney issued a statement declaring that Ms. Whitehead's personal circumstances had no bearing on the legal issues raised on appeal.

[129] In her memoir, Mary Beth explained that she published her account of the case so that Melissa and the public would know "the truth about the terrible mistake I made" and to pay off her lawyer's fees. *See* Michael Kelly, *Surrogate Makes Secret Book Deal to Finance Baby M Appeal*, The Record (Hackensack, N.J.), May 20, 1987.

[130] Elizabeth McNeil, *Mary Beth Whitehead Gould Nurtures "Baby M,"* People, March 15, 1999.

[131] Obituary, St. Petersburg Times, Nov. 29, 2001, at 10.

ness in 1993 after charges that sperm donors had not been properly tested before the insemination of surrogates. It reopened as the ICA and continues in business today headquartered in Minneapolis.

Justice Wilentz, who wrote the decision in *Baby M*, died in 1996; the case featured prominently in his obituary.[132] Harold Cassidy, Mary Beth's attorney, remains, in his own words, "an advocate and defender of the rights of pregnant mothers."[133]

What about Baby M herself? In 2005, a syndicated newspaper article featured a picture of one Melissa Stern of Tenafly, New Jersey. The article had nothing to do with surrogacy but was simply a human interest story on the use of laptops by college students. And there she was, just another freshman, working away on an assignment while plugged into her iPod.[134]

---

[132] Thomas Martello, *Author of Baby M, Megan's Law Rulings Dies*, AP Online, July 23, 1996.

[133] *See* http://www.haroldcassidy.com. One focus of Cassidy's current practice is litigation against physicians who perform abortions. *See* Acuna v. Turkish, 345 N.J. Super. Ct. 500 (App. Div. 2002) (representing a woman who sued her abortion doctor for failing to clarify that if she had an abortion "an existing family member would die.").

[134] *Gadgets Rule on College Campuses*, Shreveport Times, Apr. 11, 2005.

6

Douglas G. Baird[*]

Reconstructing Contracts: Hamer v. Sidway

Every case tells a different story. In first-year contracts, the story of *Hamer v. Sidway*[1] is among the most familiar. An uncle promises his fifteen-year-old nephew that he will give him $5,000 on his twenty-first birthday if he promises in return not to smoke, drink, or play cards or billiards for money until then. The legal question the case presents is straightforward: If the nephew keeps his end of the bargain, is the uncle legally obliged to pay? Can the nephew, in other words, sue the uncle if he breaks his promise? This question has been a central preoccupation of contracts professors for more than a hundred years. It has become the standard vehicle used to distinguish those promises that are legally enforceable from those that are not.

We are morally and ethically obliged to keep our promises, but it does not follow that promises should be legally enforceable on that account alone. Legal enforceability raises the stakes considerably. Holding a promise legally enforceable empowers one private citizen to call upon the state to use force (if necessary) against another. It is not something to be done lightly, especially when the judge must try to reconstruct the promise in question from evidence that can be conflicting and incomplete.

---

[*] Harry A. Bigelow Distinguished Service Professor, University of Chicago. I thank Vincent Buccola, Thomas Bell, and Robert Rasmussen for their help, and I am grateful to Visa U.S.A. and the John M. Olin Foundation for research support.

[1] 124 N.Y. 538, 27 N.E. 256 (1891).

We share intuitions about the cases at the extremes. The written promise of a giant corporation to sell goods to another giant corporation should be legally enforceable. A casual promise one friend makes to another in a social setting—perhaps about meeting for lunch or dinner—should not be. It would be surprising if any modern legal regime provided otherwise. But those trained in the law must learn about the cases that fall between these two extremes. *Hamer v. Sidway* is one of these intermediate cases. On one hand, the uncle's promise was not made in the marketplace. We cannot easily point to something such as the desirability of mutually beneficial trade to justify legal enforceability. On the other hand, the promise was not a casual one. The whole point of the uncle's promise was for the nephew to take it seriously. Therefore we should not necessarily treat the uncle's promise as we would an ordinary social promise.

Successive generations of legal scholars looked at the bare facts of *Hamer v. Sidway* in quite different ways. In the first half of this essay, I show how this case—or rather a hypothetical based on this case—shaped the debate over the doctrine of consideration and promissory estoppel, a debate that occupied the attention of contracts scholars for decades. In the second half of the essay, I show how removing this case from its context took away what mattered.

Understanding *Hamer v. Sidway* and the challenges it presents requires locating the uncle and his nephew in a large family group portrait. In addition to his nephew, the uncle cared also about his nieces and making sure that they were taken care of. He also had to sort out his relationship with his elder brother, someone who was financially dependent on him for much of his adult life. The nephew, far from being a wayward adolescent, appears as a responsible adult who, among other things, has to care for an elderly parent. The extended family, like many others before and since, was one in which the more well-to-do looked out for those who were less fortunate. Outside of the commercial mainstream, social relationships are inevitably intricate and laden with ambiguity. The law can play only a limited role in such an environment.

The Formalist Account

The nineteenth-century formalists who taught at the Harvard Law School believed there was an easy way to tell whether a promise was legally enforceable: A promise is legally enforceable if, but only if, it is supported by consideration. We enforce only those promises that are made in exchange for something else. A mere promise is not enforceable. (I promise to pay you ten dollars.) A promise that is subject to a condition is not enforceable. (I promise to pay you ten dollars if you are around when I get my next paycheck.) A promise that is given in exchange for a benefit you confer on me (or a detriment you incur on yourself) is enforceable. (I promise to pay you ten dollars if in return you promise to mow my lawn.) The key to consideration is that the promise is given in return for the benefit or detriment.

The crucial notion is not the value of what was given in return for the promise, but that something was part of an exchange. In the words of Lord Coke, a horse, a hawk, a robe would do.[2] There just had to be an exchange. A legally enforceable promise could not exist in the absence of a bargain. As Holmes put it,

> [I]t is the essence of a consideration, that by the terms of the agreement, it is given and accepted as the motive or inducement for furnishing the consideration. The root of the whole matter is the relation of reciprocal conventional inducement, each for the other, between consideration and promise.[3]

Hamer v. Sidway came to the Harvard Law School in the fall of 1890. The intermediate appellate court had handed down its opinion during the summer, holding that the nephew's promise to refrain from smoking, drinking, and gambling was not sufficient consideration to make a promise legally enforceable.[4] The promise had no pecuniary value to the uncle and, far from being a detriment to the nephew, probably did him considerable good. For those steeped in the teaching of Holmes and Langdell, however, this misunderstood the nature of consideration in a fundamental way.

If I commission an artist to paint a picture for a fixed sum, my obligation to pay the money is enforceable, regardless of whether I derive any value from the picture or whether the artist would have been happy to paint the picture without being paid. The fact of the bargain itself is all the matters. Further inquiry can be only a source of mischief. To return to the facts of *Hamer*, to constitute consideration it is enough that the nephew and the uncle each give up a legal right in exchange for a promise. How much performance works to the benefit of one or the detriment of the other is irrelevant so long as the performance is done *in exchange for the promise.*

In short, from the perspective of anyone who adhered to Langdell's view of contract, the intermediate court in *Hamer v. Sidway* had to be wrong. While the case was on appeal to New York's highest court, the

---

[2] Pinnel's Case, 5 Coke Rep. 117a (1602).

[3] OLIVER WENDELL HOLMES JR., THE COMMON LAW 230 (Mark deWolfe Howe ed., Belknap Press of Harvard Univ. Press 1963) (1881).

[4] 11 N.Y.S. 182 (Sup. Ct. 1890).

Harvard Law Review criticized the intermediate court opinion on just these grounds:

> [T]o say that no legal detriment is involved . . . i.e., that no legal right is parted with, would probably surprise a good many persons. . . . [T]he court's . . . suggestion, that even if there were an intention to contract the acts of the nephew, though performed at the uncle's request and in exchange for his promise, would not be a sufficient consideration, is surprising.[5]

We do not know whether Judge Alton B. Parker read the *Harvard Law Review*, but he in any event embraced the same view of consideration that permeated the halls of Harvard. It was enough that the nephew had a legal right to smoke, drink, and gamble and had agreed to give it up in exchange for the uncle's promise:

> We need not speculate on the effort which may have been required to give up the use of those stimulants. It is sufficient that he restricted his lawful freedom of action within certain prescribed limits upon the faith of his uncle's agreement, and now having fully performed the conditions imposed, it is of no moment whether such performance actually proved a benefit to the promisor.[6]

The record Judge Parker had before him included the trial transcript. It provided enough raw material to treat the uncle's promise as a bargained-for exchange. Willie (as he called him) was named after his uncle and his uncle had always been fond of him, but Willie's adolescence got off to a rocky start. By the time he was fifteen, Willie had, by his own account, "indulged in a moderate degree of playing billiards, and smoking, and drinking beer and liquor."[7] The uncle viewed these developments with some alarm, observing, "[y]ou know when a boy of his age gets to going bad it always gains on him, and I want to hold out some inducement to stop it right here and now."[8]

The uncle called Willie over to him during a family celebration and couched what he told him in the language of a bargain. "Willie, I am going to make you a proposition. . . . If you will not drink any liquor, will not smoke, will not play cards or billiards until you are twenty-

---

[5] 4 Harv. L. Rev. 237. The note appeared in the December 1890 issue of the *Harvard Law Review*, an issue that also included Warren and Brandeis's landmark article on the right to privacy. *See* Samuel D. Warren & Louis D. Brandeis, *The Right to Privacy*, 4 Harv. L. Rev. 193 (1890).

[6] 124 N.Y. at 546.

[7] Record at 93.

[8] Record at 94.

one, I will give you $5,000 that day." Willie understood his uncle to be proposing a bargain and he took it as such. After some negotiating to ensure he could still play cards and billiards as long it was not for money, Willie accepted the uncle's "proposition." Willie, by his account at least, took the promise seriously. Indeed, while he was away at college and fell quite ill, the doctor prescribed a medicine with alcohol in it, but he refused to take it.[9]

On his twenty-first birthday, Willie again used the language of a bargained-for exchange when wrote his uncle: "I believe, according to agreement, that there is due me $5,000. I have lived up to the contract to the letter in every sense of the word."[10] The uncle, for his part, responded in similar terms, "Your letter . . . came to me saying that you had lived up to the promise made to me several years ago. I have no doubt but you have, for which you shall have five thousand dollars as I promised you."[11]

Because the trial court had found in favor of the plaintiff on all the facts that pointed in the direction of there having been a bargained-for exchange, a traditional nineteenth-century formalist steeped in the Langdellian tradition would find that the intermediate court had clearly erred. As we shall see, there are many other grounds that might lead one to find against Willie, but the correctness of the lower court's narrow interpretation of consideration became the focal point of his appeal.

Far from peeking at the underlying equities of the case (which turn out not to favor Willie at all), Judge Parker simply took sides in a doctrinal dispute—the side that was then the prevailing academic fashion. Three years later, the same court found that a father's promise to give money to his daughter was unenforceable precisely because there was no quid pro quo.[12] It did not matter that the father went so far as to open an account in his daughter's name and put the money in it (something that the uncle in *Hamer v. Sidway* promised to do but never did). A promise is not enforceable in the absence of a bargained-for exchange, and the daughter had done nothing in return for the promise. Until the money (or the passbook controlling the account) was delivered, the law would do nothing to aid her.

Far from expanding the number of promises that were legally enforceable, *Hamer* did the opposite. It was the case cited to close the

---

[9] Record at 93.

[10] Record at 34–35.

[11] Record at 10.

[12] Millard v. Clark, 27 N.Y.S. 631 (1894).

door on recovery by the daughter. *Hamer* as it was first told in the academy reflected Langdellian orthodoxy. A *bargain* must exist for a promise to be legally enforceable. Inside the family, explicit bargains are the exception. Hence, most intrafamilial promises are, in Langdell's world, not legally enforceable. *Hamer* is an exception that proves the rule.

Hamer v. Sidway was included in the first edition of the contracts casebook written by Langdell's successor at Harvard.[13] It entered the canon to illustrate the idea that a bargained-for promise was enforceable, regardless of what was being promised. It was enough that the bargained-for consideration involved giving up a legal right. That the facts were extreme and unusual did not matter at all. Indeed, it underscored the idea that a principle was at work that lived apart from the particular facts of a case. It emphasized that any bargain, even over such a matter as teenage smoking and drinking, was enforceable so long as there was in fact a bargain.

Neither Holmes nor Langdell provide any justification for the principle of the bargained-for exchange. Holmes did not think it important. For him, the task of the legal scholar was simply one of being a careful observer. Like the Young Astronomer who coldly and dispassionately charts the heavens,[14] Holmes thought himself obliged only to provide a descriptive account of what the courts did. He made no claim that the law had an inner logic. For his part, Langdell had a faith that the common law had such an inner logic, one that rested upon principles, as did the physical universe. These principles were like Newton's laws, and they had an independent existence that could be discovered through careful study. Whether such things as the doctrine of consideration was good or bad was not a meaningful question. It was like asking whether gravity was good or bad. In short, although they had different reasons, neither Holmes nor Langdell sought to explain why enforcing the promise in a case such as *Hamer v. Sidway* was a sensible way to organize human affairs. The generation that followed them, however, thought such a justification necessary.

---

[13] *See* 1 SAMUEL WILLISTON, A SELECTION OF CASES ON THE LAW OF CONTRACTS 261 (1903–1904).

[14] This somewhat frosty image of Oliver Wendell Holmes Jr. as the Young Astronomer, someone who distances himself from the law and the world and looks at it remotely and heartlessly, does not, of course, originate with me. *See* OLIVER WENDELL HOLMES [SR.], THE POET AT THE BREAKFAST TABLE (1883).

The Legal Realist Account

The generation of legal scholars that followed Langdell—led principally by Arthur Corbin—rejected the idea that legal principles existed apart from the society that created them. They questioned the idea that the artificial notion of a bargained-for exchange, standing alone, could sensibly draw a line between those promises that should be legally enforceable and those that should not be. For them, *Hamer v. Sidway* was one of many cases in which courts enforced promises that fit only awkwardly with black-letter law.

Someone coming to *Hamer v. Sidway* from this perspective could take the facts as recounted at trial and tell a different story. At the family celebration, the uncle was merely adding a condition to a promise made long before. Even when Willie was as young as eight or ten, the uncle frequently told Willie's father and mother that he had $5,000 on deposit in the bank earmarked for Willie and he would have it when he came of age.[15] Rather than a deal cut to get Willie's life in order, the insistence that Willie cut out his bad habits was simply a string he tied to a promise. There was never a bargain. In the uncle's view, "when Willie came of age, if everything was favorable, he would start him in business and help him, and . . . this $5,000 would be something to look forward to that would stimulate him to do right, and if he was steady and industrious this would be a good start; and, if he was not, this would be enough for him to squander."[16]

Someone looking at the case from this perspective would see that Langdellian formalism was pernicious. It forced lawyers to labor to reshape Willie's and his father's account of the uncle's promise into the procrustean bed of a bargained-for exchange or, failing that, find another route to legal enforceability. Far from being an example of a narrow conception of what promises were legally enforceable, this case belonged to a large class of cases where courts had found in favor of promisees even though the promises were outside the marketplace. A relative asked another to come live with them and let them build a

---

[15] Record at 56. This testimony comes from a former family retainer who lived in the Midwest and had to testify through interrogatories, far away from the family lawyers. While she appears anxious to do everything she can to support her former employers, the inability of the lawyers to coach her may have led to an account that focuses more on the seriousness with which the uncle made the promise rather than on his making it as part of a bargained-for exchange. Willie's father's testimony, like Willie's, is very much couched in terms of a bargain and for that reason is at times inconsistent with the housekeeper's recollection.

[16] Record at 58–59.

house, promising to convey the land beneath.[17] A grandfather promised money to his granddaughter so that she would leave her job.[18] In dozens of cases, using a number of different theories, courts enforced promises that were seriously made and reasonably relied upon.[19]

Parties might be forced to argue for the existence of a bargained-for exchange, but it made no sense to require them to do so. The uncle made a promise, knowing that his nephew would rely upon it. In this and in many other cases, courts found such promises legally enforceable, independent of whether the promise was part of a bargained-for exchange. To describe accurately what courts did, the narrow doctrine of a consideration in the form of a bargained-for exchange was not enough.[20]

Corbin was Aristotle to Langdell's Plato. Corbin wanted to focus on the world as it was and draw conclusions about the structure of the law from "prevailing notions of honor and well-being, notions that grow out of ages of experience in business affairs and in social intercourse."[21] Corbin then was a revolutionary in a limited sense. He rejected the dogma that legal principles were like the laws of physics, things that could be derived independent of fact and circumstance. But he did not advocate dramatic change, and he still thought that the legal principles of a society were things that could be discovered. Legal principles could be derived from norms that command broad acceptance.

We can understand Corbin's approach to the question of what promises should be legally enforceable by returning to *Hamer v. Sidway*. A court might easily find that there was a promise subject to a condition, rather than a bargained-for exchange. For Langdell, which story one told was all important. For Corbin, it did not make any difference. In Corbin's view, the seriousness of the promise and Willie's reliance on it was decisive. If the promise in *Hamer* was enforceable, then so too should be an uncle's promise if a nephew went to college in reliance on the promise. What matters is that the behavior reasonably and predictably changed as a result of the promise, not that this behavior was tied explicitly to the promise.

---

[17] *See* Seavey v. Drake, 62 N.H. 393 (1882).

[18] *See* Ricketts v. Scothorn, 77 N.W. 365 (Neb. 1898).

[19] *See* Hendrik Hartog, *Someday All This Will Be Yours: Inheritance, Adoption, and Obligation in Capitalist America*, 79 Ind. L.J. 346 (2004).

[20] *See* GRANT GILMORE, THE DEATH OF CONTRACT 62–65 (1974).

[21] Arthur L. Corbin, *Does a Pre-existing Duty Defeat Consideration?—Recent Noteworthy Decisions*, 27 Yale L.J. 362, 376 (1917).

For Corbin, the idea that reasonable reliance on a promise should trigger legal liability could be derived from existing mores. The norm that a decent person keeps any serious promise that another relies upon is strongly held. Therefore, the reliance itself provides a ground for making the promise legally enforceable. There is much to admire in Corbin's work, coming as it did just a few decades after Langdell's. We must credit Corbin with the insight that consideration is itself a convention that falls far short of being an independent and immutable law that definitively establishes the domain of legally enforceable promises. Corbin's introduction of reliance as an organizing principle gave decisive shape to the way contracts was taught for most of the twentieth century. The principle of promissory estoppel—that someone in the uncle's position is legally obliged to keep serious promises that were reasonably relied on, at least to the extent of the reliance—remains firmly embedded in the modern law of contract.

In practice, however, the idea of promissory estoppel has proved far more modest than one would guess from the way it is presented in the first-year contracts class.[22] There are relatively few litigated cases in which a promise is made with sufficient definiteness that it justifies reasonable reliance and yet still lacks sufficient consideration to support enforcement along conventional lines. The reporters are filled with opinions that set out the elements of promissory estoppel, affirm its continuing vitality, and then find that it does not apply to the facts before it.

Moreover, Corbin and his heirs fell short of constructing a compelling theory of promissory estoppel. The principle that promises relied upon should be enforced demands justification. By their own account, it was contingent on fact and circumstance, not an immutable law of nature. Too many who followed in Corbin's footsteps thought the virtues of such a rule required no explanation, but this is not self-evident. We should explain *why* making such promises legally enforceable is a good idea. Given the extralegal pressures that are at work, the limited competence of courts, and the costs that come with making a promise legally enforceable, we cannot say that making promises reasonably relied on legally enforceable follows ineluctably from the notion that keeping promises is a good thing.

---

[22] *See* Alan Schwartz & Robert E. Scott, *Precontractual Liability,* 120 Harv. L. Rev. — (2007).

Recall the facts of *Allegheny College*.[23] A widow had promised to leave a bequest to a college and then changed her plans. The college sued to enforce the promise against her estate. Cardozo found that there was consideration and hence the promise was enforceable. As he showed time and time again, Cardozo could find consideration anywhere:

> The promisor wished to have a memorial to perpetuate her name. . . . [T]here was an assumption of a duty [on the part of the college] to do whatever acts were customary or reasonably necessary to maintain the memorial fairly and justly . . . .

Cardozo goes on at length to explain how this gift was part of a bargained-for exchange. Corbin wished that judges did not have to make such heroic stretches of the doctrine of consideration. He thought judges should be able to look at the reality of these situations. The presence of reliance would tell us that this promise was one we should enforce. But does the idea of reliance do the slightest bit of good here? How exactly did the college rely in this case? Was it reasonable? Moreover, Corbin thought that these promises to charities should be enforceable as a general matter. How do we arrive at this from the idea of reliance? The *Restatement (Second) of Contracts* virtually concedes this point by declaring that, in the case of charitable subscriptions, reliance is presumed.

Another classic case, *De Cicco v. Schweitzer*,[24] again forces us to ask how we should approach the question of legal enforceability. Cardozo confronted a father who promised to give his daughter and the count to whom she was engaged $2,500 a year after they married. Cardozo found the father's promise supported by consideration. Where was the consideration? What detriment did the daughter and the count incur in exchange for the promise? And where exactly is the reliance? Cardozo pointed out that even though the engaged couple were not legally bound to go through with the marriage at the time of the promise, they did so anyway. One suspects Cardozo found consideration because he thought that enforcing a promise here is a good idea. Perhaps it is. One may need to give minor European nobility a legally enforceable right in such situations. Henry James suggests as much. But we cannot reach this conclusion merely by reasoning from general principle.

Once we recognize that reliance is a constructed idea every bit as much as consideration, the mere presence of reliance somewhere

---

[23] Allegheny College v. National Chautauqua County Bank, 246 N.Y. 369, 159 N.E. 173 (1927).

[24] 117 N.E. 807 (N.Y. 1917).

should not lead to the conclusion that there should be legal liability. Reliance, to be sure, tugs at our heartstrings in a way that the presence or absence of consideration does not, but we can hardly organize the law of civil obligations on this account. In short, the same fault Corbin found in Langdell's idea of bargained-for consideration exists with his notion of detrimental reliance. We do not prove it makes sense to hold the uncle liable merely because the promise was supported by a bargained-for exchange. Nor can we say that the uncle should be bound merely because the promise was relied upon.

There is nothing inherently the matter with having simple abstract principles that set out the domain of legally enforceable promises. But the principle of reliance has led us astray precisely because people have failed to recognize that it is only an abstract principle, not a feature that we naturally find in the world around us. Just as Langdell was wrong in thinking that the doctrine of consideration was a universal law of nature, many have mistakenly thought that reliance was something other than a general principle that we have constructed ourselves.

The architects of the *Restatement (First) of Contracts* transformed *Hamer v. Sidway* into a hypothetical about an uncle who promises to give money to the nephew if he goes to school.[25] The academics who were involved approached the question from quite different starting positions, one seeing a bargain and the other reliance. Nevertheless, both could begin with a hypothetical that stripped down the case to its essentials. Either as a bargain or as a case of reasonable reliance, the nephew should win. Today we should be reluctant to make the jump so quickly from dense facts to legal conclusion. We are keenly aware that much is lost in translation.

This is not to say we should not be judicial nihilists. After all, a court with jurisdiction has to decide the case before it, and, like anything else, judicial decision making can be done better or worse. But we need to be much more concerned about taking into account the limits of judges, the laws they apply, and the way in which other forces also shape the parties' incentives. In fashioning and explicating doctrine, we need to recognize that behind *Hamer v. Sidway* and the other great cases in the canon are many possible narratives, and judges are

---

[25] We can date the time with some precision. Samuel Williston, the champion of the Langdellian tradition, gave ground and acquiesced in what became section 90 of the *Restatement (First) of Contracts* during a retreat with Corbin in the summer of 1924. *See* 2 THE AMERICAN LAW INSTITUTE: PROCEEDINGS MAY 20, 1923 TO DECEMBER 31, 1924, at 207.

limited in their ability to discover them and distinguish one from another.

Law and Possible Narratives

Corbin sought to identify the marginal cases, the instances in which
legal enforceability of a promise might make sense even though it was
not bargained for. People keep the vast majority of promises that are
seriously made and reasonably relied upon. Hence, the cases of interest, those where Corbin's revolution has traction, are those in which
someone makes a promise and then recants. To understand whether
judicial intervention makes sense, we should first understand what
might lead people not to keep (or not appear to keep) their promises.

Those cases in which promissory estoppel matters outside the marketplace are often cases where something has happened offstage that
the judge cannot see. The facts are likely to be hard to penetrate, and
the way the judge constructs the story is especially likely to be wrong.
Perhaps as important, the intricate social relationships outside the
marketplace rarely reduce themselves easily to a framework in which
the rights of A and B can be rigorously defined.

Once we leave the world of commerce, genuine misunderstandings
can easily arise. One of the other canonical cases used to illustrate the
deficiencies in the traditional doctrine of consideration presents precisely this sort of difficulty. In *Mills v. Wyman*,[26] by the usual account,
a stranger takes into his house a young man who has fallen ill. The
Good Samaritan writes to the young man's father, and the father
writes back promising to pay his son's expenses. Subsequently, the father reneges on his promise and is sued. The judge first chastises the
father for failing to honor his moral obligation, but then, again by the
standard account, rigidly and mechanically insists that the law does
not come to his aid. The father's promise is not supported by consideration.

This result is commonly criticized as an exemplar of equity being
sacrificed in the name of rigid formalism. But before reaching this conclusion, we should first recognize that we confront exceedingly odd
facts. The stranger has no obligation to the son, but takes him in and
acts as a Good Samaritan. The father has no obligation to make the
promise, but makes it nevertheless. At this point, two unusual things
happen. The father unaccountably breaks a promise he never had to
make in the first instance, and then the Good Samaritan seeks money

---

[26] 20 Mass. (3 Pick.) 207 (1825).

for his good deed. Grateful parents usually do not renege; Good Samaritans are not supposed to be in it for the cash.

Something is going on, and the question in the first instance is whether a court can enter such shoals and, by enforcing the promise, make matters better. Refusing to enforce a promise in this environment may be less a mechanical adherence to the letter of the law than a recognition that the judge may not know enough to decide the case sensibly. A good judge, like a good doctor, should always remember Hippocrates: *First, do no harm.*

What we know about the facts of *Mills v. Wyman* allows a narrative rather different from the one we see in first-year casebooks.[27] Unstated in the opinion is the crucial fact that Mills, the Good Samaritan, was by profession an innkeeper.[28] He may have kept an inn or he might have been someone who took on regular boarders. He might even have had a common law obligation to take the son in. In any event, he took in young Wyman in the expectation that he would pay for his lodging. We also know that young Wyman had long been estranged from his father and had regularly incurred debts that his father refused to pay.

This story starts when young Wyman falls ill. Mills realizes that he has a lodger who is going to require a lot of care and who can no longer foot the bill. Mills is not a bad person, and he does not want to throw this lodger out onto the street, but he is, after all, in business, and he cannot make money by taking care of total strangers who do not pay their way. Young Wyman suggests that his father can pay the bill, and so Mills writes to him and the father writes back. The letter reads, in full:[29]

> Dear Sir
>
> I received a line from you relating to my Son Levi's sickness and requesting me to come up and see him, but as the going is very bad I cannot come up at the present, but I wish you to take all possible care of him and if you cannot have him at your

---

[27] The definitive investigation into the historical record can be found in Geoffrey R. Watson, *In the Tribunal of Conscience:* Mills v. Wyman *Reconsidered*, 71 Tulane L. Rev. 1749 (1997). Professor Watson, the careful historian, resists retelling the story from any single point of view and would likely caution that the one set out in the text is only one of a number of possible narratives that can be reconstructed from the record. Anyone wishing to understand this case must begin with Professor Watson's article.

[28] *See id.* at 1759.

[29] *See id.* at 1761 n.72.

house I wish you to remove him to some convenient place and if
he cannot satisfy you for it I will.

I want that you should write me again immediately how he
does and greatly oblige your most obedient servant

Seth Wyman

Shrewsbury Feb 24th 1821
    Mr. Daniel Mills

The ambiguities in this letter suggest the following story. This case
is one of a misunderstanding between two individuals, each of whom
acted in good faith. The father mistakenly thought Mills is a gentleman and a Good Samaritan, not an innkeeper. He never thought that
Mills would charge for taking care of his son. He did, however, realize
that Mills could not be expected to put him up forever. Wyman therefore tells Mills that, if he cannot keep his son at his house (for nothing,
because a gentleman does not charge for such a thing), Mills should
put him up at an inn. If the son cannot pay for this (as yet unincurred)
expense, he will. The father does not say he will pay Mills for keeping
his son in his own home, either for the past or the future. Gentlemen
do not charge each other for such things, but, as a gentleman, the father feels obliged to cover another gentleman's out-of-pocket costs arising from the care of his son, even if he is estranged from his son and
does not cover the son's debts with tradesmen.

Mills reads the letter differently. He thinks Wyman knows he is an
innkeeper. He understands the letter to say that Wyman wants him to
continue to board his son or find for his son some other boarding house
and Wyman will make good the expenses. From an innkeeper's perspective, the natural interpretation of the letter is not that the father
will pay only for future expenses, but that he will be good for everything. After all, the father wants him to do a whole bunch of things
(such as finding his son another place to stay, if necessary, and securing medical care) that innkeepers usually do not do. Seen in this light,
the father by this letter is promising to take care of the entire bill, if
Mills continues to take care of him or finds someone else who will.

In other words, the father thinks he wrote the following letter:

Dear Fellow Gentleman:
I wish you to take all possible care of him. If you cannot have
him at your home, I wish you to remove him to some convenient place and if he cannot satisfy you for the cost of staying at
such a place, I will.

Mills thinks he received this one:

Dear Innkeeper:

I wish you to take all possible care of him. If you cannot have
him at your inn, I wish you to remove him to some convenient
place. If he cannot make you whole for everything, I will.

This retelling of the story explains why the case was litigated. Seth
Wyman had no intention of paying off another of his wayward son's
bad debts. He promised a fellow gentlemen to reimburse future out-of-
pocket costs. He never promised an innkeeper to pay for obligations his
son had already incurred, any more than he promised to pay any other
creditors of his son. By contrast, Mills thought he had a perfectly conventional bargained-for exchange. The father asked him, someone in
the business of lodging people, to take all possible care of his son, and
if the son could not pay the bill, he would. If Mills continued to take
care, he would pay for everything. Mills's undertaking to continue to
provide care was consideration for the father's promise to pick up the
entire bill. The misunderstanding—and the cultural divide between
the two—gave rise to the litigation.

This account of *Mills v. Wyman* may be no more accurate than the
conventional one, but, as mentioned before, behind any set of facts are
many possible narratives. Langdell and his successors thought all that
was necessary was to ask whether the facts could be recast as a narrative involving a bargained-for exchange; Corbin and the generations
that followed believed that one could apply principles that ensure that
promises seriously made were enforced to the extent that justice required. Neither recognized how much context matters. *Hamer v. Sidway* provides further proof—and introduces additional complications,
ones especially likely to arise outside the commercial mainstream.

Reconstructing *Hamer v. Sidway*

The record such as the one we find in *Hamer v. Sidway* allows for
multiple narratives. We can tell different stories, depending upon the
point of view we take and the facts we use. Langdell and Corbin told
two different ones—and there are many others. In the rest of this essay, I put forward two more. The first underscores the challenges of
making promises outside the commercial mainstream legally enforceable; the second shows the limited work that the law can perform in an
environment in which relationships are often (and sometimes necessarily) incompletely developed.

One way to look at the story of *Hamer v. Sidway* is from the point of
view of Franklin Sidway. William Story dies twelve years after Willie
turned twenty-one without, by Willie's account, making good on a
promise made many years before. Franklin Sidway is William's execu-

tor,[30] and he is the person in the first instance who has to decide whether there was a legally enforceable promise. Sidway is vice president of the Farmers and Mechanics National Bank, a man who is "prudent, conservative, quick of decision, and not afraid of large undertakings."[31] As a banker whose job it was to handle such matters, Sidway is used to such controversies. Precisely because he is neither a family member nor a friend who cares about sorting out the equities after the fact, his focus is narrowly on the legal technicalities. Moreover, the legal fees the case generates do not trouble him greatly.[32]

The lawyers who have represented Willie and his family for years approach Franklin Sidway and ask him to honor a promise William made to Willie long before. Formally, they are representing not Willie himself, but rather Louise Hamer. She is Willie's mother-in-law, and, Sidway is told, she is entitled to enforce this odd promise because Willie assigned it to her on the day of his uncle's funeral.

Franklin Sidway is skeptical. The evidence that the promise had even been made is not ironclad. There is only a copy, in Willie's hand, of the uncle's letter.[33] Even if Sidway believes that the letter was a faithful copy, he has to ask whether he was bound by the uncle's statement in the letter that he believed Willie kept the promise, for Sidway can reasonably doubt that Willie lived up to his part of the bargain. Willie freely admits that he smoked, drank, and gambled both before he was fifteen and again after he was twenty-one. He spent a good part of the intervening time at college in Ann Arbor, Michigan, hundreds of miles away from the eyes of anyone in his hometown. When asked about his college experiences, Willie has trouble remembering the names of his classmates or where they might be found. The only one Willie can remember and locate is, it appears, a relative of his lawyer.[34]

These problems are only the first of many reasons Sidway has for not recognizing the claim. Even if Willie had once been able to bring the action against his uncle, William seems to have satisfied whatever

---

[30] Another prominent citizen of Buffalo was appointed to act as co-executor but he declined, perhaps seeing that the matter would be a contentious one.

[31] *See* http://freenet.buffalo.edu/bah/h/sidway/index.html#Franklin8.

[32] Far from having an animus against Willie's lawyers, Sidway was using them at the same time in another piece of litigation. *See* Sidway v. Cuba State Bank, 68 Sickels 634, 20 N.E. 878 (N.Y. 1889).

[33] Willie returned the original to his uncle at his uncle's request many years before, but it was not found among the uncle's effects until later. *See* Record at 35.

[34] Record at 51–52.

obligations he owed Willie by setting him up in business, not once but twice. Shortly after turning twenty-one, Willie and his father borrowed $5,000 from the uncle as part of their efforts to run a dry goods business.[35] This loan was never repaid. When William set up his brother and his son in business a second time, he insisted that they both sign "a good strong release." The release Willie signed

> forever discharged the said William E. Story, his heirs, executors, and administrators, . . . from all . . . causes of action, . . . suits, debts, . . . sums of money . . . which against the said William E. Story [Willie] ever had, now ha[s], or which [Willie] . . . hereafter can, shall or may have, for or upon or by reason of any matter, cause or thing whatsoever, from the beginning of the world to the day of the date of these presents.[36]

Even if the uncle had not kept his promise to give $5,000 to Willie and even if he had not obtained a release from him (either one of which extinguishes any claim Willie might have against the estate), Willie lost any right to bring the action for yet another reason. When the first business failed, Willie filed for bankruptcy. In that bankruptcy, any legally enforceable right he might have had against the uncle was necessarily turned over to his creditors. And, of course, the largest of these creditors was his uncle.

In short, Sidway is convinced that, quite apart from William's having kept his promise (twice), the complaint is fatally defective for at least two independent reasons: (1) Willie gave up his right to enforce the promise when he turned over his assets (including any choses in action) to his creditors when he filed for bankruptcy; and (2) he lost whatever rights he had against the uncle when he later signed the release. Sidway moves to dismiss the complaint, believing it will disappear quickly.

The family's lawyers, however, file an amended complaint. They say they made a mistake in drafting the first one. After the uncle died, it was Willie's wife, and not Willie himself, who made the transfer to Louise Hamer.[37] Willie assigned his uncle's promise to his wife, it is

---

[35] Hamer's lawyer tried to downplay the significance of the fact that the amount equaled exactly what William promised Willie by arguing that only half the loan was to Willie. The other half was to Willie's father, Willie's partner in the business.

[36] Record at 72.

[37] Willie goes so far as to say that he never made any assignment of his rights against William to Louise. Record at 51. Like other parts of his story, Willie's assertion is not completely credible. Willie's father testifies to the con-

now alleged, *before* he filed for bankruptcy or signed the release. Once transferred, neither his own bankruptcy nor the release affected the enforceability of the promise. Willie's wife still held the promise at the time the uncle died, and her transfer of the promise to her mother, again on the day of the uncle's funeral, was therefore effective.

Sidway suspects that Willie came up with the story of the assignment to his wife only after reading the reply to the complaint. But even if he had made the assignment, it is still by no means obvious that the assignment was effective. By Willie's own account, he made the assignment gratuitously just a few weeks before his bankruptcy petition, and, again by his own account, he did it for the express purpose of keeping this asset beyond the reach of his creditors (the largest of whom was, of course, his uncle). Making a secret, gratuitous transfer to a close relative on the eve of bankruptcy is as flagrant a fraudulent conveyance as one might imagine. Failing to disclose it in the bankruptcy was a capital crime through the eighteenth century. In the nineteenth century, as in our own time, such transfers could be set aside and, if discovered, lead to a denial of discharge.[38] It is hard to imagine a principle more firmly embedded in the law. When Willie produces the release, he seems oblivious to fraudulent conveyance law and even claims that before he did it he consulted with his lawyers, the same ones involved in this litigation.[39]

---

trary, Record at 40, as does his own lawyer. (The lawyer filed an affidavit stating that he "saw an assignment in writing, made by William E. Story 2d, of this claim to the plaintiff." Record at 95. The affidavit was intended to help Willie and his family, as it was their effort to explain the error in the original complaint.) It may be that Willie made a general assignment of any rights he might have against the uncle at a time when he did not know whether his uncle might have left some modest bequest to him.

We do not know that much about the firm of Swift and Weaver, the lawyers that Willie and his family used for many years (in its various incarnations). It had its own share of problems at the time. One of the associates in the firm, indeed the one who notarized the lawyer's unusual affidavit, committed suicide just a few days after the trial ended. *See Probable Suicide at Buffalo*, N.Y. Times, July 29, 1889, at 1. The timing is an odd coincidence, but there is no other reason to think it connected with this case. Only for the mystery writer with a historical/legal bent does it present another possible narrative.

[38] *See* 14 Stat. 531–32, 534, 39th Cong., 2d Sess., ch. 176, §§29, 35 (1867). For the parallel provisions under current law, see 11 U.S.C. §§548, 727.

[39] Willie says he asked his lawyers whether, to make the assignment effective, his wife had to give him an actual dollar or whether it was sufficient to allege it in the written assignment. *See* Record at 52.

Sidway does not buy any of this. Even if Willie kept his promise, even if the uncle agreed to hold the money in trust for him, even if the uncle did not discharge his promise by setting up Willie in business the first time, even if Willie actually made the assignment to his wife, the promise should still not be honored. Because Willie's wife and mother-in-law provided no value, they cannot take free of a fraud perpetrated on the party against whom the action is being brought. Louise's rights against the uncle are no better than her son-in-law's.

Willie and his relatives now come back with a new factual claim to surmount this objection. This one too falls short of being completely convincing. They claim that the uncle was later told about the fraudulent assignment after the bankruptcy and gave it his blessing.[40] Sidway, however, had already heard enough and refuses to settle.

From Sidway's vantage point, each new explanation makes it clearer that the action Willie and his side of the family are bringing is built on sand.[41] The story as a whole does not hold together. There are too many weak links. If the uncle were still alive, it is almost inconceivable that he could have been forced to pay. At every turn, the uncle made it clear that he would turn over the money only when he thought the time was right. The decision to turn over the money was one that, in the uncle's view, was exclusively his, not Willie's, not his mother-in-law's, and not a court's. At least one of the links—that the uncle blessed the fraud Willie perpetrated on him—rests on the flimsiest of evidence that any testimony from the uncle would have dispelled.

Franklin Sidway's frustration with the case may reflect a lack of comfort with a peculiarity of Anglo-American law. It breaks causes of action into discrete elements. Each link in the story that Willie and his relatives need to tell to make the promise enforceable is weak. Nevertheless, to win they need show only that each link is more likely than not. Each of the factual claims (that there was a bargained-for ex-

---

[40] Even if we credit the father's story that the uncle blessed Willie's fraudulent assignment of the promise to his wife, it gives additional reason to think the promise was not intended to be (and was not understood by Willie to be) legally enforceable. The father reported that in the course of approving of the transfer, his brother added that he "should not let him nor her have the money until he thought they could take care of it." Record at 37. In other words, at the same time he acquiesced in the assignment, William made it clear that he retained the exclusive power to decide when to make the payment.

[41] I am inferring Sidway's frustration and refusal to believe Willie and his relatives from that of his lawyers. It becomes manifest at various points during the trial, especially when Willie and his father contradict each other or say things that strike them as especially implausible.

change, that Willie kept the promise, that the uncle did not discharge the promise either time he set Willie up in business, that Willie did make the assignment to his wife, that the uncle blessed it) leaves ground for doubt, but so long as the fact-finder believes each of them standing alone to be more likely than not, the promise is enforceable, even if in the aggregate the probability that all are true is small.[42]

In assessing the relative equities, it should be remembered that Willie's omission from the will was likely deliberate. To be sure, there was no falling out between the two, and no event that would lead the uncle to renege on his promise.[43] But Willie grew up, married, and moved away. As their paths diverged, the uncle's affections and attentions went elsewhere, perhaps to the nieces living with him at the time he died.[44]

Nor is there any evidence that the uncle was casual in keeping his affairs and simply forgot about the $5,000. If he maintained a separate account for one of his nieces, he could have easily done so for his nephew. At least from the time that Willie turned twenty-one, the uncle had made it clear that Willie would have the $5,000 only when he, the uncle, thought the time right, and that time never came to pass, most likely because the original purpose of the promise was to set up Willie in business, and the uncle had done this not once, but twice. He likely thought that doing this (something that cost him considerably more than $5,000) was sufficient to discharge whatever obligation he owed.

The story behind *Hamer v. Sidway* should make Corbin's heirs uneasy. Enforcing all promises seriously made and reasonably relied upon makes sense only if courts can engage in fact finding with sufficient precision. Even without reaching any of the other complications in the story (of which there are many), the uncertainties around whether Willie kept his side of the bargain by themselves provide a powerful counter to the intuition that promises seriously made and relied upon should be legally enforceable. Such an approach relies on a jury to decide whether the promise was kept and trusts the lawyer's skill at tracking down and then cross-examining Willie's college friends. Why would someone in the uncle's position want to risk such a

---

[42] *See* Gary Lawson, *Proving the Law*, 86 Nw. U. L. Rev. 859 (1992).

[43] Record at 45 ("They never had any words that I know of. I have never in my life know them to have a word.").

[44] Willie, however, was disappointed that "he was left out in the cold," and those in his inner circle did express their "astonishment" at what others had received. Record at 60.

thing when he makes a gratuitous promise? And why should we force it
on him?

The further the promise from the marketplace, the more likely it
has conditions implicit and explicit. Understanding what a promise
means as circumstances change in a fluid social setting is a complicated business. Moreover, making a promise legally enforceable brings
costs along with it. Litigation is expensive and prone to error. One
should not blindly accept the syllogism that if keeping promises is
good, then making them legally enforceable is even better. It is one
thing to say that I am morally bound to keep any promise I make seriously and quite another to say that when I make such a promise, I
must expose myself to a swearing contest with my nephew's fraternity
brothers.

If we look at the case again from the position of nineteenth-century
formalists, we may find the case less troubling. To be sure, at least
since the time Willie turned twenty-one, his uncle insisted that he had
complete discretion over whether to turn over the money. Willie knew
this early on and did not object over the course of more than a decade.
If either thought the promise was intended to be legally enforceable, he
would have acted differently. But we can nevertheless reconcile the
outcome with traditional doctrine in the same way one can reconcile
anomalous outcomes under any formal legal rule. Formal rules by their
nature are over- and underinclusive. The idea of a bargained-for exchange works well for the vast majority of cases. This case may be the
odd one in which it does not work well. Moreover, if the uncle had not
wanted his promise to be legally enforceable, he should not have
couched it in terms of a bargain. People who use the language of a bargained-for exchange and do not intend their promises to be legally enforceable do so at their peril.

The idea of focusing on the bargained-for exchange usually makes
sense, and if we simply direct the fact-finder to determine whether William intended to make his promise legally enforceable, we are likely to
go wrong. Indeed, by relying on the uncle's probable intent to guide us,
we may become too smug and too comfortable with what we are doing.
We shall purport to be answering the question, what did the uncle intend? but in fact we shall be continuing to ask whether we think that it
is a good idea that this promise should be enforced, given all the facts
and circumstances.

To find fault with Langdell or Corbin is not the same as coming up
with a legal rule that is better. How exactly should one identify the
domain of legally enforceable promises? If a general inquiry into intent
is too slippery, if bargained-for consideration and reasonable reliance
are unsatisfactory, what are the alternatives? In the next part of this
essay, I suggest that before answering this question, we should first

examine the larger context in which the controversy in *Hamer v. Sid-way* plays itself out.

Reconstructing *Hamer v. Sidway* (again)

Another reconstruction of *Hamer v. Sidway* focuses on William and his relationship with James, his elder brother (and Willie's father). William Story was a "man of generous impulses, and though rather brusque in manner, had really a kind heart."[45] A lifelong bachelor, he had been a successful businessman who, after earning his fortune, retired in his early fifties. James Story, Willie's father, was his elder brother. Far from enjoying his younger brother's success, James had been a failure much of his life. The two brothers, however, had always been on good terms. William visited his elder brother frequently. A room in James's house was set aside for William, and James named his son after him.[46]

James turned to his younger brother for support many times over the years. William helped him start up a business on at least two occasions. When William died after a short illness at the age of sixty-three, he left only a modest bequest to his brother and likely left the bulk of his estate to his nieces. Their father (the youngest of the three brothers) had died some years before, and two of the nieces were living with William at the time he died.

The day after William's funeral James and Willie met with the family lawyers in Buffalo and arranged for them to assert whatever legal rights they might have against William Story's estate. To do this, the two assigned gratuitously all their rights against the estate to Louise Hamer, Willie's mother-in-law. Their reasons for calling so quickly upon the family lawyers and making "arrangements for bringing suits and claims and all that sort of thing"[47] are lost to us. As in *Mills v. Wyman*, however, the record suggests one.

The relationship between William and James had always been partially business and partially familial. Money was always an issue. William was the largest creditor in his brother's bankruptcy. Indeed, he was the one who precipitated it. (In James's words, "I went into bankruptcy at the suggestion of my brother. He said if I didn't go he would compel me to go."[48]) Because he took collateral for loans to his brother,

---

[45] *See Death of William E. Storey* [*sic*], Buffalo Daily Courier, Jan. 30, 1887, at 4.

[46] Record at 37–38.

[47] *See* Record at 40, 44.

[48] Record at 89.

William ended up with most of the property, while the other creditors received 15 cents on the dollar.

Money also entered into the picture when it came to taking care of their own father a few years later. A widower, the father fell ill and became demented. William was unwilling to take care of him and persuaded his elder brother to do it in return for $150 a month (over and above his expenses, which William would also cover). When asked to explain why his brother would give him $150 a month "for taking care of your own father in your own house from your own brother,"[49] James explained, "My father was crazy. I was poor, my brother was rich."[50]

At the time William died, James was seventy and a widower. This case may be one of the many we have in which the estate planning is incomplete. William likely made a conscious decision not to leave anything to his nephew Willie, but the treatment of his brother is another matter. At the time of William's death, the relationship may have been one in which business and personal were merged. After James's business failed, we know that on more than one occasion his brother would buy a house and James would live in it while renovating it.[51] This process of "fixing over" houses may have been a way for William to support his brother without putting his elder brother in the position of taking an explicit handout.

Because William died unexpectedly after only a short illness at the age of sixty-three, he may not yet have confronted the question of incorporating this ongoing, loose arrangement into his estate plan. If James still lived in a house that his brother owned and he wished to keep it, he would have to buy it from the estate. In other words, William's unexpected death might have left James without a place to live.

James may have turned to his son for help, and Willie may have in turn gone to his mother-in-law. She might have agreed to help, but if she had, it would have made sense for them to assign whatever rights they had against the estate to her so they could be offset against whatever she had to pay for the house. This account explains why James, who was poor and who stood to inherit something under the will, would make a gratuitous assignment of this bequest to his son's mother-in-law the day of his brother's funeral. The case itself may have concluded not with a payment from Franklin Sidway to Louise Hamer, but rather a credit against money she owed the estate as a result of the purchase of a house for her son-in-law's father.

---

[49] Record at 89.

[50] Record at 90.

[51] Record at 44 ("that was the first house that we fixed over").

In any event, Willie's side of the family consolidated whatever rights it had against the uncle's estate and put them in the hands of Louise Hamer.[52] There is no doubt that at the core of *Hamer v. Sidway* is a series of intrafamilial wealth transfers. The tension, in other words, is likely between William's nieces and his indigent brother. In all of this, Willie is a bystander. Rather than the wayward adolescent being paid to hew to the straight and narrow, Willie appears as a responsible adult trying to find the means to care for his father. The complications that give rise to the litigation arise not from a gratuitous promise but from a long and complicated business and personal relationship between two brothers that comes to an end when one of them dies unexpectedly.

The larger story of *Hamer v. Sidway* is not about a single promise intended to curtail teenage smoking and drinking, but rather about a number of complicated relationships inside an extended family. In this story, what role should the law play? How, for example, would things have played themselves out if, instead of bargained-for consideration, we had a formal rule that made promises inside the family legally enforceable only when accompanied with a requisite level of formality, such as a notarized written document?

The standard objection to requiring legal rituals is that the parties will not know about them or be willing to spend the time and money they require. Willie and his family, however, provide evidence to the contrary. They were eager to take advantage of legal forms. Indeed, Willie's naïve belief in legal formalities (an eve-of-bankruptcy transfer to his wife regular in form only) is one of the sources of difficulty.

Imagine that an intrafamily promise such as the one that William made Willie is legally enforceable and assignable only if it is notarized. If we focus narrowly on the facts of *Hamer v. Sidway* as usually recounted, such a rule exhibits distinct virtues. Willie and his uncle had a number of transactions over the years (including the execution of a release) that were heavily lawyered. The uncle would have been aware of such a rule that required promises to be notarized to be enforceable. The uncle might have declined to go through the necessary ritual or he might have done so. The rule would have forced him to make his inten-

---

[52] It is clear that putting all the rights against William into Louise's hands was something that someone wanted done quickly. When Willie returned from the funeral, he stopped in Elmira only long enough to meet his wife and her mother at the train station and oversee his wife's executing the assignment of her rights against William (consisting only of the promise Willie had assigned to her) to her mother. Willie presumably brought back from Buffalo documents that the family lawyers had prepared there.

tions clear. Given the amount of money involved and the explicit quid pro quo, there seems no harm in this.[53]

But this is only one part of the story. While a formal rule would have come to the aid of the Storys in the case of the promise between the uncle and the nephew, it cannot help with what may have been the principal problem the parties faced—unscrambling the relationship between the two brothers. Some relationships in a family are not spelled out and cannot be. James may have believed that his brother participated in his various ventures at arm's length. In his own mind, he was not taking any handouts from his younger brother. For his part, William may not have thought, and may not have wanted to think, about exactly how much he was in business with his brother and how much he was supporting him. There are virtues in open-ended relationships that leave much undeveloped.[54] But there are costs as well.

There are many cases, especially from this period, in which courts confront disappointed relatives who did not receive under a will what they had been promised.[55] Courts struggle to reconcile the law of trusts and estates, contract doctrine, and the dictates of equity. The larger story of *Hamer v. Sidway* underscores that in our legal system, as in every legal system, there are limits to what the law can do. In particular, our legal culture is one in which the law reduces relationships to discrete transactions and specified rights. There are many virtues to this legal culture, but such a legal system can do little when the problem is not a broken promise, but rather a relationship that has never been formalized and perhaps could not have been. A discrete rights-based conception of law often maps poorly onto what happens inside a family and other social settings where, in our society at least, many relationships are incompletely reasoned.

---

[53] Moreover, formal legal rules governing the assignment of the promise would have dispelled one of the lingering ambiguities in the case—whether the uncle knew that Willie had assigned his claim to his wife at the time of the release.

[54] Cass Sunstein explores these in the environment of a collegial court, where incompletely reasoned agreements are the norm. *See* CASS R. SUNSTEIN, ONE CASE AT A TIME (1999). The costs of having a "completely reasoned" account are, of course, somewhat different in this environment, as they include the psychic costs of unpacking and monetizing understandings between blood relatives.

[55] *See* Hartog, *supra* note 19.

Conclusion

We have doctrines that organize the law and make it predictable and consistent across cases, but we should not pretend that these doctrines have a totemic character. Many of the legal concepts we have fashioned work well, but there is a limit to the amount of weight we can ask them to bear. It is too easy to forget that the ultimate test for whether a promise should be legally enforceable should turn not on consideration or reasonable reliance but rather on whether enforcing that promise will make the society in which it operates a better place.

The principles of reliance and bargained-for consideration may be a useful way to identify legally enforceable obligations. But they can be useful only if we understand their limits. They may make only imperfect sense of the promise between William and Willie, and they neglect (and perhaps must neglect) the far more complicated relationships between William and his brother, between William and his nieces, between Willie and his father, and between Willie and his mother-in-law. Finding that someone in Willie's position bargained with his uncle or reasonably relied on his promise as a teenager does remarkably little to unravel this web, one in which the law has only a supporting role. *Hamer v. Sidway* presents problems we cannot solve merely by uttering the magic words of "bargained-for consideration" or "reliance."

We cannot expect pat answers. The law of contracts and the world in which it operates are both too rich and too subtle to be reduced to a single metric. We must continue to reconstruct the law of contracts, remembering that the test of new organizing ideas or formal rules is whether they are useful. They will be man-made rather than God-given. The principles we fashion cannot be independent of time and place. As Aristotle reminds us, fires burn here as in Persia, but the laws are different.[56]

---

[56] ARISTOTLE, NICOMACHEAN ETHICS V.7.

7

Robert W. Gordon*

Britton v. Turner: A Signpost on the Crooked Road to "Freedom" in the Employment Contract

Britton v. Turner[1] is an old New Hampshire case that shows up in most of the major modern contracts casebooks. A farm laborer under a one-year contract to work for an annual wage of $120 quit his job without cause in the tenth month, thus breaching his contract. He then sued his employer in quantum meruit for the reasonable value of the work he had performed up to that point. The employer's defense was that completing the contract was the condition precedent to the laborer's right to payment, and that to allow a breaching plaintiff any recovery at all would promote immorality by giving people incentives to break their contracts. The New Hampshire Supreme Court, through Justice Joel Parker, held for the employee. The court said that even a

* Chancellor Kent Professor of Law and Legal History, Yale University. This is a considerably revised and expanded version of a paper first given at the Association of American Law Schools annual meeting in 2003 and subsequently published in 26 Hawaii L. Rev. 423 (2004). I see this essay primarily as a window to showcase for teachers and students of contract law some of the extraordinary recent work of legal historians on contract law. I have taken inspiration over the years from the brilliant pioneer writers of background stories to famous cases: Stewart Macaulay, Richard Danzig, and Brian Simpson. I am grateful to Elizabeth Bouvier, chief archivist of the Supreme Judicial Court of Massachusetts, and Barbara Hogan, clerk of the Cheshire County (N.H.) Superior Court, for help in searching for court records. Special thanks to Eric Tam, who provided the research on wage-payment statutes.

[1] Britton v. Turner, 6 N.H. 481 (1834).

breaching party should be able to recover the value of his services, off-set by defendant's damages, if any. Otherwise an employee who had done most of the year's work would suffer a forfeiture: "[T]he party who attempts performance may be placed in a much worse situation than he who wholly disregards his contract"; "the other party may receive much more, by the breach of the contract, than the injury which he has sustained by such breach" and thus more than he could recover in damages.[2]

This seemingly unremarkable little case has had a long and remarkable career. As we shall see, it was cited and debated by state courts throughout the nineteenth century. Writers of treatises on contracts, quasi-contracts, and employment law singled it out for special comment. In the twentieth century—even after legislation mandating regular wage payments had rendered the doctrine of the case mostly irrelevant—jurists like the great contracts scholars Samuel Williston and Arthur Corbin continued to fight over the decision and whether the American Law Institute should accept or reject its holding. Starting in the 1970s a half-dozen historians of labor and contract law revived interest in the case and contributed to studies of its origins and significance.

In the contracts casebooks, *Britton* is generally used to illustrate the current doctrine—not universally accepted but sufficiently respectable to be codified in the *Uniform Commercial Code* and *Restatement (Second) of Contracts*[3]—that even a plaintiff in default should be able to recover the value of part performance (less damages to the other party, up to the limit of the contract price or rate) in restitution. It also illustrates the more general remedial principles disfavoring forfeitures and penal or deterrent damages. And it is sometimes cited in sections of the casebooks dealing with implied or constructive conditions of exchange, to illustrate that "work first, pay later" is the default rule, if no time of payment is expressly specified, in service or construction contracts.

This chapter aims to put the case back into historical context. This will not be the usual Law Story that focuses on the immediate background to a case, the particular facts that gave rise to it, and the particular people who litigated and decided it. It turns out that not much can be discovered about those facts and personalities anyway.[4] My aim

---

[2] *Id.* at 487.

[3] UCC §2-718(2), (3); RESTATEMENT (SECOND) OF CONTRACTS §374.

[4] A search of the Cheshire County, New Hampshire, courthouse, where the records of *Britton v. Turner* would be if they still existed, failed to turn up any documents. Some records—pleadings, summary of testimony, and schedule of

here is rather to pull back to take a wider view of the case, as an incident in the long narrative of legal rules governing the worker who quits and his relationship with his employer or master. I hope to persuade you that taking the long view helps the law teacher and her students to begin to figure out: What are the real stakes of these technical issues of doctrine? Why does it matter, and for whom, what view you take?

Let me drop a short aside here on the stakes of legal rules. The very first case I read in law school was for civil procedure; it was *Sibbach v. Wilson,*[5] a case brought in the federal diversity jurisdiction. The case was meant to introduce the class to the *Erie Railroad v. Tompkins* problem, and for the next few weeks we were kept busy analyzing whether state law or federal procedural rules should govern this case and others like it brought in the federal diversity jurisdiction. The one question we never examined was why anyone—except, of course, the litigants who might find federal or state law better or worse for their side in a particular dispute—would care what the answer was. What was at stake? Not until many years later did I learn that the *Erie* problem had a history, which was that interstate corporations, especially railroads, fled from state tort law *en masse* into pro-defendant federal jurisdiction with its "federal common law." The railroads essentially used the federal courts to nullify state law more favorable to personal-injury plaintiffs. *Erie* was the Supreme Court's attempt to put an end to this practice, and cases like *Sibbach* were the dying embers of these once flaming economic and political wars.[6] The rule in *Britton v. Turner* is much the same. The particular fighting issues that made the case important in its time have faded. But the case continues to shed light on a whole range of social conflicts and ideologies, involving parties with high stakes in the outcomes, that are very much alive.

---

costs—survive of *Stark v. Parker,* the other major case discussed here: What they add of interest to our story appears below.

[5] Sibbach v. Wilson & Co., 312 U.S. 1 (1941).

[6] The (magnificent) history of these conflicts—and also of the depoliticizing of them in postwar academic writing and teaching of federal jurisdiction—is EDWARD A. PURCELL JR., LITIGATION AND INEQUALITY: FEDERAL DIVERSITY JURISDICTION IN INDUSTRIAL AMERICA, 1870–1958 (1992), and EDWARD A. PURCELL JR., BRANDEIS AND THE PROGRESSIVE CONSTITUTION: *ERIE,* THE JUDICIAL POWER, AND THE POLITICS OF THE FEDERAL COURTS IN TWENTIETH CENTURY AMERICA (2001).

A First Look at the "Entire Contract" Doctrine

Britton v. Turner—as some but not all the casebooks point out—was an outlier when it was decided. The standard rule that emerged and persisted in most American jurisdictions in the nineteenth century was the "entire contract" or "entirety" rule. A contract of hiring that did not specify its duration was presumed to be for a year and to be "entire," that is, not divisible into increments of time. Thus the worker who quits without cause before the year is out has not performed his side of the bargain and therefore forfeits all claims to unpaid wages.[7] The leading American case is from Massachusetts, *Stark v. Parker* (1824).[8] This case also involved a farm laborer who had contracted for a year's labor at $120 for the year, who walked off the job partway through his term and asked for payment for the work done so far. The Supreme Judicial Court held through Justice Levi Lincoln Jr. that serving out the year is the condition precedent for his right to recover payment for the work, and that this is a good rule because it discourages contract breach and rewards faithful service.

Stark and *Britton* make a fine matched pair for teaching purposes. The judges who wrote the opinions were strong-minded lawyers, both major public figures in their time. Levi Lincoln Jr. (1782–1868) was elected governor of Massachusetts the year after *Stark v. Parker* was decided, and later represented the commonwealth in Congress.[9] Joel Parker (1795–1875) served ten years as chief justice of New Hampshire; he went on to be a third of the Harvard Law School faculty in the 1850s and 1860s and an important writer on the constitutional issues surrounding slavery, secession, the conduct of the Civil War, and Reconstruction.

Justice Lincoln's decision in *Stark* relies partly on formal doctrinal grounds. One (he asserts, not entirely accurately[10]) is that most com-

---

[7] See (collecting cases) 2 C. B. LaBatt, Master and Servant §501 (1913); 3 Samuel Williston, The Law of Contracts §1477 (1920); Wythe Holt, *Recovery for the Worker Who Quits: A Comparison of the Mainstream, Legal Realist and Critical Legal Studies Approaches to the Problem of Nineteenth Century Contract Law*, 1986 Wis. L. Rev. 677; Peter Karsten, Heart versus Head: Judge-Made Law in Nineteenth Century America 177 (1997); Christopher Tomlins, Law, Labor and Ideology in the American Republic 273–78 (1993).

[8] 19 Mass. (2 Pick.) 267 (1824).

[9] His father, Levi Lincoln Sr., was even more distinguished. He too was briefly governor of Massachusetts, represented Massachusetts in Congress, and was President Jefferson's attorney general.

[10] Christopher Tomlins argues that the ruling in *Stark* was a "major innovation in local law," citing among other sources a contemporary newspaper report

mon law precedents, both English and American, support it. (The cases that disagree, says the court, represent a "departure from ancient and well-established principles."[11]) The other is the principle that fulfillment of the promise to work, and of the promise to pay, are dependent constructive conditions of exchange, so that the employee's complete performance of the work is a condition precedent to his right of action: "The money was to be paid in compensation for the service, and not as a consideration for an engagement to serve."[12]

So far, however, nothing explains why it's the employee who has to perform first and perform in full. The court gives some substantive reasons for that conclusion. Some of its reasons derive from custom, "[t]he usages of the country and common opinion . . . . [I]n no case has a contract [like this one] been construed by practical men to give a right to demand the agreed compensation, before the performance of the labor, and that the employer and employed universally so understand it."[13] (Note that the court is being a bit slippery here. "Practical men" may well agree that the worker is not entitled to advance payment for work not yet done. The issue is whether he may claim *any* payment for work *already done*, before it has *all* been done, especially if *most* of it is done.) Other reasons derive from policy and morality: "Nothing can be more unreasonable than that a man, who deliberately and wantonly violates an engagement, should be permitted to seek in a court of justice an indemnity from the consequences of his voluntary act. . . . The law indeed is most reasonable in itself. It denies only to a party an advantage from his own wrong."[14]

Ten years later, Judge Parker in *Britton* starts out by noting the *Stark* rule, but immediately points out that such a "technical rule . . . in its operation may be very unequal, not to say unjust," because the employer will realize a windfall by being allowed to appropriate the benefit of all the employee's work even if the damage is "trifling," while the employee who serves nearly to the end will lose everything.[15]

---

of the case that said that hitherto the right of a quitting laborer to recover his wages in quantum meruit "has generally been understood to be the common law of the State." TOMLINS, *supra* note 7, at 276.

[11] 19 Mass. at 275.

[12] *Id.*

[13] *Id.* at 274. This construction of the likely expectations of the parties would seem to be somewhat undermined by the fact that the employer in *Stark* had earlier paid three months' wages.

[14] *Id.* at 273, 275.

[15] 6 N.H. at 486, 487.

Parker bolsters his opinion with a line of cases that had softened the forfeiture effects of the *Stark* rule in the context of builders' contracts. Four years after *Stark* the Massachusetts court held that a builder, unlike an employee, could get quantum meruit for work performed if he were held in breach, since the house was "still valuable and capable of being used" and "it would be a hard case indeed if the builder could recover nothing."[16] As Wythe Holt has shown, the builders' cases were to remain for over a century a major embarrassment for jurisdictions that adopted the "entirety" rule in employment contracts: The courts had a hard time explaining why employees' labor didn't leave behind value that the employer couldn't help but accept just as contractors' labor did.[17] By importing the builders'-contract doctrine into the employment context, Parker added, he was simply carrying out the reasonable expectations of the parties, "for we have abundant reason to believe, that the general understanding of the community is, that the hired laborer shall be entitled to compensation for the service actually performed . . . and such contracts must be presumed to be made with reference to that understanding, unless an express stipulation shows the contrary."[18]

Parker concludes with a policy argument of his own about incentives: His rule will "leave no temptation to the [employer] to drive the laborer from his service, near the end of his term, by ill treatment, in order to escape from payment; nor to the latter to desert his service before the stipulated time, without a sufficient reason . . . ."[19] This last point appears to be a direct riposte to Judge Lincoln's assertion in *Stark* that "[a]ny apprehension that [the entirety] rule may be abused to the purposes of oppression, by holding out an inducement to the employer, by unkind treatment near the end of close of a term of service, to drive the laborer from his engagement, to the sacrifice of his wages, is wholly groundless," because "[w]herever there is a reasonable excuse

---

[16] The leading case was Hayward v. Leonard, 24 Mass. 181 (1828), also republished in many modern contracts casebooks. The doctrine at first applied only to cases where the builder had "substantially performed" his contract and his breaches were considered nonmaterial, but it was gradually expanded to give the builder a general restitutionary remedy for work performed, at least so long as the breach was not "willful."

[17] *See* Holt, *supra* note 7, at 681ff.

[18] 6 N.H. at 493.

[19] *Id.* at 494.

[I think he means, if the employer puts himself in breach of contract by behaving abusively or firing without cause], the law allows recovery."[20]

So we have two cases on nearly identical facts in adjoining New England states, decided ten years apart, looking at the world through two subtly different conceptual lenses. The opinions differ on customary expectations of the parties; on the likely incentive effects of different rules; and most basically on the grand eternal contest of principle within contract law: Is it to be a mechanism for forcing people to perform their promises, and to deter or punish immoral breachers? Or is it to be indifferent as between performance and breach so long as the breacher pays damages?[21] Note that in this contest the *Stark* rule straddles both sides. The employer who breaches must only pay compensatory damages, the contract wage reduced by whatever the employee earned or could have earned at another job. The breaching employee forfeits his entire wage.

On many basic matters the cases are in accord. Both cases supply implied (default) terms to the contractual relationship: Yearlong contracts are entire; payment on the contract is not due until the year's end; the worker breaches by quitting early. The parties *could* expressly spell out their own times and terms of payment in exchange for performance. The *Britton* court itself points out that the parties could if they wished contract around its holding and specify the result of the majority *Stark* doctrine—no payment until and unless a full year's work had been performed.

Since these are default rules, the party whom the rules favor can reap their benefits without having to say anything at the onset of the contract about the term in question. Under the majority *Stark* rule, unless a worker is prepared to lose a year's wages, he is effectively indentured to his employer for the entire term, even if he gets a better offer elsewhere, even if he wants to quit because the boss is abusive. If he is not deterred from quitting because he doesn't know about the secret term, he may be in for a nasty surprise when he actually quits. If the boss were abusive enough, of course, the boss would himself be in material breach of contract, which would entitle the worker both to quit work and to damages. But this is not much comfort to the worker: It leaves a farm laborer who has not yet been paid for his work with

---

[20] 19 Mass. at 275.

[21] And it touches on another grand contest: Is the role of contract law to enforce even harsh bargains to the limit? Or is it to enforce only within a range of results securing fair and equitable returns to both sides?

the burden of having to bring and finance a lawsuit.[22] Besides (as we shall see), because employment law gave masters so much authority over their servants, it was much easier for the master to put his servant in breach than the other way around: All he had to do was to give orders that the servant disobeyed, or just provoke him to insolent or defiant behavior. Anyway, the default rule allows even the manifestly abusive employer the self-help remedy of holding on to the money, to withhold back wages without going to court. Even *Britton*'s more generous rule requires the worker to incur the costs and risks of a lawsuit to recover his wage. And even if he got past those barriers, as Robert Steinfeld has pointed out, "it was always possible for an unsympathetic judge . . . to find that the damage to the employer from the worker's breach fully equaled the value of any labor performed, leaving the worker to recover nothing."[23]

A builder or contractor supplying materials and labor on a building contract, likely to be a business-savvy repeat-playing party, will, of course, usually insist on structuring the contract to get around the rule that he must finish the entire job before being entitled to any payment, and provide for periodic payments to finance the work as it proceeds. (He will also get a mechanic's lien on the realty.) A farm laborer or factory worker, we may speculate, is more likely to accept work on the terms offered, less likely to be aware of the invisible terms of the contract, and even if aware of them to be much less likely, unless labor is scarce and his skills unusual, to be able to contract around them.

In his famous lectures on *The Common Law* (1881), Oliver Wendell Holmes Jr. used the "work first, pay later" rule to illustrate his argument that the law implies conditions for "practical" rather than formal reasons:

---

[22] John Stark's experience would have been an alarming cautionary tale for any worker contemplating a lawsuit. Stark sued to recover $64. In the first trial the jury awarded him $23.37. After reversal on motion for a new trial the case was sent back for a second jury trial, and Stark won again, this time a verdict for damages of $31.68. On Parker's motion for a new trial the Supreme Judicial Court decided the case we know as *Stark v. Parker*, and sent the parties back for a third trial. This time Stark lost, and was taxed with Parker's costs, which came to $116—almost twice the amount in controversy, and very nearly his entire annual wage of $120. This does not count anything spent on attorney's fees. Records of Stark v. Parker, Supreme Judicial Court, Suffolk County, Record Book Vol. March–November 1826 (Mass. SJC Archives).

[23] Robert J. Steinfeld, Coercion, Contract and Free Labor in the Nineteenth Century 300 (2001).

How are you to decide which is to be done first, that is to say, which promise is dependent upon performance on the other side? It is only by reference to the habits of the community and to convenience. It is not enough to say that on the principle of equivalency a man is not presumed to pay for a thing until he has it. The work is payment for the money, as much as the money for the work, and one must be paid for in advance. The question is, why, if one man is not presumed to intend to pay money until he has money's worth, the other is presumed to intend to give money's worth before he has money. An answer cannot be obtained from any general theory. The fact that employers, as a class, can be trusted for wages more safely than the employed for their labor, that the employers have had the power and have been the law-makers, or other considerations, it matters not what, have determined that the work is to be done first.[24]

Holmes's practical reasons, you observe, turn out to be some mix of custom, (the employer's) convenience, class bias, and class power.[25] But clearly there are ways to justify the "entirety" rule more sympathetic to employers. One is that the risk-averse laborer gets something valuable for the deferral of his right to wages, the job security that comes with a full-year contract. (For that security he may also have to accept a somewhat lower wage than the spot price for day labor.) The farmer needs extra security for the worker's performance—in particular, that the hired hand will stick around for the harvest when he is most needed. The worker's promise to perform is not security enough, because (for reasons we will say more about in a moment) the remedy of specific performance is not available against the worker who quits, and damages may well as a practical matter be unobtainable, either because the worker is judgment-proof or because he has skipped the ju-

---

[24] OLIVER WENDELL HOLMES JR., THE COMMON LAW 263–64 (Mark deWolfe Howe ed., Belknap Press of Harvard Univ. Press 1963) (1881).

[25] The class bias explanation for the majority rule is accepted by most modern writers, e.g., MORTON HORWITZ, THE TRANSFORMATION OF AMERICAN LAW 187–88 (1977); Herbert D. Laube, *The Defaulting Employee*—Britton v. Turner *Reviewed*, 83 U. Pa. L. Rev. 825 (1935), 3A ARTHUR CORBIN, CORBIN ON CONTRACTS §676, at 209 (1952) ("Why must the employee give 'credit' and the employer not? Why must the employee carry the risk of getting nothing for his labor, while the employer does not carry the risk of getting no labor for his money? . . . No doubt this custom arose because of the superior economic position of the employers—the 'masters' "); and Holt, *supra* note 7; but resisted by others, e.g., KARSTEN, *supra* note 7.

risdiction. The farmer can provide against this risk by holding back the wage until the work is done. Also, as we shall see, farmers were often strapped for cash and had to ask their hands to advance work on credit, waiting for the crop to be harvested and sold to realize their wages.[26]

Each party can inflict harm on the other by taking opportunistic advantage of the other's situation of necessity or unrecoverable sunk costs. The worker can walk out on his employer just when his services are most urgently needed.[27] The employer (as the *Britton* court feared) can wait until the work is almost done and then try to avoid payment by inducing the employee's breach or finding a pretext to fire him. The predominance of the *Stark* over the *Britton* rule suggests most courts were more worried about protecting the employers' security than policing against their opportunism, and less confident than Justice Parker that the threat of damages for breach would keep workers from walking off the job.[28] Quite possibly one of the factors influencing these decisions was that wage labor in this period of New England's history

---

[26] *See* KARSTEN, *supra* note 7, at 180 (also noting that in many cases the farmers may have already made substantial in-kind payments such as room and board to their hired hands and may well have needed scarce cash to pay for seed, machinery, and other capital investments).

[27] He can also try to hold up the employer for a higher wage—as in another famous contracts case, Alaska Packers' Association v. Domenico, 117 F. 99 (9th Cir. 1902). In such cases the courts use consideration (preexisting-duty rule) or duress doctrine to relieve the employer from having to pay the promised higher wage or to give him back the extorted surplus if he has already paid it.

[28] An early New York case adopting what would become the majority rule that a contract is presumed to be entire even if a monthly or piece-rate wage is stipulated, put it this way:

> The general practice, in hiring labor or artisans, is, for 6 or 12 months, at so much per month: the farmer hires a man for 6 or 12 months, at monthly wages; and he takes his chance of the good, with the bad months. It is well known that the labor of a man, during the summer months, is worth double the labor of the same man in winter; but upon the principles contended for by the [worker's] counsel, if the farmer hires in the autumn, for twelve months, at monthly wages, the laborer may quit his employ on the first of May, and sue for his wages, and recover them, leaving the farmer the poor resort of a suit for damages. The rule contended for holds out temptations to men to violate their contracts. The stipulation of monthly pay, or, in this case, pay by the run, does not disjoin the contract: it is adopted as the means only of ascertaining the compensation, and does not render it less entire.

M'Millan & M'Millan v. Vanderlip, 12 Johns. 165, 166–67 (N.Y. 1815).

had recently become very mobile. Farms and households were finding it hard to hold on to hired hands and servants tempted into the burgeoning higher-paying factory economy.[29] The "entire contract" rule may have aimed to deter such defections by imposing a high penalty for quitting work.[30]

Nonetheless the "entirety" rule looks like a much blunter instrument than the employer needs to protect his legitimate interests. The rule aims for a deterrent effect that the parties could not achieve with an express term providing for liquidated damages, in the event that the employee left at any time before the year was out, in the amount of the employee's entire annual wage. Such an amount would all too obviously exceed any likely losses from an employee's departure as the end of his term approached, and would therefore be stricken as a penalty. Anyway, why wouldn't the employer's damage remedy usually suffice? If he is still holding back a year's wages anyway, he could deduct his damages—measured by what he has to pay temporary day labor to fin-

---

[29] *See* Jonathan Prude, The Coming of Industrial Order: Town and Factory Life in Rural Massachusetts, 1810–1860, at 68–69 (1983).

[30] Stark himself was not a hugely sympathetic plaintiff. From the trial record of testimony of a witness who overheard the parties: "Mr. Parker asked [Stark] why he did not go back and stay out his time. Stark I think did not give him any answer. Parker then asked if he was not used well, he said he was, that he had no fault to find out doors nor in the house—except he said he was at one time shut out doors in the evening and had to go to the barn to sleep—but he did not care any thing about it. The old gentleman [Parker] said to Stark, I advise you to go and stay out your time. . . . Mr. Parker asked [Stark] where he was going—he said he was going down east. . . . Mr. Parker told Stark he left him at a busy season of the year and it was difficult for him to get a man to supply his place—& that he ought to have given him notice of his intent to quit in season for him to find another man to take his place. . . . [Parker] said it was an injury to him because he could not procure another man—or would not get another man so cheap." Records of Stark v. Parker, *supra* note 22. Karsten, *supra* note 7, at 181, interestingly suggests that the pattern of decisions, whether courts adopted the *Stark* or *Britton* rule, seems in part to have depended on how much work the employee had performed under the particular contract being litigated. Workers who had worked for most of their contract term got quantum meruit; early defectors did not. If Karsten is right, appellate courts were making general law for the future based on the incidental equities of the cases that happened to come before them. A Legal Realist would have to acknowledge that this is not an unusual occurrence. A particularly egregious example in the contracts canon is Ortolere v. Teacher's Retirement Board, 25 N.Y.2d 196, 250 N.E.2d 460 (1969) (New York Court of Appeals feels sorry for widower left destitute from wife's pension plan election, voids election on grounds of her incapacity).

ish the job—from the annual wage and pay out the rest. Some courts thought service contracts had to be entire because the employee's work was of uneven value from season to season, which made it too hard to value a portion of it. But the law could choose a default of wages spread out evenly throughout the year, and leave to employers, who usually control the terms of contracting, to replace it with a term valuing summer work at twice or more the rate of winter work, or holding back a final bonus payment until the work was completely finished.[31]

At this point we have gone about as far as speculation can take us. So let us now bring in some more background history to expand the frame and especially to assess the wage-forfeiture penalty in the context of legal regulations of the employment relationship more generally.

The Rule in Context

The wage-forfeiture rule was not, of course, an invention of nineteenth-century New England. It was part of a complex package of much more visibly coercive legal regulations of the many varieties of labor—live-in farm labor or "servants in husbandry," day labor, domestic servants, family members, apprentices, bound or indentured labor, paupers, and slaves, among others—in England and her overseas colonies. The regime had evolved in response to severe labor shortages resulting from medieval plagues and with the main purpose of keeping laborers bound to their masters and strictly regulating their terms of service. The main features of the system were criminal penalties—imprisonment or fines—for breach of contract: leaving work, absence from work, or disobeying orders. Contracts for farm labor were presumed to be from harvest to harvest; withholding payment until the end of term was one of several means to secure work at harvests. Employers could whip their servants for disobedience or insubordination. They also had obligations to care for sick or injured workers and to pay minimum wages. All these rules were enforced by local magistrates. Servants had to apply to justices of the peace for unpaid wages or permission to leave an abusive employer; but so too did masters who wanted to dismiss their servants for cause.

In England by the early nineteenth century this regime was undergoing important modifications, many of them not that favorable to contract laborers. The system was partly deregulated. (Wage regulation,

---

[31] Seasonal wage differentials were in fact sometimes written into New England farm contracts. *See* WINIFRED BARR ROTHENBERG, FROM MARKET-PLACES TO A MARKET ECONOMY: THE TRANSFORMATION OF RURAL MASSACHUSETTS, 1750–1850, at 197–98 (1992).

both maximum and minimum, had already mostly disappeared by the mid-eighteenth century.) The English state repealed most of the detailed work rules it had enacted for many trades, and allowed employers to determine them instead. Court decisions held that masters no longer had to ask magistrates for permission to fire, allowed masters a wide discretion to define what was employee insubordination or misbehavior, and eliminated the paternalistic obligations to care for the sick and injured.

Meanwhile Parliament increased criminal penalties for contract breaching, combination to raise wages, and vagrancy or idleness. It reassigned the administration of contract breaching from magistrates to police courts exercising summary jurisdiction.[32] Workers convicted of breach could be imprisoned for up to three months at hard labor in the house of correction. Douglas Hay tells us that between 1858 and 1875, masters' prosecutions of servants for leaving work amounted to 12 to 32 percent of all annual theft prosecutions.[33] Steinfeld's definitive study of criminal sanctions for contract breach finds an average of 10,000 prosecutions a year between 1857 (when comprehensive statistics began to be collected) and 1875, when, under pressure from trade unions, Parliament finally abolished most criminal penalties for leaving work.[34]

The trajectory of legal development was very different in the United States. By the 1820s and 1830s the United States had defined itself as a republic of "free labor." This self-definition was especially important to the North, to distinguish its labor system from that of the slave South and also from that of England. More than half of the immigrants to the American colonies had arrived as indentured servants, legally bound to their masters for a term of years. The master could inflict corporal discipline on his servant and have him recaptured by the sheriff if he ran away. Indentured servitude had, however, almost completely disappeared by 1820: In American law, long terms of labor service, personal powers of discipline, and legal process to recapture defaulting servants were now thought incompatible with the worker's freedom.[35]

---

[32] For a detailed account of this regime and changes in it, see Douglas Hay, *England, 1562–1875: The Law and Its Uses, in* DOUGLAS HAY & PAUL CRAVEN, MASTERS, SERVANTS, AND MAGISTRATES IN BRITAIN AND THE EMPIRE, 1562–1955, at 67–114 (2004).

[33] *Id.* at 108.

[34] STEINFELD, *supra* note 23, at 74–82.

[35] *See* ROBERT J. STEINFELD, THE INVENTION OF FREE LABOR: THE EMPLOYMENT RELATION IN ENGLISH AND AMERICAN LAW AND CULTURE, 1350–1870 (1991).

In the American North, the use of criminal process was denounced as anti-republican.[36]

The American South was yet another country. Even after emancipation of the slaves, state legislatures enacted criminal penalties for contract breaching to try to keep freed slaves bound to their former masters or to planters who had taken them on as contract labor. The legal tools for accomplishing this were statutes making leaving work presumptive evidence of fraud if the laborer had accepted any advances (e.g., of money, seed, or tools). If freedmen under contract quit, they could be arrested, convicted, and leased back to their masters by the state.[37] In the 1911 case of *Bailey v. Alabama,*[38] the United States Supreme Court held that such criminal penalties for contract breaching violated the Thirteenth Amendment and the federal anti-peonage statutes prohibiting debt peonage, compulsory service in repayment of a debt. (This holding, unfortunately, had no actual effect on the practice of Southern planters, who were still finding ways to send farm laborers to jail for leaving work through the 1940s.[39])

In the law on the books, then, first in the North, then nationwide, a crucial implied but mandatory term of the labor contract in the United States came to be that specific performance and the criminal process are unavailable against the defaulting employee. Those remedies *define* the condition of "involuntary servitude"; their unavailability defines "free labor" contracts, the remedies for breach of which are supposedly limited to damages (or negative injunctions, in a proper case).

But as we've seen under the majority rule in *Stark v. Parker,* most employers had the additional remedy of withholding back pay for work already done, the wage-forfeiture penalty of the "entire contract" default rule. Some jurisdictions enforced the doctrine very strictly: They disallowed parol evidence, for example, to show that the contract was divisible because the parties had orally agreed on a monthly or weekly wage; they gave the worker no relief even if his breach were due to

---

[36] *See* STEINFELD, *supra* note 23, at 290–308.

[37] *See* WILLIAM COHEN, AT FREEDOM'S EDGE: BLACK MOBILITY AND THE SOUTHERN WHITE QUEST FOR RACIAL CONTROL, 1861–1915 (1991).

[38] 219 U.S. 219 (1911). Alonzo Bailey contracted to work on a farm for a year at twelve dollars a month. He quit after a month and did not return fifteen dollars advanced to him. He was convicted and sentenced to 136 days of hard labor when he could not pay the $30 fine. The Court took particular exception to a provision of Alabama evidence law that disallowed the worker to rebut the presumption of fraudulent intent with his own testimony. *Id.* at 239.

[39] PETE DANIEL, THE SHADOW OF SLAVERY: PEONAGE IN THE SOUTH, 1901–1969 (1972).

sickness or even death.[40] Disputes over whether *Stark* or *Britton* was the better rule continued to vex the minds of courts and treatise writers. As time went on, *Britton* gradually attracted more converts.[41] We have seen that breaching builders were early extended rights to restitution, first only if they had "substantially performed" their contracts, later for any performance; then contractors for services generally. Some courts found a compromise in the doctrine that eventually found its way into Samuel Williston's contracts treatise (1920) and thence into the *Restatement of Contracts* (1932) for which Williston was the chief reporter: that while restitution should be denied to "willful and deliberate"[42] breachers, it should be granted to a defaulter of "honest purpose" who had "acted in good faith though under a mistaken view of his rights."[43] The Uniform Commercial Code further advanced the cause of the *Britton* party by giving the breaching buyer of goods a (slightly qualified) right to restitution of his down payment.[44] The *Restatement (Second) of Contracts* (1981)[45] and Farnsworth's contracts treatise (second edition, 1998),[46] generalize the right to recover restitution (offset, as always, by the injured party's damages) to all plaintiffs in default—providers of services, buyers of goods or land, and employees all included—and also take the moral test out of the right, allowing it regardless of the "willful" motives of the breacher. Thus *Britton v. Turner* has finally emerged from its status as the outlier in the shadows to become the principal case illustrating the consensus position. Notwithstanding this total triumph of *Britton* among the jurists, however, it "remains a minority position" for personal service contracts in American jurisdictions.[47]

---

[40] See cases cited in HORACE G. WOOD, A TREATISE ON THE LAW OF MASTER AND SERVANT §81 & §145, at 281 n.2 (1877).

[41] For histories of the case law, see Holt, *supra* note 7, *passim*; KARSTEN, *supra* note 7, at 172–82; STEINFELD, *supra* note 23, at 291–303.

[42] RESTATEMENT (FIRST) OF CONTRACTS §357(1)(a).

[43] WILLISTON, *supra* note 7, §1477, at 2631.

[44] UCC §2-718(2),(3). The qualification is that the seller retains a right to withhold 20 percent of the contract price or $500, whichever is smaller, as a statutory penalty without having to prove damages.

[45] RESTATEMENT (SECOND) OF CONTRACTS §374.

[46] 2 E. ALLAN FARNSWORTH, FARNSWORTH ON CONTRACTS §8.14 (2d ed. 1998).

[47] 1 GEORGE PALMER, LAW OF RESTITUTION §5.13 (1978).

Did the Default Rules Matter?

The "entirety" doctrine spawned a good deal of case law and learned commentary. But how important was the "entirety" rule in actual practice? Steinfeld's pioneering history comparing sanctions for contract breaching in the United States and England suggests that it was potentially quite significant. Although the United States may have renounced criminal penalties (at least in the North), he points out, it had hardly renounced coercion: The threat of losing a year's wages could be just as or more coercive than the threat of a criminal fine or three months' hard labor.[48] But there are reasons to be cautious about the practical effects of the rule.

The rule was a default rule and could be contracted around. Winifred Rothenberg collected a sample of 692 farm labor contracts from thirty-six account books of Massachusetts farmers, 1750–1865. She found that 620 of the contracts specified length and that (varying by decade) 60 to 75 percent of the contracts were for six months or less. Whether long or short, the contracts stipulated monthly rates (mostly flat rates, but sometimes variable by season). She does not tell us whether the workers were actually paid every month (in addition to their in-kind wages of room and board), but the strong implication is that they were.

In industrial New England, by contrast, employers often inserted express terms into their contracts with factory workers specifically providing for forfeiture in case the worker quit before his term or quit without giving several weeks' notice.[49] The courts were quite explicit that the purpose of these provisions was to deter strikes and other collective action that might result in large consequential losses from work stoppages. "The only valuable protection, which the manufacturer can provide against such liability to loss, and against, what are in these days denominated 'strikes,' is to make an agreement with his laborers, that if they willfully leave their machines and his employment without previous notice, all, or a certain amount of wages that may be due them shall be forfeited."[50] Factory owners evidently expected the threat of forfeiture to do some work here, but as an express term, not a default rule.

---

[48] STEINFELD, *supra* note 23, at 310.

[49] *Id.* at 303–08. Employers chose this route rather than the default rule because they wanted to be able to terminate employees after notice rather than be presumed to hire them for the year.

[50] *See, e.g.*, Harmon v. Salmon Falls Manufacturing Co., 5 Me. 447, 452 (1853).

The default rules could also simply be ignored or waived in practice. Rothenberg rather strikingly found that although sixty-eight workers, about 10 percent of her sample, suddenly quit their work before the end of their term, the farmers paid their back wages anyway. This is especially striking because reliable farm labor was indeed getting harder to find and the price of casual day labor was actually higher than contract labor, since day laborers tended to be native Yankees rather than foreign-born and to have a higher reserve wage.[51]

Factory labor was similarly mobile. Most unskilled or semi-skilled operatives stayed on the job only for a few years when young, then moved away: the men to craftsmen's jobs, the women to marry.[52] In the years between *Stark* and *Britton*, some New England mill owners, trying to cut down on the transience of their operatives, imported the default regime used for farm labor into the express terms of their contracts with industrial labor. Contracts ran for a year, from April to April, and provided that payment would be deferred to the end of the year. But (the historian Jonathan Prude tells us) the system rapidly broke down. The employers themselves subverted it by laying off workers in slack times. Increasingly, workers left throughout the year for better opportunities. The mill owners retreated: "[W]age settlements . . . by the early 1830s . . . appear to have generally slipped into quarterly, monthly, and, in one instance, even bimonthly rhythms."[53]

Forfeiture of wages could rarely be the deterrent it aspired to be in any case, because as a practical matter farmers and factory managers had to advance their laborers money or goods over the course of the year in order to sustain them. Adam Smith explained the origins of wage labor in the fact that, after "the appropriation of land and accumulation of stock" following the "original state of things" in which every man labors only for himself, "[i]t seldom happens that the person who tills the ground has wherewithal to maintain himself until he reaps the harvest. His maintenance is generally advanced to him from the stock of a master, the farmer who employs him."[54] Laborers who skipped out on their contracts often left owing their masters money rather than having it owed them.

---

[51] ROTHENBERG, *supra* note 31, at 185–208.

[52] DAVID MONTGOMERY, THE FALL OF THE HOUSE OF LABOR 133–48 (1987).

[53] PRUDE, *supra* note 29, at 151–52.

[54] 1 ADAM SMITH, AN INQUIRY INTO THE NATURE AND CAUSES OF THE WEALTH OF NATIONS 82–83 (R. H. Campbell & A. S. Skinner eds., Clarendon Press 1976) (1776).

In any case, the wage-forfeiture rule was only one among many legal regulations constraining workers' options, and in many contexts a relatively minor one. In England and the American South after the end of Reconstruction, as we have seen, the prospect of criminal penalties—leading to convict-lease labor and the chain gang—probably deterred more laborers from quitting work than wage forfeiture, at least before they had worked out most of the year. In both regions, moreover, the worker who wanted to claim justification for quitting in the employer's own breach would have found both unfriendly doctrine and unfriendly adjudicators—in England, the summary jurisdiction of magistrates increasingly drawn from the employer rather than gentry classes,[55] in the South, a legal and political system controlled by planter interests and all-white judges and juries.[56] In both England and the American North and South, the worker who quit, and even the worker who refused wage offers because he thought them too low,[57] could be reported to police as a vagrant, arrested without a warrant and tried on summary process without a jury, and bound out to labor.[58] The common law tort of enticement (eventually evolving into tortious interference with contract relations) gave an employer a civil action against a competing employer who bid for his workers,[59] so that the employee who quit was less likely to find alternate employment in the same area. And we should not forget the sanction of extralegal but officially tolerated violence—beatings and even death—brought to bear on workers who defied their masters.

One of the biggest problems facing Southern farm laborers after emancipation turned out not to be that their employers would threaten forfeiture of their wages but that they would never be paid at all. (At least in this context, Holmes had it backward: The workers could be trusted to work, but not the employers to pay.) Planters often found it hard to get the credit to raise cash to pay their workers. Reconstruction

---

[55] On the change in composition of courts in England, see Hay, *supra* note 32, at 105–06. The hostility of Southern courts to black parties is too well known to need a footnote.

[56] *See* Laura F. Edwards, *The Problem of Dependency: African Americans, Labor Relations and the Law in the Nineteenth Century South*, 72 Agric. Hist. 313, 324–26 (1998).

[57] For examples from North Carolina, see *id.* at 327–28.

[58] On vagrancy laws and their enforcement, see AMY DRU STANLEY, FROM BONDAGE TO CONTRACT: WAGE LABOR, MARRIAGE AND THE MARKET IN THE AGE OF SLAVE EMANCIPATION 98–137 (1998).

[59] On enticement actions in the North, see TOMLINS, *supra* note 7, at 280–82 (1993); in the South, see COHEN, *supra* note 37, at 229–30.

legislatures tried to address this problem by giving farm workers a lien for their labor; but after Reconstruction ended, legislatures subordinated labor liens to those of other lienholders, and (echoes of the *Stark* rule) courts held that the worker who quit forfeited his lien. Employers addressed the problem by paying workers in goods ("truck") or scrip redeemable at the company store: This inevitably led to higher prices for necessary goods. The most durable solution turned out to be share-cropping, which attracted farmhands by promising payment in the form of a share of the crop. But these arrangements were notoriously exploitative. Landlords found it easy to cheat by controlling the accounting for shares and by taking advantage of the racially biased legal system that otherwise might have policed their cheating. The result for much farm labor was a permanent state of debt peonage: The croppers or tenants could never earn enough to repay advances of seed or tools or cash, fell further into debt every year, and were always at risk of criminal sanctions for failing to pay debts or leaving employment to avoid them.[60]

Finally, for most categories of workers, the battle over the entirety rule has been mooted for some time by two major modifications of contract law.

Sometime in the late nineteenth century, the default rule for duration of employment at common law shifted from employment for a year to employment at will.[61] (In between different state courts experimented with various other defaults, such as the presumption that an indefinite hiring could be terminated by either party with notice.) The employer may fire, or the employee quit, at any time, for any or no reason. This means, of course, that the employee does not breach the contract by quitting, and is therefore entitled to be paid for the work he has done up to that point. It also means that the employer does not need to show cause for firing.

The other development was statutory. For industrial workers, the problems of irregular or late payment, payment in truck or scrip, and the looming threat of wage forfeiture for quitting work were eventually solved by statutes. The earliest of these were truck laws, requiring

---

[60] For the details of the "long pay," see GERALD DAVID JAYNES, BRANCHES WITHOUT ROOTS: GENESIS OF THE BLACK WORKING CLASS IN THE AMERICAN SOUTH, 1862–1882, at 224–29 (1986); of labor liens generally, HAROLD WOODMAN, NEW SOUTH–NEW LAW: THE LEGAL FOUNDATIONS OF CREDIT AND LABOR RELATIONS IN THE POSTBELLUM AGRICULTURAL SOUTH (1995); of debt peonage, COHEN, *supra* note 37, and DANIEL, *supra* note 39.

[61] Jay M. Feinman, *The Development of the Employment at Will Rule*, 20 J. Am. Hist. 118 (1976).

payment in legal tender; they originated in early nineteenth-century England, where the company stores who sold workers goods on credit while they waited for wages were called tommy shops. Laissez-faire economists curiously defended the practice of payment in scrip or store credit on grounds of freedom of contract, despite their restriction of workers to employer-controlled shops; but Parliament for once ignored the economists and periodically though rather ineffectually forbade payment in truck.[62] In the United States, legislatures in the nineteenth century began to enact anti-truck and anti-scrip laws, followed by statutes requiring that workers in certain industries (usually manufacturing and mining, railroads and telegraphs) be paid at regular intervals. These statutes directly addressed the forfeiture rules by mandating that wages for work already done be paid at termination of employment.

Regular payment is now so taken for granted by parties to employment contracts that we have forgotten the decades-long pitched battles to get laws requiring it past what were often hostile courts.[63] A well-known 1886 Pennsylvania case struck down an 1881 truck law requiring ore extraction and manufacturing employers to pay wages monthly in lawful money as well as fixing the definition of a legal ton of coal, finding it an infringement of freedom of contract: "[M]ore than this [said the court], it is an insulting attempt to put the laborer under a legislative tutelage, which is not only degrading to his manhood, but subversive of his rights as a citizen. . . . He may sell his labor for what he thinks best, whether money or goods, just as his employer may sell his iron or coal, and any and every law that proposes to prevent him from so doing is an infringement of his constitutional privileges, and consequently vicious and void."[64] An Illinois decision of 1893, often quoted by other courts, struck down a statute requiring payment in weekly pay periods as a violation of liberty of contract, substantive due process, and a state constitutional provision prohibiting special or class legislation.[65] The Illinois court repeated the common formulas of the time that the right to contract freely for one's labor is part of the prop-

---

[62] P. S. ATIYAH, THE RISE AND FALL OF FREEDOM OF CONTRACT 533–37 (1979).

[63] My summary here relies on comprehensive and exhaustively researched memos from Eric Tam, Yale Law School Class of 2007 (copies on file with author). Legislation and court decisions under the Truck Acts and other wage payment laws are also summarized in 2 LABATT, *supra* note 7, at 2229–315, and Carl E. McGowan, *The Divisibility of Employment Contracts*, 21 Iowa L. Rev. 50 (1936).

[64] Godcharles & Co. v. Wigeman, 113 Pa. 431, 437, 6 A. 354 (1886).

[65] Braceville Coal Co. v. People, 147 Ill. 66, 35 N.E. 62 (1893).

erty and liberty protected by due process and that the legislation had unduly singled out special classes of corporations. It added an interesting policy argument:

> The restriction of the right to contract affects not only the corporation, and restricts its right to contract, but that of the employe as well. . . . It is a matter of common knowledge that large numbers of manufactories were [in the recent depression] shut down because of the stringency in the money market. Employers of labor were unable to continue production, for the reason that no sale could be found for the product. It was suggested, in the interest of employes and employers as well as in the public interest, that employes consent to accept only so much of their wages as was actually necessary to their sustenance, reserving payment of the balance until business should revive, and thus enable the factories and workshops to be open and operated with less present expenditure of money. Public economists and leaders in the interests of labor suggested and advised this course. In this State and under this law no such contract could be made. The employe who sought to work for one of the corporations enumerated in the act would find himself incapable of contracting as all other laborers in the State might do. The corporations would be prohibited from entering into such a contract, and if they did so, the contract would be voidable at the will of the employe, and the employer subject to a penalty for making it. The employe would, therefore, be restricted from making such a contract as would insure to him support during the unsettled condition of affairs, and the residue of his wages when the product of his labor could be sold. The employes would, by the act, be practically under guardianship; their contracts voidable, as if they were minors; their right to freely contract for and to receive the benefit of their labor, as others might do, denied them.[66]

Notwithstanding these warnings the tide turned after 1900. Between 1900 and the last serious challenge in 1937, sixteen court decisions upheld the constitutionality of wage payment statutes while nine (four of the nine in Indiana) struck them down. In 1914 the U.S. Supreme Court unanimously rejected a challenge to New York's wage payment

---

[66] *Id.* at 73–74. The court does not explain why employees who supposedly benefited from agreeing to waiving their right to present payment would then choose to void the agreement.

laws.[67] Courts carefully sidestepped the issue of whether the statutes interfered with freedom of contract, generally sustaining them on the basis of the states' reasonable use of the police power to prevent fraud or exercise of their reserved power over corporations. By 1939, thirty-nine states had enacted regular-payment statutes and their opponents basically gave up; though four states to this day have never enacted such statutes and three more have made their terms waivable by the parties.[68]

For all the reasons just given, we might conclude that the common law doctrines litigated in *Stark* and *Britton* and debated at such length by subsequent courts, commentators, and legal historians may never have had much practical impact on actual employment relations. But I think these doctrines may also be seen as a piece of a still broader tapestry, that of the evolving definitions and ideologies of "freedom" in contracting, particularly as applied to the contract of employment.

From Status to Contract and Back to Status?

The usual account of the modern law of contract relations is that it travels a path from status to contract and then back again to status—the story of the rise and fall of freedom of contract. By the late nineteenth century "free contract" relations came to be strongly contrasted to "status" relations. Status relations are described in what William Blackstone in his famous *Commentaries* called (following Roman Law) "the Law of Persons," the special obligations that the law attaches to persons occupying distinct social roles (husband and wife, parent and child, guardian and ward, master and servant, etc.), generally those of a superior to an inferior.[69] Status relations had a content (mandatory terms) prescribed by positive law or implied from custom, and usually unequal or asymmetric rights and duties. Marriage was the prime example of a status: The law's terms could not be varied by the parties; rights of exit from the contract (even by mutual consent) were heavily restricted by divorce law; in the contract relation the wife was subordinated to the husband's orders, control of their joint property, choice of dwelling place, and even citizenship; the wife owed the husband do-

---

[67] Erie R.R. Co. v. Williams, 233 U.S. 685 (1914), aff'g 199 N.Y. 525, 92 N.E. 1084 (1910).

[68] Alabama, Florida, Nebraska, South Carolina (never enacted); North Dakota, South Dakota, West Virginia (waivable).

[69] 1 WILLIAM BLACKSTONE, COMMENTARIES ON THE LAWS OF ENGLAND bk. I (1765–69).

mestic and sexual services, but the husband was also obliged to support the wife.

Thus to late nineteenth-century lawyers and treatise writers it was clear that marriage was not a contract. True contract relations were supposedly between formal equals, on terms mutually and freely agreed to by both, and alterable and terminable by mutual consent. Since the substantive content of the true contract was entirely specified by the parties, the *law* of contract could be wholly abstract, a law applying generally and indifferently to *A* and *B*, regardless of occupation or situation. The law simply specified the general default conditions (offer and acceptance, writing requirements, satisfaction of conditions, the requirement of "consideration" or exchange, absence of force or fraud, remedies, excuses, etc.) under which the legal system would supply coercive enforcement to carry out the parties' wills. "Free contract" to the nineteenth-century "classical" jurists was, of course, not simply a descriptive label but a norm, an ideal, departures from which had to be strenuously justified. In the United States the ideal was constitutionalized through the "due process" clauses of the state and federal constitutions so as to repel, as unacceptable forms of "paternalism," legislative attempts to either mandate or prohibit contract terms not agreed to by the parties.

But the regime of free contract—the story continues—no sooner triumphed than it began to be undermined. "Social" jurists, "Progressive" reformers, and interest groups who thought "free" contracts embodied the wills only of parties with better bargaining advantages or failed to protect third parties and important social interests such as the leisure, health, safety, and family responsibilities of the workforce sought legislation to mandate or prohibit specific contract terms. In short order the legal system broke up the abstraction of classical contract into specialized legislative and administrative regulation of contracts governing railroad carriage of goods and passengers; home mortgage foreclosures and exemptions; insurance; labor relations; the sale of alcohol, tobacco, firearms, narcotics, food, and drugs; consumer credit; consumer sales; professional services; liability of employers and manufacturers for personal injuries—and many more.[70] Contract, to twentieth-century observers and commentators, seemed to be returning to a miscellaneous regime of status-specific laws.

Even at the height of the "classical" period (1880–1937), American courts amiably upheld most of these new regulations of and intrusions

---

[70] For detailed summaries of these developments, see generally LAWRENCE M. FRIEDMAN, CONTRACT LAW IN AMERICA (1965); ATIYAH, *supra* note 62.

into the sphere of free contract, with the notable exception of statutes regulating the employment contract. Indeed constitutional courts (as for example in the famous case of *Lochner v. New York*[71]) suggested the employment contract was such a paradigm of freely willed relations that any direct regulation of its terms would have to be justified with special rigor to pass muster as valid exercises of the police power.

But was the employment contract ever such a great example of free contracting, even in the most formal sense? Back around 1800, employment was theorized legally as a contract relation very much like marriage. "Contract" in 1800 generally referred to relations that the parties agreed to enter voluntarily but that, once entered, bound them to prescribed terms.[72] English law in fact prescribed detailed mandatory terms—wage rates, job tasks, craft rules—for most trades and occupations. In 1799–1800 Parliament repealed these detailed rates and rules, allowing the terms of work to be set free of state regulation.[73] It did not, however, contemplate that the parties would set these terms by mutual bargaining. Work was an authoritarian relation, controlled by masters, just as marriage was controlled by husbands.

Ironically, as John Orth has pointed out, the main purpose of the English statutes that freed the content of the work bargain from direct state control was to enact stronger criminal prohibitions on a particularly threatening type of free contract—contracts among laborers to form unions.[74] The state's rules regarding labor associations, how they may organize, the tactics (strikes, pickets, boycotts, etc.) they may legitimately use, and the subjects over which they can pressure employers to bargain, underwent a long and complex history of changes. I won't dwell on these here, except to say that these rules are critical to understanding the employment contract because, along with market conditions, they ultimately determine the relative bargaining power of the parties.[75] We have also seen that the worker's freedom to move was

---

[71] 198 U.S. 45 (1905).

[72] John V. Orth, *Contract and the Common Law, in* THE STATE AND FREEDOM OF CONTRACT 52–53 (Harry N. Scheiber ed., 1998).

[73] 39 Geo. 3, c. 81, §1 (1799), 39 & 40 Geo. 3, c. 106, §17 (1800).

[74] Orth, *supra* note 72, at 56–63.

[75] For good general treatments, see JOHN ORTH, COMBINATION AND CONSPIRACY: A LEGAL HISTORY OF TRADE UNIONISM, 1721–1906 (1991) (for England); and VICTORIA HATTAM, LABOR VISIONS AND STATE POWER (1993); KAREN ORREN, BELATED FEUDALISM: LABOR, THE LAW, AND LIBERAL DEVELOPMENT IN THE UNITED STATES (1991); CHRISTOPHER TOMLINS, THE STATE AND THE UNIONS (1985); WILLIAM FORBATH, LAW AND THE SHAPING OF THE AMERICAN LABOR MOVEMENT (1991) (for the United States).

legally constrained in myriad ways, through regulation of "enticement," vagrancy, criminalization of quitting while owing debts, etc.
(and we should add to this list being subject to injunctions not to work
for others in the case of especially skilled workers[76]). The freedom of
workers to move and their capacity to organize and to engage in collective action are obviously crucial elements in their power to bargain,
and they are all affected by legal regulation. "Freedom of contract" jurists tended to ignore—or relegate to the periphery of their awareness—those external legal constraints on bargaining. They did, however, insist that once the state had pulled out of mandating and prohibiting its terms, the employment contract itself was the product of mutual free bargaining.

But there always remained a tension between the legal system's abstract ideal of contract terms as the product of mutually concurring
free wills and the doctrinal practice of treating the employment relation as one of status unequals. The way judges and treatise writers
managed the tension, as we've seen, was through implied terms that
reinforced the customary hierarchical content of the relationship, were
notionally consented to by the employees, and at least in theory could
be varied by specific agreement.

Authority and Control in the Employment Contract

In legal contemplation, throughout the nineteenth century and to a
very large extent still to this day, this relationship remains in law as
well as fact—indeed in law if anything rather more than in fact!—an
authoritarian relationship, one in which the basic terms are set not by
bargain or mutual agreement but by employer prerogative. Employers
don't just get to set the terms of the initial engagement; more important, they determine the day-to-day substantive rights and duties of
the parties to the contract.

American courts in the early republic invented the new field of "employment law" to govern work relations in industrial society. As we
have seen, they rejected English law's use of criminal sanctions for
breaching contracts and came to define free labor regimes as the absence of such sanctions. But although free labor regimes might not be
the outcome of direct state coercion, they were far from being relations
among equals. True, some of the more radical labor organizations
imagined a world in which worker-artisans and owners of capital
would sit down together and mutually hammer out the terms of their

---

[76] *See* Lea Vandervelde, *The Gendered Origins of the Lumley Doctrine:
Binding Men's Consciences and Women's Fidelity*, 101 Yale L.J. 775 (1992).

relationships; and in some industries where specialized jobs and production functions were contracted out to craft trades, something like a workplace of contracting equals actually came into being.[77] But this is a bit like saying that some feminists imagined a world in which marriage was a contract between equals, and that some women achieved marriages that were de facto equal partnerships. The legal system took quite a different view of what the relation was and should be.

As Christopher Tomlins's work has shown at length,[78] the template American courts used for the common law governance of the employment relation was lifted from the pre-industrial extended-family household—from the old domestic law of master and servant. Rather remarkably, in the republic of free labor, all wage workers were relegated to the legal status of domestic menials. Nineteenth-century treatises commonly covered industrial and domestic employment under the same master/servant categories. In this relation masters (employers) are superiors with the right of command, servants (employees) inferiors with the duty of obedience.[79] Servants, like wives, were a form of masters' property: That was the basis for the master's action for enticement against competitors who tried to lure their servants away. Servants owed their masters an unqualified duty of loyalty to their interests, and this remains an employee's duty today, though it is not reciprocated: Employers have no corresponding duty to look after their employee's interests. In the pre-industrial era, masters also owed their servants duties of care akin to the husband's duty of support, to take care of them in sickness, disability, and age; but these duties had eroded away by the mid-nineteenth century, leaving—as Southern slaveholders gleefully emphasized—masters of "free labor" free to throw injured or elderly workers out into the snow. Much of this law evolved in ways that granted masters even greater rights vis-à-vis their workers: For example, workers who invented something on the job had the rights to control those inventions until the late nineteenth

---

[77] See (for the dream) SEAN WILENTZ, CHANTS DEMOCRATIC: NEW YORK CITY AND THE RISE OF THE AMERICAN WORKING CLASS, 1788–1850 (1984), and (for the reality) WALTER LICHT, WORKING FOR THE RAILROAD: THE ORGANIZATION OF WORK IN THE NINETEENTH CENTURY (1983); David Montgomery, *Workers' Control of Machine Production in the Nineteenth Century*, 17 Labor Hist. 485 (1976).

[78] TOMLINS, *supra* note 7, at 278–92.

[79] *Id.*

century, when the law changed the rules to make such inventions "works for hire" and the property of the employer.[80]

Timothy Walker, who wrote a popular 1837 textbook on law for students, said of the employment relation:

> The title of *master and servant* . . . does not sound harmoniously to republican ears. And in fact *servitude*, strictly so-called, does not exist in this country, except in the condition of *slaves*, whose condition has already been described. But the legal relation of master and servant must exist, to a greater or lesser extent, wherever civilization furnishes work to be done, and the difference of condition makes some persons employers, and others laborers. In fact, we understand by the relation of master and servant, nothing more or less, than that of the *employer* and the *employed*. It is therefore a relation created by contract express or implied, and might properly be treated under the head of contracts; but custom has placed it among the personal relations, and I shall so treat it. Blackstone divides servants into four classes, namely, *menial servants, common labourers, apprentices, and agents*. But there is no occasion here for treating separately of [menial servants and common labourers]; because we have no provisions, as in England, relating to the duration of the contract, the amount of wages, the time of labouring each day, and the like; all such matters being here settled between the employer and employed, as matters of contract.[81]

Walker robustly comes down on the side of employment as a contract— though one between status-unequals, persons in the different "condition" (natural? or only temporary and incidental?) of employers and laborers. But he cheats a bit when he says "we have no provisions" governing the relationship, leaving it all to contract. The law's work of constructing the employment relation as one between master and servant, one who commands and one who obeys, is largely done by implying contract terms.

---

[80] *See* Catherine L. Fisk, *Removing the "Fuel of Interest" from the "Fire of Genius": Law and the Employee Inventor, 1830–1930*, 65 U. Chi. L. Rev. 1127 (1998); Catherine L. Fisk, *Working Knowledge: Trade Secrets, Restrictive Covenants in Employment, and the Rise of Corporate Intellectual Property, 1800–1920*, 52 Hastings L.J. 441 (2001).

[81] TIMOTHY WALKER, INTRODUCTION TO AMERICAN LAW 243 (1837) (emphasis in original).

The "entirety" rule of *Stark*, the implied term that the worker who quits forfeits his entire wage, may perhaps be best seen as simply another piece of the authoritarian legal constitution of the work relation. The English case usually taken (and repeatedly cited in the United States) as having decisively established the modern entirety rule is *Spain v. Arnott* (1817).[82] A waggoner about to eat dinner at his accustomed hour was ordered to take some horses off somewhere; the servant said he would go when he had finished his meal, was promptly fired, and sued for his wages. The case is partly notable because Lord Ellenborough used it to reject the traditional doctrine that the master had to apply to a magistrate before dismissing the servant: he "was not bound to pursue that course, the relation between master and servant, and the laws by which that relation is regulated, existed long before the statute."

> There is no contract between the parties, except that which the law makes for them, and it may be hard upon the servant, but it would be exceedingly inconvenient if the servant were to be permitted to set himself to control his master in his domestic regulations, such as the time of dinner. After a refusal on the part of the servant to perform his work, the master is not bound to keep him on as a burthensome and useless servant to the end of the year. In the present instance it might be very inconvenient for the master to change the hour of dinner: *the question really comes to this, whether the master or the servant is to have the superior authority.*[83]

The denial of wages for work already performed is almost an afterthought in the case, the apparently obvious corollary to a regime in which the master makes the rules, changes them at whim, and gets to decide what amounts to a violation and that a single act of disobedience is grounds for dismissal. The English court takes for granted that wage forfeiture will both deter, and be the just deserts of, faithless service. In the United States as well, plenary-discretionary powers in the master defined the status of a servant (as opposed to an independent contractor); as North Carolina's Justice Thomas Ruffin explained in an opinion of 1848,

> [H]ow do we know when two men are master and servant? . . . If the employer has a right to have the work done as he pleases, can change the plans and periods of it from time to time, to suit his fancy or his other business—in fine, if the

---

[82] 2 Stark 256, 171 Eng. Rep. 638 (1817).

[83] 2 Stark at 257–58 (emphasis added).

hired man works under the other—then one is master, and the
other is servant; but, otherwise, not. Hence, officers of companies, hands on cars or ships, deputies as well as menials and
domestics, are properly and truly servants.[84]

To reinforce the master's authority, courts repeatedly held that detailed work regulations, whether or not the worker at time of contracting was likely to have noticed them, were incorporated into the contract. Customs or customary expectations of the workers themselves or
of their trade only became part of the contract if incorporated expressly; otherwise they were displaced by the law's implied term asserting the master's plenary authority.[85] Insubordination—disobedience or defiance of the master's lawful and reasonable orders, with the
burden on the servant to show their unreasonableness by "clear and
unequivocal" evidence—was always a breach of contract.[86]

By the end of the nineteenth century, the master's prerogative to
conduct his business as he saw fit—and specifically to exercise plenary
control over the actions of employees—was being theorized by some
courts as a form of property, and inalienable property at that.[87] Labor
actions such as pickets, strikes, and boycotts directed at bringing economic pressure to bear to restrict that control thus became subject to
prosecutions for criminal conspiracy and to injunctions. A federal court
granted an injunction in 1892 against a union using pickets to pressure
a mining company into hiring union men at union wages and to prevent its recruitment of replacement labor, on the ground that if the
union succeeded, "the owner of property would lose its control and
management . . . . The enterprise would be worked by such laborers,
during such hours, at such wages, and under such regulations, as the
laborers themselves might direct."[88] Whatever happened, we might
ask, to the basic idea of freedom of contract, that terms are to be set
not by dictation but by mutual agreement?[89] These cases presumed

---

[84] Wiswall v. Brinson, 32 N.C. 554, 569–70 (1848) (Ruffin, J., dissenting).

[85] *See* TOMLINS, *supra* note 7, at 284–90.

[86] *See* WOOD, *supra* note 40, §116, at 222–23.

[87] *See* Haggai Hurvitz, *American Labor Law and the Doctrine of Entrepreneurial Property Rights: Boycott, Courts and the Judicial Reorientation of
1886–1895*, 8 Indus. Rel. L.J. 307 (1986).

[88] Coeur d'Alene Consolidated & Mining Co. v. Miners' Union of Wardner,
51 F. 260, 262–63 (C.C.D. Idaho 1892).

[89] To be fair, courts that enjoined collective action designed to pressure employers to adopt a closed union shop also used the more authentic "free contract" rationale that the union was interfering with the ability of individual

that even if employers were to contract to cede some control over basic terms of work to their employees, such concessions must have been procured by illegitimate coercion amounting to duress.[90]

In agricultural as in industrial employment the courts used strong default rules to reinforce employers' authority in relations that threatened to become egalitarian. Black sharecroppers under Reconstruction struggled to have their relations with landowners defined as partnerships, or at least as tenancies. The courts construed them as a form of wage labor in which wages were paid in kind. "Croppers not only had no voice in farm management, but found the rigorous discipline of the workplace extended into their non-working hours."[91] "White landowners who employed black croppers could thus exercise complete managerial control—determining what would be grown and how, determining the hours and pace of work, determining when and at what price to sell the croppers' shares."[92]

Employment at will, which begins to become the default duration term by the 1880s, is another implied term that largely reinforces the authoritarian contract relation. At-will employment clearly helps to set some outer limits on the employer's power to impose intolerable work conditions. If the employee just can't take it anymore, she can always quit. But quitting, of course, can be hugely costly to most workers, unless they are lucky enough to have something better lined up. The practical consequence of the at-will rule—especially in sagging labor markets—is that unless employers run afoul of some specific and *enforceable* statutory prohibition,[93] they can treat their workers pretty

---

workers to strike separate bargains with their employers. This rationale rather than the more obviously authoritarian owner's-right-to-run-his business rationale became the basis for right-to-work movements.

[90] *See, e.g.,* Hitchman Coal & Coke Co. v. Mitchell, 245 U.S. 229 (1917).

[91] WOODMAN, *supra* note 60, at 91.

[92] Charles W. McCurdy, *The "Liberty of Contract" Regime in American Law, in* THE STATE AND FREEDOM OF CONTRACT, *supra* note 72, at 161, 169.

[93] I stress this because, of course, many statutes protecting workers are good on paper only—the penalties for violating them are too low and long delayed to deter employers or attract lawyers. The influence on courts of the common law baseline presumption that employers have an arbitrary power to fire at will reaches even into settings where employers seem to be using the power for a specifically illegal purpose, such as firing union organizers. *See* Richard Michael Fischl, *A Dominion into Which the King's Writ Does Not Seek to Run: Workplace Justice in the Shadow of Employment-at-Will, in* LABOUR LAW IN AN ERA OF GLOBALIZATION 253 (Joanne Conaghan, Richard Michael Fischl & Karl Klare eds., 2002).

much any way they please. They may be restrained from firing employees by a desire to reduce turnover and create bonds of loyalty that
will give incentives to better work and a reputation as a good employer. But (unless, of course, they risk being found to have discrimi-
nated by race, sex, age, or disability) they will not be restrained by law.

The courts have pervasively imported the implied terms of managerial prerogative to control work, discipline or fire workers for insubordination, and require their (nonreciprocated) loyalty to the employers'
interests even into contracts that are the outcome of collective bargaining under the National Labor Relations Act.[94]

A historian of early twentieth-century labor called her study *Belated
Feudalism* to emphasize the prescriptive, authoritarian content of the
employment relation.[95] Ironically, while marriage has shed many of its
incidents of unequal status and been transformed into a much more
egalitarian form of contract relationship (though still heavily influenced by the customary gendered division of labor and the assumption
that whoever brings in the wage or salary income from outside calls
the shots), employment remains a domain of top-down and often arbitrary command. The feature of the work contract that distinguishes it
from virtually all other contract relations is the vast discretionary authority that the law delegates to one party to exercise near-absolute
control over the time and actions of the other.[96] Over time many different successive rationales have been used to explain the asymmetrical
authority relations of the workplace: that the masters were gentlemen
and the servants lowborn; the masters were superior in education and
attainments; that the masters had emerged on top in the Darwinian
struggle for survival, while the servant-drones had been left behind;
that servitude was a merely temporary status of workers who were
making their way up the mobility ladder to becoming self-sufficient

---

[94] This remains true even in Wagner Act (unionized) workplaces. *See* JAMES
B. ATLESON, VALUES AND ASSUMPTIONS IN LABOR LAW 95–96 (1983).

[95] *See* ORREN, *supra* note 75.

[96] One of the enduring issues in employment law is, what are the implied
limits of the employer's implied authority? If the employee is a "servant," how
much control may the employer exercise over his life "outside" the job? May the
employer require employees to pick up his dry cleaning? To come over on the
weekend and wash his car? To contribute to a lobbying effort that benefits the
employer, such as a reduction in OSHA's budget and authority? Wear tight T-
shirts on the job? Engage in dangerous work? Execute a waiver of employer's
liability for injury on the job? Undergo sterilization as a condition of continuing
employment in jobs with radiation or chemical hazards? In an at-will world,
are these questions meaningful?

producers or masters themselves; even, rather incredibly, that the masters had a preference for being bosses and workers for being bossed around.[97] These have been gradually displaced by efficiency rationales—that the coordination of work tasks necessary for efficient production requires centralized managerial control of the work process, and that employers must be free to invest or disinvest in their labor force or change its composition as production technologies and market conditions change. In short, hierarchy and "flexibility" are efficient, and the acquiescence workers give—evidenced by their staying on the job—to their employers' regime (even if induced only by fear of being fired) exhibits their consent to the regime.

This brief history should lead us somewhat to reconsider the usual account of the "freedom of contract" phase in the status-to-contract-to-status story. "Freedom of contract" in practice was not a laissez-faire regime in which the parties were left at large to bargain out the content of their contracts. It was rather a regime in which the legal system supplied implied terms largely favoring employers and in other ways threw its weight behind employers' power to impose contract terms, backed up by the sanctions of dismissal and even (in some periods and situations) criminal prosecutions and injunctions.

What Can We Learn from this History? Implications for the Contracts Course

In writing this summary of the background and context of the "entirety rule," I have shown it is but as one among many components of employers' legal powers to limit the mobility of and exercise disciplinary controls over their workforces. My principal aim is to persuade contracts teachers and their students that their subject has a rich history, one that tells us quite a lot about how our present regime of contract law came into being; and that it helps us to imagine possible alternatives to that regime.

1. Judicial technique

To begin with, for teaching purposes the *Britton* and *Stark* cases furnish a nice pair of contrasts in judicial technique—how judges go about creating implied contract terms. In each case the judge argues from precedent, from custom or convention, from policy, from both rules (form) and standards (substance), and from basic principle.

Precedent. Justice Lincoln in *Stark* asserts that his rule (that the worker who quits should receive nothing) is the settled rule, despite

---

[97] For the classic history of the rationales, see generally REINHARD BENDIX, WORK AND AUTHORITY IN INDUSTRY 13–116, 198–340 (1956).

the trial court's decision and counsel's reference to contrary cases, and simply blows off the contrary cases as wrong. Justice Parker in *Britton* recognizes that other courts have come to different conclusions but finds in the recent Massachusetts builders' cases precedent for softening the forfeiture rule.

Custom / Convention. *Stark* asserts that the "usages of the country and common opinion upon subjects of this description" is that the laborer must wait for his pay until his work is done. But (as I said above) that does not speak to the precise point at issue, whether he must finish all the work before recovering anything for work already done. On that issue evidence from social historians on actual practices of paying off quitting workers is fragmentary but cuts against Lincoln. *Britton* asserts that the custom is to pay the defaulting worker and puts the burden on the employer to contract out of it.

Policy. Parker fears that the *Stark* rule will tempt employers to contrive a pretext for firing workers just before their term is up, to avoid payment altogether. Lincoln says that if this happened, the legal system would find in it an excuse for the worker's quitting. Parker's point is that the employer's breach, being a subterfuge, would be hard to detect. Lincoln anticipated this point:

> Wherever there is a reasonable excuse, the law allows a recovery. To say that this is not sufficient protection, that an excuse may in fact exist in countless secret and indescribable circumstances, which from their very nature are not susceptible of proof, or which, if proved, the law does not recognise as adequate, is to require no less than that the law should *presume* what can never legally be established, or should admit that as *competent*, which by positive rules is held to be wholly *immaterial*.[98]

This is the kind of thing judges often say—that what ought not to happen doesn't, or that since we can't prove it does we should ignore it. Parker simply draws the opposite conclusion from the difficulty of knowing or proving the conduct: If the party has an incentive to commit bad acts, and the courts lack capacity to monitor them, let's remove the incentive.

Form versus Substance. *Stark* represents the strict application of a formal rule (though it also claims that rule is founded in justice and sound policy), *Britton* the need to temper harsh outcomes of "technical"

---

[98] 19 Mass. at 275–76.

form with substantial justice—considerations of fairness and equality in exchange.[99]

Principle. Finally, as we've seen, *Stark* rests on the sanctity of promises, the immorality of breaching them, and the need to deter breach. *Britton* rests on the equitable principle of avoiding an undue penalty to the party who has performed most of the work and an undeserved windfall to the employer.

2. Does the law matter? And if so how?

Our case study—like every other legal case study—invites us to consider what difference a given legal rule is likely to make to actual social practice. This question is particularly necessary when the rule in question is a default rule such as the implied terms of the employment contract that we have been looking at. Some implied contract terms were easily and commonly circumvented—in many work settings, as we've seen, the wage-forfeiture consequences of the "entirety" rule seems to have been one of these. Others, however, were hugely consequential, such as the "fellow servant" rule relieving employers of vicarious liability for injuries caused by co-workers' negligence. The courts simply invented a hypothetical bargain by which workers assumed all the common risks of injury on the job (in exchange for a mostly hypothetical wage premium) in their contract of employment.[100] It took many generations of political agitation, ideological missionary work, slow doctrinal erosion, and persuasion of courts with constitutional objections to replace that default regime with administrative strict-liability workers' compensation systems.[101] Another default rule of similar importance is the doctrine that unless the parties have specially contracted otherwise, employment is at will.

The default rules fairly systematically favored employers, as we have seen. If employees wanted a better contract regime, they had the

---

[99] Later in the nineteenth century, after jurists began to draw hard distinctions between promises and conditions implied-in-fact (contract) and implied-in-law (quasi-contract), classical treatise-writers argued that since it was the legal system, rather than the will of the parties, that created the no-payment-until-full-performance condition, the legal system could modify it in the interests of equitable treatment. *See* WILLIAM A. KEENER, A TREATISE ON THE LAW OF QUASI-CONTRACTS 223–24 (1893). Keener still disapproved the reasoning and result in *Britton*, however, since he did not see how it could be equitable to allow recovery to a "willful" breacher.

[100] The leading case was Farwell v. Boston & Worcester R.R., 45 Mass. (4 Met.) 49 (1842).

[101] *See* JOHN WITT, THE ACCIDENTAL REPUBLIC: CRIPPLED WORKINGMEN, DESTITUTE WIDOWS, AND THE REMAKING OF AMERICAN LAW 152–207 (1994).

burden of negotiating one, a burden that custom, their usual relative weakness, and laws limiting their capacity to act collectively made difficult to carry. But this does not mean that in actual litigation over the rules the legal system always came down on the employers' side. Like the court in *Britton v. Turner* itself, courts often concluded that an individual employee had suffered abuse, injustice, or misfortune or a good faith difference of opinion excusing his own breaches; though the courts were always markedly less sympathetic to collective action, they became intensely hostile in the great period of labor unrest after 1880, and to this day tend to interpret labor statutes to favor employer prerogatives. Dissatisfied workers could and did make end runs around the courts by pushing for statutory changes in the rules that favored their interests and challenged the employers' authority. One of the purposes of the campaign for maximum hours, the "ten-hour," then "eight-hour day" movements that began in the nineteenth century, was to mark off time that the employee could call his "own," not subject to the employer's command. (Law firm associates of the present day might want to try to revive that campaign.) Many of these amendments in the rules faced prolonged constitutional challenges and upsets in the courts, but ultimately survived them.

Moreover, as we've seen, the actual parties often ignored the default rules or contracted out of them. Relatively skilled or long-term employees inevitably achieved more control over the design and pacing of their work tasks, and demonstrated more democratic than deferential manners, than the authoritarian master-servant model supposed was appropriate to their station. They did not accept judges' notions of their inherent subservience any more than wives—even in the most traditional households—were ever likely to accept the legal system's conceited fantasy that they were inferior weak-willed vassals, fated by their gender and their status as "femes coverts" to unquestioning obedience to their lord's authority. Craft workers reached collective agreements among themselves—the recognizable ancestors of modern union work-rules—about the timing and pacing of work, production quotas, standard wages for degrees of skill and seniority, scheduling of breaks and holidays—and enforced them not by embodying them in a contract but by slowing down or walking out in a body if employers violated them.[102] They clearly did not unquestioningly accept the new scientific managers' bid to reassert total control over the workplace on the ground that management was mental work for professional men of superior intelligence, while the operatives who did the work were too

---

[102] *See* Montgomery, *supra* note 77.

"phlegmatic and stupid" to comprehend the science of it.[103] Notwithstanding the forfeiture rule and others rules like it, American workers, even black farm laborers and croppers in the Jim Crow South, walked off the job and kept on the move.

But the legal system's reinforcement of the status relations of the employment relationship, what we might call the law-of-status-repackaged-as-contract, still mattered. Employers might accept contracts on terms more favorable to workers than the default rules, or cede more authority to workers than the law did, or simply treat them more kindly in practice than their contract obligations required. Workers might evade their contracts, or defy or resist their masters' lawful orders, or set up their own counter-regimes of workplace order or mobility patterns. But the fact remained that if either of the parties resorted to law, the courts would deploy their authority, and if necessary license massive deployments of state force, to reinforce the masters' authority. Most employers might have had no interest in withholding wages of departing workers under the *Stark* doctrine. But the rule gave them the option of doing so if they pleased and, more important, the credible threat of doing so as a disciplinary measure. A master could post a detailed set of work rules on the shop floor (or even keep them in his desk), or speak them as a set of oral commands, and by that act alone have them incorporated into the employment contract that a court would deem accepted by the workers. The workers could post their own set of rules, make agreements among themselves to abide by them, establish a regular practice whereby managers would acquiesce in them, even obtain the manager's express parol consent to them; yet the courts would pay no attention to the workers' rules in interpreting the contract. If customs were in conflict in filling gaps in contracts, courts would accept the employers' customs, but not the employees'. (*Britton v. Turner* is really unusual in implying custom favorable to employees.)

Workers could and did win occasional cases complaining of individual harsh or unfair treatment. But they could not use the legal system to challenge the overarching premise that they were subordinates, and their employers superiors, in the relation. This understandably made workers reluctant to turn to the courts for redress. Willibald Steinmetz has shown that in England, even after 1870 when statutes abolished criminal penalties for leaving work, remade the employment contract on terms much more favorable to workers, and removed cases from employer-dominated magistrates' courts to professional judges in

---

[103] Frederick Winslow Taylor (the father of scientific management), quoted in MONTGOMERY, *supra* note 52, at 251.

county courts, workers rarely resorted to courts to enforce their legal rights.[104] In the United States, as William Forbath has argued, organized labor became so disillusioned with the legal system generally that its program for much of the twentieth century was collective laissez-faire or "voluntarism," trying to keep the state out of labor relations altogether.[105]

Moreover, the law finds a path into people's ways of thinking and acting in deeper, subtler ways than the direct instrumental effect of altering their legal powers and incentives. While workers were (at least partially and sporadically) resisting the law's premises of status authority,[106] they were internalizing its assumptions that freedom of contract meant freedom from direct legal regulation. In the nineteenth-century movements to limit the working day, for example, workers fought to have the ten- or eight-hour day imported into the employment relation as a default term but resisted the idea of a state-mandated work day as strongly as employers did, as inconsistent with their contractual freedom. (When statutes limiting hours of work were enacted, employers immediately and predictably contracted around the limits, and the courts supported them.[107]) From the 1860s through the 1930s, the American Federation of Labor and its lawyers urged their own constitutional theory of "freedom of contract": that the provisions of the Thirteenth Amendment outlawing the badges and incidents of slavery and peonage also outlawed "wage slavery" and that the employees could not achieve real freedom in contracting unless their rights to organize and strike were unrestricted by the state. Labor injunctions violated their freedom to contract, so they were justified in

---

[104] Willibald Steinmetz, *Was There a De-juridification of Individual Employment Relations in Britain? in* PRIVATE LAW AND SOCIAL INEQUALITY IN THE INDUSTRIAL AGE 265, 293–310 (Willibald Steinmetz ed., 2000).

[105] *See* FORBATH, *supra* note 75, at 128–66.

[106] Internalization of the law-embodied norm of employer's authority, or at least the disinclination to resist it, also seems to be on the increase. The meekness of present-day employees in the face of what is often quite authoritarian regulation of their work lives (up to the point of requiring them to ask permission to go to the bathroom, and observing them while there with surveillance cameras) would, I think, be shocking to New England factory operatives and artisans of the nineteenth century, freedmen during Reconstruction, or Detroit autoworkers of the 1930s.

[107] DAVID MONTGOMERY, BEYOND EQUALITY: LABOR AND THE RADICAL REPUBLICANS, 1862–1872, at 302–11 (1981).

defying them.[108] This argument, needless to say, got nowhere in the courts; and where it did gain some traction, in state statutes that restricted or eliminated employers' rights to injunctions, the courts promptly struck the statutes down.[109] But my point is that even in the precincts of the labor movement, the laissez-faire view of "freedom of contract"—a zone of unregulated freedom to bargain for whatever advantages one's market power and organizing capacity could win—lived on as an ideal. Some union leaders today, disillusioned with the New Deal labor-regulatory regime whose rigidities, inadequacies, and hostile court interpretations have contributed to their losses of membership, would prefer to scrap it and return to deregulated bargaining.

3. *Freedom isn't free: The role of background conventions and legally sanctioned coercion*

These cases and the history behind them also supply a useful occasion—one of the many such occasions in the contracts course—to make the Legal Realist's point that one cannot understand most contract relations simply as the products of mutually agreed-upon terms, the realm of "party autonomy." Important terms and aspects of the relation are set by customary arrangements and understandings, often reflected in implied terms or default rules, sometimes just mutely present as background conventions (for example, the gendered division of labor, which sharply restricted women's work opportunities and hence their ability to bargain for wages, and to some extent still does). Other important terms are determined by law's, or convention's, delegation of effective decisional power to one of the parties—e.g., the party who drafts and supplies the form, or (in employment contracts) the party who makes the rules and gives the orders. Since these are default terms only, they can be altered by express agreement, but for most workers, of course (other than executives or professionals), they rarely are. The terms are set by the employers in contracts that employees rarely see, or are never written down at all, and they often run strikingly counter to employees' expectations. Empirical studies of worker expectations of job security, for example, suggest that the vast majority of workers to this very day have no idea that their employer may le-

---

[108] *See* FORBATH, *supra* note 75, at 128–58; James Gray Pope, *Labor's Constitution of Freedom*, 106 Yale L.J. 941 (1997).

[109] This string of defeats in the courts was finally broken with the Norris-LaGuardia Act of 1930. But not for long. Courts interpreting the National Labor Relations (Wagner) Act have routinely construed it to permit them to enjoin secondary strikes, boycott, and even peaceful pickets, notwithstanding Norris-LaGuardia. For examples see James Gray Pope, *Labor and the Constitution: From Abolition to Deindustrialization*, 65 Tex. L. Rev. 1071 (1987).

gally fire them for bad reasons or no reason and are shocked and affronted when they find out that this is the regime to which they have purportedly all along given their free consent.[110]

The recovery of historical context also dramatizes how the law constructs the boundaries between "free contract" and "free labor"—relations that are "consented to" on the one hand and relations that are "coerced" on the other. Until the late nineteenth century the elites and legal regimes of most societies did not see how people could be induced to work at unpleasant tasks without direct legal compulsion—specific performance to recover defaulting workers, and the threat of imprisonment, whipping or heavy fines, for leaving work or leaving the lord's estate; and criminal punishment for vagrancy and confinement to the workhouse, for refusing work. Southern planters after emancipation had much the same view: The freed slaves would not stay on the plantation without the threat of the convict-lease system and the chain gang for leaving work and vagrancy prosecution for refusing work.

The great discovery of liberal societies (and the political economists and lawyers who theorized laws that constituted their ground rules) was that the state could remove all these visible compulsions and let the invisible hand of the market, the force of brute necessity, do the work of pressing workers into lifetimes of hard and disabling labor and submission to employers' authority. The extra attraction of using the "free" market as the force of compulsion was that no visible human agents seemed to be doing the compelling. Laborers entering into the wage bargain to avoid starvation were freely *choosing* work over idleness (just as it was, and by many still is, believed that the unemployed were *choosing* idleness) and were freely consenting to all the imposed and silently implied terms of the bargain. The force of necessity was by definition not coercion; giving into it was thus an exercise of free choice.

But free labor in free markets is always at some point backed up by legal coercion. To start with, the legal system obviously coerces when it enforces contracts against breaching parties. What makes contracting "free" is that the law supposedly backs by force only those contracts that were freely made and refuses enforcement to those that were themselves the product of coercion. The fragile and malleable quality of the distinction between freely made and coerced agreements is famously made manifest in the law of duress. Threats to use physical

---

[110] *See, e.g.,* Pauline T. Kim, *Bargaining with Imperfect Information: A Study of Worker Perceptions of Legal Protection in an At-Will World,* 83 Cornell L. Rev. 105 (1997); RICHARD FREEMAN & JOEL ROGERS, WHAT WORKERS WANT 118–22 (1999).

force—and even threats simply to breach existing contracts—to induce vulnerable parties to agree to onerous contract terms may constitute such duress as to invalidate the agreements. But the threat to fire or not to hire unless the worker agrees to the onerous terms—even if the consequences of refusing the deal for the vulnerable party may actually be much more severe than a fine or short jail term (unemployment, humiliation before family and friends, loss of health insurance for a sick child, etc.)—is not duress. There may be plenty of valid reasons for distinguishing the different kinds of threats, but as Robert L. Hale and John Dawson memorably pointed out, the reasons cannot be that the parties under threats of force or breach of preexisting contracts are coerced and the workers under threat of firing/not-hiring are free.[111] All are making a rational choice of the less disagreeable alternative. Some threats are held improper and others permitted because of moral, economic, and political reasons that are independent of the degree of coercion.[112]

The related points that legal Progressives such as Hale (and his present-day followers like Robert Steinfeld) emphasize is that the degree and type of freedom that people have in contracting is always in part a result of how the legal system constructs markets through the distribution of the right to use state force. The deals people are able to make are always dependent on bargaining advantages conferred by, among other factors, background legal entitlements—rules of property, tort, contract, labor law, family law, corporate law, etc. As Adam Smith pointed out, the origins of the wage labor contract lie in the simple fact that a few people are the legal owners of productive property (often as a result of legally blessed expropriations of owners of common fields or indigenous peoples or people imported as slaves), but most others are not and need to sell their labor to survive. "Freedom of contract" is a slogan whose practical meaning is that the state should not—at least, not very visibly—change the constellation of rules so as to disturb the legal system's status quo distribution of state power to coerce people

---

[111] Robert L. Hale, *Bargaining, Duress and Economic Liberty*, 43 Colum. L. Rev. 603 (1943); John P. Dawson, *Economic Duress—An Essay in Perspective*, 45 Mich. L. Rev. 253 (1947).

[112] The borderlands of duress can be found today in in modern peonage cases involving abusive treatment of illegal immigrant workers, who are easily exploited because they risk deportation by complaining. *See, e.g.,* United States v. Kozminski, 487 U.S. 931 (1988).

through its award of rights to grant and withhold valuable resources, and its conferral of organizational capacity.[113]

The corollary insight is that practical freedom in contracting may often be enhanced by state-mandated or prohibited terms rather than leaving the parties "free" to bargain away all their freedom, especially by "bargaining" in the form of tacit acquiescence to default terms they probably don't expect or know anything about. Laws that require payment in legal tender and weekly payments, prohibit personal service contracts longer than seven years, criminalize physical abuse of workers, legislate nonwaivable minimum safety standards, and refuse enforcement to the remedies of injunctions to return to work, punitive damages, and overbroad covenants not to compete are good examples; as also, of course, are laws that compel employers whose employees vote to form a union to bargain in good faith with the employees' collective bargaining agent, forbid employers to fire union organizers, grant workers a legal right to strike, or forbid discrimination in employment. All these laws coerce, but as they limit the freedom of some they expand it in others; and sometimes expand it for everyone.[114] Justice Holmes put the point with characteristic succinctness in a draft opinion he wrote (but never published, because it was clearly too radical for his colleagues) in a case upholding one of the statutes prohibiting payment of miners in scrip:

> It is now recognized by legislatures and courts as well as by everyone outside them, that as a fact freedom may disappear on the one side or other through the power of aggregated money or men . . . . [A]nd to suppose that every other force may exercise its compulsion at will but that government has no authority to counteract the pressure with its own is absurd. It is said that the power of duress has changed sides and now is with the United Mine Workers. But if it be admitted, as it certainly is established, that the legislature may interfere with theoretic [equality] in the interest of positive freedom, it would

---

[113] For a bravura description and analysis of the views of Hale and fellow Progressive lawyer-economists on coercion in contracting, see Barbara Fried, The Progressive Assault on Laissez-Faire: Robert Hale and the First Law and Economics Movement 29–70 (1998).

[114] An obvious example of expanding freedom for everyone would be the effects of the Civil Rights Acts on employers in the South, who were freed by the compulsion of those laws to hire black workers they might have wanted to hire during Jim Crow but were prevented from doing so by local custom and the fear of social sanctions.

require a very clear case before a court could declare its judgment wrong and its enactment void.[115]

The shift over the nineteenth century from the *Stark* court's "entirety" rule, which denied restitution to the worker who quits, to increasing acceptance of the *Britton* court's rule, which permitted restitution, was a tiny redistribution of state force in favor of practical freedom for the worker who wants to quit his job. (How consequential it
actually was would, of course, depend on things that study of appellate
cases mostly does not reveal, such as the importance of the default rule
in practice or whether any but the exceptional worker could actually
sue to enforce his rights.)

Our last lesson under this subheading is that the background conventions, legal doctrines, and common understandings of contract relations change over time—and do so because parties or their interest
groups or supporters or reformers and their institutional and managerial practices, lobbies, and social movements, as well as lawyers,
judges, and jurists, act to change them. The rules in force are not often
generally accepted, at least not for long; the shape they eventually take
is the result of political struggles, contingent social forces, and—not
least—conflicting legal interpretations of convention, policy, and principle like the ones we saw at work in *Stark* and *Britton*. The rules are
unstable, contestable, perpetually in motion. The content of implicit
workplace contracts in the primary sector of employment in the United
States, for example, seems to have changed dramatically in the past
generation from a norm of expected lifetime employment security to a
norm in which (ideally at least—the reality is considerably more dis-
appointing) the employer promises no security but does undertake to
equip workers with general, flexible skills they can take to the next
job—although none of these implicit bargains is legally enforceable.[116]

We are best positioned to see the contingent, constructed nature of
our legal-social relations by comparing them to what they were in the
past or to those of other societies. What we now learn as the law of contracts was not always thus, nor will it be the same twenty years from
now, depending on how the people concerned go about altering their
conventional expectations and building them into institutions, and

---

[115] Draft opinion in Keokee Consolidated Coke Co. v. Taylor, 234 U.S. 224
(1917). Holmes's draft opinion was unearthed by ALEXANDER M. BICKEL &
BENNO C. SCHMIDT JR., THE JUDICIARY AND RESPONSIBLE GOVERNMENT, 1910–
1921, at 298 (1984). I am grateful to McCurdy, *supra* note 92, at 183, for bringing it to my attention.

[116] *See* KATHERINE V. W. STONE, FROM WIDGETS TO DIGITS: EMPLOYMENT
REGULATION FOR THE CHANGING WORKPLACE (2004).

how, in response, their lawyers and the legislatures, courts, and agencies, and the people their actions are designed to influence, decide to act.

8

Lea S. VanderVelde*

The Gendered Origins of the *Lumley* Doctrine: Binding Men's Consciences and Women's Fidelity

Introduction

In the familiar case of *Lumley v. Wagner*,[1] the English Court of Equity held that although opera singer Johanna Wagner could not be ordered to perform her contract, she would be enjoined from singing at any competing music hall for the term of the contract. *Lumley* is usually lauded in first-year contracts courses as a just and fair decision, one that illustrates the proper distinction between equitable orders that force performance (unworkable and unjust) and equitable orders that prevent performance (sometimes workable, usually practical, and not necessarily unjust).

Contracts classes, however, rarely consider the central labor issue: whether an injunction preventing an employee from quitting and working elsewhere violates the American tradition of free labor and the right to quit employment. In American employment law, the *Lumley* rule was a regressive development. The beneficial side of the rule, that

* Josephine R. Witte Professor of Law, University of Iowa College of Law. Reprinted by permission of The Yale Law Journal Company and William S. Hein Company from *The Yale Law Journal*, Vol. 101, pages 775–852.

[1] 1. DeG., M. & G. 604, 619, 42 Eng. Rep. 687, 693 (Ch. 1852).

the opera singer would not be ordered to perform, was already secured by the Thirteenth Amendment. Before *Lumley* took hold in American courts, employers had considerably less leverage to compel the continued service of employees under contract. With the *Lumley* rule in effect, employers could shut employees out of work unless they returned to work for them for the remainder of the employment contract, a term which sometimes lasted several years. An employer holding the power of an injunction over an employee could dictate the terms on which that employee would be free to work elsewhere.

The *Lumley* rule's regressive effect was expressly denounced by a leading American jurist at its first introduction in the labor emancipatory era following the Civil War; yet it quiescently attained the status of the dominant common law rule in American courts by the 1890s. How did the rule of *Lumley v. Wagner* come to be incorporated into the canon of rules pertaining to equitable intervention in cases of departing employees? Why, of all the nineteenth-century opinions on the subject, was *Lumley*, rather than other rulings decided by equally eminent American judges, constructed into the canon of law?

The answer appears to be related to the gendered context in which the rule was examined at the time that American courts constructed the canon. Suits involving the services of women constituted the core of cases and provided the central contextual focus in which the rule was examined. Many more actresses than actors were sued under this cause of action.[2] Indeed, in the nineteenth century, all of the prominent cases in this line involved the services of women, and only women performers were subjected to permanent injunctions against performing elsewhere for the duration of the contract. In the corpus of reported cases, no male performer was ever permanently enjoined from quitting and performing elsewhere during the entire nineteenth century.

The fact that suits over women dominate this line of cases is more than a coincidence. On no other topic of employment litigation, save the tort of seduction, do women figure so prominently in the leading cases.[3] This concentration of women litigants is anomalous in the nine-

---

[2] The two-way table below illustrates the courts' differential treatment of male and female performers over the period 1860–1900.

Negative Injunctions Involving Performers, 1860–1900

	Actresses	Actors
Enjoined	5(6)	0
Not enjoined	7(6)	6
Sued	12	6

[3] *See* Lea S. VanderVelde, *The Legal Ways of Seduction*, 48 Stan. L. Rev. 817 (1996).

teenth century, an era when women were unlikely to be parties to any employment litigation. Both legal and cultural constraints discouraged women from working for wages. If they were married, the doctrine of coverture submerged women's legal identity under their husbands'. Thus, it is indeed unusual to find that on a gender-neutral legal issue like an employee's right to quit, women's cases would so considerably outnumber men's cases in a profession where women worked alongside men. Moreover, it is unusual that these women's cases would be raised to establish the standard.

The *Lumley* rule's reception in the United States was a gendered phenomenon—"gendered" because the term covers a broad range of gender-specific elements that recur in this line of cases. These include sexist behavior, sex role typing, unequal treatment, charged language of a gender-specific nature, and sexual harassment. However, the pattern is complex. The phenomenon was not a simple one of misogyny or sexism, and it did not appear uniformly in every case involving a woman employee. Deeper cultural constructions of the role of women in the public workplace, particularly the very public workplace of the stage, explain the phenomenon better than would attributions of sexism to the few key individuals involved. A woman appearing in public on the stage posed a particular challenge to the dominant norm of the Victorian era that women were supposed to remain in the privacy of the home.

Unlike male actors, nineteenth-century women performers were less likely to be viewed as free and independent employees. Nineteenth-century women were generally perceived as relationally bound to men. In this line of cases, that perception of women manifested itself in the *need* to bind actresses to their male theater managers. Moreover, in the view of the dominant culture, women performers were more likely to be perceived as subordinate than were their male counterparts. This conceptualization of women in the nineteenth century paved the way for the adoption of the *Lumley* rule in America.

The story that emerges is one of reversal of a legal rule due in large part to the increasing presence of women in the acting profession. When *Lumley* first appeared in the United States, the cultural repulsion to anything that even hinted of slavery led to its unequivocal rejection. But later in the century, the cultural aversion to mastery had lessened and no longer seemed to apply to men's domination of women in particular. In the later cases, courts were harsher upon women defendants who attempted to leave their employment than they were in the few parallel cases involving men. And in the later cases, courts were harsher upon women than they had been earlier in the century. By the end of the century, the courts' subjugation of actresses to the control of theater managers surpassed even the language of their con-

tracts and became an incident of a status classification constructed
largely by the courts, sometimes in contradiction to the express agreement of the parties.

Although no court articulated gender as a factor influencing its decision, the tone of the opinions as well as the pattern of results shows
that the courts of New York, where the core cases were litigated, were
unable to ignore differential cultural constructions of women's proper
behavior as reflected in the larger society and in other legal rules.
Women's attempts to control their worklives and to assert their agency
and independence by terminating employment that they no longer
found desirable was no more to be tolerated than the emerging trend of
women's attempts to divorce their husbands. Although courts deciding
employment cases spoke of "binding men's consciences," they rarely did
so when presented with male defendants. The courts appeared more
willing and even eager to sanction what they perceived as women's infidelity to their male employers.

What we can know of the general legal history of working women
must be extrapolated from the glimpses we get from cases such as
these. Acting was one of the few professions open to women in the
nineteenth century. Actresses vastly outnumbered professional women
in most other fields. Thus, these cases represent the best evidence of
nineteenth-century legal treatment of relatively independent, professional working women. In certain respects, the status of actress was
the highest working women could hope to attain. No other profession
in the nineteenth century offered women greater autonomy and income. The freer atmosphere of the theater community allowed women
to enjoy lifestyle privileges and liberties forbidden to other middle-
class American women.

To discover that actresses were more constrained by the courts than
were actors is to demonstrate the bounds of their employment liberty.
To discover that actresses were more constrained than actors is to illustrate that access to a profession on terms basically parallel to those
offered men does not guarantee full equality of privileges and liberties.
Hence, what follows is a cautionary tale of women seeking and gaining
greater independence in a profession.

As the *Lumley* rule gained prominence, it eventually came to apply
to all professional performers. A legal rule originally accepted in the
heavily gendered context of actresses' cases eventually came to subordinate male performers to their employers as well. The point is not
only that, in keeping with prevailing cultural biases, some courts and
employers accorded actresses disparate treatment based on gender.
Rather, gender was a catalyst that transformed this aspect of the legal
status of an entire class of professional working people. What *Lumley*
wrought came to apply to all manner of employed people: actors, ac-

tresses, dancers, singers, musicians, radio commentators, booking
agents, baseball players, boxers, jockeys, public school music teachers,
artists, inventors, retail salespeople, and managers.[4] Courts of equity
no longer viewed employees under contract as partners or free laborers; instead, they became legally subordinate to their employers.

The Case Histories

The nineteenth-century employment cases can be divided into
roughly three periods. In the early period, 1800–1860, equitable courts
refused to intervene on behalf of employers who attempted to sue for
specific performance of performers' contracts. In the second period,
1860–1890, two shifts occurred as the English *Lumley* rule struggled to
take root in hostile soil. First, although suits involving men had pre-
dominated during the first half of the century, beginning around 1860,
suits against women were brought with far greater frequency than
suits against men. Second, in 1874, near the end of Reconstruction, the
first American court actually enforced the *Lumley* rule.

The third period is marked by the publication of John W. Pomeroy's
second edition of *Specific Performance* in 1897. This treatise, as well as
similar treatises, had a tremendous impact in disseminating legal
rules in an era when few courts or lawyers had access to legal libraries
or other means of researching precedent.[5] After 1900, the canon's edi-
fice was fully constructed, if only freshly set, in stone. Following the
canon's construction, cases tended to cite Pomeroy as the standard,
accepting without examination the treatise's judgment that *Lumley*
was the most significant case of the century. After 1900, the free labor
tradition surfaced only sporadically in cases and only as a counterpoint
to the established *Lumley* rule. The relatively high proportion of suits
involving women continued, but after 1900, men were enjoined as well
as women.

*1. The cases of the first period: Equity courts' nonintervention in a
man's world*

During the colonial and revolutionary periods of American history,
there were no reported instances of employers restricting the mobility
of an individual retained under general employment contracts of the
sort involved in the *Lumley* cases. Personal service contracts such as
apprenticeships and indentures were, of course, another matter, and

---

[4] For a comprehensive overview of these cases, see Lea S. VanderVelde, *The
Gendered Origins of the Lumley Doctrine: Binding Men's Consciences and
Women's Fidelity*, 101 Yale L.J. 775 (1992).

[5] JOHN N. POMEROY, SPECIFIC PERFORMANCE OF CONTRACTS (2d ed. 1897).

they could be enforced in a variety of ways, including specific performance. For those contracts, an employer held a quasi-property right in an employee's services in much the same way that a master held a property right in a slave.

In the early nineteenth century, American courts decided six general employment cases and regularly borrowed from four additional British decisions. Eight out of the ten cases concerned the services of white men, primarily actors and opera singers, but also a playwright, an office clerk, and a circus giant. In these cases, the respective employers unsuccessfully asked the courts for specific performance of the employment contracts. In only one of these cases, *Morris v. Colman*,[6] did a court actually grant any equitable relief. That case set the pre-*Lumley* standard for determining when equitable intervention was appropriate in contracts for services.

The distinguishing feature of *Morris* was the equality of the legal relationship between the playwright and the theater. The two parties were characterized as equal partners: Colman's creative contribution to the partnership, in writing plays, was considered equally important to Morris's contribution of capital. "[I]n partnership engagements," the court stated, "a covenant, that the partners shall not carry on for their private benefit that particular commercial concern, in which they are jointly engaged, is not only permitted, but is the constant course."[7] Presumably, the court would have equally enjoined either of the partners from competing with the partnership—Colman from writing for another theater, Morris from opening another playhouse. Morris may have had claims on the commitment of Colman's labor, but Colman had reciprocal claims on the commitment of capital controlled by Morris. Injunctions, and even specific performance, could be used to bind partners together, but the power was mutual and reciprocal.

In none of the remaining nine cases did the court enjoin the employee from performing his or (in two cases) her unique services for another employer. As one court put it, equity will not enforce a "hard bargain."[8] One defendant argued that he could not be enjoined from quitting and working for another firm expressly because he was *merely an employee* and not a partner. The court concurred: "Nothing could be more harsh towards a young man dealing with great traders than that

---

[6] 34 Eng. Rep. 382 (Ch. 1812).

[7] *Id.* at 383.

[8] Kimberley v. Jennings, 58 Eng. Rep. 621, 625–26 (1836).

he should be allowed to enter into an agreement which placed him so entirely in their power."[9]

The opinions of this period viewed employment contracts as a whole. The *Lumley* line of cases involved primary agreements to perform where covenants not to work elsewhere were incidental to the primary agreements. The covenant not to perform for another firm merely guards the "active" covenant of promised performance for the employer. This covenant could be enforced while the primary contract was still in effect and while the professional was still providing services, but not as a separate and independent covenant when other aspects of the contract could not or would not be carried through.

Equity courts of this period stated that they would not enforce part of a contract if they could not enforce all of the contract. They did not pick and choose between a contract's clauses based on their enforceability. Once an employee repudiated a contract, the theater or other hiring firm was left to its remedies of damages at law. Characteristic of the opinions during this period is the reasoning that specific performance cannot issue absent a partnership; therefore, the court will not attempt to produce indirectly a result that it cannot achieve directly.

As artisans under contract, these working individuals occupied a niche between the higher status of partners and the lower status of indentured servants, apprentices, and slaves. In the higher status, either partner could be ordered to continue the partnership, and the relationship was characterized as one of equality and reciprocity. In the lower status, the relationship was expressly unequal and marked by the formalities of indenture and bondage.

Unlike the strata above and the strata below, the contractual relationships of these talented or skilled tradesmen could not be specifically enforced, nor could they be enjoined from quitting and going elsewhere. The relationships between these free individuals were easily created and fairly easily dissolved. Once one of the parties to the relationship chose to repudiate the contract, he was free to go his own way, subject only to the limitation of possible damages for breach of the agreement.

a. Attending to the women

Three American cases involving women performers straddled the 1856 British decision of *Lumley v. Wagner* and the American Civil War. These cases—*Burton, Burke & Wife v. Marshall* in 1846,[10] *Dela-*

---

[9] *Id.* at 625; *see also* Hamblin v. Dinneford, 2 Edw. Ch. 528, 529 (N.Y. 1835).

[10] 4 Gill 487 (Md. Ct. App. 1846).

van v. Macarte & Wife in 1847,[11] and *Ford v. Jermon* in 1865[12] — are significant in that the courts refused to countenance employers' attempts to obtain orders preventing the actresses from quitting and performing elsewhere. The first two opinions demonstrate a marked sympathy to the circumstances of the women performers. All three stand in stark contrast to the generally punitive judicial treatment of actresses later in the century.

Burton v. Marshall was the earliest American case involving the services of a woman performer. Because the actress, Margaret Burke, was a married woman, the principal defendant in the case was her husband. As a married woman, Margaret Burke was classified as a *feme covert*. Under coverture, she was disabled from entering contracts; instead, her husband was the party to the contract for *her* services.

In many respects this case parallels the other cases of the first period, with Margaret Burke's husband occupying a role parallel to that of the male defendants in the other cases. Like them, Mr. Burke stood on an equal footing with the theater managers in his ability to repudiate the contract and refuse to order his wife to return to the first theater.

In other respects, however, this case is distinctive. This theater manager attempted to constrain Margaret Burke under a contract that contained no negative covenant. He attempted to gain equitable control over Margaret Burke on the strength of her employment contract alone. That the theater even attempted to secure an injunction in her case is curious because no previous court had agreed to interfere in an actor's decision to quit. On what basis could this theater, faced with negative precedent in the actors' cases where exclusive clauses were present in the contracts, have expected a court to impose additional restrictions on a contract for Margaret Burke's services? On what grounds could this theater have sought specific performance against a woman who was not bound by the formalities of indenture, apprenticeship, or slavery?

One explanation is that despite the fact that there were no cases actually ordering specific performance of actors, the courts sometimes sent ambiguous messages in their opinions. In 1833, for example, one court said, somewhat facetiously: "Upon the merits of the case, I suppose it must be conceded that the complainant is entitled to a specific performance of this contract; as the law appears to have been long

---

[11] 4 W. L.J. 555 (Ohio C.P. 1847).

[12] 6 Phila. 6 (Dist. Ct. 1865).

since settled that a bird that can sing and will not sing must be made to sing."[13] Nonetheless, the court did not order the singer to perform.

Another explanation is that the theater managers may not have considered Margaret Burke to be entitled to the same degree of independence that characterized the professional men in the other cases. Under the predominant legal conception of the day, private life was ordered in households in which the free male head of the household held a right and privilege of patrimony over all those residing therein and dependent upon him. This included his wife, his children, his servants, and, where the relationship existed, his slaves. Although legal and social differences existed between the different members of the master's household, the master's right to direct and control the labors of all members of his household, and his right to enjoy and profit from the fruits of their labors, was essentially similar.

As a wage-earning, married woman, Margaret Burke served two masters, her husband and the theater manager. The dispute between them over whether she should stay with the original theater owner or go to the second employer, as her husband directed, had less to do with her free choice of labor than it did with the competing hierarchies of her masters' conflicting directives. Like the other dependents in the master's household, a woman under coverture occupied a diminished status of limited autonomy and independence. In this respect, Margaret Burke's position was quite unlike that of the free professional men involved in the other cases. Margaret Burke was not free to make her own contracts. She did not even have a right to her own earnings. She was subordinated to all of the parties in the lawsuit, including her husband.

The law allowed masters to regain the services of other persons of diminished autonomy. Compelled service in the United States still existed for significant numbers of workers, such as indentured servants, apprentices, and slaves. The Constitution contained an enforceable clause permitting laborers who breached employment contracts and fled to other states to be extradited to their home state for whatever punishments or sanctions the home state allowed. Most of the actual enforcement under fugitive labor statutes fell upon fugitive slaves or apprentices. Nevertheless, like slaves, youths, and apprentices, women—particularly married women—were often perceived in their social station as subservient individuals. In their legal station, they were similarly disabled from self-ownership and control of their own energies and services.

---

[13] De Rivafinoli v. Corsetti, 4 Paige Ch. 264, 269 (N.Y. 1833).

The suit against Margaret Burke's husband parallels suits brought by masters against apprentices' fathers to resecure the services of underage apprentices. Perhaps for this reason, her employers had the temerity to sue for specific performance and injunction, in the absence of an exclusivity clause, when all the previous precedent ran against them, and despite the fact that she was not bound to them under the formalities of bondage.

The judge did not share the theater's view of Margaret Burke. In the judge's eyes, her subordinated position appeared to have the opposite effect; her low station evoked the court's sympathy even more poignantly than the other cases of this early period. The Maryland court seemed to give closer attention to Margaret Burke's circumstances as a working person. The court stated that she was entitled to the right to earn her own bread. It reasoned that if she were to be enjoined from performing, "she must either beg her bread, or be incarcerated within the walls of a public prison."[14] "Is it not unjust," the court asked rhetorically, that "she may be stripped of all means of subsistence, or be consigned to loathsome imprisonment in jail?"[15]

Burke was the first case in this line in which a court directly confronted the life necessity that impels a person to work. Because none of the other courts came close to ordering an injunction, they need not have paused to ponder the effect on the individual of being enjoined from working. Yet when confronted with the multifaceted subordination of Mrs. Burke (employee-servant, female, and married, hence *feme covert*), the Maryland court responded sympathetically by offering her protection from need and recoiled at the inhumanity of reducing her to a beggar as a consequence of the plaintiff's request.

Delavan v. Macarte & Wife,[16] decided in Ohio in 1847, followed the same pattern as *Burke*. Mrs. Macarte, "one of the most celebrated equestrians in the United States," was retained by Delavan under a written contract to give traveling performances for a year. As in *Burke*, Mrs. Macarte's husband was the party to the contract and the contract did not contain a negative covenant. The complaint alleged that the contract with Mrs. Macarte was of great pecuniary importance to them, that the circus owner had spent more than $2,000 preparing bills announcing her performances, and that the Macartes had left and joined "Spalding's Monster Circus," which was traveling just ahead of the Delavan circus. The complaint further alleged that "the defendants were

---

[14] Burton v. Marshall, 4 Gill 487, 491 (Md. Ct. App. 1846).

[15] *Id.* at 492.

[16] 4 W. L.J. 555 (Ohio C.P. 1847).

aliens, without any permanent locality, and without property within the reach of law or execution" and that their actions "would produce great and irreparable injury to plaintiffs." The defendants, for their part, alleged as their reason for leaving that "the conduct of Mr. Delavan in many respects had rendered Mrs. Macarte especially, very uncomfortable and unhappy."[17] The court's opinion was brief. Citing a few of the earlier cases, it simply stated, "[E]quity will not interfere by injunction to enforce a contract for personal services. It certainly seems to be a high stretch of power to interfere with a person in following his ordinary and regular business, upon an application for an injunction."[18]

b. A decision from across the water: Lumley's special significance for American law

The *Lumley* case had particular significance for the American tradition of free labor. In *Lumley v. Wagner*,[19] the English Court of Equity for the first time subjected a professional performer to her employer's control for the term of the contract. Soprano Johanna Wagner was enjoined from appearing anywhere on the London stage rather than simply held to damages for breach of contract. In one respect, *Lumley* was only a small step from *Morris v. Colman*'s notion of reciprocal commitment. Johanna Wagner's contract *did* contain a reciprocal clause securing the singing role exclusively to Madame Wagner. Should Benjamin Lumley have offered anyone else the part, Johanna Wagner could have sued, and possibly enjoined, the theater.

In other respects, however, the case was a break with the past. *Lumley v. Wagner* was actually one of two cases, based on the same incident, that played an important role in imposing conditions on an employee's right to quit. In the related case, *Lumley v. Gye*,[20] Benjamin Lumley sued the rival theater that enticed Madame Wagner away. He sued under the partially statutory, partially common law cause of action for enticement, which allowed an individual who had an interest in the services of another to sue anyone who interfered with the employee's services by enticing the employee away from his or her contract. Naturally, a rival employer, who hired the departing employee, fell within the scope of potential defendants to these actions.

When the English courts ruled against Johanna Wagner in both cases, they legitimated the employer's use of enticement actions and injunctions to control a class of workers: the professional class under

---

[17] *Id.* at 556.

[18] *Id.* at 558.

[19] 1 DeG., M. & G. 604, 42 Eng. Rep. 687 (Ch. 1852).

[20] 2 El. & Bl. 216, 118 Eng. Rep. 749 (Q.B. 1853).

general employment contracts, who had never before been subject to either type of employer control. Historically, only menial laborers had been subject to these actions. Taken together, the effect of these two causes of action was to impose legal and equitable constraints on a performer's election to quit employment. The injunction prevented the performer from using her talents and skills elsewhere. The enticement action discouraged demand for currently employed performers. In essence, these sanctions increased the employer's leverage over employees contemplating quitting. In Johanna Wagner's case, even though the original contract term was only three months long, the combined effect of these suits kept her off the London stage for four years.

In the American context, the sanctions legitimated by the two *Lumley* cases presented a particularly significant obstacle to employees because they burdened the constitutionally guaranteed right to quit employment. *Lumley* appeared before American courts at precisely the same time that the Civil War brought the issue of slavery, and the concomitant right to be free from mastery, before the American people. The problematic relationship between the two types of *Lumley* actions and the abolition of slavery was more than theoretical. Considerable discussion of the right to be free from an employer's control occurred in the Reconstruction debates. In the context of considering the rights of the newly emancipated freedmen, the Reconstruction congressmen repeatedly expressed their desire to guarantee that working people be able to quit their jobs and seek new employment without their former employers' permission. The notion of former masters being able to enjoin freedmen from seeking new employers was antithetical to the Reconstruction Congress's concept of free labor.[21]

In the nineteenth century then, the two common law causes of action that had the most impact in continuing to bind unwilling employees to their employers and in conditioning the right to quit are epitomized in *Lumley v. Wagner* and *Lumley v. Gye*—injunctions against employees and enticement actions against competing employers who would hire them. That these two cases gained acceptance in the United States for use against professional performers under contract represents a legal development counter to other free labor reforms occurring at the time.[22] In the century that witnessed the abolition of slavery and

---

[21] *See* Lea S. VanderVelde, *The Labor Vision of the Thirteenth Amendment*, 138 U. Pa. L. Rev. 437, 487–95 (1989).

[22] *See, e.g.*, W. J. RORABAUGH, THE CRAFT APPRENTICE 16–75 (1986) (describing disappearance of apprenticeships); ROBERT J. STEINFELD, THE INVENTION OF FREE LABOR: THE EMPLOYMENT RELATION IN ENGLISH AND AMERICAN LAW AND

the disappearance of apprenticeship and other forms of bound labor, the scope of employers' equitable power against contract employees actually expanded.

c. The free labor concept in full bloom

Ford v. Jermon,[23] which expressly rejected the *Lumley* rule, is perhaps the most significant American case of the early period. *Ford* is the first American case in this line of employment injunctions decided after the Civil War, after the enactment of the Thirteenth Amendment, and after the *Lumley v. Wagner* decision. Moreover, *Ford v. Jermon* is the first case in this line in which an American working woman was sued in her own name. As a widow, Mrs. Jermon had no husband; the doctrine of coverture was inapplicable. Perhaps because no man stood as a party principal protecting Mrs. Jermon's interests, the court went further to protect her interests. Most important, the free labor principle was the basis of the decision. The *Ford v. Jermon* opinion unambiguously affirmed Mrs. Jermon's independence and her right to be free from her employer's control, based expressly upon the distinctively American principle of free labor.

Mrs. Jermon, who had contracted to perform a play, decided, for her own unstated reasons, not to go through with the performance. Her contract contained clauses providing both that she would perform on Ford's stages and that she would not appear for any other competing theater for the season's duration.

In his complaint, Ford initially requested an order compelling Mrs. Jermon to perform the play. The case came before Judge John Innis Clark Hare, an eminent jurist of the day. He was one of the authors of a well-known series entitled *Leading American Cases*, and he lectured on contracts at the University of Pennsylvania Law School. He concluded that it would be inequitable to force the actress to perform her labor contract. Judge Hare's reasons for not attempting to force an unwilling performer before the public generally tracked the policy reasons against specific performance listed in *Lumley*. In addressing the request for an injunction barring Mrs. Jermon from performing at other theaters, Judge Hare emphasized that the very policies for not compelling performance explained why no injunction should issue. It would be harsh to compel obedience by imprisonment, and it would be difficult, if not impossible, to evaluate the quality of obedience when a performer reluctantly consented to appear. Hare explained: "I am unable

---

CULTURE, 1350–1870 (1991) (describing disappearance of indentured servitude).

[23] 6 Phila. 6 (Dist. Ct. 1865).

to see that these difficulties are likely to be less, because the mode of compulsion is the indirect one of obliging the actor to remain idle until necessity forces him to comply."[24]

Moreover, Judge Hare saw in the request for an injunction the attempt to force Mrs. Jermon back to her employer by her need to earn her living.

> We are asked to say that Mrs. Jermon shall not play at all, unless she will consent to play for the complainant; are we also to declare that she shall not sing? shall not earn her bread by writing or by her needle? To debar her from one pursuit would be vain and futile, unless she were also excluded from others, that might, so far as we can tell, be more profitable.[25]

Embedded in this argument was a recognition of the significance of "earning one's bread" and doing so by one's chosen trade. Judge Hare questioned why the actress should be compelled indirectly to come to terms with a theater owner for whom she now refused to work. He rhetorically questioned to what lengths the court should go in keeping her to a contract that had the effect of preventing her from earning her daily bread.

Judge Hare also predicted that forcing employees back to their employers would spread to other types of trades: "Are such decrees to be made solely with reference to actors, or shall lawyers be held to their clients, mechanics to their employers, and servants to their masters, by the same process[?]"[26] The emphasis was not on the court's powerlessness to enforce an order, but on the underlying importance of protecting the right of the employee to quit and to engage in her trade elsewhere.

Finally, Judge Hare articulated the free labor principle in relationship to slavery.

> Is it not obvious that a contract for personal services thus enforced would be but a mitigated form of slavery, in which the party would have lost the right to dispose of himself as a free agent, and be, for a greater or less length of time, subject to the control of another?[27]

Judge Hare viewed the distinction that the English Court of Chancery had drawn in *Lumley*, between equitable orders that compel and

---

[24] *Id.* at 7.

[25] *Id.* at 6.

[26] *Id.*

[27] *Id.*

those that prevent performance, as exalting form over substance. Both equitable orders had the same purpose or effect. Similarly, the terms of the contract were not the relevant issue. It would do theater managers no good to come up with stronger language in future contracts because it was the substance of the provisions, the fact that the individual "would have lost the right to dispose of himself as a free agent, and be, for a greater or less length of time, subject to the control of another," that was objectionable.

By looking beyond the form of the contract to its intended effect, Judge Hare acknowledged that the parties had unequal bargaining power and that "the sympathies of mankind would be all with the weaker party."[28] He effectively neutralized any argument that the actress should be enjoined because she had voluntarily contracted for such a result. The court viewed the injunction request as a grudge suit, an attempt to cut off her ability to earn a living elsewhere, without necessarily obtaining for the plaintiff the benefit of her performance.

The free labor principle was asserted to shield a professional actress from her employer's attempt to enjoin her. This particular employment context was one in which the performer presumably had somewhat greater bargaining power than the average working-class individual and the greater legal status of a written contract. Notwithstanding these status indicia, she still had to work to eat. The free labor principle came to her aid as a means of analyzing her relative powerlessness with respect to Ford. The court squarely considered the consequences of an injunction for her autonomy from Ford and for her ability to earn a living. Significantly, the court never asked her to produce or justify her reasons for quitting. It was her right.

Moreover, the court considered the precedential consequences for other employees. If Mrs. Jermon was enjoined, that type of employer prerogative might then spread to affect other service providers. Thus, in Judge Hare's eyes, Mrs. Jermon was not just a poor widow to be excused or pitied; she was a representative of an entire class of service providers, a class that spanned the constituency of the Republican party, from lawyers to mechanics to servants. Not only were Judge Hare's instincts the instincts of a Republican free labor adherent, but he allowed a woman to be a representative of their class interests and analogized from her situation to theirs. If she were subordinated to her employer, others too would be at risk. The fact that the defendant was a woman was not a sufficient reason to deny her free agency.

---

[28] *Id.* at 7.

Ford v. Jermon is an interesting and noteworthy case because, from a perspective of compartmentalized labor statuses, one would not have expected the court to analogize the defendant's circumstances to slavery—taking the analogy across gender lines, across race lines, and across class lines. Before the Civil War, the compartmentalization of separate labor statuses—one for slaves and another for nonslave laborers—could be considered complete and intact. But with the emancipation of the slaves, the edges of the compartmentalized labor system were coming unraveled. The oppression of slaves was in many ways a unique situation. The experiences and legal consequences of former slaves were different from those of a white actress like Mrs. Jermon. But that makes Judge Hare's opinion all the more remarkable. He saw the interests of working people as unified in this respect: Mrs. Jermon had a right to be free from the mastery of Ford.

2. *The cases of the second period: Binding women's fidelity and contracting their freedom to quit*

During the second period, women were coming into their own in the theater. Broadway was expanding and flourishing, and the American theater was becoming big business. As never before, women were performing more openly in public, forming theater companies, designing careers, commanding top billings and top dollars, and heading up touring companies. There were opportunities for income, travel, independence, and autonomy.

Outside the theater, however, the Victorian ideology was prescribing a stricter code of propriety and conduct for middle-class women than that of earlier decades. The notion that a woman's life should be limited to hearth and home became more and more generally accepted. When women did not comport themselves according to the strictures of propriety, the standard reproach was to label them prostitutes.[29]

By the very act of performing in public, actresses defied the social norms that the place for women was in the home and that the proper roles of women were as faithful mothers, wives, and daughters obligated to serve. Moreover, actresses appeared in a mode of dress that violated the expectations of the piety of "true womanhood." As a result, despite the banishment of prostitutes from the theaters, actresses as a group were still apt to be characterized as fallen women.

Their precarious social position was reflected in their legal position. Female performers were being sued for specific performance and injunction in greater numbers than were men during the period. They

---

[29] MARY P. RYAN, WOMEN IN PUBLIC: BETWEEN BANNERS AND BALLOTS, 1825–1880, at 3–5 (1990).

were also less able to make clean breaks from their employment contracts with only liability for damages. After 1860, cases involving women performers dominated the litigation: Annetta Galetti, Auguste Sohlke, Fanny Morant, Loie Fuller, and most important, Lillian Russell, who appears in three of the major reported cases of the period.

The canon of negative injunction was based on *Daly v. Smith* and two cases involving Lillian Russell, but the broader litigation base included a number of other cases, most of which involved women performers. During this critical period when American courts were deliberating whether they would exercise any equitable jurisdiction over quitting performers, there were roughly twice as many cases involving actresses as cases involving actors. In the cases involving actors, no permanent injunction for the term of the contract was ever issued; the only equitable orders ever granted against actors were preliminary injunctions, and none survived appeal. Significantly, the only cases during the entire century that permanently enjoined performers from appearing elsewhere for the duration of the contract term were five cases involving women performers.

a. Hayes v. Willio *and* Daly v. Smith: *The Daly brothers chart a new course for American law*

The 1871 opinion in *Hayes v. Willio*[30] illustrates the beginnings of a change in judicial attitude regarding the free labor implications of holding performers to their contracts of employment. By the early 1870s, the momentum of Reconstruction reforms had begun to diminish. Moreover, American courts were less sensitive to certain incidents of mastery in employment relationships and more concerned with protecting the aggregation of capital. The lower court decision in *Hayes v. Willio* was the only reported case in which a court actually decided against a male performer. Although the injunction was only preliminary and the decision was quickly reversed on appeal, the case laid the basis for the actress cases that followed.

The case is interesting for three reasons. First, the author of the lower court opinion, Judge Joseph Francis Daly, could not really be said to be neutral on this issue; he was deeply involved in theater management himself. Second, Daly's opinion marks the ascendancy of the capital interest as a policy element influencing the rule of decision. And third, the court of appeals beat a hasty retreat when confronted with Judge Daly's injunctive order restraining the defendant's employment and his personal liberty.

---

[30] 11 Abb. Pr. (n.s.) 167 (N.Y.C.P. 1871), rev'd on other grounds, 4 Daly's Rep. 259 (N.Y.C.P. 1872).

Judge Daly collaborated closely throughout his life with his famous brother, Augustin Daly, who was the manager of one of the major theaters of the time. Judge Daly was in some sense his theater-manager brother's alter ego. He had served as his brother's lawyer before being appointed to the bench. The two brothers met every day to discuss details of the theater's management, including Judge Daly's specific instructions for dealing with actors. Given this degree of involvement in his brother's affairs, it is not surprising that Judge Daly was able to elaborate so expansively and protectively upon the interests of theater managers. In fact, at the time he wrote the opinion, Judge Daly was also consoling his brother Augustin, whose own acting company was beleaguered by the first of a series of desertions.[31]

Not surprisingly then, Judge Daly's opinion emphasized the efforts of theater managers, the capital that theater managers have at stake, and the competitive nature of their business in relation to other theaters. He wrote language that would be seized upon in the next decision:

> [W]hen theatrical managers with large capital invested in their business, making contracts with performers of attractive talents, and relying upon such contracts to carry on the business of their theaters, are suddenly deserted by the performers in the middle of their season, the resort to actions at law for damages must fail to afford adequate compensation. It is not always that the manager is deprived of his means of carrying on his business, but that his performers, by carrying their services to other establishments, deprive him of the fruits of his diligence and enterprise, increase the rivalry against him, and cause him an injury. It is as much his right, if he have a contract to that effect, that no other establishment shall have the services of his performers, as that he shall have them himself.[32]

This statement established a new legally cognizable interest—that of depriving other establishments of the services of performers. It also identified a new relationship as the critical interest in the situation, the competitive position of the plaintiff theater as compared to other theaters. No longer was the primary balancing of equities between the employee and the theater. Instead, the competitive rivalry between one theater and another was considered the crucial interest to be protected and the interest that tipped the scales.

---

[31] MARVIN FELHEIM, THE THEATER OF AUGUSTIN DALY 9, 15, 19 (1956). In his later years, Judge Daly wrote a glowing biography of his elder brother. JOSEPH F. DALY, THE LIFE OF AUGUSTIN DALY (1917).

[32] 11 Abb. Pr. (n.s.) at 176.

Moreover, in this passage, the free labor principle was inverted. According to Judge Daly, the actor's desire to quit threatened to deprive the theater manager of "the fruits of *his* diligence and enterprise," rather than the reverse. The free labor principle—the rights to the fruits of one's labor—had from its inception appealed to both small entrepreneurs as well as laborers; in this case, the free labor principle came to the aid of capital in its disputes with labor and its rivalries with other capital interests.

As for fairness to the performer, Judge Daly stated without elaboration that there was no hardship in enjoining the performer because every man expects to be held to his agreement. Willio was sent to jail on a *ne exeat* order.

On appeal the decision was reversed by the New York Court of Common Pleas, sitting as a three-judge panel. The court determined that the agreement Willio originally made with a talent scout to accept employment with Hayes, if the agent could procure it, did not allow Hayes any enforcement rights as an employer. This irregularity of agency gave the appeals court a reason to reverse the preliminary injunction against Willio, freeing him from jail and from an injunction against performing elsewhere. Notwithstanding the reversal on other grounds, Judge Daly's lower court opinion became the basis for the legal cases that were to follow.

The permanent injunction threatened in *Hayes v. Willio* was actualized in *Daly v. Smith*, a case involving Judge Daly's brother, Augustin, and an actress in Augustin's company.[33] *Daly v. Smith* marked the first time an American court issued an equitable order permanently preventing a highly skilled performer from repudiating her contract, paying damages, and leaving. The opinion in *Daly v. Smith*, decided in 1874, was as biting in spirit toward the notion of her free agency as the opinion in *Ford v. Jermon* was magnanimous.

The case involved Fanny Morant Smith, "a distinguished actress, and a great artistic acquisition,"[34] who was also a wealthy woman and financially able to contemplate buying her way out of her contract. Mrs. Smith had decided that remaining with Augustin Daly was injurious to her career. A previous theater season had been canceled early without warning, leaving her without work, and she complained that her roles as a character actress cast her below her talents. Although she had signed on for another three years, she had come to believe that Daly's true motive was not to produce her, but to keep her off the stage

---

[33] 49 How. Pr. (n.s.) 150 (N.Y. Super. Ct. 1874).

[34] *Id.* at 161.

and away from rival theaters. Realizing her mistake, she approached Daly about getting out of the contract and posted a $20,000 surety bond against any damages for breach of contract.

Augustin Daly was called "The Autocrat of the Stage."[35] Modern historians consider him the most dictatorial of all the nineteenth-century theater managers, and his dictatorial fervor was most frequently directed at women in his company. Augustin Daly prized obedience over most other virtues, particularly in women. Fanny Morant Smith was the sixth major actress to attempt to leave his company in two years. This string of desertions by women performers caused Augustin Daly (and his brother Judge Daly) considerable consternation. In his own theater records, Augustin Daly used the language of matrimony to describe the actresses' departures, writing that they had "annulled" their contracts.[36]

In *Daly v. Smith*, Judge Freedman drew heavily on Judge Daly's reversed opinion in the prior case. The judge's sympathies favored the theater manager's capital interest from the outset. Judge Freedman stated that he could conceive

> of no reason why contracts for theatrical performances should stand upon a different footing than other contracts involving the exercise of intellectual faculties; why actors and actresses should, by the law of contracts, be treated as a specially privileged class, or why theatrical managers, who have to rely upon their contracts with performers of attractive talents . . . should, with the large capital necessarily invested in their business, be left completely at the mercy of their performers.[37]

By framing the issue in this way, Judge Freedman followed Judge Daly's lead and reversed two of the customary equities between performers and managers. First, he redirected all the equities of unequal power to run in favor of the unfortunate theater owner, rather than the "shrewd" Mrs. Smith. Second, he characterized the right to quit without intervention of a court of equity as a special privilege or preferred status claimed by actors and actresses to which other litigants were not entitled.

Judge Freedman continued by expressing regret that he could not order performance of the contract:

---

[35] GLENN HUGHES, A HISTORY OF THE AMERICAN THEATRE, 1700–1950, at 231 (1951).

[36] *See* FELHEIM, *supra* note 31, at 19–20, 32–33.

[37] 49 How. Pr. (n.s.) at 164.

I am of the opinion that actors and actresses, like all other persons, should be held to a true and faithful performance of their engagements, and that whenever the court has not proper jurisdiction to enforce the whole engagement, *it should*, like in all other cases, *operate to bind their consciences, at least as far as they can be bound*, to a true and faithful performance.[38]

This passage paraphrases a similar statement in *Lumley* about binding consciences, but Judge Freedman made two significant departures. Unlike *Lumley*, which had delicately stated that binding consciences contributed to the "wholesome tendency" to maintain good faith, Judge Freedman was concerned with the maintenance of the employer's capital, or more specifically, the income earned by the capital. Secondly, Judge Freedman introduced the word "faithful" in describing the actress's duty, asserting that "persons should be held to a true and faithful performance of their engagements." This evoked the notion that employees ought to be faithful to their employers, a notion not present in *Lumley*.

In justifying the use of equitable power to restrain Mrs. Smith, Judge Freedman ignored her willingness to pay damages for breach. The usual justification for equitable intervention was that the plaintiff is unable to obtain adequate relief at law. But Judge Freedman questioned why a theater manager must seek his remedy at law and take the chance of proving his damages to a jury. And how would the manager benefit, the judge asked, if the defendant were wholly insolvent?

This argument was interesting for three reasons. First, it represents a shift in judicial attitude about a performer's need to work to eat. When confronted with the possible insolvency of Margaret Burke and Mrs. Jermon, earlier courts paled at the notion of depriving them of their livelihood by equitable orders. In this case, the hypothetically insolvent performer led Judge Freedman to worry instead that the theater manager would go uncompensated. Second, Judge Freedman's hypothetical was counterfactual. There was little chance Augustin Daly would go uncompensated; Mrs. Smith stood ready to pay. Third, there is further irony in characterizing the plaintiff's possibility of obtaining an adequate remedy from the jury as "chancy." Judge Freedman appeared not to have trusted the jury to see the equities the same way that he did, even though he described the equities as running so clearly in favor of the theater manager.

Borrowing Judge Daly's language from *Hayes v. Willio*, Judge Freedman reiterated the view that "performers, by carrying their ser-

---

[38] *Id.* at 160 (emphasis added).

vices to other establishments, deprive [the manager] of the fruits of his
diligence and enterprise, increase the rivalry against him, and cause
him irreparable injury."[39] Like Judge Daly had, Judge Freedman focused on the theater manager's interests rather than on those of the
actress.

When Judge Freedman did consider Mrs. Smith's defense that Daly
was acting in bad faith and that remaining with Daly would injure her
reputation, he dismissed it emphatically, calling it "too preposterous to
raise an equity in her behalf." He considered her claims insincere, stating that her allegations seemed to "owe their origin to an afterthought
. . . produced by a desire on her part to find some excuse for breaking
her engagement."[40] According to the judge, since Mrs. Smith was a
"shrewd lady of great business capacity and mature age and judgment," he found it "safe to assume" that "she made the best bargain for
herself that could be got under the circumstances."[41] Judge Freedman
simply refused to take seriously Mrs. Smith's arguments or her attempts to get out of a contract she found burdensome.

The new equities and interests that the court was willing to credit to
Augustin Daly were not applied equally to Mrs. Smith. The judge did
not require the theater to provide "particulars" supporting its claim
that rivalry would be increased or that a jury would not take these issues fully into account in assessing damages. He did not notice that
Mrs. Smith's midseason withdrawal closely tracked the theater's midseason cancellation the year before. Each party's interests were similarly injured by the other's withdrawal. Only their remedies were different.

b. *Lillian Russell*

One actress's litigation fate seemed to shape and reinforce judicial
and public attitudes regarding the breach of employment contracts by
women. Lillian Russell's losses in two major cases during the next decade reinforced the rule adopted in *Daly v. Smith*. By 1897, on the authority of Fanny Morant Smith's case and one of Lillian Russell's suits,
Pomeroy's *Specific Performance* could state that the English rule of
Lumley v. Wagner was followed in the United States.[42] More important,
the opinion in one of Lillian Russell's cases indicated that something
beyond the abstract application of a capital-protective legal rule was at

---

[39] *Id.* at 161.

[40] *Id.* at 165.

[41] *Id.* at 164.

[42] POMEROY, *supra* note 5, at 31 & n.2. Pomeroy also cited Judge Daly's
lower court opinion in *Hayes v. Willio*.

work. The opinion in the second case carried *Lumley*'s rationale to the point of legal absurdity.

Lillian Russell, both as a popular symbol and as an individual, was the ideal foil for reinforcing this more restrictive legal rule concerning the freedom of women performers. She was a larger-than-life symbol of American femininity in the American consciousness. Her face adorned cigar boxes, and her voice was chosen for the first publicized long distance telephone conversation to demonstrate Alexander Graham Bell's new invention; the cable was laid from her dressing room on Broadway to the White House. She was the woman who made all men swoon, America's sweetheart, the major attraction of the Columbian Exposition of 1893. Her public presence was feminine *non plus ultra*, sweet, gracious, youthful, and, above all, submissive. She never played serious roles.

Despite her popularity as an actress, she belonged to a suspect profession, and both her private and professional life were major topics of the gossip newspapers. Although billed as America's sweetheart, the public still considered her scandalous and risqué. Russell appeared on the stage wearing tights and décolleté costumes. She fully enjoyed the independence that her fame and power gave her. But most important, Lillian Russell broke off her four unhappy marriages and her unhappy contracts with equally innocent abandon.

Russell's habit of breaking off contracts led to *McCaull v. Braham*[43] and *Duff v. Russell*,[44] litigation that spanned a decade.[45] Russell's first experience in court occurred early in her career. Russell was sued not because she would not perform for the plaintiff theater but because she proposed to sing at other engagements on off-nights. Since Lillian Russell was seeking not to repudiate the contract but merely to retain her ability to perform outside of scheduled performances under the contract, the issue of her right to quit was not squarely presented in *McCaull v. Braham*. Nonetheless, this case was used as precedent in later cases where employees did seek to quit.

The theater manager, Colonel McCaull, sought to enjoin her from performing *anywhere* without his consent. McCaull, who had begun his

---

[43] 16 F. 37 (C.C.S.D.N.Y. 1883). Lillian Russell was sued under her then married name, Mrs. Helen Braham.

[44] 14 N.Y.S. 134 (Super. Ct. 1891), aff'd, 31 N.E. 622 (N.Y. 1892).

[45] Lillian Russell was also involved in Canary v. Russell, 30 N.Y.S. 122 (Sup. Ct. 1894).

career as an attorney for Ford's Theater,[46] had drafted an ironclad contract with three different clauses spelling out the theater's desire to maintain exclusive control over Russell's singing engagements. One of the clauses stipulated that she would forfeit either a week's salary or the entire contract, at McCaull's option, if she sang at a competing theater during the season. Another stated that McCaull would have additional rights to pursue remedies notwithstanding the forfeiture clause. The only serious legal issue the court saw was whether the forfeiture clause constituted a liquidated damages provision or an additional penalty. The court took the latter position.

In contrast with the *Jermon* court, the *McCaull* court never considered whether it should look beyond the language of the well-drafted contract to the substantive effect on the young actress. In interpreting the language of the agreement, the *McCaull* court did not evaluate who had the upper hand in drafting the contract's terms. Not only did the court enforce the exclusivity clause by ordering an injunction, even when the defendant's performance for the plaintiff theater would continue undisturbed, it enforced the forfeiture as a special penalty in addition to the injunction rather than as a provision for liquidated damages. The court used the difficulty in evaluating damages for breach to justify invoking its equitable powers.

Ten years later, there was a subsequent case against Lillian Russell. In that case, *Duff v. Russell,* Judge Freedman actually set new precedent. He ignored the language of the contract and turned the equitable rules into parodies of themselves. The basic justification for issuing negative injunctions was first, that injunctions were necessary because legal damages were inadequate and could not be accurately estimated, and second, that the parties had bargained for an express negative stipulation in the contract. Without an express clause limited as to time and place, the general rule was that no injunction could issue. In *Duff v. Russell*, Judge Freedman bent both of these conditions out of shape in order to enjoin Lillian Russell.

Before trial, the parties reached a stipulated agreement about the amount of damages. They agreed that Russell would be allowed to go ahead with the rival performance, but if the injunction was deemed valid at trial, Russell would pay Duff $2,000. Clearly, the damages in this case could be estimated. But Judge Freedman gave no more heed to the condition that injunctions should issue only when there was no adequate remedy at law here than he did when deciding *Daly v. Smith*.

---

[46] *Five Years a Manager: Col. M'Caull's Experience with Comic Opera*, N.Y. Times, Aug. 16, 1885, at 3.

He stated the facts of the agreement concerning damages and then, as if in parody, ruled that an injunction was appropriate because damages could not be determined.

The second distortion occurred with regard to the contract language. Unlike her contract with McCaull, Russell's contract with Duff contained no negative covenant of any kind. The absence of such a covenant did not give Judge Freedman pause, however; he was prepared to imply one. He stated:

> [A]s was shown in *Daly v. Smith*, . . . the court is bound to look to the substance, and not to the form, of the contract. As the defendant had agreed to appear in seven performances in each week (exclusive of Sundays) which the plaintiff's company might give in New York, it was not possible for her to perform elsewhere in New York without a violation of her contract with the plaintiff, and a negative clause was unnecessary to secure to the plaintiff exclusively the services of defendant.[47]

It did not occur to Judge Freedman that if the defendant sought to get out of a contract that lacked an exclusivity clause, it made no difference whether the contract called for seven performances a week or two. Nothing in the contract specified that she should not perform elsewhere, either while the engagement continued or if, and when, she quit.

c. The nineteenth century's last decades: Binding women as a consequence of their uniqueness rather than their consent

With the canon constructed, American courts continued to press the *Lumley* rule even further to prevent women from breaking off their employment contracts. What followed were cases that expanded on *Duff v. Russell* and enjoined women from performing elsewhere, even when the contract failed to include a negative covenant, and even when the employee was not a superstar. This expansion on the *Lumley* rule occurred primarily in cases involving women. This tendency suggests that the strength of the cultural impulse to subordinate women surpassed even the formal limits of the language of their contracts.

There were two other cases in which New York courts issued injunctions preventing the women defendants from performing at other theaters despite the lack of negative clauses in their contracts. Moreover, the defendants in these cases were not well paid, were not featured as starring attractions, and were much less famous than Fanny Morant Smith. These women were held in a subservient employment status

---

[47] 14 N.Y.S. at 136 (emphasis added).

constructed largely by the courts rather than by the terms of their contracts.

Loie Fuller created a new dance, the Serpentine Dance. As a performing artist, she was a self-made woman. She designed her dance, her sets, and her costumes to create a particular effect. Under her contract with Hoyt, she appeared on the stage to dance for only a few minutes as a part of a much longer production. This contract never conveyed to Hoyt the exclusive rights to the Serpentine Dance. In fact, Fuller had attempted to copyright it and defend it against imitators.[48] Nonetheless, her vigilance in keeping the dance her own was turned to her disadvantage; instead of securing her ownership rights, it demonstrated her uniqueness. On the strength of her uniqueness, the court ruled that if she performed the dance elsewhere, it would result in irreparable harm to the theater. Once again, in a woman's case, the court declared a written covenant was not necessary for a theater to enjoin the performer. Moreover, Fuller's contract lacked mutuality: the theater could terminate her services on short notice, but the contract did not provide a way for her to terminate her relationship with the theater. The *Fuller* court had several options. It could have found the lack of an exclusivity clause to be a material defect to a suit in equity. It could have refused to enforce the contract at all because of the lack of mutuality. It could have reformulated the bargain to allow Loie Fuller to terminate the contract on terms equal to those on which she could be terminated. The court chose none of these options. Instead, the court held that "the defendant cannot complain of that [condition] after obtaining employment on the strength of that special condition"[49] and enjoined her from dancing elsewhere.

Edwards v. Fitzgerald further highlighted the significance of gender under the *Lumley* rule.[50] Cissy Fitzgerald, a dancer who received an extremely modest salary, was restrained, despite the absence of any contract provision. Fitzgerald appeared as a "Gaiety Girl" in a dance revue. The court restrained her, stating that although "[h]er talents may not be so exceptional as to render it impossible to replace her[,] . . . [s]he has a charm peculiar to herself. . . . The plaintiff would undoubtedly find it difficult to procure a substitute who would be likely to produce a similar impression. . . ." In this turn of language, the court expanded the definition of uniqueness to include charm. For Fitzgerald to

---

[48] *See* Hoyt v. Fuller, 19 N.Y.S. 962, 962 (Super. Ct. 1892).

[49] *Id.*

[50] The opinion in Edwards v. Fitzgerald (N.Y. Sup. Ct. 1895) was reported only at Hammerstein v. Sylva, 124 N.Y.S. 535, 539–40 n.1 (Sup. Ct. 1910).

be unique did not mean that she was exceptional or irreplaceable. The court conceded that she was not. It meant simply that no one else could be found who looked or moved exactly like her or who could produce *the same charm or impression*. The social construction of women, much more than of men, valued them for their charm, appearance, or femininity. Every woman, particularly actresses and dancers, was encouraged to distinguish herself by her looks or her graces.

As a result of *Edwards's* interpretation of uniqueness, almost any woman performer, except the most indistinguishable member of a background chorus, was susceptible to injunction, notwithstanding the lack of contract language. Any woman performer whom the judge might find had a charm "peculiar to herself" could be considered sui generis and was vulnerable to the *Lumley* rule.

Ms. Fitzgerald had come with the revue from London to New York. She wished to stay in New York, but Edwards planned to send her on a long tour to the West and Australia. In a manner reminiscent of earlier actresses' cases, the judge characterized her reasons for wishing to quit as "flimsy in the extreme." His final words emphasized the newly constructed theme of one-sided fidelity: "Is it not apparent that the success of the [producer's] entire enterprise is dependent upon the fidelity of his employ[ee]s, and—if that be wanting—upon the assurance that desertion will be checked by the strong arm of the law?" The *Lumley* rule had become an instrument to enforce a performer's fidelity to her employer.

d. The men's cases

The men's cases were far fewer in number than the women's were. Most of the male performers won on appeal, if not in the first instance. In the men's cases, actor Moritz Hahn, baritone Giuseppe Del Puente, acrobats Lassard and Lucifer, actor William Ferguson, tenor Agostino Montegriffo, and even performer Henry Willio, who was initially jailed and then released, all successfully defended themselves against their theater managers' attempts to enjoin them. In fact, the first permanent injunction of a male performer of any kind was that of a baseball player, Napolean Lajoie, which did not occur until 1902, almost thirty years after the decision in *Daly v. Smith* and fifty years after *Lumley*.[51]

The men's cases generally were not resolved by repudiating the *Lumley* rule, but instead were decided by excusing the male performer from the operation of the rule through one of a number of exceptions.

---

[51] Philadelphia Ball Club v. Lajoie, 202 Pa. 210, 51 A. 973 (Pa. Sup. Ct. 1902).

For example, in 1875, in *Hahn v. Concordia Society*,[52] an actor who was the featured performer was able to cancel his performance for the plaintiff and proceed to another theater by paying the fine as a liquidated damages amount.

Although the greatest concentration of the men's cases involved theatrical performers, some cases involved men in other trades. Noteworthy among those were the baseball players' cases, which litigated the closely related issue of the player reserve system. The baseball disputes followed a slightly different pattern than the theater cases, however, because the lawsuits tended to respond to collective action taken by the players. In these cases, almost all the baseball players avoided injunction. In fact, *American Association Base-Ball Club v. Pickett*[53] was the only reported nineteenth-century baseball player's case where an American court, this time a Pennsylvania county court, issued a preliminary injunction against a baseball player. Because the case was not appealed, it was also the only nineteenth-century case against a male defendant of any vocation in which the preliminary injunction was allowed to stand. The case made virtually no contribution to the *Lumley* canon, and it was not played out on the grand public stage as were Lillian Russell's three cases.

Although *Pickett* never surfaced in the canon, its existence illustrates that by 1890, men were not completely immune from injunctive control by their employers and that the seeds of Augustin Daly's success in *Daly v. Smith* had begun to sprout. Nevertheless, the preliminary injunction ruling in *Pickett* ran counter to the dominant trend of denying injunctions in men's cases.

From a gender perspective, the most interesting of the men's cases is one in which both traditional gender roles were reversed. In 1890, Louise Dudley Carter formed her own theater company, retained William Ferguson, and, when he left, commenced suit against him to restrain him from breaking his contract to perform services exclusively for her company.[54] The court ruled against Carter despite the contract language and despite Carter's allegations that Ferguson was unique and could not be replaced.

---

[52] 42 Md. 460 (1875).

[53] 8 Pa. C. 232 (C.P. 1890). Pickett refused to play for Kansas City because its membership had been transferred from the American Association to the Western Association and because some of his fellow teammates had been released.

[54] Carter v. Ferguson, 12 N.Y.S. 580 (Sup. Ct. 1890).

The talent and box office draw of these male defendants may not have matched that of superstar Lillian Russell. But many, if not most, of them were at least as attractive talents as Fanny Morant Smith. Certainly, most of them were as valuable theatrical attractions as mid-level women performers like Loie Fuller and Cissy Fitzgerald. It must be concluded then that uniqueness was neither an objective determinant nor a gender-neutral legal criterion. Instead, it was an artifact of subjective social understanding, and in these cases one that could be deployed most easily to the disadvantage of performing women.

The Influence of Gender in the Legal Texts

A close reading of the case histories suggests that the gender ratios reflected in the case results were not purely coincidental. Simply put, without the women's cases, there would have been no *Lumley* rule in the United States in the nineteenth century. Not only did women performers lose more cases than men did, women performers were sued more often than men were. This is not to suggest that gender was the only factor in canonizing the *Lumley* rule. Clearly, legal formalism, legal preferences for capital over labor, and class stratification were all at work in the late nineteenth century, and all contributed to the conditions for the American acceptance of the *Lumley* rule. However, the distribution of results along gender lines cannot be explained adequately by reasons such as preferences for capital over labor or differences in labor markets.

When examined collectively, the women's cases demonstrate that judges treated women defendants differently than their male counterparts. In cases involving women performers, the legal reasoning was frequently distorted, essential preconditions were dismissed as irrelevant, burdens of proof were reversed, and counterfactual circumstances were assumed in order to justify the issuance of injunctions. By contrast, in cases involving men, the legal reasoning was consistently stretched to allow male performers greater latitude in breaking their contracts.

The malleability of the legal doctrine was manifested in three ways. First, when male performers argued that they were leaving because the theater managers had breached agreements, their reasons were taken seriously and found to justify departure. Women, by contrast, were never excused from the operation of strict contract language, and their reasons for wishing to quit were usually found to be unjustified. Their reasons were labeled pretexts and described by such adjectives as "flimsy in the extreme" and "preposterous."

Second, the doctrine of mutuality was disparately applied in the cases of male and female performers. The lack of mutuality in con-

tracts that denied baseball players the right to quit while allowing the
team managers the right to release players was found to preclude injunctions against most male baseball players. In contrast, when this
argument was raised in Loie Fuller's case, the lack of mutuality was
dismissed as irrelevant.

Third, the specific language in men's contracts was deemed material
if it could be interpreted to avoid issuing an injunction and deemed
nonbinding if it could not. Women, on the other hand, were repeatedly
held to their employers, even in the absence of the requisite contract
language. The courts were willing to presume an intention on the part
of the women's employers to bind them. Indeed, in *Edwards v. Fitzgerald*, the court invoked a definition of uniqueness that applied to virtually any attractive woman.

Because late nineteenth-century society imposed cultural bounds on
the roles open to women, it was unthinkable that women could be fully
free laborers, as fellow or equal partners engaged in a joint enterprise
with the theaters. The image of the independent, yeoman-free laborer
was distinctly masculine. Masterless men may have been exalted in
the earlier Republican ideology of self-reliance, but masterless women,
or women who chose for themselves between two masters, were an inherently suspect group. The social construction of gender in the Victorian ideology precluded the image of working women as independent,
self-owned, free agents. This culturally constructed barrier to contemplating women as autonomous parties, who legitimately pursued their
own career interests independent of socially imposed relational obligations to male theater managers, contributed to the acceptability of the
Lumley rule as a legal barrier.

1. Gender in the nineteenth-century legal culture

Obviously, women performers swam against the current in violation
of several of the norms of Victorian ideology. What was particularly
significant about the behavior of actresses in this line of cases is that
they did not seek to get out of their contracts for socially approved reasons: in order to marry, to bear children, or to retire to the privacy of
the home. These actresses sought to be free of their contracts in order
to reenter the public stage under terms or conditions that they found
more desirable. When they chose to leave one theater's employ for another, their actions played into the stereotype of actresses as unfaithful, duplicitous, loose women.

Of the legal models available to a nineteenth-century judge, there is
no model that tracks the *Lumley* rule's methodological and remedial
structure more closely than does divorce law. During this era in New
York, where most of the cases occurred, most divorce decrees entailed
orders barring remarriage. Marital infidelity was the principal ground

for a divorce. The bar on remarriage was motivated by the belief that allowing wrongdoers to remarry rewarded them for their adultery.

Functionally, the bar on remarriage paralleled the distinction drawn by the *Lumley* rule between specific performance and a negative injunction. These divorces relieved the parties of the obligation to cohabit and relieved wives from the obligation to provide domestic services. American courts would not and could not force cohabitation, but they could and did forbid the remarriage of the unfaithful party to anyone else.[55] The *Lumley* rule split the burdens imposed on the performer accused of unfaithfulness in *exactly* the same way that divorce law split the burdens imposed on the unfaithful spouse. Unfaithful women performers could be prevented from performing for any employer for the term of the contract, just as unfaithful wives could be prevented from remarrying for life.

There were procedural parallels as well. The cause of action to protect an employer's interest in his employee was virtually identical to the cause of action to protect a husband's interest in his wife's services. It would not be surprising then if New York judges, who were most apt to observe women litigants who attempted to sever their relationships to men primarily in divorce proceedings, responded to women's attempts to break off their employment contracts in the same way. Judge Freedman decided a divorce case, granting a divorce a mensa et thoro the same day he decided *Daly v. Smith*.[56] Given the strength of the analogy between the legal frameworks for marriage and for employment, it would be more surprising if judges could have ignored these parallels. Just as nineteenth-century judges were more harsh on women charged with marital infidelity than on men, so too, they appear to have been more harsh on women whose actions were perceived as employment infidelity.

B. The core cross-gender dispute

No discussion of gender in this line of cases would be complete without considering whether gender played a role in the creation of these disputes. The core issue is not simply why courts ruled the way they did, but why more women performers wished to quit and why their

---

[55] This bar could be avoided by going to a state where divorce laws were more liberal. One of Lillian Russell's divorces entailed such a decree, causing her to elope to New Jersey, a state that did not recognize the conditions against remarriage imposed in her New York divorce. *See* P MORRELL, LILLIAN RUSSELL: THE ERA OF PLUSH 141 (1940).

[56] *See Law Reports*, N.Y. Times, Sept. 11, 1874, at 2.

male employers sued to enjoin them—especially in greater numbers than men.

The women in these cases gave a variety of reasons for wishing to quit. In general, women alleged less often that they quit for money and more often that they quit for more satisfying work opportunities or because they disliked their circumstances.

Managers' motives are less apparent from the texts because plaintiffs were not called upon to give reasons why they chose to sue. No doubt, most of the employers involved in this line of cases were disappointed commercially. But unless the actress changed her mind, an injunction would not recoup the theater manager's losses; an action for damages would. Surprisingly, employers rarely made claims for damages in these disputes.[57] This lack of resort to actions for legal damages suggests that economic losses may not have been foremost on the theater managers' minds. Indeed, the remarkable feature of these cases is the evidence that something more was at stake for the plaintiffs than simply their commercial interest in profits. Perhaps, the explanation for the phenomenon of more women's cases than men's may, in fact, be found in behavior that was not commercially rational at all.

In several of the cases, there is evidence that the manager seemed to have bonded with the actress. This is not to say that men did not bond with other men in certain circumstances, for example, as mentor to protégé, but the nature of that bond, so far as the records reveal, was substantially different. The departure of a valuable woman employee may have been more of an affront than was the departure of a man. Women were expected to be obedient and subordinate. A woman's decision to leave her employer, especially for a competitor, may have seemed more like a betrayal and threatened what the manager felt were his legitimate prerogatives. To protect his prerogatives, the manager may have been more likely to seek revenge by lawsuit. The possibility that an actress's departure would be a public event, announced in advertisements, covered in the press, and subject to public commen-

---

[57] *But see* H.W. Gossard Co. v. Crosby, 109 N.W. 483, 485 (Iowa 1906) (demanding $10,000 in damages and injunction against traveling saleswoman). I have been unable to find evidence of any enticement action for damages arising out of any of these disputes, as, for example, Lumley v. Gye, 2 El. & Bl. 216, 118 Eng. Rep. 749 (Q.B. 1853), arose out of the same incident as Lumley v. Wagner, 1 DeG., M. & G. 604, 42 Eng. Rep. 687 (Ch. 1852). On several occasions, managers did dissolve injunctions with the payment of money, however. *See* Duff v. Russell, 14 N.Y.S. 134 (Super. Ct. 1891), aff'd, 31 N.E. 622 (N.Y. 1892); Canary v. Russell, 30 N.Y.S. 122 (Sup. Ct. 1894).

tary, would only have amplified his injury. The more public the departure, the higher the stakes would have been for the theater manager.

For example, when Lillian Russell eloped and fled to London, her American managers pursued her to England with legal actions. One told the press that "my only object in getting the injunction out against her in London was to show her that the American law was powerful even in England, and that when she made an engagement in this country we could hold her to it across the sea."[58] These theater managers had no credible claim that Lillian Russell performing in London would affect their New York box office receipts. Nor could they force her to return. And yet, they made the extraordinary effort to teach her a lesson and to demonstrate their control over her.

Other cases demonstrate that the actresses did not like the conditions in which they were ordered to perform or the way they were ordered to present themselves. Lillian Russell's rejected suitor made her wear tights in circumstances to which she objected. Fanny Morant Smith's notoriously autocratic manager had driven away five actresses before her; he cast her in character roles that she believed were below her talents as a leading lady. Cissy Fitzgerald, having traveled with her manager from London to New York, did not wish to be sent still further to San Francisco and Australia. Ms. Crosby did not wish to be required to travel with a man who was a stranger to her. Several incidents entail the theater managers' objections to men whom the actresses wished to marry. This pattern of testimony suggests that at least some of these women had legitimate grievances against their working conditions.

This evidence suggests important issues of employee satisfaction, privacy, and autonomy. The employee's right to quit is her protection against employer abuses. The ability to threaten to quit gives her voice greater authority in raising grievances and in resisting unfair demands or uncomfortable situations.[59] Uncomfortable incidents may have prompted actresses to seek greater distance from their employers by seeking the protection of positions elsewhere. Being able to reestablish oneself in a new job provides the employee with a place of refuge from distressing circumstances. Certainly in these contexts, giving employers the threat or power of injunction over the actresses' future employment, once they had repudiated their contracts, accorded them an undue advantage. Moreover, the very conduct of a male employer pur-

---

[58] *The Law After Lillian Russell: What Her American Managers Think of Her*, N.Y. Times, July 29, 1883, at 12.

[59] ALBERT O. HIRSCHMAN, EXIT, VOICE, AND LOYALTY 82 (1970).

suing a woman who wished to repudiate an employment contract at some point crosses the professional line and could constitute harassment. Even a dispute that began over money could become ego engendered under the right conditions.

If male employers bonded more closely to important women they employed, and if the actions of women in quitting engendered stronger feelings on the employer's part, then women may have found themselves more often in circumstances from which they needed to exit and to exit quickly and cleanly. Applied in these circumstances, the *Lumley* rule has the unfortunate effect of tying the individual in greatest need of independence to her employer's continuing consent.

Conclusion

It is not surprising to find discrimination against actresses in this line of nineteenth-century cases. After all, during the nineteenth century, the Supreme Court itself openly upheld the exclusion of women from the legal profession based on the ideology of domesticity.[60] Given that social climate, more subtle forms of discrimination against women could flourish as well.

What is more remarkable about this particular history is the evidence that gender discrimination created the pathway for the adoption of a more regressive legal rule. The ground first eroded under women, and subsequently free laboring men lost parity with their employers. Once women were enjoined, their cases served as the linchpin of precedent for extending this rule to other working people. Thus, culturally constructed attitudes about gender subordination had real consequences, not only for the lives and legal rights of these actresses, but also for the development of law as a whole. In this instance, unarticulated gender biases appear to have influenced the selection of legal rules for the treatment of all other employees under similarly restrictive contracts, even for free white working men.

Examining a history such as this raises several questions about the present. Recognizing that *Lumley* was a contested issue of employment policy and knowing the circumstances of its adoption undermine one's belief in the rule's presumptive legitimacy. That the *Lumley* rule's origins were suspect may not be sufficient grounds to abandon the rule. To the contrary, one might think that a rule that has survived for one hundred years in American law has proved its usefulness. Its survival, however, is no greater reason to exonerate it than its origins are to indict it. One must examine closely how the rule works in context.

---

[60] *See, e.g.,* Bradwell v. Illinois, 83 U.S. (16 Wall.) 130 (1872).

A major benefit of examining context and history is that they shed light on our own time. We may be able to see patterns in the light of history that we are unable to perceive with the limited consciousness of our own experiences. As the late nineteenth century shaped present assumptions about the employment relation, so too, it has shaped many of our basic assumptions about gender and the appropriate roles of men and women in society, in the household, and in the workplace. If we were able to step back and comprehend the full scope of contemporary disputes, would we observe the same patterns taking shape, now as then? In occupations in which women coexist with men, do more women become caught in restrictive rules such as *Lumley*?[61] If this phenomenon continues to be the norm, does it continue to be explained by expectations of gender domination in the workplace? Do the forms continue to replicate themselves?

Seeing a rule in its broader context poses the ethical question of whether the law's response to a pattern of disputes was the appropriate one. An ethically responsible legal rule must take into account the private injustices that flourish in its wake. As an issue of employment policy, the *Lumley* rule prescribes a certain legal setting between the related matters of employees' abilities to exit when dissatisfied with working conditions, their exercise of voice to raise issues of dissatisfaction, and their loyalty. By limiting employees' abilities to exit to substitute employment opportunities, the rule necessarily dampens the authority of employees' voices in raising and resolving grievances. As a consequence, the rule has the potential to condone or actually to invite employer abuses.

Finally, history offers us the freedom to imagine other futures, other possibilities for rules whose acceptance has become habit. Imagine a rule formulated upon the norm of these working women's experiences. Imagine a rule formulated on understanding that employment contracts are agreements in principle, subject to modification and adjustment, but reserving always to the employee a private sphere of auton-

---

[61] There were no people of color in the cases to which the *Lumley* rule was applied in the nineteenth century. Nonetheless, it cannot go without saying that the analysis developed here raises the question whether people of color were more likely to be caught in restrictive rules such as *Lumley* once they entered this particular employment market. For cases applying the *Lumley* rule to African American performers in the twentieth century, see Okeh Phonograph v. Armstrong, 63 F.2d 636 (9th Cir. 1933) (jazz trumpeter Louis Armstrong); Foxx v. Williams, 52 Cal. Rptr. 896 (Ct. App. 1966) (comedian Redd Foxx); Beverly Glen Music v. Warner Communications, 224 Cal. Rptr. 260 (Ct. App. 1986) (singer Anita Baker in related cause of action for enticement).

omy guarded by the employee's right to exit. Such a policy would assure employees a greater voice in the conditions under which they
work. The loyalty that the employer received would be the loyalty that
the employer earned in its continuing dealings with employees, rather
than a loyalty enforced by the courts upon contracts that were often
more standardized than the products of negotiated consent.

Most individuals enter into employment contracts with hopes and
dreams. Few enter with the end of the relationship clearly in mind.
Still fewer anticipate that their employer will be able to prevent them
from working elsewhere should they wish to leave. Would employees
willingly enter employment relationships that so compromised their
satisfaction, their personal autonomy, and maybe even their dignity if
the situation unexpectedly deteriorated? Or would they enter these
relationships only if they had no real choice, if they were impelled by
necessity to work, and if they were unable to influence the terms? Perhaps they would remain, despite unsatisfactory working conditions,
only for the income or for love of the work, if the alternative was not to
be able to do the work at all. But that is a far cry from the American
ideal of free labor.

9

Judith L. Maute[*]

The Unearthed Facts of *Peevyhouse v. Garland Coal & Mining Co.*

Students often want to skim over the messy, confusing facts of a case, preferring to find a "rule of law" set forth by the court—an abstract principle to put in their outline, memorize, and dutifully repeat in the final exam. *Peevyhouse* teaches the important lesson, "if you don't get the facts right, you can't get the law right." Clients come to lawyers asking for help with thorny problems; they don't know what facts are legally significant, and they may tell rambling stories that omit or gloss over crucial facts. It is the lawyer's job to elicit a complete and accurate recount of what happened, to evaluate and accurately assess the significance of those facts to the various possible legal principles that could apply, and then seek an appropriate resolution in light of the relevant facts and law. If litigation ensues, the lawyer's job is to "re-present" the client's story in the most favorable light, making sure that critical evidence gets in the record by anticipating and responding effectively to any objections that could exclude the evidence. An effective advocate presents a compelling, plausible story, persuading the fact-finder to rule in the client's favor, based on strong legal

[*] William J. Alley Professor of Law, University of Oklahoma Law Center. Copyright 2006 by Judith L. Maute. This chapter is based on an earlier work, Peevyhouse v. Garland Coal & Mining Co. *Revisited: The Ballad of Willie and Lucille*, 89 Nw. U. L. Rev. 1341 (1995). Assistance in the preparation of this chapter was provided by Brian M. Childs (J.D. Suffolk 2004), Jennifer Pruchnicki (J.D. University of Oklahoma 2004), and Ivan L. London (J.D. expected 2007, University of Oklahoma, M.S. Colorado School of Mines 2004).

theory that withstands challenges both at the trial and on appeal. This 1963 Oklahoma Supreme Court decision is a story that underscores the importance of understanding factual context and its influence on legal doctrine. *Peevyhouse* cautions against blind faith in the litigation process, a process sometimes filled with systemic defects that distort facts and produce bad law.

While the Peevyhouses' lawyer represented them with exceptional zeal, he lacked the legal expertise the case required. Primarily a tort lawyer, he did not do the research that he needed to grasp the relevant principles of contract law and theory, and he did not know or appreciate the significance of critical facts about the contract terms, its performance, and the possible remedies. His misunderstanding of the facts and law doomed their case. Correctly understood and effectively presented, Willie and Lucille Peevyhouse's breach of contract action against Garland Coal Company should have produced a sizeable recovery.

Blame for the decision does not lie solely with failure of advocacy by plaintiffs' lawyer. The American adversary system assumes that both parties are represented by counsel with equal skill, dedication, and resources, and that courts rule impartially, without regard to disparities in the quality of partisan presentation and unswayed by any political, professional, or economic considerations. The reality is often otherwise. Where Peevyhouses' lawyer was a solo practitioner with modest litigation experience and little knowledge of contract law, Garland's defense counsel had vast litigation experience in contract matters, ample resources, and strong professional and political connections. The mismatch of counsel is yet another example of why we have come to understand that in so much litigation, the "haves come out against the have-nots."

The court system also bears responsibility for this miscarriage of justice. At trial, the judge allowed defense counsel to run roughshod over plaintiffs, bullying them into a stipulation that was then used to exclude relevant evidence crucial to plaintiffs' case. The Oklahoma Supreme Court ignored obvious contract language demonstrating materiality of the breached provisions and ruled that because these promises were immaterial, plaintiffs' damages were limited to diminution in value. Questions of improper judicial bias further taint the decision.

The Deal

Willie and Lucille Peevyhouse were both born and raised outside of Stigler, in the rolling hills of southeast Oklahoma where their families had lived since before statehood. In 1951 the young couple bought eighty acres of land from her parents, the Krumscicks, and soon added to their homestead another forty acres of adjoining land. They built a house, cultivated a large vegetable garden, and put in a pasture for grazing a small herd of cattle. After their son was born, Lucille left her job with a local canning company to tend their home and farm. Besides working the land, Willie worked at an ammunition depot and later did construction work.

The natural energy industry has always played a central role in the Oklahoma economy and political landscape. In the 1950s, surface mining of coal came second in importance only to oil and gas. Coal from the rich Hartshorne vein around Stigler, the Haskell County seat, accounted for nearly 20 percent of the state's total coal production. Garland Coal Company, headquartered in Fort Smith, Arkansas, was a major player in the mining industry. It maintained a local office in Stigler, then a bustling commercial center for outlying farms, ranches, and mining operations. At the time in question, several different companies were mining the area under a loose joint venture arrangement—sometimes in cooperation with each other, and sometimes in underhanded competition or self-dealing between the companies and their principal actors. Garland was, by far, the largest producer. It appears the community was familiar with local industry's personnel, mining activities, and whispered shenanigans.

Coal was king. Mining was important to the local economy, providing jobs, revenue to vendors, and cash to landowners. Most landowners passively accepted whatever terms the operators offered, pocketing the cash. When the mining ended, they still owned surface title to the disturbed land, stripped of all its value and future usefulness. Payment to landowners under the standard agreement had two components: (1) advance payment for surface damages in an amount equal to the fair market value of the property, in exchange for release of liability for those damages; and (2) advance royalty for coal to be removed, typically set at fifteen cents per ton. When a landowner refused to lease, the operators could either try to buy the property outright or skip over that parcel, moving the equipment to the next leased property along the coal seam. No existing law required reclamation, and landowners were seldom willing to forgo sizeable upfront cash payments in exchange for an operator's promise to do some remedial work when the mining ended.

The Peevyhouse land consisted of 120 acres, all contiguous, and it had an unusual footprint, with 100 of the acres bought from her parents' homestead forming a square-shaped "U" and a smaller 20-acre parcel lying horizontally on top of the "U." The Peevyhouses cared deeply about the land, both that which they owned and lived upon and the surrounding area. Even today, their love for the land is made obvious by the pristine condition of their house and garden, located on the left side and bottom of the "U," and the undisturbed pasture acreage. "Car farms" are sometimes seen in rural areas—where landowners keep in the field a collection of old, beat-up trucks and cars just waiting for a city slicker to come by and pay a lot of money for a vintage auto. There is no car farm on the Peevyhouse land. The small, well-maintained house has a neatly arranged front porch and yard with landscaped flowers, clay geese, a picnic table, and several chairs. It looks like a gathering place for friends and family. Farm equipment is stored in a side-barn, set back and hidden from view. The sixty acres eventually leased to Garland included a large stand of trees and fertile soil suitable for farming, which the Peevyhouses had used for pasture.

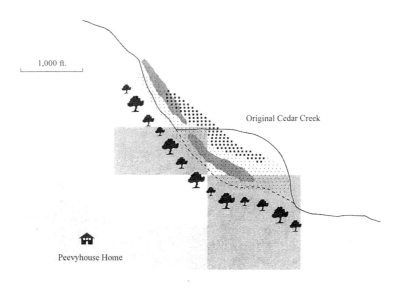

1,000 ft.

Original Cedar Creek

Peevyhouse Home

-- Diverted Cedar Creek

:: Land disturbed by stripmining before lease

Land disturbed as a result of lease

🌳 Tree line

☐ Peevyhouse land but not leased

▨ Peevyhouse land leased to Garland

▧ Pits left by stripmining after lease

The Peevyhouse Farm

The Peevyhouse land, while small in relation to the total acreage and quantity of coal Garland expected to mine, was key to a profitable operation. The targeted coal vein cut through their back twenty-acre parcel (top of the "U") and a small portion of their forty-acre parcel (east side of the "U"). Only by leasing those sixty acres could Garland move its mining operation efficiently from northwest to southeast. Diverting Cedar Creek also provided strong motivation to obtain the Peevyhouse lease. Cedar Creek naturally ran north of the property, passing through the heavily mined land owned by their neighbors and eventually flowing onto the northeast corner of the Peevyhouses' forty-acre parcel to the east. Diverting the creek to flow onto Peevyhouse property south of the planned mining site was essential so water did not interfere with the mining operations.[1]

The Peevyhouses had seen and heard of the disruption to their neighbors' property from noisy trucks on mining roads that passed right by their homes and dynamite blasts that damaged the homes and surrounding property. An earlier mining operation stopped at their north property lines, leaving behind the disturbed land, a dangerous pit, highwall and unsightly overburden. No amount of money was worth the disruption to their personal lives or permanent harm to their land, leaving it unsightly, unusable and worthless. Besides their sentimental attachment to the land, they also had moral concerns with the proposed mining. As Willie told me during my first meeting with him, "It's just not right to do something with land that makes it useless for the future."

Given that stance, why did they agree to permit any mining on their land? Mining had already reached the northern boundary of their top twenty acres; the natural course of the seam lay north to a line of trees that would shield their personal acreage from the view and disruption caused by the mining activities. Other nearby landowners had received tidy sums for leasing their land, disturbing much of the local terrain. The expected operation would affect only a small portion of the acres they would lease, and at the northern boundaries of their land. If Garland would do modest remediation that assured future use of that land, it made sense to them to allow the mining to continue on to their land.

From the outset the Peevyhouses insisted that Garland do some remedial work after the mining: leveling the disturbed land so it could again be used as pasture and providing safe access across the pit, which would fill with water, so their cattle could graze on their undisturbed land north of the planned pit. They refused to lease any land that Garland did not intend to mine or to permit Garland to bring its

---

[1] Its importance is evidenced by the fact that Garland began pumping water from the creek onto their land even before the lease was signed. An aerial view of the Peevyhouse farm at the present time can be found on Google. *See* http://www.google.com/maps?f=q&hl=en&q=stigler,+oklahoma&ie=UTF8&t=k &om=1&z=18&ll=35.17465,-95.142851&spn=0.001995,0.005322&iwloc=A.

equipment across unleased land. That is, the Peevyhouses insisted that Garland would have no rights to enter or mine the sixty acres on which they lived and gardened, and a portion of the land they used for pasture. They would only consider leasing the north twenty and east forty acres directly involved in the planned mining.

The negotiations took some time, with Willie negotiating directly and Lucille participating behind the scenes, helping to identify issues and desired terms. Contrary to some folklore, Willie and Lucille were not naïve country bumpkins deceived into relinquishing control of the family farm by Garland's slick verbal assurances. Despite their limited formal education, they were sensible and astute, having acquired sound judgment and survival skills from living off the land. Garland offered the standard deal: advance payment of $3,000 for surface damages based on the current market price of fifty dollars an acre, plus $2,000 as advance royalty based on fifteen cents a ton, with any future royalties payable only if required by the actual amount of coal removed.[2] Rather than accept $5,000 up front when the lease was signed, the Peevyhouses gave up $3,000 advance payment for surface damages in return for Garland's promise to perform specified remedial work when the mining ended.

It is not known whether Garland prepared cost estimates for the remediation work. Garland had planned to stop mining that strip while on the Peevyhouse land, leaving behind a pit that would interfere with access to several acres of virgin land. But Garland's heavy earthmoving equipment already would be on site and available to do much of the promised work at a fraction of the cost of hiring outside contractors. By smoothing off the spoil banks and removing unstable shale and dirt from the highwalls, Garland could use that leftover material to stabilize the diverted creek crossing and make fills across the pit, giving the owners access to their undisturbed back acreage. In short, Garland agreed only to the remediation work that it was well positioned to do with the equipment it had in place. In exchange, Garland was able to divert the creek immediately and acquired rights to mine the Peevyhouse land without incurring the usual cash outlay of $3,000.

---

[2] Later on, after the mining began, the Peevyhouses and other landowners suspected that operators manipulated records on amounts removed in order to cheat landowners of additional royalties.

The Contract

The contract was signed November 23, 1954, in the Stigler law office of J. F. Hudson, Garland's local counsel.[3] Although the Peevyhouses were not represented by counsel in the lease negotiations or execution, the final agreement demonstrates their savvy and practical wisdom. The signed agreement revised Garland's preprinted form lease and included a one-paged typed addendum containing specially negotiated terms. It limited the lease term to five years, striking the lessee's standardized renewal option. It promised an additional five cents per ton royalty, increased from fifteen cents printed in the form lease. It also deleted standard language giving the lessee rights of passage over all the lessor's property, including that not subject to the lease, meaning that Garland had no right to disturb the sixty acres of adjacent land on which the Peevyhouse home, pasture, and garden were located.

Paragraph six of the standard form contract granted Garland broad authority to alter the Peevyhouses' property without liability for damages, providing:

> . . . Lessors agree to furnish Lessee, in consideration of said royalty, all surface as may be necessary to be used by Lessee in the operation of strip pits, and may be used by Lessee for drainage ditches, haulage roads, spoil banks, tipples, tracks, and any other structures that Lessee finds necessary in the operation of said strip pit or pits or coal mine and the lessee agrees that all such structures shall be located consistent with good operating practice so as to cause the least damage or inconvenience to the owner or user of such surface; . . . Lessors agree that they will save harmless and indemnify the Lessee from any claim or liability arising from any damage to the surface of these lands caused by such operations; it is further recognized the Lessee shall have the right without liability to the Lessor, wherever it may be necessary in conducting such operations, to change the course of any streams or water courses and to erect and maintain such drainage ditches as it shall deem advisable having due regard for the successful operation of said strip pit and damage to the remainder of the property.

---

[3] The negotiations, however, had been with Burrow ("Burl") Cumpton. Cumpton was a native of Stigler and Garland's main contact with the Peevyhouses. This middle-aged civil engineer seemed to play a role in some questionable activities involving coal, land, and money. He had already acquired experience testifying in court.

In sharp contrast with this boilerplate language, the typewritten insert containing paragraph seven was conspicuously the result of individualized negotiations. Three of the eight subparagraphs acknowledged that the Peevyhouses received $2,000 in advance royalties; prohibited any transfer or assignment of the lease without their written permission; and required that Garland survey the property and fix boundary lines before starting to mine. The following five clauses specified Garland's remedial obligations:

> 7b. Lessee agrees to make fills in the pits dug on said premises on the property lines in such manner that fences can be placed thereon and access had to opposite sides of the pits.

> 7c. Lessee agrees to smooth off the top of the spoil banks on the above premises.

> 7d. Lessee agrees to leave the creek crossing the above premises in such a condition that it will not interfere with the crossings to be made in pits as set out in 7b.

> 7e. Lessee agrees to build and maintain a cattle guard in the south fence of SW [fr1/4] SW [fr1/4] of Section 7 if an access road is made through said fence.

> 7f. Lessee further agrees to leave no shale or dirt on the highwall of said pits.

Performance, Breach, and Settlement Negotiations

Garland started work near the Peevyhouse land in October 1954, a month before the lease was signed. The day after signing, Garland began blasting to dam Cedar Creek and build the channel diverting the creek onto the leased Peevyhouse land south of the current mining activity.

Although Garland continued mining in Haskell County until January 1958, it mined this particular segment during 1956 and 1957. It removed substantial quantities of coal from the other leased properties but comparatively little coal from the Peevyhouse land, paying them only about $500 beyond the initial $2,000. Based on figures Garland used in court to obtain an accounting from a co-tenant on nearby land then being mined, its likely profits from the sale of Peevyhouse coal ranged from $25,000 to $34,500, not including any intangible value received from creek diversion or other economic benefits from access to their land.

Actual mining on Peevyhouse land possibly lasted only three months. Exceptionally heavy spring rains ended a six-year drought, causing widespread flooding. Cedar Creek's proximity made the pit on their land especially vulnerable. Garland pulled the dragline from the worksite and resumed mining at a higher and drier site. When preparing to relocate, Garland's principal contact person, Burl Cumpton, told Willie that the coal depth fell from forty-five to seventy feet below the surface just as the seam reached their land. He also claimed that the price was not high enough to justify the increased costs of extracting the coal from the lower depth.[4] Garland's decision to stop operations when it did, however, made little difference. Garland never planned to make more than one or two additional cuts on the Peevyhouse land, and the exact number of cuts would not greatly change the costs of remediation.[5]

As Garland prepared to leave the site, Burl and Willie discussed the remedial work, and tentatively agreed that Garland would smooth off the spoil banks, stabilize the highwall, redirect the creek into the pit, and level the diversionary channel. A bulldozer spent one day smoothing off the sharp peaks on the spoil banks and building a dirt levee across the pit. These makeshift efforts ended when more heavy rains worsened already unstable ground conditions. Because it had relocated the equipment to another profitable site, Garland decided not to return to complete the remedial work. This suggests its breach was perhaps not in bad faith, but prompted by a change in conditions. While this was nothing close to justify a legal excuse of nonperformance, it was enough to tempt Garland into walking away from its promise.

Willie offered to accept $500 so he could hire a bulldozer and level the ground himself. Garland refused. He then told Cumpton that the price of settlement would increase by $500 each time he returned to Garland's Stigler office about the incomplete work. Six fruitless visits later, Garland presented a check for $3,000, conditioned on full release and indemnification.

Willie and Lucille knew of Oklahoma City attorney Woodrow McConnell, who had grown up in Stigler and was representing a neighbor in a pending tort claim against Garland. They traveled three

---

[4] As I show below, Cumpton's testimony on this score is not strong. *See infra* note 9. Moreover, Garland's own operations map shows mining on depths ranging from thirty to sixty feet from the surface, and the coal bed on the Peevyhouse land was about twenty-five to forty-eight feet deep. In addition, Garland continued to mine on property directly to their east, with comparable coal depths owned by a family with mining interests closely linked to Garland. It is unclear where Garland moved its equipment, but court opinions from other Garland-related litigation suggest this was an expedient opportunity to relocate to other properties in which its actors owned some stake and stood to personally profit.

[5] I discuss this point in greater detail below.

hours to Oklahoma City to get his advice on the proposed settlement. McConnell advised against signing the release unless a certain paragraph was deleted. They recall his explanation: "If you sign [this], you take full responsibility to your neighbors for damage [being done to their land from the creek], and your neighbors will look to you." Settlement discussions ended when Garland refused to delete the indemnification clause.

The Trial

McConnell had been a solo practitioner for five years, mostly handling tort claims at the trial court level. He made do, best as possible, with limited resources to pursue fact investigation, conduct in-depth legal research, and develop sophisticated trial exhibits and expert witnesses. When we spoke about the case many years later, he conceded that contracts was not his strong suit in law school, an assessment confirmed by his professor. Alas, had he understood contract law better, he could have created a strong record that would have made it much harder for the state supreme court to rule as it did. He demonstrated to me how his tort bias influenced his judgment in *Peevyhouse*, that one ought not be allowed to walk away from one's contract duties and escape punishment. If he had understood that contract remedies seek to protect expectations—and not inflict punishment—he would not have pursued a misguided strategy of grossly exaggerating the cost to complete the remedial work. His likely contingent fee agreement also influenced that strategy. Had he understood the transactional details and that the remedial goal of contract damages was to protect the injured party's defeated expectations, McConnell would have realized why the diminution measure—or any other that yielded less than $3,000—was plainly inadequate since the Peevyhouses valued the work at least in the amount they gave up to ensure it was done. Had McConnell only understood the parol evidence rule and its exceptions, he could have countered defendant's objections at trial, filling gaps in the record or preserving the issue for appeal.

In February 1960, three years after Garland quit the site, McConnell brought suit for money damages in the state trial court located in Oklahoma City. Although the breach occurred in spring of 1957, McConnell waited until after the five-year lease expired. The two-count complaint sounded in contract and tort, identifying only the specific parcels Garland had leased, mistakenly alleging that the Peevyhouse home was located on the leased premises. The contract claim demanded $25,000 as the cost to complete the remedial work promised in the breached provisions. The tort claim demanded recovery of $1,750 for the damage to their home and water well caused by dynamite blasting performed in an unworkmanlike manner.[6]

It is doubtful that McConnell gave serious thought to seeking specific performance, influenced both by his tort orientation and contingent fee. Had he considered the possibility of equitable relief, he might reasonably have predicted the court would deny it, given equity's historical reluctance to supervise performance of construction. The Peevyhouses wanted the remedial work done and did not need or want money in its stead. McConnell told them that if they prevailed in an action to recover money damages based on cost to complete, they could buy substitute performance with the proceeds. (Although theoretically the cost measure fully compensates for plaintiffs' defeated expectations, the net recovery after absorbing litigation costs is less than what it would cost to obtain substitute performance.) Strategically, had plaintiffs also sought specific performance, it would have forced closer attention to the intended purpose of the breached remedial provisions, their importance to the parties' agreement, and why the diminution measure was inadequate. Regardless of McConnell's reason for not seeking specific performance, defense counsel perceived that decision as evidence of opportunistic, strategic behavior.

Garland Coal was an experienced, repeat litigant, knowing which firms had the best litigation track records, professional, and political connections. It retained the Oklahoma City firm of Looney, Watts, Looney & Nichols (hereafter, "Looney, Watts"), which it had often used before, and in all prior suits brought by McConnell. Clyde Watts, lead defense counsel, was an outstanding litigator with nearly twenty years of experience in federal and state, trial and appellate courts, including many cases involving contract law.

Garland answered the petition by general denial, asserting the mining operations complied both with proper custom and practice and with the lease requirements. No discovery was taken. The pretrial conference order identified the case as a simple breach-of-contract action, involving neither negligence nor novel questions of law or statute. No one thought it presented important questions of theory or policy.

The Honorable W. R. Wallace Jr. presided at the two-day jury trial. He was thought to have an average legal mind but was considered conscientious, fair, and politically astute. Like most judges of that era, he

---

[6] The blasting did cause lasting but relatively minor damage to walls in the house, and significantly damaged a water well. Timely suit on the tort claim for damage to land that was not leased might also have forced Garland to pay attention to its obligations under the existing lease terms. One can only speculate.

generally did not intervene to correct imbalances arising from one party's weak partisan presentation. Nevertheless, at one point he interrupted McConnell's cross-examination of a witness, stating, "I don't think the jury knows what you are talking about. They can't see that exhibit and this conversation you are having doesn't have any meaning." His unusual intervention typifies the confusing and garbled record, reflecting McConnell's deliberate but misguided strategy to focus exclusively on cost as the only possible damage measure, using grossly inflated estimates of the work required by the contract. Long known for being stubborn, McConnell refused to acknowledge the possible applicability of the diminution measure and presented nothing to counter the defendant's evidence of minimal lost value. Because McConnell thought that the $2,500 in royalties paid to the Peevyhouses was irrelevant and maybe prejudicial, the record is silent on that aspect of the bargain. Most critical, McConnell did not show that the Peevyhouses gave up a $3,000 payment for surface damages in exchange for Garland's promise of remedial work. That material omission does not seem based on deliberate strategy. McConnell likely did not understand that aspect of the bargain, and, even if he had, he did not see that it provided a floor for the damages to which the Peevyhouses were entitled under contract law.

At the outset of trial, during Willie's opening testimony, counsel stipulated that the defendant had not performed the remedial work in paragraph seven, leaving in dispute only the measure and proof of damages.[7] McConnell tried to elicit testimony from Willie on direct, and from Burl on cross-examination, about the negotiation of the remedial provisions, the scope of work as understood by the parties, and that the Peevyhouses insisted upon those provisions as essential to the contract. Watts objected each time, invoking the stipulation and the parol evidence rule. McConnell did not counter with recognized exceptions to support admissibility of the evidence, with citation to relevant Oklahoma precedent holding that contract purpose is a fact question for the jury, needed to determine whether the contract was substantially performed or materially breached.[8]

McConnell should have argued that under the parol evidence rule, the evidence on the customary practice of paying in advance for surface

---

[7] The stipulation provided "that all covenants and agreements in the lease contract had been fully carried out by both parties, except the remedial work mentioned above; defendant conceded that this work had not been done." Additionally, the tort claim was voluntarily dismissed because suit was filed after the limitations period expired.

[8] Ardizonne v. Archer, 178 P.263 (Okla. 1919).

damages was generally admissible, aiding to interpret the materiality of the remedial provisions agreed to instead of the usual arrangement. Likewise, he should have pointed to the obvious conflict and facial ambiguity between printed paragraph six, absolving Garland of any liability for disturbing the land, and typewritten remedial provisions in paragraph seven. The proffered testimony should have been allowed to aid the fact-finders' interpretation in accordance with the parties' probable intent. Hearing nothing to justify the testimony, Judge Wallace sustained Watts's objections, finding "the contract speaks for itself." This very strict application of the parol evidence rule left gaping holes in the trial record. Willie's limited testimony described the current condition of the leased property and its impact on his use of the land. An engineer provided detailed, but unrealistic specifications supporting their claim it would cost $29,000 to have the work done.

Garland's defense challenged plaintiffs' claim for $29,000 as excessive and beyond the required scope of work, and stated that the necessary work could be done for $400. Alternatively, Garland claimed plaintiffs' recovery should be limited to diminution in value because the cost measure far exceeded actual harm. Although its four supporting witnesses differed on specific land values before and after mining, they generally agreed that the remedial work would add little value to plaintiffs' land. Cumpton's testimony briefly alluded to a possible impracticability defense, which was not pled, supported by evidence, or argued on the main appeal to the Oklahoma Supreme Court.[9] No evi-

---

[9] Burl Cumpton's testimony provides scant factual support for a possible defense based on impossibility doctrine. He said Garland did not fully strip the coal from the Peevyhouse site before it quit mining this segment in 1957 because the vein ran a bit thinner on their land, and Garland's equipment was too small to continue mining at greater depths. Some modern contract scholars point to this testimony as support for the nascent defense:

Watts:	Mr. Cumpton, did you strip all the coal from under that pit that you were able to get?
Cumpton:	No, we didn't.
Watts:	Why?
Cumpton:	Well, the machine, for one thing, was a little small for any deeper than we did go. And we ran into some thin coal on that southwest.
Watts:	Down this area here?
Cumpton:	There's a fault in there.
Watts:	Did you go toward the southwest as far as, in this direction, as you officially could?
Cumpton:	No. If this coal hadn't turned out thin on that 40 acres in the southwest-southwest, we would probably have made another pit or two in there.

dence was offered to show that the end of the drought increased its performance costs.

Because the parties stipulated to breach, Judge Wallace directed that the jury find for plaintiffs, along with instructions allowing latitude to fix damages. In determining what sum would reasonably compensate plaintiffs, the jury could consider the costs of doing each item of remedial work, "together with all of the evidence" offered by either

---

On cross-examination, McConnell tried to establish that the Peevyhouses' insistence upon the remedial work influenced contract negotiations. He did not, however, ask whether Garland estimated the costs of completing the remedial work before entering the contract, or whether the claimed change in coal depth substantially increased those costs.

McConnell:	Isn't it true Mr. Peevyhouse insisted upon those provisions being included in that lease?
Cumpton:	That's true.
McConnell:	Before he agreed to sign it?
Cumpton:	That's right.
Watts:	May I have the same objection?
The Court:	The objection will be sustained in that connection. The contract speaks for itself.
McConnell:	Mr. Cumpton, when you negotiated and obtained that lease from the Peevyhouses, did you intend to comply with the terms of that contract, those specific terms of the lease that are included in there?
Cumpton:	Yes, we did.
McConnell:	Your company hasn't complied with them?
Cumpton:	No, that's right.
McConnell:	Could you, with the equipment you have, could you have complied with those terms of that lease?
Cumpton:	Yes, we could, but I want to qualify that statement.

Watts pursued the matter on redirect.

Watts:	. . . I will ask you if you had been able economically to mine further coal toward the southeast, would you have been able to establish that fence on the spoil bank?
Cumpton:	Yes, we could have.
Watts:	Having stopped when you ran out of coal down in here, can you now establish that fence line without putting in a very useless and expensive fill?
Cumpton:	No.

This reference to "useless and expensive fill" is part of an argument Garland used to show that part of the remediation—"to make fills in the pits . . . on the property lines in such manner that fences can be placed thereon"—would be wasteful. Garland asserted that these fills (one running north-south and the other east-west) would meet in the middle of the pit that would fill with water and would hence be pointless. The Peevyhouses maintained the fills would not meet in the middle of the pit.

party. After brief deliberations, the jury returned a verdict for $5,000. The jury, it appears, was not fooled by either side's exaggerated damage evidence, nor by the truncated evidence that told a badly incomplete story. It saw the pictures of plaintiffs' damaged land and the actual contract with typewritten remedial terms, and it heard testimony from Willie, who presented well: soft spoken, honest, and sincere. While the jury was not inclined to inflict punishment on the defendant, part of an important local industry, it aimed to compensate plaintiffs fairly for their defeated contract expectations. In retrospect, its $5,000 verdict was probably just about right, except for plaintiffs' litigation costs. Perhaps the legal system should place more trust in the common sense of just plain folks, and worry less about constraining their judgment.

Considering Garland's potential liability, defense counsel viewed the low sum as a victory. Thereafter, its formal litigation conduct was precautionary, guarding against the downside risk that the plaintiffs might prevail on appeal. Both sides filed motions for new trial, which, after argument and briefs, were overruled in December 1960. Although both parties appealed, dissatisfaction on the plaintiffs' side propelled the case forward to the Oklahoma Supreme Court. Kenny Rogers's song, "The Gambler," offers wise counsel to litigants: "You got to know when to hold them, [and] know when to fold them."[10] Without some basis for thinking that an appeal would lead to a new trial and a more generous jury verdict, they should have accepted the $5,000 verdict.

Appeal: Tilting at Windmills

The wheels of appellate justice turned slowly: initial briefing dragged on for sixteen months; the Oklahoma Supreme Court finally disposed of the case a year later. Such delays were then common; lawyers routinely obtained multiple extensions for filing briefs. In many ways, the parties' briefs are a study in contrasts: in professional writing styles, legal argumentation, polish, and rhetoric. A well-written brief persuasively tells a credible story, organizes legal arguments in order of their strength and importance. Opposing arguments are acknowledged, addressing factual and legal distinctions. Policy analysis is woven throughout.

Plaintiffs' brief was ineffective. Lengthy excerpts from the trial transcript enhanced adverse testimony that the promised work would add negligible value to the land. To win, plaintiffs had to persuade the

---

[10] *See* Kenny Rogers, *The Gambler*, on KENNY ROGERS, GREATEST COUNTRY HITS (EMI Records 1990).

court that the cost measure was necessary to protect their subjective expectation interest, supported by the limited record evidence reflecting their personal interests. Instead of beginning with this essential argument, their brief began with the argument that the trial court erred in admitting testimony on diminution in value. Its crucial argument on the cost measure came later. It paid scant attention to the statutory damage limit, which became so important to the state supreme court.[11] Rather than selectively quoting from precedent to develop strong legal arguments supported by the evidence, key points were buried in lengthy quotes.

Substantively, the plaintiffs' brief cited relevant, helpful precedent but did not use the cases to develop reasoned arguments. It made little of the policy issues significant to modern contracts scholars, such as a landowner's personal and idiosyncratic values and how market values undervalue such concerns. The brief did quote extensively from *Ardizonne v. Archer*,[12] an Oklahoma case awarding the cost measure for breach of a contract to drill a test well, despite lack of proof that the well could produce oil, in order to protect the injured party's subjective expectation interest. Dictum suggested the importance of accurately determining the parties' intended purpose for breached provisions, a fact question critical to whether substantial performance doctrine applied.[13] It also quoted the classic language from *Chamberlain v. Parker,* evoking image of the proverbial "ugly fountain."[14] Buried toward the end, it argued that *Groves v. John Wunder Co.*[15] was "the majority rule . . . unquestionably supported and followed in Oklahoma." The strongest argument, also near the end, urged that Garland's willful and bad faith breach "should not . . . be handsomely rewarded." If damages were limited to diminution in value, Garland "could enter into similar contracts, reap the benefits to be realized from the mining operations

---

[11] They needed to convince the court that the statute prohibiting "unconscionable and grossly oppressive damages" did not preclude the cost measure. Ultimately, the court interpreted this as a mandatory, policy-based limit on recovery.

[12] 178 P. 263 (Okla. 1919).

[13] *Id.* at 266. "It does not lie with the plaintiffs in error, who engaged and were compensated for drilling the well, to say that their performance would not be beneficial to the lessor. It has been held that the loss may be sustained in a legal sense for the breach of a contract, notwithstanding it can be shown that the performance would have been a positive injury, as in the case of a failure to erect a useless structure upon another's premises."

[14] 45 N.Y. 569, 572 (1871).

[15] 286 N.W. 235 (Minn. 1939).

by removing the mineral deposits, dispose of them and pocket the money, and then limit liability by selecting their own method of compensation to the injured party." The consequence of assessing such nominal damages "would open the door for the legal practice of fraud . . . ."

Tom Capshaw, the junior associate who wrote Garland's brief on appeal, believed the remedial work would increase the land's value by only $300 and considered possible expenditure of $30,000 as "appalling social waste." Because he was not familiar with the coal industry's customary practices and contract terms, he did not appreciate that this contract was unique but did think it strange the contract set no dollar limits on the remedial work.

Well written and persuasive, Garland's brief concisely stated the facts and proposed analytical framework. Its first proposition contended: "The measure of damages for the breach of a mining lease covenant to make specified restorations in the surface market of the land should be the cost of performance, limited, however, to the total difference in the market value before and after the work was performed."[16] The instant case was one of first impression, distinguishable from *Ardizonne* and the Minnesota court's plurality decision in *Groves,* because the cost of performance far exceeded the increased value to the property. An Oklahoma statute limited recovery to the amount plaintiffs could have gained from full performance, and never more than reasonable damages. Accordingly, it asked the Oklahoma Supreme Court to reverse and remand the judgment below with directions to grant remittitur for $4,700.

Garland conceded it did not complete the promised remedial work and offered no legal justification to excuse the breach. The sole question on appeal concerned damages. Its legal argument mislabeled a valuation figure, which misled and confused the court, hampering sound economic analysis of the case. This distortion of facts was made possible by plaintiffs' trial strategy and general failure to present a coherent, plausible economic analysis.

Defendant's brief summarized testimony on the loss in value caused by mining: Before mining, the land was worth sixty dollars per acre; after mining, the value dropped to eleven dollars per acre. In parentheses, it calculated "(60 acres at $49.00 per acre is $2,940.00)." This sum represented the loss in value caused by the mining. Regarding diminution of value caused by the breach, the brief stated that if the repairs were done, the land value would have increased only by two to five dol-

---

[16] Defendant's Brief at 4.

lars an acre, or $300 for the leased acreage. Standing alone, each calculation accurately portrayed evidence presented at trial: the mining stripped $2,940 in market value from the leased acreage, and the remedial work would increase the present value of that land by $300. In the following legal arguments, the brief erroneously characterized $2,940 as representing either the pre- or the post- mining value of the leased acres (as opposed to the loss in value caused by the mining). The $2,940 sum became central to Garland's main argument that plaintiffs' recovery was limited to $300, representing the "total difference in the market value before and after the [promised remedial] work was performed."

Both labels were wrong. Using Garland's figures, the pre-mining value of the sixty leased acreage was $3,600; its post-mining value was $660. The promised remedial work would have increased the post-mining land value by almost 50 percent. When one considers that mining stripped $2,940 in value from the land and other financial aspects of the bargain, the economic analysis appears quite different, even without evidence that the remedial promises were given in return for valuable consideration.

Plaintiffs' reply brief was more effective than the first. It dismissed diminution precedent as outmoded and distinguishable, involving immaterial and nonwillful breaches. Plaintiffs had insisted upon the remedial provisions in order to assure functional use of their land. At last, it presented an economic analysis of the transaction, that the Peevyhouses received minimal royalty payments while Garland's reaped about a half-million dollars in gross sales from the coal removed from plaintiffs' land.[17]

Confidential court records demonstrate that this case, involving relatively low stakes, commanded unusual attention by the Oklahoma Supreme Court. It was discussed in court conference eight times in as many months, where typical cases were presented and disposed of in one conference. Whatever the cause, it was a troublesome case for the court. On December 11, 1962, the Oklahoma Supreme Court affirmed judgment on liability but reduced plaintiffs' damages to $300.[18] The case was initially decided by a 5–3 vote, with Justice Williams voting with the majority, and Justice Welch not participating.

---

[17] This analysis was used to support an extraordinary request to amend the complaint, adding tort claims of trespass and wrongful conversion, to support recovery of both compensatory and punitive damages.

[18] Peevyhouse v. Garland Coal & Mining Co., 382 P.2d 109 (Okla. 1962).

Justice Jackson, writing for the majority, considered this a case of first impression. *Ardizonne*, awarding the cost measure, was distinguishable because drilling gives the landowner valuable geological information, even where no oil or gas was found. Here, however, performance would only add a few hundred dollars to the farm's market value, and that is "all plaintiffs have lost."[19] The majority refused to consider future appreciation in value or potential future use that would only be possible if the remedial work were done, deftly avoiding any scrutiny of the actual contract. The "unrealistic fact situation" was deeply troubling.[20] The expectation principle usually requires compensating the lessee for the reasonable cost of the work. In this case, where the breached provision was

> [m]erely incidental to the main purpose in view, and where the economic benefit which would result to lessor by full performance of the work is grossly disproportionate to the cost of performance, the damages which lessor may recover are limited to the diminution in value resulting to the premises because of the non-performance.[21]

Attorneys for both parties filtered, shaped, and distorted the evidence presented at trial, which led the appeals court to make several mistaken assumptions. The majority opinion assumed that the Peevyhouses leased their entire farm to Garland Coal and that after mining, the farm was worth approximately $3,000, which remedial work costing $29,000 would increase by only $300. It assumed the damage estimates on both cost and diminution were reasonably accurate. Most critical, it assumed the parties' primary purpose for the contract was mutually profitable recovery and sale of coal and that the remedial provisions were "merely incidental" to the main object involved.

Justice Irwin's dissent examined the record in light of the specific breached provisions and concluded they were a material part of the consideration promised to payments, in addition to royalties. "[D]efendant had knowledge, when it prevailed upon the plaintiffs to execute the lease, that the cost of performance might be disproportionate to the

---

[19] *Id.* at 111.

[20] "It is highly unlikely that the ordinary property owner would agree to pay $29,000 (or its equivalent) for the construction of 'improvements' upon his property that would increase its value only about ($300) three hundred dollars. The result is that we are called upon to apply principles of law theoretically based upon reason and reality to a situation which is basically unreasonable and unrealistic." *Id.* at 112.

[21] *Id.* at 114.

value or benefits received by plaintiff for the performance."[22] Defendant admitted that plaintiffs would not agree to lease their land unless the remedial provisions were included, could reasonably approximate the costs of performance before entering the contract, and presumably found the contract was advantageous, or it would not have agreed to it. No record evidence indicates defendant could not perform, or that there was any change in conditions "which could not have reasonably been anticipated."[23] Garland's breach was willful and not in good faith; it received full performance from Peevyhouses and offered no excuse for its failure to perform. Plaintiffs were entitled to specific performance, or the cost of performance. "Any other measure of damages would be holding for naught the express provisions of the contract; would be taking from the plaintiffs the benefits of the contract and placing those benefits in defendant which has failed to perform its obligations; . . . and would be completely rescinding the solemn obligation of the contract . . . by making an entirely new contract for the parties."[24]

On February 1, 1963, seven weeks after the initial decision, ten prominent local attorneys and academics filed an amicus brief urging the court to reconsider and award plaintiffs the cost measure. Because they represented clients who enter contracts with comparable future risks, they were concerned with proper legal development. In three pages, the amicus forcefully argued for the sanctity of contracts. McConnell petitioned for rehearing and oral argument. His supporting brief buried otherwise viable arguments in excess prose or abrasive attacks on the court. It addressed the factual errors arising from the deficient record, such as the excluded evidence of plaintiffs' personal acreage, and asked for a full hearing on remand, allowing plaintiffs opportunity to show their loss in value in light of the economic benefits they expected to receive from the remedial work.

On March 25, with all nine justices voting, the court voted 5–4 to deny rehearing.[25] Justice Williams had switched his vote to the dissent. Justice Welch, who had not previously participated in a dispositive

---

[22] *Id.* at 115.

[23] *Id.*

[24] *Id.* at 116.

[25] Justice Jackson's supplemental opinion on rehearing catalogued the litany of errors by plaintiffs' counsel at trial and on appeal, including failure to appeal the trial court's exclusion of evidence and impermissible change of theory on appeal. *Id.* at 116–19. (Original opinion dated March 26, 1963.)

vote in the case, cast the deciding vote for Garland Coal. Had he not voted, the resulting 4:4 split could have left intact the $5,000 verdict.[26]

McConnell refused to accept defeat and filed a second petition for rehearing, which prompted the court to hear oral arguments. His supporting brief fought to preserve the $5,000 verdict, arguing that the supreme court should not have accepted verbatim defendant's diminution figure, and at least should hear oral arguments in the case. Watts's reply to the second petition for rehearing, for the *first time in the litigation*, asserted impossibility as justification for the breach. Garland's breach was not arbitrary and unreasonable. Cumpton's testimony indicated that at time of contracting, Garland intended in good faith to fully comply with its terms. Only after partial performance did it become apparent that the amount of coal under the leased property was limited, and the operations were not extended far enough toward the southeast to permit economic compliance with the terms of the lease requiring remedial work. Two weeks later the court denied the petition. McConnell fought on. He petitioned for writ of certiorari to the United States Supreme Court, asserting unconstitutional impairment of contract and due process and equal protection violations. It was promptly denied. McConnell then sued in federal court, seeking specific performance or, in the alternative, money damages. The district court dismissed on summary judgment; res judicata barred any further action. The Tenth Circuit affirmed. After six years of litigation, the case was over.

Legal Analysis

The majority opinion focused on the "main purpose" of the contract as central to determining the measure of damages. Had the facts been competently presented they should have significantly altered doctrinal and policy analysis. Besides the remedial questions, the unearthed facts would impact analysis of three major issues: (1) contract interpretation; (2) materiality of the breach and substantial performance doctrine; and (3) excuse of Garland's nonperformance under mistake and impracticability doctrines.

1. Interpretation and parol evidence rule

The primary focus of any contracts litigation should be to determine the parties' intent—what they intended to accomplish through the

---

[26] Had Justice Welch formally recused from participating in the case because of his close connections with the defense firm, Oklahoma law would have required the governor to appoint a substitute judge; this undoubtedly would have caused further delay in disposition of the case.

agreement—as fundamental to ascribing the meaning given their words of agreement. Standard interpretive process focuses on the exact words of agreement, especially when the agreement is reduced to writing. Notwithstanding the parol evidence rule, courts routinely admit evidence that puts the agreement in context, to best discern the parties' probable intent. Recognized exceptions to the parol evidence rule permit extrinsic evidence on surrounding circumstances and to explain any ambiguities in the contract itself.

The barren trial record left few clues on the underlying circumstances that resulted in the specially negotiated remedial provisions. Because plaintiffs' counsel did not understand the underlying transaction as it related to contract law, he was unprepared to argue for admissibility of evidence on the surrounding circumstances to explain and interpret the remedial provisions. The trial court, presumably finding the contract a clear and complete integration, excluded any testimony of the personal acreage, the circumstances explaining why the remedial provisions were included, what they were intended to accomplish, and details on the intended scope of work.

Even after counsel's stipulation to breach, this evidence should have been admitted as relevant to interpreting the parties' intent and its bearing on the proper measure of damages. Given the lack of a merger clause, the contract's relative informality, and the side agreement regarding surface damages, the written contract was only a partial integration. Moreover, the conflicting language in lease paragraphs six and seven created a facial ambiguity that would support admission of extrinsic evidence to aid interpretation. Even if plaintiffs' counsel countered the objection with sound argument to permit this evidence in aid of interpretation, that still might not have worked. Often such evidentiary rulings bear witness to courts' deep-seated judicial reluctance to admit time-consuming evidence on extended background information. When courts generously admit contextual evidence to show the parties' intent, they lose the ability to streamline issues, to shape the law, and to determine outcome. The modern neo-formalist, textualist movement suggests renewed vigor of that judicial stance.

The court's holding, limiting recoverable damages to the diminution in value, is premised on its interpretation that the breached provisions were "merely incidental to the main purpose in view." The opinion recognized "the property owner's right to do what he will with his own . . . ." Where such result is in fact contemplated by the parties and is a main or principal purpose of those contracting, the measure of damages for breach would ordinarily be the cost of performance. By imputing contract intent without any individualized focus on the actual bargain or evidence of actual intent, the court's opinion negates this passing nod to freedom of contract. Its interpretive efforts were pure abstractions without regard to the parties' actual intent.

The scant trial record made it easier for the court to reach its own conclusion on the primary purpose of the contract. While acknowledging that Garland "specifically agreed" to perform certain remedial work, the majority did not examine the actual contract language or invoke other rules of interpretation to determine what the parties actually sought to accomplish. Instead, it treated contract purpose as an abstract finding that could be imputed to the parties, not as a factual question warranting closer examination. The supreme court thought it obvious that mutually profitable extraction of mineral resources was the main purpose; it made no reference to the record, to the actual writing, or to standard rules of interpretation. Before reaching this fact-based conclusion, the majority should have examined the actual writing and circumstances surrounding its execution. It ignored conspicuous differences between the printed lease and the typewritten addendum and the interpretive maxim that places greater weight on individually negotiated remedial provisions. It ignored evidence of surrounding circumstances, including Garland's admission that the Peevyhouses insisted upon the remedial provisions as a condition of entering the lease. Despite reasonable inferences that Garland drafted the actual contract language, including the remedial provisions, the court disregarded the usual interpretive guideline that any ambiguities would be construed against the drafter. Although sparse, ample evidence in the record supported a contrary conclusion—that the remedial provisions were a material part of the exchange, requiring compensation based on cost to complete.

2. Material breach or substantial performance?

A more complete trial record and effective appellate argument should have precluded a finding that Garland's breach was only partial, warranting the clemency of substantial performance doctrine. Substantial performance doctrine primarily applies to service contracts, where the service provider essentially completed performance, with only insignificant defects or incomplete items remaining. The doctrine allows recovery of the unpaid contract price, less any damages owed the payor from defective or incomplete performance. Equitable principles allow the contractor's recovery notwithstanding its nonmaterial breach. Assuming substantial performance fulfills the payor's principal purpose for the contract, anti-forfeiture doctrine protects the contractor's expectation interest. Conversely, if the remaining work is significant, the defects serious, or the breach willful, courts may determine the breach was material. Material breach doctrine would allow the payor, as the injured party, to cancel the contract and seek damages. Usually the contractor's right to recover requires a fact-intensive analysis of whether the injured party received substantially what it sought to obtain in entering the contract, and whether its disappointed expectations can be compensated adequately with money damages measured by either cost or diminution. Correct doctrinal application requires the court to interpret whether any of the breached provisions were material elements of the exchange that would defeat the injured party's intended purpose for the contract.

Once again the *Peevyhouse* majority glossed over standard methods of interpretation, this time to invoke the substantial performance damage formula. Its conclusory analysis—that the breached provisions were incidental to the main purpose of the contract—enabled it to assume that Garland substantially performed. Citing *Jacob & Youngs v. Kent*[27] and Charles McCormick's damage treatise, the court used the doctrine as precedent for adopting a "relative economic test" to deny recovery for work costing an amount "grossly and unfairly out of proportion to the good to be attained." It again avoided focusing on the actual bargain to determine the materiality of the breach to the underlying exchange.

Peevyhouse is not a substantial performance case. It does not fit the pattern triggering the anti-forfeiture doctrine. Garland had already received full performance from the Peevyhouses and was not at risk of forfeiting agreed compensation for work done under the contract. Garland materially breached by not performing the remedial work for which it received valuable consideration. The case is analogous to a construction dispute where the contractor abandons without cause a half-completed building. No court would find this constitutes substantial performance and require the owner to pay the remaining contract price, less any diminution in value between the completed and half-completed structure. Unless the owner receives a substantially complete and serviceable building, substantial performance doctrine does not apply. Garland's failure to perform essential duties deprived the Peevyhouses of the benefit they reasonably expected to obtain from the agreement. Other factors, including Garland's willful breach and plaintiffs' risk of undercompensation, further support the conclusion that Garland materially breached.

3. Nonperformance excused by mistake or impracticability

Contract duties are generally absolute, requiring that each party perform as promised or respond with damages. However, a contract may allow for escape by making a duty conditional or subject to dis-

---

[27] 129 N.E. 889 (N.Y. 1921).

charge upon occurrence of specified events. Absent such a provision, the law of mistake or impracticability will occasionally excuse a party's failure to perform. To establish mistake or impracticability, the party claiming excuse must show that the mistake or supervening event went to a basic assumption of the contract, that it severely increased the burden of performing, and that the burdened party did not bear the risk of its occurrence.

The record includes limited testimony and a brief but tardy appellate argument that impracticability excused Garland's failure to complete the remedial work. Citing these excerpts, some commentators suggest that unexpected difficulties excused Garland's liability for breach.

Two related factual matters might raise issues of mistake or impracticability to excuse Garland's liability for breach: (1) the presence and location of sufficient coal on Peevyhouse land, and (2) the location of the northern Peevyhouse boundary. Garland presented meager evidence at trial that might support an excuse, but it did not expressly assert this defense. Nor were the issues directly raised on appeal to the Oklahoma Supreme Court. Garland first alluded to impracticability after the court's original decision, in its brief opposing plaintiffs' second petition for rehearing. Examination of the available data reveals no factual basis for excuse doctrine.

Some evidence in the record suggests that Garland may have removed somewhat less coal from the property than it had anticipated. A smaller quantity of retrievable coal would leave less overburden for Garland's use in constructing the promised fills. The record is silent on whether this affected the cost to perform. Because the pit represents the last cut, and cuts are comparable in size, the precise location where the mining stops does not affect the distance across the pit. Had Garland made additional cuts, it would have had more overburden and spoil banks to grade. The reduction in available fill material would have been offset by the expanded scope of work required and would have a negligible effect on performance costs.

Garland's nascent impracticability defense must have focused on the increased costs of constructing fills along both property lines. Repeated reference in the contract to plural "fills" makes it very unlikely that Garland assumed it would stop mining on the northern boundary in order to construct just one fill. A more reasonable interpretation would have required fills along any property lines that intersect a pit, for the full distance across the pit. Given where Garland stopped, performance would have required two fills, with that on the east-west property line to span the full distance across the pit.

Garland's impracticability defense seems more a wishful cost-savings rather than a severe and unexpected increase in performance costs. Garland specifically promised to construct fills allowing access to land beyond the pit, and to take necessary measures to protect those fills from the diverted creek. It cannot later complain that a shortage of accessible coal prevented it from saving the costs of constructing one fill. By disputing the true property line, it was able to argue that the L-shaped fills would intersect in the middle of the pit and hence be useless, thereby justifying not doing any of the work promised in paragraphs 7b and 7f.

Garland presumably calculated the projected costs of performance as weighed against the benefits to be obtained. Assuming that it originally intended to perform, one must infer that the estimated cost of the remedial work was less than the value of benefits Garland expected to obtain from the lease. That the agreement contemplated that one or more pits would remain on the Peevyhouse land proves that Garland did not intend to mine all of the leased sixty acres. Assuming Garland projected that performance costs exceeded $3,000, it must have decided the intangible benefits from creek diversion justified the expenditure. Garland should bear the risk of increased performance costs.

Without question, Garland was the more efficient insurer. As an experienced surface mining operator with nationwide operations, technical skill, and equipment, it had the capability to predict the costs of performing the promised remedial work under the best and worst of possible coal conditions. Garland conducted test borings to predict subsurface coal conditions. Nothing suggests that remediation costs fell outside the range Garland should have reasonably anticipated at the time it entered into its agreement with the Peevyhouses.

Remedies

1. Measuring expectation damages

Peevyhouse is all about remedies. Litigation deficiencies left the *Peevyhouse* court with an incomplete or inaccurate understanding of the parties' exchange. Suppose these matters were fully litigated. The economics of the exchange might be depicted as follows, allowing latitude for credibility judgments and valuation difficulties. The Peevyhouses bought land in 1947 for $12 per acre; in 1954, when they entered the lease, each acre was worth $50. Accordingly, their 120-acre ranch was worth $6,000 before the mining. The Peevyhouses' negotiation behavior in rejecting the customary advance surface-damage payment signaled that they valued the sixty leased acres for more than the $3,000 market value. Just how much more, in dollar terms, will remain a mystery. Nevertheless, the Peevyhouses clearly communicated their subjective (or idiosyncratic) values to Garland, which could somewhat anticipate their probable loss from breach and hence gauge appropriate breach precautions. Moreover, Garland representatives knew that the Peevyhouses were not rich and yet rejected a lucrative cash payment readily accepted by their neighbors. Because present cash is worth more to poorer persons, Garland must have known at the time of contracting that the Peevyhouses valued the future remedial performance at a sum much higher than $3,000 in present value.

Assume that Garland bargained rationally and in good faith, fully intending to perform. Having estimated the restoration costs, Garland would enter the exchange only after concluding the net benefits outweighed the total performance costs. Theoretically, Garland was indifferent to paying the Peevyhouses at the time of contract formation an amount equal to the restoration costs discounted to present value, or to promise future performance and risk fluctuations in the actual cost. By promising to do the work, Garland avoided immediate cash outlay of $3,000 for surface damages and deferred payment of the projected costs until expiration of the lease term. In return for Garland's promises and $2,000 in advanced royalties, the Peevyhouses granted permission for creek diversion and coal removal. Under the terms of exchange, the Peevyhouses effectively paid in advance for the remedial work.

Consider the relative economics when the lease expired. Garland removed at least 12,500 tons of coal, which it sold for an estimated net profit between $24,000 and $34,500. In exchange for the coal and valuable right of creek diversion, Garland paid the Peevyhouses a total of $2,500 in royalties. Garland stood to gain handsomely from breach if it could both avoid doing the remedial work and paying the Peevyhouses the cash to obtain substitute performance. In postbreach negotiations, Garland essentially offered to pay $3,000 in restitution for the forgone surface damage payment, thus leaving the Peevyhouses in a position comparable to their neighbors who accepted the standard default terms. The Oklahoma Supreme Court's diminution award saved Garland from doing work that it had always known would cost it thousands of dollars.[28]

While Garland captured significant gains from its breach, the Peevyhouses' special bargaining efforts left them worse off than they would have been if they accepted the default provisions. Had they refused to bargain with Garland, their untouched 120 acres would have

---

[28] Because both parties presented exaggerated evidence of cost (both high and low), there is no reliable information on what it would have cost to do the work at that time. Thirty years later, in 1993, the remedial work would have cost somewhere between $52,000 and $96,000.

been valued at about $7,200 in 1960. Instead, their total farm was worth perhaps $4,260. If restored, based on 1995 property values, it could have been worth around $45,000.

Contracts remedial doctrine seeks to protect the injured party's defeated expectations with money damages as a substitute for the promised performance, giving preference to the subjective loss in value unless that cannot be proved with sufficient certainty. A wealthy injured party can prove with certainty its subjective loss in value by purchasing substitute performance from a third person and presenting the bills in court. In cases like this, where plaintiffs lack the resources to purchase substitute performance, courts are left to speculate on their subjective loss in value. Because litigants can seldom prove this measure with the required certainty, they are relegated to cost or diminution as alternative measures to protect their lost expectancy. Lacking reasonably certain proof of subjective loss, *Restatement (Second) of Contracts* §348(2) allows a plaintiff to recover at most the reasonable costs of repair or completion, or at least the diminution in market value caused by the breach. The cost measure might give the plaintiff a windfall exceeding actual loss, while punishing the defendant for what might have been an efficient breach. Diminution reverses the situation, risking undercompensation to the plaintiff while possibly rewarding the breaching defendant, who is allowed to retain the surplus performance costs. The *Restatement* formulation prefers the cost measure, provided that the sum "is not clearly disproportionate to the probable loss in value" to the injured party.

Diminution represents the lowest possible loss in value to the injured party, who might not specially value the property but could sell it on the open market. When property owners contract for specific improvements, they seek (and pay for) actual performance and not merely an increase in market value. Consider the amounts home owners spend on landscaping, remodeling, and other long-term improvements that enhance their quality of life but do not necessarily produce corresponding increased market values. A contractor's material breach deprives them of the benefit of their bargain unless they are compensated for what it costs to obtain substitute performance. The contractor cannot take the home owner's money, break its promise, and then insist that it owes in damages only the amount by which the landscaping would increase the home's market value. The position of Garland and the Peevyhouses is no different from that of the contractor and the home owner.

The *Restatement* formulation theoretically prefers the cost measure over diminution except when it results in "unreasonable economic waste" or recovery "clearly disproportionate to the [injured party's] probable loss in value . . . ." This policy preference promotes contract stability, encouraging full performance on both sides. The diminution alternative directs courts to consider whether a plaintiff's likely subjective harm from breach is disproportionately small in relation to the probable cost to complete, so as not to punish the breaching defendant and allow a windfall to the plaintiff.

Theory notwithstanding, courts often conservatively limit plaintiff's recovery to diminution, making assumptions about (or distorting) the record to justify the result. The diminution measure is often a token remedy that preserves the illusion of protecting expectations while systematically undercompensating plaintiffs. Thus, the *Peevyhouse* court conceded there was no economic waste, defined as the expense of tearing down and rebuilding a completed structure. Nevertheless, it constructed a new test of "relative economic benefit" and assumed facts necessary to limit the plaintiffs' recovery to $300, the amount by which Garland's breach diminished the current market value of the leased acreage. Despite Garland's undisputed breach and the plaintiff's nominal victory, the Peevyhouses received nothing after the litigation costs were deducted. Even with no enforcement costs, the diminution measure for sixty acres was inadequate to enable purchase of a comparable 120-acre homestead.

In resorting to the diminution measure, the court ignored strong indications of plaintiffs' higher subjective value for the land. Despite deficiencies in the official record, it was obvious that the leased parcel joined land on which plaintiffs lived. By definition, homestead property embodies personal, moral, and aesthetic concerns distinguishing it from real estate held for commercial purposes. The court should have inferred that the mining impaired both the going concern value of the entire farm and the plaintiffs' personal valuation of their homestead. The record showed the plaintiff-landowners rejected the standard or "off the rack" agreement to obtain the promised remedial work in order to protect their idiosyncratic moral and aesthetic values.

In the real, imperfect world, legal rules matter. Although they only apply absent contrary agreement, default rules strongly influence incentives to bargain in good faith and to perform as promised. Enforcement costs may grossly imbalance what seemed a perfect (and efficient) agreement, if voluntarily performed. Moreover, as demonstrated here, courts may not strictly enforce agreements even where parties have explicitly bargained around an existing legal rule to reach an efficient outcome that reflects their preferences. Legal rules should serve as disincentives to strategic or opportunistic behavior. Where parties bargain in the shadow of law that encourages performance except when breach is truly efficient, most contracts are fully performed. Where the legal consequence of breach is liability to compensate fully the injured party for any gains expected from performance, the promisor stands to gain nothing from breach. An inefficient default rule can reverse the situation, providing strong incentives to breach.[29]

Consider the effects of a strong, practically immutable default provision limiting the landowner's damages to diminution in market value. Contrary to policies promoting stability and good faith in the formation and performance of contracts, the rule encourages operators to promise restoration work fraudulently, knowing that they would be held liable only for diminution. By keeping this information secret from the landowners, operators would exact somewhat smaller price concessions from landowners, albeit still for empty promises. The resulting bargain is grossly inefficient. To the extent landowners give consideration for the remedial promises, they unwittingly give surplus benefits to the operators. The price concessions bear little relation to the operator's projected performance costs (minimal, absent intent to perform). Operators have no incentives to take reasonable precautions against events that could cause a breach.

Moreover, consider the incentives if operators knew that they were required to perform the restoration regardless of cost or be liable for expectation damages based on performance costs. A cost default rule places informational burdens on the better-informed party (often a repeat player), requiring that an operator first inform the landowners of their legal entitlement and then seek an exchange that efficiently reflects the parties' respective utilities for the land. Thus, before contracting, the operator would take precautions in estimating performance costs, including geological surveys and test boreholes to determine project feasibility. After contracting, the operator could take precautions against breach by retaining a landscape architect, buying topsoil, and taking other actions evidencing intent to perform.

Many policy reasons support the cost measure of damages in cases like this, where the contractor's incomplete or defective performance constitutes a material breach and the owners lack sufficient proof of their subjective loss in value. The likelihood that diminution will both undercompensate the injured party and reward the breacher should discourage its use as token protection of the expectation interest.

---

[29] Indeed, some knowledgeable observers perceive that is exactly how the *Peevyhouse* doctrine is being used by companies specializing in extracting natural resources from private land, promising remedial work to landowners without ever intending to perform, knowing their damage liability would be limited to diminution in value.

2. Restitution alternative: Preventing unjust enrichment

Although traditional doctrine strongly prefers money damages to approximate defeated expectations, the *Peevyhouse* facts would also support restitution and specific performance as viable alternative forms of relief. If Garland's failure to perform the remedial work constituted a material breach and was not substantial performance, then the Peevyhouses were entitled to treat the contract as discharged and to seek restitution for benefits conferred that would unjustly enrich Garland. Restitution could have provided an alternative to the nominal recovery for lost market value. Because Garland owed future duties of performance (and not merely the payment of money), the expectation principle would not fix an upper limit on their recovery.

Three distinct restitution claims were possible. Under the first theory, the Peevyhouses were entitled to recover, at a minimum, the $3,000 they relinquished as advance payment for the promised remedial work. Had they proven the true bargain and claimed restitution, basic equitable principles would have required Garland to disgorge this amount. Their recovery under the second restitution theory could exceed the cost of completion. If they could have shown that Garland fraudulently induced the contract with false promises of remedial work, then they might have sought contract rescission. Because such fraud would vitiate contract consent, Garland's mining activities could support claims of tortious breach or wrongful conversion. Under such a theory, the Peevyhouses might have recovered the fair market value of the coal, less the value added by Garland's labor. As a condition to this relief, the injured party must return any benefit received under the contract. Allan Farnsworth suggested a third possible restitution claim, for disgorgement to redress abuse of contract.[30] Garland failed to perform the remedial work even though it received advance payment as consideration. Disgorgement of gain resulting from such an abuse of contract is necessary to prevent undercompensating the injured party. If, during the bargaining process, Garland accurately estimated and reflected the cost to perform in the price terms, its breach could realize a gain equal to the avoided performance costs. Unless required to disgorge this sum, Garland is unfairly enriched. Even if its cost estimates were inaccurate, its breach avoided the expense of performing or of modifying the contract to buy out of the remedial provisions. Although Professor Farnsworth's proposed standard might present challenges to

---

[30] E. Allan Farnsworth, *Your Loss or My Gain? The Dilemma of the Disgorgement Principle in Breach of Contract*, 94 Yale L.J. 1339, 1384–1385 (1985).

fix damages where the disgorgement damage liability is less than the cost measure, it could be used by courts opposed to awarding costs.

3. Equitable protection of contract expectations: Specific performance

Plaintiffs raised no claim to equitable relief in the trial court. Regardless whether they made an informed decision to seek money damages, it probably was correct. Courts then (and now) were likely to find damages an adequate legal remedy, thus avoiding difficulties in fashioning an equitable remedy and supervising its performance. Some modern courts might find specific relief preferable on moral and economic grounds. It is the remedy best calculated to protect contract expectations through performance or post-breach settlement for an amount reflecting the injured party's lost value.

If damages do not enable replacement performance and further permit the breacher to save the performance costs, the legal remedy upsets the agreed exchange. Where the contract called for Garland to perform remedial work, the Peevyhouses are entitled to receive either performance or cost of obtaining comparable substitute performance. After deducting for enforcement costs, even the cost measure nets less than that needed to replace the breached services. Absent litigation cost-shifting mechanisms, only specific relief can assure the replaceability of Garland's performance.

Specific performance would squelch nagging concerns that the cost recovery confers a windfall far exceeding plaintiffs' subjective loss in value, which they would not use to obtain substitute performance. Were specific relief the routine—and not the extraordinary—remedy, it would promote efficient outcomes by directing the parties to bargain over their relative preferences. If the Peevyhouses valued restoration less than Garland's cost to perform, their post-decree bargaining would produce settlement that accurately reflected their subjective loss in value. If, however, the Peevyhouses subjectively valued performance higher than what it would cost Garland to do the work, they could prove this by terminating postjudgment negotiations and insisting on compliance with the court order. By exercising this exit option, plaintiffs could show with their conduct their high utility for actual contract performance.

At least in the context of postmining restoration, specific relief protects the public interest in a manner comparable to environmental law. If coal operators can avoid reclamation obligations with damage payments, society's long-term preservation interests remain unsatisfied. Federal and state statutes have already struck the balance, dictating that the work shall be done, with administrative enforcement mechanisms to handle supervisory burdens. Where a private breach of contract creates public risk of harm that may be remedied at public cost, the parties should not be allowed to relinquish reclamation obligations in exchange for payment to the landowners.

Strains on the Quality of Justice

The unearthed facts in *Peevyhouse* raise disturbing questions about the quality of justice. The Peevyhouses bargained to obtain contractual protection of their idiosyncratic interests. When Garland breached, they sought legal redress but were denied meaningful contract enforcement. Meanwhile, the adversary system maintained the illusion that diminution damages protected their expectations of contract performance.

Several factors combined to produce a legal ruling based on facts far removed from the truth. Richard Danzig's important work on litigation incapacities identifies structural constraints in the litigation system that influence and sometimes distort the presentation.[31] Inaccuracies result from the formal rules of litigation, witnesses' varying abilities to testify clearly and credibly, and gaps in evidence that leave the fact-finder to fill in the blanks. In *Peevyhouse,* these constraints served to present an incomplete or inaccurate picture of the relevant facts. Evidentiary rulings excluded testimony about the entire affected land, the negotiation context, and the purpose for the remedial provisions. Garland's technical exhibits and better-educated witnesses communicated its version of the facts more clearly and persuasively than did the plaintiffs' side.

By definition, the adversary process requires partisan presentation of evidence and legal argument. Each side presents its strongest case under the facts and law and tries to rebut the opponent's contrary assertions. The impartial judge or fact-finder passively receives what is presented and, when thus informed by the parties, renders a considered judgment. Impartiality is an essential element, requiring both absence of bias and nonparticipation in presentation of the case. Justification for the adversary system assumes that each party can participate effectively, usually through counsel. It assumes that counsel are roughly equal in legal skill and dedication to their client's cause and have equivalent resources to support the litigation. *Peevyhouse* illustrates how capability problems strain the quality of justice and the flawed assumptions underlying the adversary system.

The client's financial resources, business and social connections, and prior experiences as a litigant influence who is retained as counsel and

---

[31] RICHARD DANZIG, THE CAPABILITY PROBLEM IN CONTRACT LAW: FURTHER READINGS ON WELL-KNOWN CASES 1–2 (1978).

the fee arrangement. The fee arrangement, in turn, may affect counsel's dedication and resources devoted to the case. For one-time individual litigants, the Peevyhouses knew a good bit about Woodrow McConnell before retaining him. Like most occasional litigants (and some lawyers), they did not appreciate the impact of doctrinal distinctions between tort and contract law. McConnell's accumulated legal knowledge and expertise concerned tort law, which did not translate to adequate knowledge of contract law.

The fact that McConnell represented Peevyhouses and most of his clients on a contingent fee basis probably influenced the representation. On appeal, McConnell demonstrated exceptional, at times quixotic, dedication to their cause, valiantly fighting a losing battle to reverse the court's initial decision. Sadly, the effort came too late. Had he taken greater care gathering facts, researching, and preparing for trial, the record would not have left room for the grossly inaccurate assumptions made by the court. The Peevyhouses' limited resources and McConnell's legal skill, effort, and knowledge were no match for Garland's strong defense team. By contrast, Garland had direct experience with Looney, Watts, which had successfully represented it in prior lawsuits. As a repeat litigation player, Garland could better evaluate whether the firm had the advocacy skills, legal knowledge, and professional resources to mount an effective defense.

Premised as it is on partisan advocacy, the adversary system assumes a fair fight with litigants roughly balanced in their ability to present their sides effectively. Overall, a significant disparity in dedication, skills, and resources can tilt the outcome. Judged by modern standards of competence, McConnell's representation fell short in fact gathering, legal knowledge, and advocacy skills. A lack of financial and other resources to aid the litigation furthered the imbalance. Although he could do nothing to revive the time-barred tort claim, he could have framed the pleadings to allege that the breach caused lost utility and value to the entire farm, including acreage not leased to Garland. The complaint should have differentiated between the leased and unleased parcels and specifically alleged the separate consideration the Peevyhouses gave to obtain the remedial promises. This trade-off in lieu of payment for surface damages strongly related to contract interpretation and substantial performance doctrine. A more able advocate would have anticipated parol evidence objections and acquired mastery over the legal issues key to admission: nonintegration of the writing, the failure of consideration challenged the existence of a legally enforceable contract, and the general admissibility of evidence of surrounding circumstances to aid interpretation.

Watts understood Garland's viewpoint enough to suggest the impracticability excuse and property line dispute, both of which triggered waste considerations and risk allocation. McConnell never stood "toe to toe" with Watts on these issues and failed to pierce the defense with demands for proof. If plaintiffs' counsel had understood the law of impracticability and mistake, he could have gathered information before trial to defeat those claims. Mastery of contract law, damages, and policy would have enabled him to develop a coherent theory and trial strategy to create a strong record and supporting legal arguments. The *Peevyhouse* opinion would be quite different if the trial record clearly established the parties' actual intent and revealed data showing the relative economic and other benefits sought to be achieved by the contract.

Availability of adequate resources to support the litigation strongly affects the quality of representation. If a litigant cannot pay in advance for the services and costs, it must depend on counsel's resources to pay or obtain credit. Garland and its defense firm clearly had superior resources devoted to the litigation as compared to plaintiffs. No clear distinction can be made between quality differences affected by disparities in resources or legal skills. Garland's professionally drawn maps and aerial photos were more helpful and persuasive than plaintiffs' snapshots and sketch of the affected land. Its polished presentations at trial and on appeal reflected extensive investments of professional time—by Watts and associates working behind the scenes and also by Cumpton and Curry, the engineers who testified.

There were significant disparities between the advocacy skills of the parties' respective counsel. Watts was well prepared. He adeptly planned a trial strategy with supporting witnesses and documentation, knew the weaknesses in his case, and formulated a plan to limit unfavorable evidence. Watts's aggressive tactical maneuvers may have blindsided plaintiffs' counsel. By drastically limiting triable issues, perhaps he upset their trial strategy, leaving them little to present. Although McConnell and his co-counsel were fairly skilled in questioning witnesses, they seldom countered Watts's evidentiary objections, even when strong contracts arguments supported admissibility. Their litigation style was characteristic of lawyers who "shoot from the hip," who have an intuitive sense about how the trial should proceed, formulate a general trial strategy, and obtain the necessary witnesses who receive limited advance preparation to testify. They defer most research until needed to prepare documents filed with the court. Those with great instincts may thrive without the painstaking efforts of their more compulsive colleagues. Many clients, however, bear the brunt of their lawyers' lackluster preparation.

But it may not have been the lawyers alone who failed in this case. Democratic politics heavily dominated Oklahoma's early history. In sixty years of statehood, government scandals were commonplace.

Folklore suggested the prevalence of backroom, often shady, political deals. Some national journalists referred to the pervasive corruption, suggesting that at election time there was always "an aroma in Oklahoma." Nor was the judiciary isolated from politics. Oklahoma courts had a climate ripe for influence peddling. Ex parte communications between judges and lawyers appearing before them were common. Those with political influence would use it. For years, rumors persisted that several members of the Oklahoma Supreme Court were corrupt and accepted bribes.

The bribe scandal, involving under-the-table payments to insure "fine justice," began unraveling in 1957. After seven years of discomfiting investigation, two supreme court justices were indicted for federal income tax evasion and another impeached from office.[32] Two of the implicated judges, Welch and Johnson, voted with the Peevyhouse majority in favor of Garland Coal.

Was *Peevyhouse* tainted by the Oklahoma Supreme Court bribe scandal? Definitive proof is impossible. There is no evidence that a bribe was paid in *Peevyhouse* or that Ned Looney (senior partner in the Looney, Watts firm) sought favorable treatment from the court. However, the evidence strongly suggests that Justice Welch voted in favor of interests represented by the Looney, Watts law firm, especially in close cases where his vote could make a difference. *Peevyhouse* is such a case. Supreme court conference minutes show Welch did not participate in a dispositive vote on the case until March 1963, when the court denied the plaintiffs' second rehearing petition. In September 1963—after the case had ended—a court order retroactively added Welch to the original decision, which became necessary to preserve the original majority opinion after Williams switched to the dissent.

Examination of Justice Welch's overall voting pattern reveals a moderate but statistically significant correlation reflecting a pro–Looney, Watts bias. This bias is most striking in the seventeen close cases decided by the Oklahoma Supreme Court where his vote could

---

[32] Eighty-year-old N. S. Corn, under a partial grant of federal immunity, gave a statement implicating the others. He resigned from the bench, pled nolo contendere to the pending charges, and spent a short time in prison. Seventy-two-year-old Earl Welch (Chickasaw), a strong and persuasive member of the court, fought the charges. In October 1964 he was convicted of five counts of income tax evasion, sentenced to three years in prison and a hefty fine. Welch continued to deny any wrongdoing until his death in 1969. In May 1965, a bare majority of the Oklahoma Senate voted to impeach N. B. Johnson (Cherokee). During the impeachment proceedings, Johnson called Corn "an evil old man" whose allegations against Johnson and Welch were motivated by deep-seated bias against Indians.

have affected the outcome.[33] Welch voted in every close case, and in all but one, he supported the interest represented by the Looney, Watts firm. In each case where the Looney, Watts interest lost, Welch dissented. In seven of the eight cases where the Looney, Watts interest prevailed, Welch voted with or authored the majority opinion. He was consistently loyal to the firm interest when it mattered. He never voted dispositively to defeat a Looney case, and he cast the deciding vote in three cases, including *Peevyhouse*. Welch's conference votes in *Peevyhouse* suggest that he stayed his hand and did not participate in any dispositive vote until necessary for Garland to prevail. An answer to the question whether *Peevyhouse* was tainted thus depends upon how one defines that concept. If the definition is limited to bribery, *Peevyhouse* is probably unblemished. If one considers suspect all cases with outcomes affected by improper judicial bias, then *Peevyhouse* appears tainted.

Epilogue

Zeal does not necessarily translate into competent representation. At its best, legal education equips students with the technical skills needed for competence, a firm grounding in lawyers' ethical obligations, and a passion to have their professional lives make a positive difference in the legal system. Lawyers must develop the legal skills to understand a case in its industrial, economic, and theoretical context in order to represent clients competently.

Mr. and Mrs. Peevyhouse still live on that land. Time has not healed the wounds inflicted by the mining, which ended nearly fifty years ago. When last visited in 2004, the diversionary channel was badly eroded and overgrown with aggressive bramblebush. Steep embankments on the spoil banks were unstable and muddy. The condition of the land in 2004 was significantly worse than when I had last seen it several years ago. Mr. Peevyhouse said he hadn't been on that land in years; about thirty acres is completely useless. The last time I spoke with Lucille she was bitter and distrustful of the legal system. Willie still wants the land fixed.

The Porter family owned and operated Sallisaw Stripping, or its successor, Garland Coal Company, since the middle 1950s. An acrimonious strike produced ongoing labor disputes, ultimately prompting Garland's president, J. F. Porter III, to sell the Haskell County operations to Alpine Construction Company around 1982. When Garland stopped

---

[33] A close case is defined as one where the court was split on the final vote, with five or six justices in the majority.

mining, it incurred withdrawal liability to the United Mine Workers Trust Fund. Payment disputes caused the trust fund to file an involuntary Chapter 7 bankruptcy petition against Garland in 1984. In 1986, the bankruptcy court found Garland was insolvent and entered an order for relief. Thereafter, Porter decided to liquidate the company and move on to other pursuits. In an extraordinary turn of events, the trustee paid in full all claims filed in the bankruptcy case, and a surplus of $1.4 million was returned to Garland Coal shareholders.

Diverted creek bed (2004)

For some time, federal courts sitting in diversity cases were uncertain about whether *Peevyhouse* remained the law in Oklahoma. A federal court certified to the Oklahoma Supreme Court the question concerning the measure of damages for breach of a settlement agreement to reduce water pollutants following an oil and gas drilling operation. The facts on record were also extreme. A litigation settlement agreement provided an $80,000 payment to plaintiffs for damages and litigation expenses and about $180,000 in attorney's fees. The oil company also allegedly agreed to achieve a specified reduction in water contaminants. The plaintiffs sought an estimated $1.3 million to complete remediation to that standard, while Apache Corporation estimated that the lost market value from the breach was only $5,175 (damages sought more than 250 times the loss in value). In 1994, in *Schneberger v. Apache Corp.,*[34] by a 5–4 vote the Oklahoma Supreme Court reaffirmed and extended *Peevyhouse.* Regardless of whether the damage to real property was abatable or permanent, and regardless of whether the breached provisions were material or incidental, where the cost to restore the land exceeds the loss in value, diminution in value is the correct measure. Dictum suggests a possible way out for very sophisticated parties, or alternatively supports the view that *Peevyhouse* states an almost immutable rule. The court assumed that the parties to the settlement were aware of Oklahoma law on measure of damages and that they "were free to specify in the contract what the measure of damages would be in the event of a breach."[35] Because they did not include such a provision, the diminution measure would serve as the default rule. Of course, the default rule gives no disclosure incentive to industrial negotiators.

Since *Schneberger,* groups representing the interests of surface owners have pressed for legislative reversal, to provide that diminished property value is only one factor to be considered in determining whether the cost measure is reasonable. Unfortunately, the *Peevyhouse* principle survives in Oklahoma, with even broader application.[36] It is of dubious origin, made possible by the vagaries of the adversary process, yet has remarkable longevity against the weight of criticism. *Peevyhouse* opponents must patiently await another opportunity to seek its reversal.

---

[34] 890 P.2d 847 (Okla. 1994) (answering certified questions from federal court sitting in diversity jurisdiction).

[35] *Id.* at 854.

[36] Other jurisdictions have declined to follow, preferring instead the cost measure. See Corbello v. Iowa Production, 850 So. 2d 866 (La. 2003) (holding that mining lessor's damages for lessee's breach of contractual obligation to reasonably restore property need not be tethered to the market value of the property; cost measure upheld); Ruddach v. Don Johnston Ford, Inc., 644 P.2d 671 (Wash. 1982); Miller v. C.K.L., Inc., 1988 WL 106637 (Ohio Ct. App. 1988); American Standard, Inc. v. Schectman, 439 N.Y.S.2d 529 (App. Div. 1981).

10

Barak D. Richman*

The King of Rockingham County and the Original Bridge to Nowhere

Miles from anywhere with no approaches and no connecting roads, the most beautiful bridge in the south springs in three magnificent arches across the historic Dan, a silhouette in virgin alabaster against the green hills of a wilderness.

    Leaksville News, Aug. 11, 1932

On October 15, 1929, Horace Williams, the University of North Carolina's famed professor and founder of its philosophy department, wrote a letter to his friend and former student, Judge John J. Parker of the Fourth Circuit Court of Appeals of the United States, asking, "I

---

* This chapter is adapted from *A Bridge, A Tax Revolt, and the Struggle to Industrialize: The Story and Legacy of* Rockingham County v. Luten Bridge Co., 84 N.C. L. Rev. — (2006).

have had in mind for some time to write and ask for copies of one or two of your decisions. It is stimulating to read them, also they give me pleasure."[1] Parker wrote back eleven days later with a copy of his recently published opinion in *Rockingham County v. Luten Bridge Co.*

Williams, who taught a course on logic to generations of UNC undergraduates, including Parker, and was an enthusiast of logical reasoning, was thoroughly impressed with Parker's work. He wrote back effusively, "There is something in your manner of reaching a decision that reminds me of Marshall. It is the analysis. If I had made a decision in the lower court on this case, then read your analysis, I should resign."[2] Indeed, since its publication in 1929, the opinion has proceeded to leave an impression on generations of law students. *Luten Bridge*, a staple in most contracts casebooks, is known today as the paradigmatic case that demonstrates the duty to mitigate damages in contract law, whereby a nonbreaching party is not compensated for performance that occurs after the other party announces an intention to breach. But no matter how impressive the analysis, neither Williams nor Parker had any reason to suspect that *Luten Bridge* would reach generations of contracts students, for the case only tangentially involved a dispute over contract law.

When sending his *Luten Bridge* opinion to Williams, Judge Parker remarked that it was "a case involving an important question of county government in North Carolina."[3] This chapter revisits the history of this famous case and reveals that Parker was exactly right—the core of the dispute was not over the calculation of damages for contract breach but instead implicated important issues in local government law. Moreover, those legal issues were of great importance to Parker and his fellow North Carolinians at the time the case was decided. They reflected the new challenges to local governments as industrialization took hold, and they demonstrate how legal rules played a significant role during that seminal historical era.

This chapter has three objectives: It identifies the case's original importance, uncovers the opinion's political and jurisprudential significance, and tells a remarkable story, one that arose within a heated tax revolt pitting the county's farmers against its most celebrated industrialist. Much more than a crisp illustration of the duty to mitigate,

---

[1] Letter from Horace Williams to John Parker (Oct. 15, 1929), in John J. Parker Papers, Box 23, Folder 426, Southern Historical Manuscripts Collection, University of North Carolina, Chapel Hill, NC.

[2] Letter from Horace Williams to John Parker (Oct. 31, 1929).

[3] Letter from John Parker to Horace Williams (Oct. 26, 1929).

Rockingham County v. Luten Bridge Co. offers a window into a southern community's struggles with a divided social order, the introduction of wealth into local politics, and a changing economy.

A View from the Casebook

The case taught in most first-year contracts courses and textbooks goes as follows. On January 7, 1924, the Rockingham County Board of Commissioners decided by a 3–2 vote to award a contract to the Luten Bridge Company to build a bridge over the Dan River. The opinion notes that "[m]uch feeling was engendered over the matter" and that a "result" of the vote was that W. F. Pruitt, one of the commissioners who had voted in favor of the project, resigned on February 11, 1924. The next day, the county clerk appointed W. W. Hampton as a member of the board to succeed him, and on February 21, Hampton and the two commissioners who opposed the contract passed a resolution "declaring that the contract for the building of the bridge was not legal and valid, and directing the clerk of the board to notify [the Luten Bridge Company] that it refused to recognize same as a valid contract, and that [the company] should proceed no further thereunder." But, "notwithstanding the repudiation of the contract by the county, the bridge company continued with the work of construction." On November 24, 1924, the Luten Bridge Company sued Rockingham County for $18,301.07 for its completed work on the bridge even though the company's incurred costs as of February 21 were estimated at only $1,900.

Judge Parker, hearing the case on appeal to the United States Court of Appeals for the Fourth Circuit, wrote on behalf of a unanimous panel and ruled that the Luten Bridge Company was entitled only to the damages it had incurred prior to the county's announcing its anticipatory breach. He held, "after plaintiff had received notice of the breach, it was its duty to do nothing to increase the damages flowing therefrom." Judge Parker continued:

> In the case at bar, the county decided not to build the road of which the bridge was to be a part, and did not build it. The bridge, built in the midst of the forest, is of no value to the county because of this change of circumstances. When, therefore, the county gave notice to the plaintiff that it would not proceed with the project, plaintiff should have desisted from further work. It had no right thus to pile up damages by proceeding with the erection of a useless bridge.[4]

---

[4] Rockingham Co. v. Luten Bridge Co., 35 F.2d 301, 307 (4th Cir. 1929).

And thus, *Luten Bridge* has come to illustrate the duty to mitigate damages.

A Tale of a Bridge

The central figure in Rockingham County's decision to build a new bridge at Fishing Creek, near the three mill towns of Leaksville, Draper, and Spray, was Colonel Benjamin Franklin Mebane Jr. Throughout the first quarter of the twentieth century, Mebane, a flamboyant industrialist living in a changing South, was the undisputed king of Rockingham County. In his time, Mebane's power and notoriety seemed limitless, with one contemporary saying:

> It is quite safe to say that no story-book hero ever has a more romantic history than B. Frank Mebane, industrial tycoon, town builder, millionaire, philanthropist, and patron of the arts. He was the most fabulous and colorful character to appear on the Leaksville community scene during the life of the town, and its mightiest personal force for a generation.[5]

Mebane exploited this power and his oversized personality to reign supreme over a wide variety of local industries. The Rockingham industrialist's vast enterprises included raising cattle, running a variety of publishing companies, managing the Imperial Bank and Trust Company, and establishing the Spray Institute of Technology. But Mebane's primary enterprise, and the one in which he left an indelible imprint on the county, was textile manufacturing. In 1893, the same year he charmed and married Lily Connolly Morehead, the granddaughter of former North Carolina governor and textile industrialist John Motley Morehead,[6] he bought 600 acres of land in Spray, in northern Rockingham County, with the ambitious goal of building one new mill in the area every year. Mebane did not achieve this goal but he came close, building six new mills by 1905 and employing nearly all of Spray's five thousand residents in some capacity. During his reign,

---

[5] C. P. Robertson, *A Character Sketch of B. Frank Mebane* (1955), *reprinted in* 29 J. Rockingham County Hist. & Genealogy 25, 26 (2004). Although Mebane was educated at the Bingham Military School, in Mebane, N.C., he never served in the military; he earned the nickname "Colonel" from his friends.

[6] Although the Moreheads were rich and powerful, the family legend has it that Mebane met Lily at an auction featuring many items that originally belonged to the Morehead family, which had fallen on hard times. Seeing an opportunity to impress the beautiful young woman, Mebane said to her, "Ma'am, you'll not lose a thing at this auction today," bought all of her possessions, and then promptly returned them to her.

Mebane saw northern Rockingham transform from a sleepy rural community into a thriving industrial center, featuring new factories, roads, and bridges. Indeed, much of Rockingham County's growth was a byproduct of Mebane's own industry.

Even as the price of expansion caught up with him, forcing a declaration of bankruptcy in 1910, Mebane's aspirations continued to grow in ambition and audacity. Mebane's next plan, developed in the early 1920s, was to build a massive chemical factory in "the Meadows," a large series of fields that Mebane's Spray Water Power & Land Company owned between Spray and Draper. However, Mebane's oversized dream, which might also have included attracting new residents near the chemical factory and laying the foundations to a new town, was hindered by the lack of infrastructure in the immediate area. At the time of Mebane's initial scheming, the only modern bridge across the Dan was the Highway 87 bridge (scheduled to be completed in 1924), which was upstream from the Meadows. To get to the bridge and across the Dan from the Meadows, one would have to take the cumbersome path through the towns of Spray and Leaksville. Seeking to facilitate this route, Mebane decided an additional bridge should be built, this one near the confluence of the Dan River and the Fishing Creek.[7]

Even though Mebane would be the primary beneficiary of the new bridge, he considered the project to be part of the county's larger plan for industrial growth and thought the county should pay for it. So in 1922, Mebane, himself an avid Republican in heavily Democratic Rockingham County, recruited three Democrats to support his industrial agenda and run for the county's board of commissioners: Josiah Ferre

---

[7] It is possible that Mebane demanded the new bridge in order to have efficient access to Reidsville, the County's largest city and home to a railroad depot, so raw materials and manufactured products could be transported into and out of the Meadows' factories. However, nearby Leaksville and Spray had railroad depots as early as the 1880s. Mebane feuded frequently with the railroad operators, who did not offer him the discounts he demanded, and at one point Mebane founded the North Carolina–Virginia Railroad simply to challenge the railroads' pricing policies. But road access to Reidsville would not have posed an effective challenge to the railroads in Leaksville and Spray in the 1920s. Perhaps Mebane accurately foresaw the time when trucks would replace railroads. This conjecture all indicates that it is not entirely clear why Mebane pursued the expensive bridge. Indeed, a local Rockingham County historian recently concluded that Mebane's true plan was "never released to the public and is still unknown to this day." Bob Carter, *The Bridge to Nowhere: The Great Mebane's Bridge Controversy*, 29 J. Rockingham County Hist. & Genealogy 1, 4 (2004).

McCollum, Thomas Ruffin Pratt, and William Franklin Pruitt. Both Pruitt and McCollum were farmers, Pratt was a local merchant, and all three were late in years. Newspapers later reported that Mebane royally entertained the three at his lavish home, romancing the modest men with his wealth and personal charm, and persuaded them to align their interests with his own. His appeal was successful, and all three signed on to Mebane's plan.

Mebane quietly helped Pratt, Pruitt, and McCollum get elected to the five-member board of commissioners in the 1922 election along with two other Democrats—R. B. Chance and J. R. Martin. Pratt, Pruitt, and McCollum promptly initiated Mebane's bridge plan, issuing a proposal to build a new bridge near Mebane's Meadows property. Chance and Martin, however, were quite reluctant to fund the project, especially since another bridge would soon be completed only a mile and a half upstream. Initially, the three Mebane loyalists were undeterred. In a March 19, 1923, resolution introduced by Commissioner W. F. Pruitt, the board of county commissioners deemed it "a public necessity" to build a bridge across the Dan River near its juncture with the Fishing Creek.[8] The proposal, receiving the support of Commissioners Pratt and McCollum while encountering strong opposition from Commissioners Martin and Chance, authorized the board to spend $50,000 on the bridge and to employ an engineer to lead the construction effort. At the same meeting, the board (led by Mebane's commissioners) voted 3–2 to build a hard surface road from the town of Madison to Settle's bridge at an additional cost of $250,000—this second project has been described as Mebane's bait to get support for his bridge plans from western Rockingham County, or a payoff to Pratt who lived in Madison. Neither of those dollar figures, however, included the additional $100,000 that would be needed to build a road to and from the Fishing Creek site—the bridge plan was initiated without a plan to provide road access.

These very substantial public expenditures were unprecedented for Rockingham County and forced dramatic changes in the county's finances. The county commissioners raised county property taxes to bankroll much of these new public works projects, and in 1923 alone increased county taxes from 0.95 percent to 1.35 percent, with 0.30 percent designated as "road taxes." The commissioners also issued new bonds at significant interest rates, increasing the county's debt by nearly one-third and leaving Rockingham County in 1925 with the third-highest indebtedness of North Carolina's ninety-eight counties.

---

[8] Meeting Minutes from the Rockingham County Bd. of Comm'rs (Mar. 19, 1923).

Some feared that if these public expenditures continued unabated, financing the debt taxes would require raising the tax rate to 2.7 percent, the highest in the state.

The rising taxes, and the apparent cronyism behind the projects they financed, quickly drew the ire of many of Rockingham County's citizens. The heavily Democratic county was like many Democratic bastions of the time in the South, composed primarily of rural voters opposed to government spending on public works and generally hostile to taxes, especially property taxes. Moreover, the board of commissioners had been elected in 1922 on a platform of fiscal restraint, so the additional spending was seen as both extravagant and a breach of the voters' trust. The *Reidsville Review*—the county's largest newspaper—joined the opposition, launching repeated attacks on the commissioners who supported Mebane's plan. The newspaper, reflecting the political preferences of county Democrats, warned "taxpayers [to] sit up and take notice—[the commissioners' plan is] said to be only a start of some great program of county expenditures." Suspecting Mebane's role behind the plan, the *Review* added, "[I]t is pointed out that the new bridge is not needed for public traffic and it is freely asserted that it will be built solely for the benefit of a very few private property owners."[9]

The Opposition Takes Shape

Mebane's opponents first launched a legal attack on the project. A group of local lawyers—acting "on their own part as citizens and taxpayers of Rockingham County, and on the part of all other citizens and tax payers"—filed for an injunction in state court to prevent the county board from entering into a contract to build the proposed bridge. The bill of complaint went on to state that the bridge was being built

> for the benefit largely of one person, solely, and at his demand and request[.] [O]rdering said bridge to be built is a flagrant abuse of the discretion vested in said Board of Commissioners by law, and is in violation of the rights of each plaintiff and all other taxpayers of said county and this action is brought for the purpose of restraining said Board of Commissioners from proceeding with the construction of said bridge and road . . . .[10]

The complaint successfully convinced Judge H. P. Lane of North Carolina's Eleventh District Court (and a native of Leaksville) to impose a temporary injunction to prevent the county board from entering into a

---

[9] *County Fathers Start Something!* Reidsville Rev., March 26, 1923, at 1.

[10] *Judge Grants a Temporary Injunction*, Reidsville Rev., May 9, 1923, at 1.

contract to build the Fishing Creek Bridge. The county appealed, and Superior Court Judge Thomas J. Shaw overturned the injunction, declaring that the county's elected officials could decide matters of public expenditures as they saw fit. With preemptive legal options exhausted, opponents of the bridge opted instead to arouse political pressure and called for a series of "mass meetings" to organize and defeat the Mebane plan. These meetings were each held at the county courthouse in Wentworth and open to all citizens, who, as the *Leaksville News* reported, were encouraged to attend: "[L]et everyone come and show by your presence the interest you feel in your county and the expenditure of your money."[11]

Three mass meetings were held in the summer of 1923 and were organized by a "Citizens Committee," led by R. S. Montgomery, a prominent Reidsville businessman, owner of farmland, president of Rockingham's First National Bank, and director of the eleventh district of the Tobacco Grower's Association.[12] Meetings drew residents from across the county, packing many as two thousand people into the six-hundred-seat courthouse, and were scheduled to coincide with meetings of the county commissioners. Speakers used the mass meetings to gather information from across the county (they conducted informal polls of public opinion, which consistently claimed that 95 percent of the electorate in Rockingham County was opposed to the bridge), channel organizational force into their opposition, and send coherent messages—and unveiled threats—to the county commissioners.[13] But the meetings served primarily as a device through which the county's irate farmers and indignant politicians could express outrage at profligate government spending.

---

[11] *Mass Meeting at Wentworth*, Leaksville News, Apr. 4, 1924, at 1.

[12] As an owner of farmland, Montgomery chiefly identified with interests south of the river and was resistant to public expenditures to build up Mebane's industrial base at the expense of the entire county. He was described by the *Reidsville Review* as a "tower of strength" and "a conservative, level headed business man." *R. S. Montgomery New Director*, Reidsville Rev., May 14, 1923, at 1.

[13] At both the second and third mass meetings, the Citizens Committee demanded the resignations of the three pro-bridge county commissioners, and overtones of violence began to emerge. The *Reidsville Review* reported that organizers planned to have a "committee" of fifty men visit the three pro-bridge commissioners and refuse to leave until the bridge issue was settled. It was also at this time that reports surfaced that at least two of the three commissioners began missing county commissioners meetings due to illness.

Yet while the first two mass meetings focused on sentiments that the bridge was a poor use of public dollars, with additional anger at rising taxes, it was at the third mass meeting that public opposition struck a theme that elevated its cause. The theme was captured by A. D. Ivie, an eloquent attorney and former North Carolina state senator who earlier had represented B. Frank Mebane in business affairs. Ivie, standing before the overflowing courthouse in North Carolina's summer heat, told the angry crowd:

> There has been established and is now existing in Rockingham county an invisible government, dominated and controlled by one individual, administered from the dark, based upon the same arbitrary, autocratic, and imperialistic principles as those put forth by George III of England and William II of Germany. So bold and notorious is this invisible government established and maintained in the interest of special privilege and the conduct and relationship and domination of certain officials of the county and particularly three commissioners that the people feel that a further submission thereto would be a sacrifice and surrender of the sacred principles of government vouchsafed by the blood of our fathers.[14]

Ivie's rhetoric transformed the opposition from angry taxpayers—the proverbial peasants with pitchforks—into citizens demanding government accountability, transparency, and integrity. The uprising now focused on the very legitimacy of the county government, which citizens had felt was usurped by a local tycoon. Ivie concluded his oration by urging the citizenry to "pledge each to the other, and to the people of Rockingham county, our every power to the overthrow of this invisible special interest . . . and restore to the people their government!"

News related to the bridge disappeared almost entirely from the pages of the county's newspapers for the rest of 1923. Anti-bridge commissioner R. B. Chance resigned from the board on October 23, 1923, and was replaced by George E. Barber, a Reidsville native and a fellow opponent of the Fishing Creek project. The commission shuffle occurred without incident, in stark contrast to what would follow in 1924.

A Contract, a Company, and a Divided County

Public opposition throughout 1923 was sufficiently fierce that by January 1924, many people in Rockingham County assumed that Mebane's bridge would not be built. Then on January 7, 1924, in what

---

[14] *Resolutions by Mass-Meeting*, Reidsville Rev., July 4, 1923, at 4.

the *Reidsville Review* described as "a bolt from the clear sky," the board
of county commissioners voted to approve the construction of a bridge,
to be known as the Fishing Creek Bridge. A contract in the amount of
$39,670 was awarded to the Luten Bridge Company of Knoxville, Ten-
nessee, calling for the bridge company to

> furnish material for and to construct complete and ready for
> traffic, a reinforced concrete bridge over Dan River, near Fish-
> ing Creek, of three arches 105'0" each with 18'0" roadway . . . .
> In consideration of the for[e]going, the [county] hereby agrees
> to pay the [bridge company] the sum of Thirty Nine Thousand
> six hundred and seventy five $39,675.00 as follows, on monthly
> estimates made up by the County Engineer and to be paid at
> the regular meeting of the Commissioners at their meeting the
> first Monday in each month . . . .

Voting in favor of the contract were Commissioners Pratt, Pruitt, and
McCollum, and voting against were Commissioners Barber and Mar-
tin.[15] Rockingham County had made a contract with the Luten Bridge
Company.

The contract was another in a long line of transactions between
southern communities and the Luten Bridge Company. The company
built a significant number of bridges throughout the South in the first
half of the twentieth century, many of which still stand today.[16] The
company was one of several in the country with the name "Luten
Bridge Company," all named after Daniel B. Luten, a professor of engineering at Purdue University who created and patented an arch-
based design for reinforced concrete bridges.[17] By 1920, more than

---

[15] After losing the vote, Martin and Barber proposed that the bidding process be reopened, arguing that the Luten Bridge Company's bid had been submitted to the county on July 2, 1923, and that circumstances had changed in
the meantime such that the contract price was outdated. That proposal was
rejected, again in a 3–2 vote.

[16] Many of the remaining Luten-designed bridges are reaching the end of
their life cycle, forcing state and local officials to choose between replacing the
bridges with newer models or restoring the historic spans. For example, the
Worsham Street Bridge in Danville, Virginia (located only twenty-five miles
from the Fishing Creek Bridge), has been the subject of a heated political dispute, pitting historical preservationists against developers and city planners.
See Emyl Jenkins, *Worsham Street Bridge Update*, Evince, July 2004, at 13.

[17] Professor Luten had no proprietary stake in any of the firms that bore his
name, but he received lucrative royalties from licensing his patented design.
Luten himself worked instead for the rival National Bridge Company, which he
founded in 1902.

17,000 bridges nationwide were built in the United States with Luten's arch-based design, and the Luten Bridge Company of Knoxville—which had experience dealing with county governments and less-than-cooperative citizens—viewed this as a routine contract with a community.

County residents, however, met the news with public outcry, and political pressure swelled to fever pitch by February 1924. It, would prove to be the pivotal month for the bridge debate. On February 11, 1924, W. Franklin Pruitt sent a letter of resignation from the board of county commissioners to Hunter K. Penn, the Rockingham County clerk:

> As my health has so failed me that I fear that I cannot attend the meetings of the Board of Co. Commissioners as I should have and feeling that it would be to the best interest of my health I hereby tender my resignation as a member of said Board, my resignation effective at once. I have desired to do my duty as one of the Board, and do hope that a good man will be chosen as my successor.[18]

Pruitt, however, promptly reconsidered and, that same afternoon, telephoned the clerk's office requesting to rescind his resignation. He later explained, in a remark that suggests Mebane's forceful hand, that "friends" had "urged upon [him] that it was his duty to remain faithful to the County interests to which he had been elected." Pruitt posted a letter the same day, addressed to the board and sent to Clerk Penn, saying that "after due consideration I request the Board not to take any action on [the resignation], and I still consider myself a member of said Board."[19]

Penn disregarded both Pruitt's call and letter and instead accepted Pruitt's resignation. The next day, Penn wrote to W. W. Hampton, a Leakesville businessman, appointing him "as a County Commissioner for Rockingham County to fill the unexpired term of W. F. Pruitt, resigned." Hampton was described by the *Reidsville Review* as "a dyed-in-the-wool democrat" and "a booster at all times for this great

---

[18] Transcript of Record at 34, Rockingham County v. Luten Bridge Co., 35 F.2d 301 (4th Cir. 1929) (No. 2873). Pruitt later testified that he resigned "on account of local political dissentions in the County [and that] certain disorderly elements of the county sought, by intimidation, threats and mob action to intimidate the Commissioners and prevent the Commissioners from going ahead with the contract."

[19] Transcript of Record at 21.

county."[20] His loyalties to the county's Democrats ensured that Hampton would oppose construction of the bridge, thus changing the balance of power on the five-member board.

For the following eleven months, both Pruitt and Hampton claimed to be on the County Board of Commissioners, leaving the actual membership of that body in dispute. But while Pruitt continued to claim a place on the board, he, Chairman Pratt, and Commissioner McCollum stopped attending board meetings. The three men met only one more time, toward the end of 1924 as a shadow board of commissioners, without the other members, solely to discuss the lawsuit later filed by the Luten Bridge Company against the county and the commissioners. Pratt and McCollum explained their own continued absences from their rightful place at the board meetings with claims of poor health.

Meanwhile, the anti-bridge commissioners—Martin, Barber, and Hampton—immediately asserted control over Rockingham County matters and started implementing a traditional Democratic agenda. In its first meeting, on February 21, 1924, the newly constituted board agreed to cut spending projects throughout the county, promptly resolving that the Fishing Creek Bridge was "not in the public interest, but on the contrary against the public interest." As such, they ordered the clerk to notify the Luten Bridge Company that the county "refuses to recognize the said paper writing as a valid contract and to advise said Bridge Company to proceed no further thereunder . . . ."[21] These three commissioners continued to meet every two weeks at the county courthouse in Wentworth to conduct the county's business, including the many mundane matters of county governance that had nothing to do with the bridge controversy. In total, the three men met as the board of county commissioners twenty-five times between February 12 and December 1, 1924.

The two parallel boards, and the confusion over who spoke for the county, wreaked significant uncertainty over county policy. When the "anti-bridge" board met on March 3, the three commissioners noted that they had "been informed that a member of this Board was privately insisting on the Luten Bridge Company building the Fishing Creek Bridge in opposition to the action of this Board." Notwithstanding this claim, the board reiterated its refusal to pay for the bridge, resolving that the Luten Bridge Company should be notified that

---

[20] *Commissioner Pruitt Resigns; Will Hampton Sworn in This Morning*, Reidsville Rev., Feb. 13, 1924, at 1.

[21] Meeting Minutes from the Rockingham County Bd. of Comm'rs (Feb. 21, 1924).

any and all work or expense incurred by it in regard to said bridge will be done by it at its own hazard and risk. The contract with the Luten Bridge Company for the construction of this bridge is not a valid and legal contract as heretofore expressed by resolution of this Board, but if this Board should be mistaken about the legality of said paper writing, this Board does not desire to construct this bridge and will contest the payment for same if constructed.[22]

Nonetheless, the Luten Bridge Company continued to build. The *Tri-City Daily Gazette* reported, "[I]t is thought that attorneys for the bridge company were looking into the legal status of the matter and found that the only safe thing to do, was to fulfill their contract signed by themselves and the commissioners."[23] Some believed that the reason the bridge company continued to build was that B. Frank Mebane promised to pay for the bridge if the company was unable to secure payment from the county. Indeed, years after the incident, it was discovered that Mebane personally gave the Luten Bridge Company $25,000 in Liberty Bonds to continue building the bridge. Mebane, with all he had invested in the bridge to this point, remained determined not to let his bridge die.[24]

Whatever its reason, the Luten Bridge Company appeared steadfast in its plans to build the bridge. Even after Rockingham County indicated that it would not pay for the bridge, W. H. Long, vice president of the Luten Bridge Company, traveled to Rockingham County and defiantly proclaimed in an interview with the *Reidsville Review* that not only would the bridge be completed, but it also would be "the finest bridge in this county." The company also issued a more direct response to the county's rescission by sending a letter to the board of county commissioners:

> We are unable to agree with you that this contract is for any reason invalid or illegal, and we cannot consent to its recision [*sic*] or cancellation or to any other conduct upon your part which will excuse you from the full and complete execution and compliance therewith upon the part of the Board of Commis-

---

[22] Meeting Minutes from the Rockingham County Bd. of Comm'rs (Mar. 3, 1924).

[23] *A Tale of a Bridge (Series No. 18)*, Tri-City Daily Gazette, Mar. 8. 1924, at 1.

[24] Mebane's determination to build the bridge resembled the same cavalier spirit that led to his earlier bankruptcy. His injudiciousness in pursuing the bridge project led many to name the bridge "Mebane's Folly."

sioners of Rockingham County. We have already assembled a
lot of material, organized our forces and performed a portion of
the contract. It shall be our purpose to live up to and carry out
the contract upon our part, and this is to advise you that we
shall expect you to do the same upon your part and that we will
be paid by the county in accordance with the contract for the
material and work done by us in the completion of the construction of the said bridge. We shall proceed at once and vigorously the construction of this bridge in fulfillment of our contract with full confidence that the county will fulfill its part
and pay for the same.[25]

The Luten Bridge Company and the three opposing commissioners
continued to play a slow-paced cat-and-mouse game throughout the
spring and summer of 1924. After each board of commissioners meeting, the board passed a resolution, and gave notice to the company, de-
creeing that the county refused to meet its end of the contract. Meanwhile, County Engineer J. S. Trogdon came to the courthouse each
month, in accordance with the contract, with a new estimate of what
the county owed the Luten Bridge Company, and every month the
county rejected the bill on its face. County Attorney P. W. Glidewell,
who would later help Pratt, Pruitt, and McCollum with their response
to the Luten Bridge Company's suit against the commissioners, resigned from his post, and the county's residents grew increasingly divided.

Rhetorical attacks became more vicious as well, as each side of the
bridge debate tried to lay the blame for the struggle on divisive figures.
Those opposed to the bridge vilified B. Frank Mebane, while the pro-
bridge faction laid the blame on A. D. Ivie and on J. M. Sharp, another
lawyer active in the anti-bridge movement. The county's newspapers
also delved into the fray and fueled the divisive debate. The *Tri-Daily
Gazette*, which was called by one of its competing newspapers "the or-
gan that speaks for [Mebane]," was rife with constant negative references to the lawyers. In "A Tale of a Bridge," a regular column that
editorialized the benefits of the bridge and lauded its proponents,[26] the

---

[25] *A Tale of a Bridge (Series No. 20)*, Tri-City Daily Gazette, Mar. 12, 1924,
at 1.

[26] The *Gazette*'s editor, M. E. Murray, explained that he was intent on using
the column as a method of exposing the facts underlying the bridge controversy:

Today, there is controversy in Rockingham County. More lies are
told and retold in one day than has ever been put in one book. Men

newspaper wrote, "[s]ome lawyers can get a man into more trouble in an hour, than he can get out of in ten years" and displayed a front-page political cartoon portraying Ivie as a crony for special interests.[27] In another column, the *Gazette* described Ivie and Sharp's opposition to the bridge as just a small part in a larger campaign to dominate the county:

> The Ivie-Sharp faction wants to gain control of the Democrat party in Rockingham County and in this way they think, they will control the county, the Board of Commissioners, the County Board of Education, the County Offices, the Jail and Poor Farm, the Road Force and the Convict Camps, the County Playgrounds, Welfare Officers and all the vast army of men under the High Sheriff, some of whom are hired and paid by private interests, and when they thus gain control of everything, including our schools, the whole thing will become a political machine before whom every citizen must bow in blind subjection or be run out of the county.[28]

Meanwhile, as the *Gazette* ridiculed bridge opponents, it portrayed Mebane and the pro-bridge commissioners as saintlike figures. On March 6, 1924, the paper glorified the bridge supporters with a poem "Building at Eventide:"

> An old man going a lone highway,
> Came at evening, cold and gray,
> To a chasm vast, and deep, and wide.
> The Old man crossed in the twilight dim—
> The sullen stream had no fear for him—
> But he turned, when safe on the other side,
> And built a bridge to span the tide.
> "Old man," said a fellow pilgrim near,
> "You are wasting your time with building here.
> Your journey must end with the ending day;
> You never again will pass this way.
> You have crossed the chasm deep and wide,

---

charge others with doing and saying the wrong thing. Threats are heard on county officials. Serious charges are lodged at the doors of the Board of Commissioners. On the other hand three Commissioners are suing certain individuals because of these charges. The fight is on and the county is all torn up over the facts and the truth.

A Tale of a Bridge, Tri-City Daily Gazette, Feb. 8, 1924, at 1.

[27] *Political Triumvirate*, Tri-City Daily Gazette, Apr. 5, 1924, at 1. 3.

[28] *A Tale of a Bridge*, Tri-City Daily Gazette, Mar. 4, 1924, at 1.

> Why build this bridge at eventide?"
> The builder lifted his old gray head:
> "Good friend, in the path I have com," he said
> "There follows after me a throng
> Whose feet must pass this way.
> This stream, which has been but naught to me,
> To that hurrying throng may a pitfall be,
> They, too, the flowing stream should stem.
> Good Friend, I am building this bridge for them."[29]

The *Reidsville Review* was also an active participant in the debate, strongly opposing Mebane's bridge and encouraging readers to attend the various mass meetings in the context of news stories covering past meetings. The *Review* was so active in opposing the bridge project and denouncing its proponents that in February 1924, the *Review*, along with the Citizens Committee, was sued for libel by Pratt, Pruitt, and McCollum. The lawsuit claimed that the Citizens Committee was "wantonly, maliciously, and recklessly" attacking the pro-bridge commissioners and that the *Review* was their soapbox.[30]

The anti-bridge faction stepped up its campaign and planned another mass meeting in April 1924, where rhetoric became particularly intense. At this mass meeting, which again coincided with a meeting of the board and at which a Luten Bridge Company representative was in attendance, Citizens Committee Chairman Montgomery vigorously attacked the proposal, promised that the Citizens Committee would not back down, and then invoked the image of the Ku Klux Klan,[31] which reputedly counted among its ranks members of the Citizens Committee leadership. He declared, "I don't know much about this organization. But when we have to go after anything we are not going to mask but we will go if it is necessary."[32] The *Gazette* also noted an as-

---

[29] *Bridge to Span the Tide*, Tri-City Daily Gazette, Mar. 6, 1924, at 1.

[30] Summons for Relief, Brooke, Parker & Smith, Graves, Brock & Graves, J. C. Brown, attorneys for plaintiff, *reprinted in* The Reidsville Rev., Feb. 4, 1924, at 4.

[31] The KKK often participated in local politics in the South during the 1920s, making their presence known when they felt that the government was not representing what they perceived as the public interest. Klansmen often asserted their will, and often justified their violence, when there was a perceived need to demand more responsiveness from a municipality or county government. *See* ARNOLD S. RICE, THE KU KLUX KLAN IN AMERICAN POLITICS (1972).

[32] *Mass Meeting Now in Session at Wentworth*, Reidsville Rev., Apr. 7, 1924, at 1.

sociation between the Klan and the anti-bridge movement, referring to their mass meetings as "mask-meetings."

The battle over the bridge became even more contentious in late 1924 when the county commissioners were up for reelection. When Pratt, Pruitt, and McCollum all declined to seek reelection, Mebane (who, after all, was a Republican himself) pledged his support behind the 1924 Republican campaign and the Republican challengers for county commission. As the November election approached, it clearly became a referendum on the bridge project and also on B. Frank Mebane himself. The lead editorial in the *Leaksville News* on October 31, 1924, titled "Do Not Be Deceived," stated that B. Frank Mebane was "pulling the wires" on behalf of the Republican candidates for the board of county commissioners and encouraged readers to be wary of these candidates.[33] The *Reidsville Review*, which generally referred to Mebane as a "special interest" rather than referring to him by name, published a number of direct political advertisements in the lead-up to the election, denouncing Mebane specifically, including one that read: "Don't scratch the Democratic county ticket. It might act as a soothing balm toward healing the twisted political spine of B. Frank Mebane."[34] Commissioners Barber, Martin, and Hampton—understanding that the election would quell any dispute about the board's membership— took great pains to point out that they were pursuing a traditional Democratic agenda, curtailing spending in every way possible, including (but not limited to) their opposition to the bridge. And the Republican candidates desperately tried to avoid being labeled as Mebane's cronies. Some responded directly with advertisements of their own that warned, "Voters Do Not Be Deceived" or that advised readers, "Watch B. Frank Mebane."

The election clearly reflected the county's anger. With a record voter turnout and in a categorical rebuke of Mebane's plan, the previous anti-bridge commissioners—Barber, Martin, and Hampton—were all reelected, J. H. Benton and C. H. Dalton, two Democrats firmly opposed to the construction of the Fishing Creek Bridge, won election, and the Republican candidates were handily beaten. The morning after Election Day, Rockingham citizens were greeted with the headline, "In Rockingham County Republicans and Mebane are 'Snowed Under'" splashed across the cover of the *Reidsville Review*. The newly elected board promptly put into action their anti-bridge campaign promises

---

[33] *Do Not Be Deceived*, Leaksville News, Oct. 31, 1924, at 1.

[34] Advertisement, *Watch B. Frank Mebane*, Reidsville Rev., Oct. 31, 1924, at 2.

and even resolved to prohibit either the Luten Bridge Company or J. S. Trogdon from leaving a bill at the office of the county auditor.

Mebane's Rockingham County

In addition to igniting a political firestorm, Mebane's bridge plan exposed some underlying structural fissures that divided Rockingham County. The Dan River, as it flows eastward from the Appalachian foothills toward Albemarle Sound and the Atlantic Ocean, cuts through Rockingham County to separate two distinct communities. To the south lay an agrarian economy. Reidsville, the epicenter of southern Rockingham County, was populated largely by tobacco farmers and became a bustling agricultural center that contributed to North Carolina's production of more than 90 percent of the nation's tobacco supply. To the north of the Dan lay Leaksville, Draper, and Spray, which were emblematic of Rockingham County's burgeoning textile industry prominence. The emergence of North Carolina as a textile leader occurred largely between the 1880s and 1920s, and by a conservative estimate, more than six new mills were built each year in North Carolina between 1880 and 1900, enabling the state to quickly supplant New England as the leading region for textile production. Rockingham County contributed its share to the industry's growth. In Leaksville, Draper, and Spray—which in 1967 were consolidated into a single municipality, Eden—the textile mills employed almost half of the county's residents, and the number of looms in the county nearly doubled between 1900 and 1920.

Reidsville and Eden—separated by a mere 12 miles—represented Rockingham County's dominance in two former staples of the southern economy, tobacco production and textile milling. In 1920, as Mebane began devising his plan, the balance of economic power began to shift across the Dan, toward industrialization, and precipitated changes in the county's social fabric. Industrialization led to greater creation of wealth for the industrialists, including substantial trickling down to mill and factory workers, and by 1920, the state's small manufacturing workforce was creating goods valued at twice the combined production of the state's agricultural sectors. Industrialization also meant a growing discrepancy in wealth that was enjoyed by a relatively small minority. Yet even as industrial employment grew, still only a small percentage of North Carolinians worked at mills, and agriculture remained the dominant political force in North Carolina. This created a landscape ripe for societal and political conflict, pitting enshrined and traditional majoritarian forces against increasingly wealthy individual entrepreneurs.

These tensions were not new, and North Carolina's political parties were forced to navigate between the conflicting interests of agriculture and industry from the post–Civil War era. Generally, the Democratic party stood for traditional agrarian interests, and because of the large percentage of agricultural workers in the state, the Democratic party maintained a stronghold over state government. But opposition to the Democratic leadership was steady and constant. One of the early political leaders who battled successfully against Democrats was John Motley Morehead, the Whig governor of North Carolina from 1841 to 1845. With Morehead as governor, North Carolina made significant investments in its schools, railroads, and waterways, generally against intractable Democratic opposition.

The Republican party inherited the Whig policy priorities, emphasizing the creation of civic improvements to pursue economic growth and stimulate industrialization, and one of the party's leaders in the early twentieth century was John Motley Morehead II, the Whig governor's grandson. Morehead II defeated a Democratic incumbent for Congress in 1908 and assumed the chairmanship of North Carolina's Republican party in 1910. Because of Morehead II's appeal to the state's emerging business leaders, his ascendancy to the party chairmanship "was hailed as the inauguration of a new era in the political affairs."[35]

One of Morehead II's strongest supporters was a bright young attorney named John J. Parker. At age twenty-three, having just graduated from the University of North Carolina with an A.B. (graduating with a G.P.A. higher than any previous UNC undergraduate)[36] and an L.L.B., Parker managed Morehead II's successful congressional campaign. Drawn at an early age to the party's progressive vision and its belief in constructively harnessing the power of government, Parker remained actively involved in state Republican politics. He ran, unsuccessfully, for Congress in 1910, state attorney general in 1916, and governor in 1920.[37] But Parker's loyalty to, and connections with, the

---

[35] Joseph F. Steelman, *The Trials of a Republican State Chairman: John Motley Morehead and North Carolina Politics, 1910–1912*, 43 N.C. Hist. Rev. 31, 31 (1966).

[36] He received only one C, in a logic course taught by his eccentric mentor Horace Williams, who later was forced to explain, "my A's are saved for that person who is interested in philosophy as a professional matter." Judge Harold R. Medina, *John Johnston Parker, 1885–1958*, 38 N.C. L. Rev. 299, 300 (1960). Williams would say about Parker, "We fought like tigers from the first day of the course as John would accept no thought unless it was made a part of his own thinking." *Id.*

[37] One of Parker's colleagues said many years later, "He must have known that he was renouncing the hope of speedy advancement as a member of the

Republican party finally reaped returns in October 1925, when President Calvin Coolidge granted the forty-one-year-old Parker a recess appointment to the Fourth Circuit of the U.S. Court of Appeals. The position was made permanent two months later, and he remained on the court until his death in 1958, serving as chief judge for the final twenty-seven years of his tenure.[38]

---

opposite party in a town and country where the majority of people vote the straight Democratic ticket almost as a religious duty." *Id.* at 302.

[38] For a time, it looked as though Parker's tenure on the court was going to be significantly shorter, as he was nominated by Herbert Hoover to the United States Supreme Court in 1930. Parker's confirmation hearings were highly contentious and—in what political scientist Peter Fish called "a Senate confirmation process run amuck," *The Hushed Case Against a Supreme Court Appointment: Judge Parker's "New South" Constitutional Jurisprudence, 1925–1933*, 9 Duke L. Mag. 12, 12 (1990)—ultimately led to his nomination's rejection by a two-vote majority.

Two groups played a central role in Parker's ultimate rejection for a seat on the Supreme Court: the labor and civil rights movements. The labor movement took issue with Parker's decision in *United Mine Workers of America v. Red Jacket Consolidated Coal and Coke Co.*, 275 U.S. 536 (1927), in which the Fourth Circuit upheld a lower court's injunction against a union from fighting yellow-dog contracts. The "opinion ignited massive opposition from members of organized labor and their putative allies in academe, the press, and the Senate." *See* Peter G. Fish, *John Johnson [sic] Parker, in* 2 GREAT AMERICAN JUDGES: AN ENCYCLOPEDIA 583, 585 (John R. Vile ed., 2003). Parker later defended his rulings, saying he had simply followed two recent Supreme Court rulings that left him without any latitude or discretion. *See* Richard Kluger, *The Story of John Johnston Parker: The First Demonstration of Negro Political Power Since Reconstruction*, 46 J. Blacks Higher Educ. 124, 125 (2005).

The more damaging accusation came from civil rights leaders, who mobilized against Parker's nomination because of comments Parker made during his 1920 gubernatorial campaign. Parker, in response to a Democratic race-baiting campaign that painted Republicans as champions for Black Americans, was reported to have said the following while accepting the Republican nomination:

> The Negro as a class does not desire to enter politics. The Republican Party of North Carolina does not desire him to do so. We recognize the fact that he has not yet reached that stage in his development when he can share the burdens and responsibilities of government. This being true, and every intelligent man in North Carolina knows it is true, the attempt of certain petty Democratic politicians to inject the race issue into every campaign is most reprehensible. I say it deliberately, there is no more dangerous or contemptible enemy of the state than men who for personal and political advantage will attempt to kindle the flame of racial prejudice or hatred.

When *Rockingham County v. Luten Bridge Co.* finally reached Parker's desk in 1929, Parker had been fully immersed in the multidimensional political battles between Republican industrialists and Democratic agrarians for nearly two decades. Aside from being politically aligned with (and indebted to) the Morehead family and maintaining friendships with both Lily Morehead Mebane and her husband, B. Frank Mebane, Parker firmly believed in a progressive vision of good governance and investments in public works that would facilitate North Carolina's industrialization. As a judge, he became a leader of the judicial administration movement, which promoted legal reforms to enhance judicial autonomy, administrative expertise, and judicial pragmatism. He also was known to subscribe to a "Madisonian-Marshallian model of American government" that argued that democratic institutions should be designed to resist "the tyranny of temporary majorities."[39] And he developed a pragmatic jurisprudence that sought to empower public institutions to tackle modern economic and social challenges, including the daunting task to realize economic development in the South. Thus, by the time Rockingham's political crisis spilled into the Fourth Circuit, Parker had a thoroughly developed view of the role local government should play when corrupt interests, majoritarian passions, and legal uncertainty combine to create political confusion and hamper proper government.

The Suit

On November 24, 1924, only a few weeks after Election Day delivered a resounding defeat to Mebane and his political allies, the Luten Bridge Company sued Rockingham County and its commissioners in the Western District of North Carolina for breach of contract and de-

---

46 J. Blacks Higher Educ. at 124. NAACP leaders seized upon the first part of this statement and led the campaign against his confirmation. Recent scholarship has suggested that civil rights leaders might have mischaracterized the judge's beliefs. The judge left behind a long judicial record that expressed contempt for regional chauvinism and white supremacy, and he also became a member of North Carolina's branch of the Commission on Interracial Cooperation. Regardless of his true position on race relations, Parker would never escape the lasting effects of his comments from his time in partisan politics.

[39] Peter G. Fish, *Guarding the Judicial Ramparts: John J. Parker and the Administration of Federal Justice*, 3 Just. Sys. J. 105, 107 (1977). Parker later served as an alternate member of the military tribunal in Nuremberg from 1945 to 1946, and, in many respects, the lessons from Nazi Germany confirmed important tenets of Parker's judicial and political philosophies: his fears of democratic excesses and his estimation of the courts as essential arbiters in negotiating the balance of powers.

manded payment for work on the bridge. The bridge had not been completed when the lawsuit was filed, but substantial work had been done, and the company sued for $18,301.07, which was the sum of the county engineer's estimated monthly payments minus 10 percent.[40]

The named defendants were Rockingham County and the individual commissioners who were on the board at the time the original contract had been signed: Pratt, Pruitt, McCollum, Barber, and Martin. The complaint portrayed the dispute as a simple breach of contract: it set forth that the Luten Bridge Company and Rockingham County, acting through its board of county commissioners, entered into a contract to build a bridge; the latter party hired an engineer to oversee the work and present it with a monthly bill; the county refused to pay the bill; and the action at hand was intended to recover these debts. There was no mention of the turmoil that preceded the suit, and the complaint stated that Pratt, Pruitt, and McCollum, along with Martin and Barber, "are the duly elected, qualified and acting members of the Board of Commissioners" of Rockingham County.[41]

On November 27, the three pro-bridge commissioners—Pratt, Pruitt, and McCollum—met in Wentworth with a lawyer and filed an answer.[42] Claiming to act in their official capacity as duly elected county commissioners, the three commissioners conceded to all the charges made in the Luten Bridge Company's complaint, admitting that the county had entered into a contract with the company and that the company had performed its obligations. Without consulting the other commissioners named in the suit, Pratt, Pruitt, and McCollum "asked that the action be dismissed as to them as individuals, and that the defendant Rockingham County be required to pay such sum as was justly due and owing the plaintiff."[43]

Before a court could address the pro-bridge commissioners' answer, the newly elected board, also claiming to speak for Rockingham County, issued its own response to the suit. The board moved to dismiss the suit and quash the service of process, arguing that since the

---

[40] Under the original contract, the county was allowed to withhold 10 percent of the purchase price until the completion of the contract.

[41] Transcript of Record at 3, *Luten Bridge*, 35 F.2d 301 (4th Cir. 1929) (No. 2873).

[42] The immediacy between the filing of the Luten Bridge Company's complaint and the filing of the Pratt, Pruitt, and McCollum answer suggests that there was a coordinated effort behind the two legal actions, though this is not confirmed by the court record or other primary sources.

[43] Brief of Appellee at 2, *Luten Bridge*, 35 F.2d 301 (4th Cir. 1929) (No. 2873).

summons was addressed to Chairman Pratt and Commissioner Pruitt at the time when Martin was serving as the board's chair and Hampton had replaced Pruitt, the summons was improperly presented. Similarly, the county argued that Hampton should have been presented with a summons instead of Pruitt because of Pruitt's resignation earlier in the year. Last, the county argued that the contract was made by undue influence and therefore was not binding. It further stated that "there was a preponderate opinion . . . that it was not in the public interest to build said bridge, but on the contrary that its construction would be making use of public funds for the private gain and good of one or a few citizens of the county."[44]

The matters went before District Court Judge E. Y. Webb. On June 2, 1927, Judge Webb, without addressing the county's argument that Pruitt's resignation should be enforced, issued a terse two-page ruling that accepted that Pruitt had remained a member of the board of county commissioners through 1924. Accordingly, Judge Webb ruled that the November 1924 meeting of Pratt, Pruitt, and McCollum constituted a quorum of the board of county commissioners, and he refused to admit into evidence testimony contending that the anti-bridge commissioners were, in fact, the county's official body. He then concluded as follows:

> The Court is of the opinion that the defendants, T. R. Pratt, Chairman, W. F. Pruitt and J. F. McCollum, were the duly elected and regularly constituted Commissioners for the County of Rockingham, and possessed the necessary power and authority to speak and act for the County in this litigation, and that their answer herein filed is a valid and lawful act for and on behalf of said County, and constitutes the regular and legal answer to the complaint herein filed.[45]

The ruling undermined the core of the county's case, severely handcuffing any chance of challenging the validity of either the contract or the authority of the anti-bridge board's repudiations. And it proved to be determinative. A brief one-day jury trial, held on January 11, 1929, resulted in a verdict that the county was liable to the Luten Bridge Company for breach of contract in the amount of $18,301.07.[46]

---

[44] Transcript of Record at 19 (Answer of Rockingham County).

[45] *Id.* at 16 (Findings of Fact, Conclusions of Law, and Judgment Upon the Foregoing Motion).

[46] Judge Parker later expressed disappointment over Judge Webb's handling of the case, remarking to his colleagues hearing the *Luten Bridge* case

Rockingham County appealed to the Fourth Circuit on April 17, 1929. The county's primary objection aimed at Judge Webb's decision to treat Pratt, Pruitt, and McCollum's answer as one that spoke for the county. The county's appeal rested on sixteen separate grounds, but the arguments fell into three categories. First, it argued that Pruitt had lawfully resigned and ceased being a member of the board of county commissioners at the moment he submitted his resignation. As such, the answer he filed with Pratt and McCollum did not reflect a majority of commissioners and thus could not be the answer for the county. Second, the county argued that the lawfully constituted board of county commissioners included Hampton de jure, and thus could not include Pruitt. Alternatively, if Hampton was not a member de jure, then he acted as a de facto member of the board of county commissioners and thus acquired official status. Finally, the county argued that even assuming arguendo that Pruitt was still a member of the board when the answer was filed, the three commissioners meeting outside of a formal board meeting could not act in their official capacity, and thus the answer the three filed was not the county's answer. The county requested that the appeals court reverse the lower court's judgment and remand for a new trial, in which it could admit into evidence its version of events and discredit the answer offered by Pratt, Pruitt, and McCollum.

In response, the Luten Bridge Company, the appellee, countered that Pruitt's resignation had not been properly accepted and that the three pro-bridge commissioners were entitled to act on behalf of the county at the meeting in November 1924. But the crux of the bridge company's argument remained simple: the duly elected board of commissioners of Rockingham County entered into a contract with the company, and since the latter performed its end of the contract, the former must perform as set forth in the contract. The appellees' brief stated succinctly that "the bridge has been built and completed in accordance with the contract, and now spans the stream in Rockingham County, and for which not one cent has been paid by the County."[47]

Thus, ironically, none of the issues on appeal focused on any material question of contract law. The county, in contrast to its position in the district court, did not dispute the validity of the contract and instead challenged the validity of the pro-bridge commissioners' answer and requested a remand. The bridge company's arguments defended the authority claimed by the three pro-bridge commissioners while

---

that Webb "virtually directed a verdict for the plaintiff." *See* No. 2873—Memorandum, John J. Parker Papers, *supra* note 1, at Folder 1234.

[47] Brief of Appellee at 6.

challenging the county clerk's decision to accept irrevocably Pruitt's resignation. And, most interesting of all, neither party proffered an argument challenging the lower court's calculation of damages.

The case was assigned to a three-judge panel of the United States Court of Appeals for the Fourth Circuit. The panel included Judges John J. Parker of North Carolina, George McClintic of West Virginia, and Morris Soper of Baltimore. Judge Parker chaired the panel and would ultimately write the decision that would make *Rockingham County v. Luten Bridge Co.* famous.

Rockingham County v. Luten Bridge Co., Revisited

With the details of the underlying dispute as background, Parker's complete opinion, including the bulk that is neglected by the casebooks, comes into focus, and its intended meaning and historical significance become evident.

Judge Parker began the opinion by stating that there were three issues before the Fourth Circuit on appeal. The first was whether the answer filed by Pratt, Pruitt, and McCollum was the answer for the county. Thus, the court would have to decide whether Pruitt was still a member of the board of county commissioners when he signed the answer, and even if Pruitt were a member of the board, whether the three men could act as the county's governing body in an informal meeting. The second issue was whether the county's resolutions and notices to repudiate the contract were official actions on the part of the county. The question for the court was whether a board of commissioners that included Hampton had the authority to conduct the county's business after Pruitt delivered his resignation. And the final issue was, if the repudiations constituted official county actions, whether the Luten Bridge Company could recover damages for work done after the repudiations were received.

In an opinion that received virtually no negative comments from the other members of the Fourth Circuit panel, Judge Parker concluded that Rockingham County had indeed terminated the bridge contract. He first ruled that the lower court had erred in treating the answer by Pratt, Pruitt, and McCollum as the answer of the county. Even if all three (including Pruitt) were still members of the board of county commissioners, they could not act on the county's behalf unless their November 1924 meeting was properly held in "legal session." In noting that "[t]he rule is well settled that the governing board of a county can act only as a body and when in legal session as such," Parker ruled that "Commissioners casually meeting have no power to act for the county" and thus "[i]t is unthinkable that the county should be held bound by such action."[48]

Next, Parker ruled that Hampton had the authority to act officially as a Rockingham County commissioner. This conclusion rested on two independent grounds. First, Pruitt's resignation was properly accepted by the county clerk before it was rescinded, and thereafter the clerk had duly sworn in Hampton as the new commissioner. Each step of this resignation and reappointment process was proper, and though "[t]he mere filing of the resignation . . . did not itself vacate the office of Pruitt, . . . after its acceptance, he had no power to withdraw it."[49] In the alternative, even if Hampton's appointment was not valid, Parker ruled that Hampton enjoyed authority as a de facto officer. Under either argument, the board of county commissioners as constituted by Hampton, Barber, and Martin could, in Parker's view, speak for the county. As such, their declarations that the county no longer wanted the bridge and their instructions to the Luten Bridge Company to halt construction constituted official county actions.

Then, in the final two pages of the nine-page opinion, Parker famously ruled that the Luten Bridge Company had a duty to mitigate the damages from the county's breach. Parker chiefly cited Samuel Williston's treatise, which observed that a number of cases, dating back to the New York 1845 case of *Clark v. Marsiglia*, have held that "after an absolute repudiation or refusal to perform by one party to a contract, the other party cannot continue to perform and recover damages based on full performance."[50] The case was then remanded to the lower court with instructions to award the Luten Bridge Company its expenses up through the time of the county's repudiation, plus its expected profits.

Rereading the entirety of this famous opinion—viewing it through the lens of its contextual history—makes a number of lessons immediately apparent. First, Parker expresses concern for the problem of democratic instability, which had the potential to wreak genuine havoc in Rockingham County. The lack of clear rules governing Pruitt's resignation and replacement created political uncertainty that hampered

---

[48] *Luten Bridge*, 35 F.2d at 304–05.

[49] *Id.* at 306.

[50] *Id.* at 307. The British rule has long been different. Parker declined to follow the 1872 British case of Frost v. Knight, (1872) 7 L.R. Exch. 111 (Ex. Ch.), in which Lord Cockburn permitted nonbreaching parties to continue performing even after a repudiation. British courts have continued to follow the rule in *Frost*, including the post-*Luten* decision of White & Carter (Councils) Ltd. v. McGregor, [1962] A.C. 413 (H.L.) (appeal taken from Scot.).

county government, and Parker used the opinion to devise legal rules that could decisively denote the boundaries of legitimate authority and thus shore up administrative stability. Specifically, Parker handed down a bright-line rule to govern succession, holding that a commissioner's resignation becomes official and irrevocable upon its acceptance by the county clerk. Parker additionally vested the power of reappointment in the county clerk, reasoning that if a resignation is inextricably linked to a reappointment, then the lines of authority will not be blurred. The ruling reinforces additional administrative stability by insulating the reappointment process from elected officials and centralizing the temporary power in the hands of a bureaucrat.

By no means did the relevant case law dictate this conclusion—to the contrary, Parker resorted to some creative reasoning. Relying on a passing reference in an 1883 North Carolina Supreme Court opinion stating that a resignation must be accepted by an authority to become official, Parker extended the logic to vest in the county clerk the power both to enforce a rescinded resignation and to reappoint a successor. Parker's reason for overstating the clarity of the law is obvious, for it was the law's lack of clarity that contributed to the political chaos (even the Luten Bridge Company—resorting in the end to "the only safe thing to do"—was uncertain whom to follow). The reasoning reveals both Parker's pragmatic jurisprudence and his concern for protecting municipal authority.

Second, the *Luten Bridge* case illustrated the dangers of unrestrained political corruption, not just by showcasing the influence of money in elections but, much more important, by revealing the possibility that informal actions have the potential to improperly replace formal government acts. Indeed, the answer issued by Pratt, Pruitt, and McCollum in a secret backroom setting, organized outside standard procedures and beyond the view or supervision of the county's electorate, was an exercise in arbitrary rule that correlates with purchased politics. Parker's ruling admonished the pro-bridge commissioners for their meeting in late 1924 and declared that "commissioners casually meeting have no power to act for the county." Instead, a "single entity, the 'board,' alone can by its action bind the county," and he noted pointedly that board authority is exercised only when it is convened in "legal session" that is subject to standard procedure and not by the whims of certain individuals.[51]

---

[51] *Luten Bridge*, 35 F.2d at 304. Note that Parker did not have to reach this ruling. He could have rested his holding on enforcing Pruitt's resignation and deciding that Pratt, Pruitt, and McCollum therefore did not constitute a majority of the commissioners. Parker's decision to issue the additional ruling to

At the same time, Parker did not want legal formalism to impede important government affairs, and he embraced a de facto rule of governmental authority. Consequently, "discharging the duties of a county commissioner" was enough to confer legitimate authority if the "want of power or irregularity [is] unknown to the public."[52] In Parker's view, Hampton earned this de facto authority by dutifully assuming the responsibilities of county commissioner. Parker emphasized that the highest priorities—the efficient operation of government and all its indispensable duties—were at stake, for legal formalities cannot be divorced from the essential public functions that legal institutions are charged with fulfilling:

> The only government which the county had for a period of nearly 10 months was that which [Hampton] and his associates, Martin and Barber, administered. If their action respecting this contract is to be ignored, then, for the same reason, their tax levy for the year must be treated as void and the many transactions carried through at their twenty-five meetings, which were not attended by Pruitt, Pratt or McCollum, must be set aside. This cannot be the law. It ought not be the law anywhere; it certainly is not the law in North Carolina.[53]

If a fidelity to formalism could impede county leaders from assuming important governmental functions during a time of legal uncertainty— a time when their leadership and decisiveness are needed most—then legal rules need to both stabilize and endorse the exercise of de facto authority.

Last, and perhaps most important, Parker's opinion cemented the notion that county boards must have the full authority to enter into, and credibly commit to, contracts with private parties. This authority extends especially to politically unpopular contracts and contracts for long-term projects that last into the reign of succeeding boards (who might prefer different policies). Such agreements must be insulated from political upheaval, shifts in power following subsequent elections, and the tyranny of temporary majorities, such as the angry tax revolt engineered by Rockingham County's citizens. Accordingly, Parker concluded that although the county's repudiation of the contract meant the Luten Bridge Company should have stopped construction, and thus the district court miscalculated the damages, "[i]t is true that the

---

deny authority to the informal meeting reflects his strong objection to arbitrary governing.

[52] *Id.* at 307.

[53] *Id.* at 306.

county had no right to rescind the contract, and the notice given plaintiff amounted to a breach on its part."[54]

Though this final point is tucked away in Parker's reasoning, its importance should not be understated. Residents understood that this issue was at stake. The *Leaksville News*, for example, identified the central issue in the case to be one of local government contracting: "The case will probably make clear whether one board of county commissioners can arbitrarily repudiate the contract of another and 'get by' to the loss of the outside party," or similarly make disingenuous promises it knows future commissioners will refuse to keep.[55] Indeed, Rockingham County originally denied that it was obligated to any legally binding contract, arguing that the contract was entered into under undue influence and was contrary to public interest. However illegitimate Mebane's usurpation of power might have been, permitting Rockingham County to advance such a defense would damage all counties' credibility when committing to contracts. This would undermine a source of authority that counties need most to meet the demands of industrialization, since contracting with private parties—bridge companies, railroads, and educators—is essential to meet demands for public improvements.

Consequently, to Parker, the *Luten Bridge* case did indeed (as he wrote to his mentor Williams) address important issues of county government law and implicated policies that were critical to a changing North Carolina. In this respect, sensible rules that govern North Carolina's counties went hand-in-hand with sensible rules for contract law. But perhaps the most striking lesson is the simplest—that *Rockingham County v. Luten Bridge Co.* was only incidentally about the law of contract damages. To the contrary, the case was not so much about what to do once counties got out of contracts but, rather, about enabling counties to enter into contracts.

Afterword

Even though *Rockingham County v. Luten Bridge Co.* was indeed more about North Carolina county law than contract law, the case's lasting image—the unwanted bridge arching gracefully through the forest—continues to intrigue curious contracts students, and every so often anonymous law students and lawyers make a pilgrimage to Eden, North Carolina, in hopes of finding the concrete span.

---

[54] *Id.* at 307.

[55] *Fishing Creek Bridge to Get the Spotlight*, Leaksville News, Jan. 4, 1929, at 1.

B. Frank Mebane never saw any of the trials related to his bridge. He died suddenly on June 15, 1926, after three days of illness in New York City, while traveling en route to London to meet his wife. Dying without children, Mebane left her his entire estate, then valued at $2 million. News of his death received national attention and was the major news story of the week in the North Carolina piedmont, with headlines such as "His Name Is Written Large in Economic History of Rockingham County."[56] And retrospective history has been quite kind to Mebane. Later writings have called Mebane "as sharp a promoter, an entrepreneur, as the Gilded Age produced," have concluded that "that no man before or since ever lived in that area to possess such brilliant capacities to do great deeds," and have described Mebane as "[s]o great and powerful that he could build a bridge to nowhere and from nowhere and leave people wondering whether he paid for it or got the county to pay for it."[57] Perhaps most vindicating, some current residents of Rockingham County are thankful that the flamboyant, impatient, and politically manipulative Mebane confronted the county's traditional agrarian culture and brought technological and economic progress to the county.

Judge Parker lived into his thirty-third year as a circuit judge, dying in 1958 while still on the bench and leaving behind an accomplished career that few judges have rivaled. But Parker was unlikely to know of the fame and legacy he would enjoy from his most famous opinion. Though the case appeared in Williston's casebook two years before Parker's death, it was not until the early 1960s that it became a staple in first-year contracts texts. And the penultimate testament to the case's lasting significance did not arrive until 1979, fifty years after Judge Parker wrote the famous opinion, when *Luten Bridge* was included in the *Restatement (Second) of the Law of Contracts* to demonstrate the duty to mitigate.

The Fishing Creek Bridge's colorful history continued long past Parker's 1929 decision. The bridge sat quietly over the Dan River for about a decade, unencumbered by traffic and alone in the woods. Occasionally the remote bridge played host to picnics and parties attended by young people from the area, including some elegant dinners and dances. Still, the legal wrangling continued. The Luten Bridge Company evidently continued construction on the bridge long past its November 1924 lawsuit and eventually completed the bridge. In a last-

---

[56] *B. Frank Mebane, of Spray, Is Dead After Three Days Sickness*, Greensboro Daily News, June 16, 1926, at 1.

[57] Russ Edmonston, *Bridge Is Tribute to Entrepreneur*, Greensboro Daily News, Dec. 26, 1976, at G-1.

ditch effort to reclaim its losses, the company instituted another lawsuit in 1936, this time against the state highway commission for $9,800. The company stated that "the bridge cost $44,000.00 and that only $34,200.00 had been paid, with $9,200.00 of it coming from the county and $25,000.00 from the Spray Water Power and Land Company."[58] But the Luten Bridge Company failed to appear at an assigned court date, and the suit was dismissed. The company does not appear in any further public records in Rockingham County.

In 1935, the North Carolina Department of Transportation finally connected the bridge to dirt roads leading to Spray and Leaksville, and in 1968, when the department connected both sides of the bridge to paved roads, the Fishing Creek Bridge was renamed Mebane's Bridge (many still call it "Mebane's Folly"). What might be the bridge's final chapter arrived in the fall of 2003, when the famous bridge was permanently closed to traffic. The single-lane bridge still crosses high above the Dan River and remains available for pedestrians, and it now ingloriously supports a sewage pipe leading to Eden's water treatment facility. There had been threats that North Carolina's Department of Transportation might decide to demolish the bridge, but that sewage pipe might just save the bridge from destruction. However long it remains above the Dan River, Mebane's Bridge will serve as a monument to industrial ambition, cronyism, a countryside in transition, Judge Parker's most famous opinion, and one of the most bizarre and heated moments in Rockingham County's history.

---

[58] *Bridge Concern Again Lost Its Fight Last Fri.*, Leaksville News, Aug. 6, 1936, at 1.

11

Debora L. Threedy*

A Fish Story: *Alaska Packers' Association v. Domenico*

Introduction

A persistent criticism leveled against legal education is that it fails to teach cases in context.[1] The lack of context arises in two ways. First, the statement of facts in judicial opinions is extremely truncated and is usually presented as if the facts of the case are not problematical or in dispute. Second, appellate decisions are presented in textbooks and analyzed in classroom discussion with little or no discussion of the historical, economic, and social context in which the litigation arose and was pursued.

This article explores the context of one of the canonical first-year contracts cases, *Alaska Packers' Association v. Domenico*.[2] The case involves a wage dispute between a group of Alaskan salmon fishermen and their employer, the operator of a salmon cannery. In the first section, I present a traditional, straightforward analysis of the district and circuit court opinions. I also examine how jurists and other legal scholars, relying solely on the written opinions (in fact, apparently relying almost exclusively on the appellate court opinion), have inter-

---

* Professor of Law, University of Utah, S.J. Quinney College of Law. An earlier version of this chapter appeared as *A Fish Story:* Alaska Packers' Association v. Domenico, 2000 Utah L. Rev. 185.

[1] *See, e.g.*, LANI GUINIER, MICHELLE FINE & JANE BALIN, BECOMING GENTLEMEN: WOMEN, LAW SCHOOL AND INSTITUTIONAL CHANGE 14–15 (1997).

[2] 117 F. 99 (9th Cir. 1902), rev'g 112 F. 554 (N.D. Cal. 1901). The complete record on appeal, which includes the trial transcript, is available and is at: http://old.law.utah.edu/faculty/bios/threedyd/threedyd_alaska_transcript.pdf.

preted the case, what it means and what it stands for. In other words, the "traditional" interpretation of the case is explicated.

In the second section, I present the "background story." I attempt to situate the legal decision in the context of the growth of the salmon industry and the formation of the Alaska Packers' Association ("Alaska Packers")—"the fish trust" that operated the cannery at Pyramid Harbor. I also provide details about the cannery operation at Pyramid Harbor, which is where the "action" of the case occurs.

In the third section, I propose several alternative interpretations of the case. These alternative interpretations are based upon the methodology of "legal archaeology."[3] Approaching a case as if it were an archaeological site, the legal archaeologist digs beneath the reported facts and reconstructs the fuller context of the case using other sources. As part of the reconstruction of *Alaska Packers*, I have turned to the trial record, the company's corporate records, and contemporaneous government reports. I use information revealed by these sources to question assumptions made by the judges in the case and commentators since then. By doing so, I hope that students and scholars of the law will view the case in a new and more informed light.

The Traditional Story

1. The district court opinion

The published opinion by the District Court for the Northern District of California is dated December 9, 1901. It is authored by District Judge De Haven. John Jefferson De Haven was born in St. Joseph, Missouri, in 1845.[4] He was brought to California in 1849, grew up in Eureka, attended public schools, was admitted to the bar in 1866, and was married in 1872. He had a long political career including terms as a district attorney, county assemblyman, state senator, city attorney, congressman, state supreme court justice, and finally, in June 1897, he was appointed a federal district court judge.

The facts of the case, as summarized by Judge De Haven, are these: Libelants, fishermen and seamen, sued to recover $50 each on a contract alleged to have been entered into on May 22, 1900, in Pyramid Harbor, Alaska. Previously, on March 26, 1900, before departing San

---

[3] The term was coined by Professor Brian Simpson.

[4] *See* HISTORY OF THE BENCH AND BAR OF CALIFORNIA: BEING BIOGRAPHIES OF MANY REMARKABLE MEN, A STORE OF HUMOROUS AND PATHETIC RECOLLECTIONS, ACCOUNTS OF IMPORTANT LEGISLATION AND EXTRAORDINARY CASES, COMPREHENDING THE JUDICIAL HISTORY OF THE STATE 658 (Oscar Tully Shuck ed., 1901).

Francisco for Alaska, the libelants had signed a contract with Alaska Packers in which they agreed to work for $50 for the season plus two cents for each red salmon caught. (Some of the libelants had signed shipping articles on April 5, 1900, which provided that they would be paid $60 plus two cents for each red salmon.) Libelants, in addition to their duties as fishermen, also were required to sail the ship to and from Alaska and to discharge and load the ship's cargo at Pyramid Harbor.

Shortly after arriving in Pyramid Harbor, libelants "became dissatisfied" and refused to work unless their pay was raised to $100 for the season, plus two cents for each red salmon caught. The court noted that Alaska Packers had $150,000 invested in the cannery and that "no other men could be engaged to take the places of libelants during that fishing season."[5]

In these circumstances, the superintendent of the cannery agreed to the raise in wages, but at the end of the season, back in San Francisco, the company refused to pay anything beyond the amounts of the original agreements. Under protest, the fishermen took the payment and executed releases. The fishermen then brought suit for the difference between what they were paid and what they argued they were entitled to under the May contract.

Alaska Packers' answer raised three defenses: (1) There was no consideration for the contract sued upon and thus it was unenforceable; (2) the superintendent was without authority to bind the company; and (3) the releases signed by the fishermen when they were paid precluded suit on the disputed contract.

The district court briefly disposed of two of these issues. Although Hugh Murray, the superintendent at Pyramid Harbor, argued he had no authority to enter into a new contract, the court found that Alaska Packers was estopped from denying his authority. Finally, as to the releases, the court applied the admiralty rule: Because "seamen are usually improvident, and often ignorant of their rights, they are frequently tempted by their necessities to take less than is due them,"[6] and thus signing a release does not bar their suit for wages.

The bulk of the district court's analysis focused on the enforceability of the May contract. First, the court considered the question of the nets. The fishermen argued that Alaska Packers failed to provide them with "serviceable nets in which an average catch of fish could be taken" even though it had agreed to do so. They further argued that this de-

[5] 112 F. at 555.

[6] *Id.* at 560.

fault justified their refusal to work unless additional compensation was given to them. The court's treatment of this argument is worth quoting in full:

> The contention of libelants that the nets provided them were rotten and unserviceable is not sustained by the evidence. The defendant's interest required that libelants should be provided with every facility necessary to their success as fishermen, for on such success depended the profits defendant would be able to realize that season from its packing plant, and the large capital invested therein. In view of this self-evident fact, it is highly improbable that the defendant gave libelants rotten and unserviceable nets with which to fish. It follows from this finding that libelants were not justified in refusing performance of their original contract.[7]

Thus, the court rejected the fishermen's argument that Alaska Packers was the first party to breach the contract by failing to provide serviceable nets.

Since the fishermen were not justified in refusing to perform the original contract and thus it continued in force, the court agreed with Alaska Packers that there was no new consideration for the May contract. That contract required the fishermen to do what they were already obligated to do under the previous agreements.

The district court, however, drew a distinction between executory contracts and contracts where performance has been rendered; the court agreed that in the latter class of contracts any modification would require new consideration. But with regard to executory contracts, where prior to the completion of performance one party refuses to perform unless additional payment is made, the court noted that there was a split of authority. In such circumstances, some courts had found the modification to be without consideration and thus unenforceable, while other courts had found that the parties implicitly terminated the original contract and entered into a "new" agreement. The court then sided with the novation cases.

In particular, the district court relied upon the case of *Goebel v. Lin*.[8] In *Goebel*, the Belle Isle Ice Co. promised to provide brewers with all the ice they needed for the season at $1.75 per ton unless there was a scarcity of ice, in which case the price was to be $2 per ton. Halfway through the term of the contract, the ice company refused to deliver any more ice unless the brewers agreed to pay $3.50 per ton. Since the

---

[7] *Id.* at 556.

[8] 11 N.W. 284 (Mich. 1882).

brewers had a considerable stock of beer on hand which would be ruined if not kept chilled, and because they were unable to procure ice
elsewhere, the brewers agreed to the price increase. As in the present
case, however, the brewers subsequently refused to pay the additional
price, arguing that there was no consideration for the new contract and
that it had been obtained by duress.

The *Goebel* court ruled in favor of the ice company. It reasoned that
"[i]f the ice company has the ability to perform their contract but took
advantage of the circumstances to extort a higher price from the necessities of the brewers, its conduct was reprehensible."[9] The court, however, noted that the brewers thought it was better to accede to the ice
company's demand for a higher price than to bring suit for breach of
the original contract. The court noted that the brewers' reason for doing this was not explained. The court then created a hypothetical case
where there has been an unforeseeable change in circumstances: "Suppose, for example, the [brewers] had satisfied themselves that the ice
company under the very extraordinary circumstances of the entire failure of the local crop of ice must be ruined if their existing contracts
were to be insisted upon, and must be utterly unable to respond in
damages."[10] The *Goebel* court thought that in these circumstances a
reasonable person would renegotiate the contract. Implicitly, the court
presumed that the brewers had some such reason for agreeing to the
new contract, and thus upheld it.

Finally, the *Alaska Packers* district court considered whether the
new contract was obtained by duress, and concluded that "the facts
appearing here do not show that the defendant acted under duress, in
making [the new] contract."[11] The court reasoned that because defendant could have sued on the original contract, they had another option—even though the court acknowledged that the libelants were
judgment proof.

Alaska Packers moved for rehearing after the district court issued
its opinion, and on rehearing the court elaborated on its reasons for
finding no duress:

> It is clear that no legal duress can be found in the circum-
> stances under which the new contract was made. The libelants
> were not guilty of intimidation, and did nothing whatever to
> prevent the defendant from securing other men to take their
> places. If there had been an attempt upon their part to intimi-

---

[9] *Id.* at 285.

[10] *Id.*

[11] 112 F. at 558.

date other men from taking the places which they voluntarily quit, a very different case would be presented, but nothing of that kind appears, and the fact that there were no other men there, who could be engaged for that service, does not alter the case.[12]

The district court ordered Alaska Packers to pay each fisherman an additional fifty dollars plus interest.

2. *The appellate court opinion*

Alaska Packers took an appeal from the adverse decision in the trial court. The Ninth Circuit rendered its decision on May 26, 1902, five months after the final order in the trial court. The panel was made up of Circuit Court Judges Gilbert and Ross and District Court Judge Hawley. The opinion was authored by Judge Ross. His background was very different than that of Judge De Haven.

Judge Erskine M. Ross was born in Culpepper County, Virginia, in 1845, "the son of a planter."[13] He attended the Virginia Military Institute and fought on the Confederate side during the Civil War. He came to California in 1868 and lived with his uncle, a state senator and prominent attorney. After studying law under his uncle for two years, he was admitted to the bar and achieved "professional fame and financial prosperity at an exceptionally early age."[14] At the age of thirty-four he was chosen justice of the state supreme court, where he served until 1887, when he was appointed a U.S. district court judge and then circuit judge in 1895. Married with a son, he owned one of the largest and most profitable orange orchards in the state, Rossmoyne. "His enlightened firmness in the discharge of judicial duty . . . was well evidenced during the great railroad strikes of 1894."[15] In that year, then District Judge Ross entered an injunction requiring striking railway workers "to perform all of their regular and accustomed duties,"[16] thus effectively enjoining the workers from striking.

Regarding the issue of the nets, the appellate court said that "the evidence was substantially conflicting, and the finding of the court was

---

[12] Record at 161 (citation omitted).

[13] *See* HISTORY OF THE BENCH, *supra* note 4, at 657.

[14] *Id.*

[15] The "great strikes" referred to are, of course, the Pullman strike, "the largest concentrated labor action in the nation's history." J. ANTHONY LUKAS, BIG TROUBLE: A MURDER IN A SMALL WESTERN TOWN SETS OFF A STRUGGLE FOR THE SOUL OF AMERICA 208 (1997).

[16] Southern California Railway Co. v. Rutherford, 62 F. 796, 798 (C.C.S.D. Cal. 1894).

against the libelants." Because the evidence was conflicting, the appellate court deferred to the district court, "who heard and saw the witnesses."[17]

The appellate court then noted that the "real questions in the case . . . are questions of law."[18] The court found it necessary to consider only one such: whether there was consideration for the May contract. The court's analysis of this issue is based upon its determination of the weight to be given to the opposing precedents. The court noted that the district court, in holding that there was a novation of the contract and thus consideration, relied upon eight cases: five from Massachusetts; two from Michigan, which relied upon the Massachusetts authority; and one from Vermont, which was impliedly overruled by a later Vermont Supreme Court case. Conversely, the court noted that the "weight of authority" holds that there is no consideration for the new contract when one party promises only to do what it was previously bound to do, and cited cases from fifteen jurisdictions. Additionally, the appellate court briefly distinguished the *Goebel* case, upon which the district court had relied heavily, by saying that it "presented some unusual and extraordinary circumstances."[19]

The court did state that it thought the Massachusetts rule "wrong on principle" but did not explicitly state what that principle might be. Clues to the court's policy decision can be found, however, both in the way the court summarized the facts of the case before it and from language quoted from other cases. Both of these sources come very close to characterizing the case as one involving duress.

For example, the court summarized the facts in the *Alaska Packers* case as follows:

> [The fishermen agreed to serve] in remote waters where the season for fishing is extremely short, and in which enterprise the appellant had a large amount of money invested; . . . and at a time when it was impossible for the appellant to secure other men in their places, the libelants, *without any valid cause*, absolutely refused to continue the services they were under contract to perform . . . . The case shows that they *wilfully and arbitrarily* broke that obligation . . . . Certainly, it cannot justly

---

[17] 117 F. at 101.

[18] *Id.* at 102.

[19] *See id.* at 105. Although ambiguous, the court's comment seems to accept as a fact the failure of the entire ice crop. The *Goebel* court's statement about the failure of the ice crop, however, was part of the court's hypothetical.

be held . . . that there was any voluntary waiver on the part of the appellant of the breach of the original contract.[20]

Additionally, the court quoted the Minnesota Supreme Court:

> No astute reasoning can change the plain fact that the party who refuses to perform, and thereby coerces a promise from the other party to the contract to pay him an increased compensation for doing that which he is legally bound to do, *takes an unjustifiable advantage of the necessities of the other party.*[21]

In a similar vein, the court quoted a Missouri case in which the court held that to permit a party to refuse to perform a contract unless additional money is paid "would be to offer a premium upon *bad faith*, and invite men to violate their most sacred contracts that they may profit by their own wrong."[22]

The appellate court does not technically hold that the new contract is void due to duress; its holding is that the new contract is unenforceable due to a lack of consideration. Nevertheless, the court's rhetoric is that of bad faith and coercion on the part of the fishermen.

3. Modern interpretation

The Ninth Circuit's implicit characterization of the case as one involving duress has become the accepted reading of the case. For example, Judge Richard Posner has called *Alaska Packers* "a classic case of duress."[23] In fact, Judge Posner has had a great deal to do with the case being considered a duress case. In the last twenty-five years, *Alaska Packers* has been cited thirteen times. Twelve of those citations appeared in cases decided by the Seventh Circuit, and eight of those Seventh Circuit decisions were authored by Judge Posner.

In these cases, Posner characterizes *Alaska Packers* as a monopoly case. Due to the short season and the remote location, he concludes that the fishermen have a temporary monopoly on the supply of labor, and thus fish. He also assumes that without their labor the fishing season would be ruined and that the company has no effective remedy.

---

[20] *Id.* at 102 (emphasis added). The court's conclusions that the fishermen broke the first contract without cause is a consequence of the district court's factual finding that the nets were sufficient. *See id.* at 101.

[21] *Id.* at 102 (quoting King v. Duluth M. & N. Railway Co., 63 N.W. 1105, 1106–07 (Minn. 1895)) (emphasis added).

[22] *Id.* (quoting Lingenfelder v. Mainwright Brewery Co., 15 S.W. 844, 848 (Mo. 1891)) (emphasis added).

[23] Trompler, Inc. v. NLRB, 338 F.3d 747, 751 (7th Cir. 2003).

"[T]he exploitation of temporary monopolies is," he concludes, "the functional meaning of the legal concept of economic duress."[24]

In *Trompler, Inc. v. NLRB,*[25] his most recent opinion invoking *Alaska Packers*, which also involved a labor dispute, Posner notes that today employees have a statutorily protected right to engage in work stoppages. He then discusses how economic duress is a limitation on this right, but cautions that the concept must not be too freely invoked, as then "no strike would be protected activity, since the entire purpose of a strike is to exert economic pressure on the employer by withholding labor services that he needs."[26] The line dividing legitimate economic pressure and illegitimate economic duress is marked by the exploitation of a temporary monopoly. He distinguishes the case before him from *Alaska Packers* because he sees no evidence of such a monopoly.

Posner also distinguishes the monopolistic refusal to comply with a contract from cases involving changed circumstances, in which latter category he puts the *Goebel* case. In doing so, he assumes the failure of the ice crop as a fact. He contrasts a threat to repudiate, which is "a response to external conditions genuinely impairing the promisor's ability to honor the contract" with a threat of nonperformance, which is "merely a strategic ploy designed to exploit a monopoly position" and concludes that there should be a "firm rule of nonenforceability" in the latter type of cases.[27]

Marvin Chirelstein, a contracts scholar from Columbia University, offers a similar reading of *Alaska Packers*, which he discusses under the rubric of duress. Chirelstein, like Posner, examines the context of a threat not to perform in order to determine whether it is legitimate bargaining behavior or extortion. He does not consider the threat of nonperformance in *Alaska Packers* to be difficult to classify, comparing it to the classic "gun-to-the-head case" of extortion:

> Plainly, the defendant's consent to the pay raise was a forced consent, the alternative being the loss of much of its investment in the cannery itself. The plaintiffs apparently timed

---

[24] *Id.* at 751–52.

[25] 338 F.3d 747 (7th Cir. 2003).

[26] *Id.* at 751.

[27] Richard A. Posner, *Gratuitous Promises in Economics and Law* 57, *in* 56 THE ECONOMICS OF CONTRACT LAW (Anthony T. Kronman & Richard A. Posner eds., 1979). *See also* Mary Lou Serafine, Note, *Repudiated Compromise After Breach*, 100 Yale L.J. 2229 (1991) (advocating changed-circumstances rule for determining whether to uphold repudiated compromise).

their threat so as to maximize the defendant's vulnerability—plaintiffs had received no competing offer and no change had occurred in the market for their services or the conditions of their work that would explain or legitimate an effort to get an increase in compensation. [T]here appears to have been considerable justification for applying the doctrine of duress. [28]

The traditional reading of *Alaska Packers* is one in which the wily fishermen took calculated and unfair advantage of the vulnerable cannery, conduct coming close to if not actually constituting economic duress.

The Background Story: Alaska Canneries in the Gilded Age

Between 1850 and 1900, the population swelled; the cities grew enormously; the Far West was settled; the country became a major industrial power; transportation and communication vastly improved; overseas expansion began. New inventions and new techniques made life easier and healthier; at the same time, the social order became immeasurably more complex, and perhaps more difficult for the average person to grasp. New social cleavages developed . . . . When the blood of the Civil War dried, the Gilded Age began. This was the factory age, the age of money, the age of the robber barons, of capital and labor at war.[29]

In the last twenty-two years of the nineteenth century, a new industry came into being: the Alaskan canned salmon industry. Those years saw an amazing explosion of canneries in Alaskan waters, from two in 1878 to forty-two in 1900, with thirty opened in a single year, 1889. The industry owed its existence to technological innovations introduced only decades before. Huge fortunes were made in the course of a season or two. Packing companies, threatened by this exponential growth, entered into combinations known as "the fish trusts." What was happening in Alaska was merely an outgrowth and reflection of what was happening across the United States. And with this growth came social unrest. Class and ethnicity, race and language, all served to fragment society, to create "us" and "them." This, too, was occurring in Alaska.

1. The birth of the salmon industry

In the second half of the nineteenth century, large-scale exploitation of salmon as a food resource began. The spur to large-scale exploitation was the development of a reliable method of canning. Canning allowed salmon to be transported over long distances and stored for extended

---

[28] MARVIN A. CHIRELSTEIN, CONCEPTS AND CASE ANALYSIS IN THE LAW OF CONTRACTS 77 (5th ed. 2006).

[29] LAWRENCE M. FRIEDMAN, A HISTORY OF AMERICAN LAW 338 (2d ed. 1985).

periods without spoiling, and canned salmon was more palatable to consumers than salted salmon.

In 1864, Hapgood, Hume and Co. established the first salmon cannery, on the Sacramento River in California. "The cans were hand-soldered and the secret of sealing the cans was carefully maintained: Andrew Hapgood, who had worked at a lobster cannery in Maine, sealed all the cans himself behind closed doors."[30] Two years later, the company moved to the Columbia River. That year the company packed and sold four thousand cases of salmon for sixteen dollars per case. The success of this pioneer company led to the development of other canneries; by 1873, there were seven canneries operating on the Columbia. Two years later, there were fourteen.

During the 1870s, salmon canning on the Columbia River was a prosperous business. During this period there were no failures among the canning companies. However, in the following decade, canneries saw profits decline: "the competition for fish and markets resulted in higher prices for fishermen and lower selling prices for the finished product."[31]

Many of the pioneers who began on the Columbia River spread to other localities because of growing concerns that the Columbia was "fished out." Alaska salmon canning began in 1878; the first two canneries were built at Old Sitka and Klawak. In 1887, the Alaska Commercial Company established a cannery on the Karluk River, which made an "immense" pack in 1887 and 1888, "the fame of which quickly extended to San Francisco."[32] The next year, more than thirty new canneries were established, for a total of thirty-seven canneries.

2. The fish trust

In the late 1880s, production far outstripped demand for canned salmon. In 1889, 1890, and 1891, canneries packed more salmon than they could sell. At the beginning of the 1891 season, "it was reported that 600,000 cases of canned salmon were in San Francisco warehouses

---

[30] IAN DORE, SALMON: THE ILLUSTRATED HANDBOOK FOR COMMERCIAL USERS 196 (1990).

[31] *See* COURTLAND L. SMITH, SALMON FISHERS OF THE COLUMBIA 18 (1979). In 1866, fishermen on the Columbia River received fifteen cents per fish; by 1880, they were receiving fifty cents. During the same period, the price of a case of canned salmon dropped from sixteen dollars to five dollars. *See id.* Canneries on the Columbia River knew by 1883–84 that they had saturated the market. *See id.* at 21. The Columbia River Packers Association, however, was not formed until 1899. *See id.* at 54.

[32] MARSHALL MACDONALD, REPORT ON THE SALMON FISHERIES OF ALASKA, H.R. MISC. DOC. NO. 122, at 2 (1893).

and that in London about 400,000 cases . . . were still on the market."[33]
This represented about two-thirds of the total average annual pack for
the entire Pacific Coast. This over-supply inevitably led to a drop in
price. "Finding that the market was overstocked and the price of
canned salmon reduced in consequence, so that in many cases business
became unprofitable, the [Alaskan] canners decided to make a combination and curtail the fishing in the season of 1892."[34]

In 1892, a majority of the Alaskan canneries formed a loose association, the Alaska Packing Association; the members agreed to operate
only about nine canneries and divide the profits among the members.
This experiment was successful and, in February 1893, twenty-two
companies incorporated as the Alaska Packers' Association. In the first
year, Alaska Packers operated thirteen canneries at nine locations.
From 1893 until the turn of the century, it averaged 70 percent of the
annual Alaskan salmon pack.

The first year Alaska Packers operated, it had a net profit of
$420,470. In 1900, never having operated at a loss, the net profit, ac-
cording to Alaska Packers' own records, was $770,536. In 1900 there
were forty-two canneries operating in Alaska; Alaska Packers operated
eighteen of these. Alaska Packers eventually became a division of Del
Monte.

3. Pyramid Harbor

The cannery at Pyramid Harbor was the site of the confrontation between the fishermen and the company that led to the lawsuit. The
Pyramid Harbor cannery was one of eighteen canneries Alaska Packers
was operating in 1900. Pyramid Harbor is located on Chilkat Inlet,
about eighty miles north of Juneau. It is on the western side of the
inlet, a mile and a half south of Pyramid Island. The harbor "consists
of a small cove in which two or three vessels may find anchorage."[35]

The cannery was located on the southern shore of the cove. It was
built in 1883, changed hands once, and was burned in the spring of
1889 but immediately rebuilt so that it operated during the 1889 season. In 1892 it was a member of the Alaska Packing Association. In
1893 it became part of the Alaska Packers' Association. Alaska Packers' records show the purchase price of the cannery to be $100,745, but

---

[33] *Id.* at 10.

[34] *Id.*

[35] JEFFERSON F. MOSER, THE SALMON AND SALMON FISHERIES OF ALASKA: RE-
PORT OF THE OPERATION OF THE U.S. FISHERIES COMMISSION STEAMER *ALBATROSS*
FOR THE YEAR ENDING JUNE, 1898, H.R. DOC. NO. 308, at 125 (1899) [hereinaf-
ter MOSER 1898].

that was most likely a transfer from the original owners to the corporation in exchange for Alaska Packers' Association stock.

The cannery at Pyramid Harbor was operated by Alaska Packers from 1893 until 1904; it was closed for the 1905 season but ran again from 1906 until 1908, when it closed for good. It was abandoned in 1912 and eventually dismantled in the early 1930s. Pyramid Harbor was one of only three canneries closed in the first decade of the twentieth century. The one-year break in operations in 1905 is unexplained, but the closing of the cannery at the end of the 1908 season appears to have been driven by economics: Pyramid Harbor was one of the more expensive canneries to operate.

At the turn of the century, a case of salmon from Pyramid Harbor often cost more to produce than a case from other Alaskan canneries. At the same time, the pack from this cannery was considered "the choicest in Alaska."[36] Pyramid Harbor produced salmon mostly for export, and the cannery was meticulously run.

Moreover, Pyramid Harbor rather consistently spent a disproportionate amount on fishing gear. For example, in 1899 Pyramid Harbor spent $7,863.08 on fishing gear when it was outfitting to pack 50,000 cases, while Karluk, another cannery, spent $12,180.12 to outfit for 200,000 cases, and the Chignik cannery spent $3,650.15 to outfit for 50,000 cases.[37] The explanation for this seems to be that at Pyramid Harbor the fishing was done almost exclusively with gill nets, whereas other canneries used seine nets or traps. It took more men to operate gill nets; thus, Pyramid Harbor's labor force tended to be disproportionately large.

Not surprisingly, the wages paid per man at Pyramid Harbor were consistently among the lowest in Alaska. In 1901, Alaska Packers began keeping records on fishermen's average earnings, and for every year after that when the cannery was in operation (except the final year) Pyramid Harbor's fishermen earned one of the lowest averages in Alaska.[38] For example, in 1901, Pyramid Harbor fishermen averaged $183.95 for the season, when the average for all of the Alaska Packers' Alaska canneries was $273.24.

---

[36] JEFFERSON F. MOSER, SALMON INVESTIGATIONS OF THE STEAMER *ALBATROSS* IN THE SUMMER OF 1900, H.R. DOC. NO. 706, at 254 (1902) [hereinafter MOSER 1900].

[37] *See* APA Microfiche No. 336, "Cannery Costs 1893–1946."

[38] *See* APA Microfiche No. 310, "Alaska Packers Association Fishermen's Average Earnings 1901 to 1910, inclusive."

In 1900 the cannery was equipped with the following machinery: six retorts, two fillers, two toppers, two solderers, one cutter, and one can-making set. Each filling machine could fill 800 cases per day, setting the maximum daily capacity for Pyramid Harbor at 1,600 cases, which was rarely attained. The packing was done entirely by a Chinese crew who lived and ate separately from the fishermen. The Chinese crew was highly specialized at filleting the salmon in pieces sized to fit in the one pound cans. A small number of Native American women, called "klootchmen," also worked in the cannery doing less specialized work.

Pyramid Harbor packed primarily "redfish," which was the name given to sockeye salmon. The fish for the cannery were caught in the Chilkat, Chilkoot, and Taku Inlets, although most of the fish came from the Chilkat and Chilkoot Inlets. The average annual catch for the cannery fishermen for 1894–98 was 300,000 redfish. The run was about forty-five days in length.

In addition to fish caught by the cannery's salaried fishermen, the cannery bought fish from the local Chilkat and Chilkoot tribes. From 1896 through 1900, the cannery bought an average of 147,000 fish annually from about 200 Chilkat and Chilkoot fishermen.[39] However, these tribesmen were not employees of the company. The Native Americans employed their traditional fishing methods: they would fish from canoes or from a platform built over the stream, using a "gaff" (a long pole ten to twelve feet long with an unbarbed hook on the end, about four inches across the bend). The gaff was thrust into the water and the salmon impaled on the hook; when the fish were plentiful, the gaff could simply be dragged through the water. Although the cannery purchased a large part of its supply from the Native Americans, certain individuals complained that the Native Americans were unreliable.

In 1900, Pyramid Harbor employed ninety-two white and ten Native American fishermen. Eighty-two of the fishermen joined in the lawsuit. From the names on the libel, it appears that a majority of these were Italian. It also appears that at least the Italian fishermen were recruited by a "labor contractor" named G. Viscecova. Labor contractors were more prevalent in other sections of the canning industry, such as among cannery workers. By and large, the fishermen avoided the system of labor contractors, but "intermittently . . . Italians recruited in San Francisco for the Alaska fisheries had fallen into the clutches of boss contractors of their own nationality. Whenever this occurred a

---

[39] *See* MOSER 1898, *supra* note 35, at 126–27; MOSER 1900, *supra* note 36, at 254, 320.

general lowering of living standards resulted."[40] Generally, labor contractors received a fee from the fishermen they recruited. It appears that Viscecova may also have run the messhouse at Pyramid Harbor.

With this understanding of how the cannery at Pyramid Harbor operated, as well as a broad brush picture of the Alaskan canned salmon industry, it is now possible to consider some alternative narratives to the "traditional story" enshrined in the two court opinions.

Alternative Stories

In this section, alternative readings of the *Alaska Packers* case are put forth. First, a theory suggested by a reading of the trial transcript is explored: that the nets were indeed serviceable for fishing in Pyramid Harbor, but because the nets were unique to that fishery and because a large majority of the fishermen were both new to Alaska and not fluent in English, they mistakenly believed the nets were inadequate. Conversely, the possibility that the nets were indeed substandard is considered, along with an examination of why Alaska Packers had a motive to supply inadequate equipment. The assumption that Alaska Packers was at the mercy of the fishermen is challenged in the next section. Finally, changes in the labor market are examined as a source of the fishermen's dissatisfaction.

1. The question of the nets

At trial the fishermen justified their refusal to work by arguing that Alaska Packers had provided them with substandard nets. The trial court, however, rejected this argument. Although all three of the libelants' witnesses testified that the nets were in poor condition, the court found that this contention was "not sustained by the evidence."[41]

One possible reading of the trial transcript in the *Alaska Packers* case is that the nets provided by Alaska Packers were indeed serviceable, but that the fishermen did not realize this, due in large part to differences in language and experience. A review of the individual libelants quickly reveals that most were Italians. Testimony at the trial indicated that most were immigrants and that the majority did not speak English. An interpreter was present and, on at least one occa-

---

[40] L. W. Casaday, Labor Unrest and the Labor Movement in the Salmon Industry of the Pacific Coast 263 (1938) (unpublished Ph.D. dissertation, University of California–Berkeley) (on file with author). Even after the fishermen became generally unionized, the system of labor contracting continued, resulting in union agreements that contained express provisions prohibiting the practice. *See id.*

[41] 112 F. at 556.

sion, used at trial. The transcript itself indicates some language problems.[42]

In addition, it appears that for most of the fishermen this was their first year fishing at Pyramid Harbor, although they testified they had experience in other places. The trial testimony strongly suggests that the type of nets used at Pyramid Harbor was different than the type used at other places, such as on the Columbia River.

The Pyramid Harbor fishermen used gill nets exclusively, which were supplied by the company.[43] The nets from top to bottom are sixteen to eighteen feet deep (also described as thirty-two meshes deep). At Pyramid Harbor, each year the top sixteen meshes of the net were new; however, the bottom meshes were not. The bottom meshes were recycled from the top of the preceding year's net.

Apparently, reusing the nets in this way was unique to Pyramid Harbor. There was testimony at trial that on the Columbia River in Oregon and at Orca in Alaska the nets were new each year. The fishermen's complaints about the nets at trial appear to have focused on the old, reused portion of the nets. They testified that the nets were hanging in the cannery and that they could tear the meshes by pulling on them with two fingers. One testified that the fish broke right through the bottom of the nets where the mesh was old.

Murray, the superintendent of the cannery, testified that the reason for reusing the nets in this way was because fish are only caught in the upper portion of the net, the top seven or eight meshes. The lower part of the net is there merely to keep the net hanging properly. The reason that fish are only caught in the upper portion of the net at Pyramid Harbor had to do with the conditions of the water where they were fishing. At the point in the channel where they were fishing, the fresh river water floats on top of the denser salt water to a depth of six or seven feet. Because the salmon were found only in the muddy, nutrient-rich, fresh water, there was new netting for the top six or seven feet of the net, where the fish would be. The fish did not strike in the clear salt water that lay below the fresh river water.

Murray testified that when the men first complained to him about the nets, on May 19, "I explained the way we fished, and the way we got our fish."[44] He also was of the opinion that the few fishermen who

---

[42] *See, e.g.,* Record at 19, 39, 49, 65, 66 (illustrating language difficulties).

[43] *See* MOSER 1900, *supra* note 36, at 254. "[W]here the water is discolored gill nets are used . . . where the water is clear, drag seines give the best results." MOSER 1898, *supra* note 35, at 22.

[44] Testimony of Hugh Murray, Record at 108.

had been at Pyramid Harbor before understood about the nets and "could fully explain the kinds of nets we used," although he did not know whether they had.[45] Given the fishermen's language difficulties, and assuming that Murray did not speak Italian, the possibility exists that the men's understanding of what Murray was saying was incomplete.

Assuming for the moment that the fishermen did not understand that the nets were perfectly adequate for fishing at Pyramid Harbor, the case takes on a different complexion. Their misunderstanding might not have affected the ultimate outcome of the case because, after all, there still would not have been justification in fact for their strike. However, any suggestion of duress would have disappeared, as the fishermen would have had a good faith, albeit mistaken, reason for refusing to work.

A recent Seventh Circuit case illustrates how *Alaska Packers* might have played out if the fishermen were found to have such a mistaken belief. In *Contempo Design, Inc. v. Chicago & Northeast Illinois District Council of Carpenters*,[46] a union mistakenly believed that the collective bargaining agreement had been terminated and called a strike for higher wages. At the time, the company was in the middle of negotiating a multimillion-dollar contract with a potential client and so agreed with the union's demands in order to resolve the labor dispute. Subsequently, the company sued the union for damages caused by the strike.

The Seventh Circuit rejected the union's argument that the parties had rescinded the old agreement and adopted a new one. The court ruled that since the original agreement had not expired as the union mistakenly believed, there was no consideration for the new agreement, citing *Alaska Packers* and the preexisting-duty rule. Pursuant to the majority's reasoning, the fishermen would still have lost on the consideration issue, even if they had a good faith belief that the nets were inadequate.

The dissent, however, argued that the majority was "disguising what really is a finding of duress in lack-of-consideration's clothing."[47] The dissent then concluded there was no economic duress. The dissent conceded that the union had the company "over a barrel"[48] but distinguished the present case from *Alaska Packers* because the union had a good faith, albeit mistaken, belief that the collective bargaining agree-

---

[45] *Id.* at 98.

[46] 226 F.3d 535 (7th Cir. 2000).

[47] *Id.* at 555 (Evans, J., dissenting).

[48] *Id.* at 556.

ment was no longer in force. In the absence of duress, the dissent reasoned, the settling of a bona fide, albeit mistaken, dispute constituted the consideration for the new agreement. Ironically, assuming the fishermen honestly but mistakenly believed the nets were inadequate, the dissent's reasoning would result in a judgment for the fishermen.

2. Divergent interests: An assumption called into question

Another distinct possibility is that the nets were indeed substandard. The court disbelieved the fishermen because the court assumed that Alaska Packers' self-interest would lead it to furnish the fishermen with good nets. The court took it as a "self-evident fact" that Alaska Packers would provide adequate gear "for on [the fishermen's] success depended the profits defendant would be able to realize that season from its packing plant, and the large capital invested therein."[49] The court thus assumed that the fishermen and Alaska Packers both wished to maximize the number of fish caught. This line of reasoning, however, oversimplifies the economics of the salmon canning industry at the turn of the century. While the fishermen certainly wanted to maximize the number of fish they caught, it should not be assumed that the cannery wanted to as well.

Certainly, the fishermen's self-interest would lead them to want to catch as many fish as possible. At the turn of the century, Alaskan fishermen's wages were made up of two components: "run money" and the price paid per fish.

> From the earliest days of the industry fishermen sent to Alaska from the United States proper customarily have manned the company vessels on the voyage to and from the salmon fields. For this service they are paid what is known as "run money"— a flat sum for the season negotiated in advance. . . .[50]

The run money included payment for anything that was not fishing. As the testimony at trial showed, the fishermen were expected not only to sail the vessel from San Francisco to Pyramid Harbor, but also to unload supplies for the cannery, clean and mend the fishing nets and other equipment, close up the cannery at the end of the season, and load the packed cases of canned salmon onto the ship.

The greatest part of the fishermen's earnings, however, came from the price paid per fish. The original contract gave the men fifty dollars in "run money" and four cents per red salmon per boat. As two men manned each boat, this worked out to two cents per man per fish.

---

[49] 112 F. at 556.

[50] Casady, *supra* note 40, at 267; *see also id.* at 24 (defining "run money").

Conversely, the canneries needed the fishermen to catch sufficient fish, but not too many. There were no facilities in 1900 for preserving the fish until they could be canned. Moreover, canning the fish was a very labor intensive operation. If the salmon harvest was too bountiful, the cannery workers would not be able to keep up and fish would rot before they could be canned.

Exactly this situation occurred in British Columbia in 1897: "[s]almon ran in vast numbers that year . . . . The vast numbers of fish delivered each day exceeded the cannery capacity. Until strict limits per boat were imposed on the fishermen, large amounts of salmon lay rotting in trenches dug to receive the overflow."[51] One scholar has noted that "failure to make use of caught salmon used to be very common."[52] In 1900, the government inspector for the Alaskan canneries commented that the waste in the Bristol Bay district was "strikingly large."[53]

As it turned out, the salmon run during the 1900 season was exceptionally large. "From all parts of Alaska come reports of a large and steady run of salmon: The number of cases packed this year in Alaskan waters will be the greatest on record."[54] At least for Alaska Packers, this prediction proved true: in 1900 for the first time the total pack exceeded one million cases. Of course, in May when the fishermen made their demands, no one could know what the run would be like for that season, but they knew the possibility existed that the run could be very large.

There is very little in the trial testimony that sheds any light on the relation between the catch and the Pyramid Harbor cannery's ability to can that catch. Murray, the superintendent, testified that the pack in 1900 was 1,500 to 2,000 cases better than in 1899. He indicated that 2,000 cases represented about 20,000 fish. Murray also testified that the run in 1900 was about the same as the run in 1899. However, E. J. Banning, the attorney for the fishermen, failed to pin Murray down on the comparison between 1900's catch and that from 1899.

If the catches in the two years were comparable while the pack for 1900 increased by 2,000 cases, that would suggest that in 1899 the

---

[51] JOSEPH E. FORESTER & ANNE D. FORESTER, FISHING: BRITISH COLUMBIA'S COMMERCIAL FISHING HISTORY 21 (1975).

[52] Casaday, *supra* note 40, at 331 n.74.

[53] MOSER 1900, *supra* note 36, at 187.

[54] Coast Seamen's Journal, Aug. 1, 1900, Microform v.12–13.

cannery was unable to process at least 20,000 salmon.[55] It also would suggest that the company had a motive for making sure the fishermen's catch did not exceed the cannery's capacity.

This motive is reinforced by Alaska Packers documents indicating the number of cases for which Pyramid Harbor was outfitted. Due to the distance between Alaska and the mainland, cannery superintendents had to plan for the season months before it began and without knowing what the run would be like. In 1900, Pyramid Harbor was outfitted (with materials such as tin, solder, labels, cases, etc.) to can 55,000 cases. In fact, that year it canned 55,601. This suggests that in 1900, Pyramid Harbor was operating pretty much at capacity for the season.

Moreover, in both 1898 and 1899 the pack at Pyramid Harbor had either met or exceeded the number of cases for which the cannery had been outfitted. This suggests that the cannery would not have had many extra supplies on hand from previous seasons. None of these facts, however, came out in the trial.

There is another possible reason for why the cannery might have provided substandard nets. As was pointed out above, Pyramid Harbor's cost per case of salmon was higher than most of the other Alaska Packers' canneries, and it spent more on fishing gear than other canneries of a comparable size. The reason for the disproportionate gear expenditure may have been the need to fish with gillnets, which are an inefficient means of fishing for salmon. Thus, if Murray, the superintendent, felt the need to reduce the cost per case, he may have chosen to economize on the nets by recycling portions of last year's nets.

Murray may have been willing to economize on the nets, even though this reduced, to some extent, the fishermen's catch, because he knew he could purchase fish from the local tribes. Each year, the cannery obtained a significant percentage of its fish from the Chilkat and Chilkoot fishermen. The records show that Pyramid Harbor regularly obtained 25 to 40 percent of its fish from the tribes. In 1900, it purchased more than 200,000 fish from them.

Perhaps what Alaska Packers really needed the fishermen for was not fishing, but for sailing the vessel to and from San Francisco, unloading supplies upon arrival in Alaska, and loading the pack at the end of the season. In fact, Murray testified that it was "just as necessary" to have the men discharge the ship as it was to have them fish.[56]

---

[55] The increased pack cannot be explained by any increase in the size of the cannery crew as it was exactly the same size in both 1899 and 1900.

[56] Record at 131.

The possibility that Alaska Packers was not concerned with maximizing the fishermen's catch due to the availability of fish from the local tribes was not raised at trial.

I suspect that Banning's failure to establish any credible motive for the cannery to provide its fishermen with substandard equipment is an example of what has been called "litigation incapacity."[57] Our adversarial system posits two opposing sides with relatively equal resources. In reality, of course, the two sides frequently are mismatched. In several places, the transcript suggests that Alaska Packers' attorney was very familiar with the salmon canning industry, while Banning was not. This is hardly surprising, given that Alaska Packers was a large, well-funded conglomerate, certainly with more financial resources than the largely illiterate wage laborers on the other side of the case. Indeed, what is surprising is that the fishermen were able to obtain counsel at all.

Banning's trial strategy focused on comparing what the fishermen caught elsewhere and what they caught at Pyramid Harbor in the 1900 season. For example, Banning attempted to present evidence showing that one of the fishermen had caught 29,000 fish at Copper River, Alaska. At Pyramid Harbor, this same fisherman caught 5,600. From this, Banning wanted to draw the implication that substandard equipment at Pyramid Harbor led to the reduced catch. This strategy, however, triggered objections from Alaska Packers' counsel and rebuttal testimony that called into question the abilities of the fishermen. Ultimately, Banning's strategy did not persuade the trial judge.

Hindsight, of course, has perfect vision, but if Banning had focused on the cannery's capacity and had been able to establish that the 1900 catch met or exceeded the cannery's capacity, then he would have established a motive for the cannery to limit the fishermen's catch. Similarly, if he had been able to bring out the disparities between Pyramid Harbor and other canneries in cost per case and expenditures for fishing gear, along with the extent to which Pyramid Harbor relied on the local tribes, he could have suggested a motive to cut corners on the nets. Either strategy would have bolstered the credibility of the fishermen who testified that the nets were substandard. Moreover, if Banning had been able to bring out the extent to which local tribal fishermen contributed to the cannery's operation, he would have been able to

---

[57] Judith L. Maute, *Peevyhouse v. Garland Coal Mining Co. Revisited: The Ballad of Willie and Lucille*, 89 Nw. U. L. Rev. 1341, 1448 (1995); *cf.* RICHARD DANZIG & GEOFFREY R. WATSON, THE CAPABILITY PROBLEM IN CONTRACT LAW: FURTHER READINGS ON WELL-KNOWN CASES (2d ed. 2004) (referring to the same phenomenon as the "capability problem").

argue that the cannery could have operated even if the fishermen had refused to work during the season. This leads into the "duress" issue.

3. The question of duress

As discussed above, jurists and scholars examining the court's opinion categorize this case as one involving duress. They point to the short fishing season, the impossibility of obtaining other fishermen, and the significant amount of money Alaska Packers invested in the cannery at Pyramid Harbor. As a result, they conclude that the company had no feasible alternative to agreeing to the fishermen's demands. As Chirelstein phrases it, the company's only other alternative was "the loss of much of its investment in the cannery itself."[58] The company's vulnerability, however, never rose to such a level.

There are at least three reasons why Alaska Packers was not completely without options. First, Pyramid Harbor would still have been able to pack a substantial number of salmon even without the fishermen's catch. Moreover, even if Pyramid Harbor had operated at a loss for the 1900 season, that would not have caused Alaska Packers to post a loss. Finally, the fishermen were just as isolated as the cannery and their isolation could have been exploited by the company.

At trial, there was actually not much testimony about the availability of substitutes for the fishermen. Murray was asked if he needed the men's "services as fishermen," and he answered yes.[59] He was also asked if he could have obtained other fishermen, and he answered no. On cross, he was asked whether "there were Indians there that you could have got?" Murray responded that there were "[o]nly a limited number" who come every year.[60]

He was being somewhat disingenuous at this point. While there were only a few Native Americans who were actual employees of Pyramid Harbor, in the five years between 1896 and 1900, the cannery purchased fish from approximately two hundred Native Americans every year. As discussed in the preceding section, these nonemployee Native Americans supplied the cannery with significant numbers of fish. Thus, it was highly unlikely that the season would have been a complete failure even if the fishermen had refused to fish. Given that the cannery bought over 200,000 fish from the local tribes in 1900 and that it took approximately ten salmon to fill a case, at a minimum the cannery should have been able to produce about 20,000 cases. Certainly the assumption that the company's only other option to acceding

---

[58] CHIRELSTEIN, *supra* note 28, at 65.

[59] *See* Testimony of Hugh Murray, Record at 108.

[60] *See id.* at 121–22.

to the fishermen's demand for increased wages was to lose its entire investment in the cannery is not supported by these circumstances.

As suggested in the preceding section, perhaps the company really needed the men's services as sailors. It is unlikely that the Native Americans would have had the skill, not to mention the desire, to man the sailing vessel back to San Francisco with that season's pack. If the primary concern was with shipping the pack to San Francisco, however, there would have been no time pressure, as there was with the short fishing season. In other words, the company could have brought up replacement sailors, and it would not have mattered that they arrived after the run of salmon.

Furthermore, what is overlooked in this picture of the company at the mercy of the recalcitrant fishermen is that Alaska Packers was a trust, a combination of a number of independent canneries. In 1900, Alaska Packers operated eighteen canneries in Alaska and two more on Puget Sound. Part of the purpose of Alaska Packers was to protect individual canneries from catastrophic losses, such as the loss of the ship bearing the entire season's pack, which were part and parcel of the salmon industry. Even if the cannery at Pyramid Harbor had not canned a single tin of salmon and its entire season had been a loss, it would not have had a profound effect on Alaska Packers' bottom line.

The cannery at Pyramid Harbor did not represent a major part of Alaska Packers' operations. In 1900, Pyramid Harbor packed 55,601 cases of canned salmon, which as it turned out was the cannery's best year. Alaska Packers' total pack for Alaska and Puget Sound that year was 1,004,318. Thus, in 1900, Pyramid Harbor represented only about 5 percent of Alaska Packers' total output.

Alaska Packers' net profit for 1900 was $770,536. The market value of Pyramid Harbor's 55,601 cases was approximately $230,000. It cost Alaska Packers $170,190 to pack the 55,601 cases. This indicates that Alaska Packers' profit from the Pyramid Harbor pack was about $58,885. Subtracting that from Alaska Packers overall net profit still leaves a net profit of more than $700,000.

Moreover, assuming that Pyramid Harbor produced about 20,000 cases from the fish caught from local tribes, it may still have had a profitable season, even if the fishermen had refused to fish. The cannery's cost of production per case in 1900 was $3.06 and the market value of a case of red salmon was $4.12, so the cannery might have still turned a profit even if the cost of production per case rose. The largest single operating cost was for labor, and the cannery would have saved the unpaid wages to the fishermen. The next largest operating cost was for durable supplies (tin, solder, cases, etc.), and the unused supplies could have been stored for use the next season.

Of course, even if the entire operating cost of $170,190 was lost, which would not have been the case even if the cannery did not operate at all during the 1900 season, there would not have been the catastrophic loss the court envisioned. Alaska Packers would still have had a net profit in excess of $500,000.

In other words, from this perspective, Alaska Packers could have called the fishermen's bluff. Given the disparity in their economic resources, the fishermen would have suffered far more from the loss of a season's income than Alaska Packers would have.

It has been suggested, however, that evaluating the coerciveness of the fishermen's threat not to work from the point of view of Alaska Packers is inappropriate.[61] Certainly, perception of coercion depends upon the frame of reference. From the point of view of Hugh Murray, the superintendent of Pyramid Harbor, the situation may have seemed coercive; his compensation and perhaps even his job may have depended upon the success of the cannery's season. But this only establishes that his self-interest may have conflicted with the company's.

There is an additional reason why the distribution of bargaining power between the fishermen and Alaska Packers was not all on the fishermen's side. The messhouse operator, once he found out that the men were not working, refused to serve them meals, and only Murray's intervention persuaded him to continue to do so. This suggests that the company could have leveraged the fact that the men had no other source of victuals in the same way the men were leveraging the company's lack of substitute fishermen. During labor unrest in the mid-1930s, packing companies "threw [striking fishermen] on the beach," "that is, they deprived the men of board and lodging and forced them to shift for themselves."[62] This may not have been an option for Murray; he testified that the fishermen threatened to break into the messhouse and help themselves, and that he ordered the messhouse operator to feed them because he did not want any trouble.

Even putting aside the company's ability or desire to withhold food, the historical record suggests that Alaska Packers was not faced with a Hobson's choice when the fishermen threatened a work stoppage. The company had access to a substantial number of salmon as a result of the efforts of the local Native American fishermen. Moreover, Alaska Packers had more financial resources than the immigrant fishermen and could have absorbed the loss of Pyramid Harbor's season.

---

[61] This suggestion was made by a member of the audience at the symposium at which an earlier version of this paper was given.

[62] Casaday, *supra* note 40, at 460–61.

4. Changes in the labor market

There was a cartoon hanging in the lobby of the "Scandinavian Rooms" in Juneau in the early part of this century. The cartoon, entitled "A Fish Story," shows a thin, bedraggled fisherman in his boat, holding up the tail of a salmon. The fisherman is saying, "Is this my share[?]"[63] On the dock stands a large-bellied, grinning man, dressed nattily in a suit with top hat and spats; on his suit coat appears the legend "Fish Trust." He answers the fisherman: "It's the same as you always get—what ya kicking about?" In the waters of the bay, a mermaid pleads with Neptune, the god of the sea: "Father Neptune can't you help that poor fisherman?" And Neptune, pipe in hand, muses, "You can't help anyone who won't help themselves." Neptune is, of course, referring to the failure of the fishermen to organize.

In Alaska Packers' view of the case, the fishermen had gone on strike solely to get more money. At the end of the trial, Warren Gregory, the attorney for Alaska Packers, called a G. Viscecova to the stand. He was the labor contractor who recruited the fishermen for Pyramid Harbor. Gregory sought to have this witness testify as to a letter he had received, apparently from some of the libelants, but the court excluded the letter as hearsay. In the letter, according to Gregory, the writer or writers admitted that they had "gone on strike" for better wages.[64] Moreover, Murray testified that there was some talk at the time of the work stoppage that the fishermen should have had a hundred dollars for run money from the beginning.

One explanation for the Pyramid Harbor fishermen's demand for an increase in wages could be that when they agreed to the original terms, they were proceeding with imperfect information regarding Alaskan wages. Then, when they arrived in Pyramid Harbor, they discovered that other fishermen in the immediate vicinity of Pyramid Harbor were earning more than they were.

In the spring of 1900, two new small canneries had opened in the vicinity of Pyramid Harbor. Neither was a member of the Alaska Packers' Association. One was the Chilkoot Packing Company, located at the head of Chilkoot Inlet, and the other was Taku Packing Company, located in Taku Inlet, where Pyramid Harbor fishermen fished for king salmon early in the season.

The company that opened the Chilkoot cannery was from Aberdeen, Washington.[65] It employed twenty-four white and eight native fisher-

---

[63] *See id.* at 261.

[64] *See* Record at 145.

[65] *See* MOSER 1900, *supra* note 36, at 255.

men and purchased fish from another sixteen natives. The fishermen were recruited from the Puget Sound area and were paid twenty-five dollars per month from the time of departure from Puget Sound to the date of return, plus five cents for each redfish per two-man boat. Even accounting for the fact that it probably did not take as long to sail from Puget Sound as it did from San Francisco, the Chilkoot Packing Company fishermen were making more than the Pyramid Harbor fishermen, probably at least seventy-five dollars in run money plus the extra half-cent per man per fish.

The Taku Packing Company was organized in Astoria, Oregon, and thus probably recruited fishermen from that port. It employed thirty white and fourteen native fishermen. The Taku fishermen received eighty dollars for the season and five cents per redfish per two-man boat. Again, these men were earning more than the Pyramid Harbor fishermen.

It is highly probable that after arriving at Pyramid Harbor, the fishermen discovered that they were being paid less than the fishermen at the two closest canneries. Moreover, these other fishermen were getting more run money even though they were traveling less distance. Perhaps the men also discovered that as little as two years previously, the cannery at Pyramid Harbor was paying $100 in run money, though only three cents per fish per boat.

The following demonstrates a likely scenario: In San Francisco, the men were not organized. They were of different nationalities, although predominantly Italian. They probably did not belong to a union. They scarcely knew their fellow fishermen. They were new to Alaska. After they arrived in Alaska, for the first time they had the opportunity to talk with the few fishermen who fished at Pyramid Harbor in the past, and they discovered that the average catches were not what they thought they would be. The nets were different, not like any they had used before. Accordingly, their concerns about their ability to earn a living wage increased. In addition, they discovered that other nearby canneries were paying their fishermen more than Pyramid Harbor. Together in a foreign place, isolated from outside influences, they coalesced into a group and went on strike.

Interestingly, there appears to have been a repeat of the Pyramid Harbor strike two years later at Bristol Bay, in western Alaska. On June 24, 1902, seven hundred fishermen went on strike, demanding an increase in pay per fish, from two to three cents per red salmon. The strike lasted four days, at which time the cannery gave in to the men's demands.[66] Apparently, however, just as with this case, the company at the end of the season refused to pay the increased amount, and the courts upheld the company. According to the *Coast Seamen's Journal*, there was a lesson to be learned here: "[t]heir present experience should teach the Alaskan fishermen that the proper place to raise wages is in San Francisco, and the proper time when they are signing articles. To wait until they are on the grounds and the fish begin to run is to take bigger risks than fish, to say the least."[67]

Conclusion

Although history is interesting for its own sake, the point of developing as fully as possible the history of the *Alaska Packers* case is to contribute to our understanding of the law. This article attempts to do that by looking beyond the authoritative narrative enshrined in the judicial opinions to a more complete, and more complex, story.

An important lesson that emerges from this work is the insidious way in which assumptions about how the world works influence litigation outcomes. Because District Judge De Haven assumed the "self-evident fact" that Alaska Packers would want the men to catch as many fish as possible, he did not find the men's testimony regarding the inadequate nets to be credible. Because of his assumption, he could see no motive for the company to provide substandard nets. The possibility that there could be too many fish, or that the cannery was trying to cut corners on its equipment, did not occur to him.

Other assumptions have led to this case being thought of as a case of duress. Assumptions about language, experience, and perhaps class led to the conclusion that the men were motivated solely by a desire for more wages and obscured the possibility of honest misunderstanding. Crucial to seeing this case as one of coercion is the assumption that if the men had refused to work, Alaska Packers had no other means of obtaining salmon and would have lost its investment in the cannery. The substantial contributions of the Native American fishermen to the cannery's operation, as well as the resources of the fish trust, are not seen.

By developing the social and economic history of the case, I have tried to call these assumptions into question. My goal is not to "prove" the outcome of the case wrong. Rather, it is to "shake things up," to destabilize the received wisdom about the case and to suggest other ways of looking at the litigation. I hope that this fuller historical narra-

---

[66] *See* Coast Seamen's Journal, August 6, 1902, Microform v.14–15.

[67] Coast Seamen's Journal, September 17, 1902, Microform v.14–15.

tive will enrich classroom discussion and provoke debate, both about the merits of the case and about our adversarial system of justice.